FIGURES OF WAR AND FIELDS OF HONOUR:
ISAAK BABEL'S *RED CAVALRY*

Figures of War and
Fields of Honour:
Isaak Babel's *Red Cavalry*

Christopher Luck

Essays in Poetics Publications: Volume 3

Series Editor: Joe Andrew

KEELE UNIVERSITY PRESS

First published in 1995 by
Keele University Press
Keele, Staffordshire

© Christopher Luck

Composed by KUP
Printed on acid-free paper
by Hartnolls, Bodmin,
Cornwall, England

ISBN 1 85331 088 3

For Lin, Heidi, Nikolai and Natalya

Contents

Part Three: The Tropes of War

Preface

In this book I intend to make a close examination of Isaak Babel's two cycles of war stories *Na pole chesti* and *Konarmiya*. My first purpose is to draw the reader's attention to the former cycle, which has received the scantiest notice and practically no serious analysis from scholars of Babel. Yet not only does it afford unique insights into Babel's literary method, for special and surprising reasons that will become apparent, but it also greatly helps our understanding of his major cycle, *Konarmiya* – one of the acknowledged masterpieces of twentieth-century literature.

In the second place I have examined journalistic writing that Babel undertook in 1922 between his two war cycles. It was in this period that he further developed his technique of *skaz* writing. I have also examined extant portions of a diary that Babel wrote in 1920 when he worked as a war correspondent assigned to Budyonnyy's cavalry. These, together with the plans and sketches for *Konarmiya* that are available, have enabled me to trace developments between source materials and finished cycle, a process that reveals the distance both between Babel's immediate impressions and those which Lyutov later conveys, as well as between the author himself and his central narrator. Personal contacts that I made with two of Babel's widows, T. V. Ivanova and A. N. Pirozhkova, have also helped me in this respect.

Finally, I have conducted a detailed statistical and expository analysis of Babel's use of metaphor in both cycles. *Konarmiya* is a work that abounds in imagery. The brilliance and succinctness, the pithiness and unexpectedness of its images have aroused interest and evoked comment from all who have written about Babel. Yet no accurate and detailed analysis has been undertaken of Babel's use of figurative language in his masterpiece. Mendelsohn's work *Metaphor in Babel's Short Stories* (Ann Arbor, 1982) is defective in a number of ways, not least of which is her skimpy treatment of *Na pole chesti* and more surprisingly, of *Konarmiya* itself. Individual stories have been examined by others, articles have been published on Babel's style and the principal trope types have merited fleeting comment in the monographs that have appeared, such as Falen's *Isaac Babel – Russian Master of the Short Story* (Knoxville, 1974) or Carden's *The Art of Isaac Babel* (Ithaca, 1972), yet it is as if Babelists have been unwilling to move beyond cursory statements of admiration and brief exegetic forays into his world of imagery. Perhaps our apparent unease stems from the enigmatic or ambivalent qualities which many of his figures embody, or from the desire merely to appreciate the sensuous shocks which Babel deals us without delving below the often harsh and glittering surface, lest the impression of brilliance be destroyed.

My purpose is thus not to assess in any general way Babel's place in world literature or the literary scene of the 1920s, a task that has been satisfactorily undertaken by several scholars, but to overcome the reserve that has persisted in examining Babel's formation and use of figurative language, for the latter is the single most significant aspect of the masterpiece of one of the twentieth century's greatest short story writers, an aspect which many have applauded but none yet anatomized.

*   *   *

I would like to express my thanks to Robin Milner-Gulland and Joe Andrew for their respective help and advice to me in my research and in the preparation of the text.

I also wish to thank the All Saints Educational Trust for their financial assistance which enabled me to complete my research and the BASSEES Research and Development Committee for their sub-grant from the Ford Foundation which enabled me to finance this publication.

NOTES ON SYSTEM OF TRANSLITERATION

In my transliteration of Russian quotations and names I have adopted the former *Slavonic and East European Review* (Matthews) scheme in which 'e' equals 'ye' initially and after vowels and the hard and soft signs but is 'e' otherwise; 'ё' is 'o' after 'ж, ч, ш, щ', otherwise 'yo'. But I have adhered to 'i' for 'и' and 'y' for 'ы' or 'й' even when in combination at the end of proper names. Both the hard and soft signs I have transliterated by an apostrophe. However, references to Babel and other familiar figures omit the apostrophe, except in any quotations from Russian.

Part One

PEREKHOD CHEREZ POLE CHESTI
(Crossing the Field of Honour)

PROLOGUE

Isaak Babel was described by his sister Maria as gentle, affectionate, taciturn, observant and very myopic.[1] Paustovskiy writes of the striking quality both of his voice and his eyes: 'In the gentle sound of his voice could be heard a pervasive irony. Many people could not look at the burning gaze of Babel's eyes. By nature Babel was one who laid things bare.'[2] Perhaps Babel's myopia was instrumental in the piercing observations and ironic exposés of life that he produced. The heavy lenses of his spectacles symbolize the distorting filter of a mind whose unique world-view is simultaneously 'ironic, poetic and pictorial'.[3] Yet his prose does not appeal only to the reader's visual sense, but also to his ear. Like the author's voice it has a pleasing auditory effect.

Nor is the reader spared Babel's irony: 'I have no imagination ... I cannot invent. I must know everything to the last jot, otherwise I can write nothing.'[4] This wry admission to Paustovskiy might well explain why Babel found inspiration for his *Na pole chesti* cycle amid the memoirs of a French soldier of the First World War.[5] Yet a remark made in a letter to his mother concerning two childhood stories[6] might equally well apply to the above mentioned cycle, for although the subject matter has been copied, the treatment of it is uniquely Babel's: 'of course I have invented a lot of things and I have changed others'.[7]

When talking of Kipling, Babel is reported as saying: 'A story should be precise, like a military report or a bank cheque'.[8]

The image of a war report is an apt choice to illustrate what Babel sought from and in a story, for it is his 'reporting' of war that constitutes his major masterpiece and displays his creative talent at its best.

INTRODUCTION

In 1920, when Babel was making notes in his diary[9] for his subsequent *Konarmiya* cycle, four stories were published in the Odessan journal *Lava*.[10] They were Babel's first stories about war and exemplify themes that were to be developed in his later masterpiece. What is particularly significant, however, is the fact that three of them have been adapted from the work of another author. Consequently, one is able to examine both raw source material and the finished work, a rare and hitherto neglected opportunity in the case of a writer whose legacy of manuscripts is minimal.

Babel states in a short introduction to the cycle that these stories constitute the beginning of his observations on war, that their contents are borrowed from books written by French soldiers and officers, and that, in certain extracts, the plot and form of recounting are changed, while in others he has tried to keep closer to the original.[11] From this one might presume that Babel intended a series of war stories based on many episodes from a variety of works, but such is hardly the case.

Only three stories are developed from two of a cycle of thirty-five written by a French army captain, Gaston Vidal. The setting of Vidal's book, *Figures et anecdotes de la Grande Guerre*, is the German front in the First World War.[12] The stories, the eleventh and fifteenth in the cycle, are respectively entitled 'Deux actes devant une conscience' and 'Histoire Shakespearienne'. Babel changed the former into two stories, transforming the two acts of the French title into 'Na pole chesti' and 'Dezertir' respectively, while the latter is entitled 'Semeystvo papashi Maresko'.

The source of the fourth story, 'Kvaker', is not to be found in the remaining thirty-three chapters of Vidal's work. Babel, however, does state that the contents of his cycle are borrowed from books; one may well think therefore that his inspiration for 'Kvaker' emanates from another writer on the First World War. No facts have yet emerged concerning its source; indeed the story, as well as the cycle, has elicited very little comment among scholars of Babel.

Nathalie Babel is unable to shed any light on the source of 'Kvaker'.[13] Other scholars such as Carden, Falen and Sicher, whom I have consulted, also do not know, although the latter, in an unpublished thesis, notes a strong resemblance between 'Kvaker' and Maupassant's 'Coco'.[14] Sicher comments on the theme of malevolent cruelty committed on a defenceless horse which both stories share and also on Babel's affection for Maupassant's works and style of writing. The implication by Sicher that 'Coco' may be the source of 'Kvaker' is necessarily tentative since nowhere in the former story does a figure resembling Ston appear, nor does such a protagonist emerge in the Maupassant stories of similar theme, such as 'Pierrot' or 'L'âne'. More recently, Danuta Mendelsohn wrongly ascribes Babel's *Lava* stories to incidents of the Franco-Prussian War of 1870–1, and also claims that they are based on a single French source.[15]

A theory worth expounding is that Babel was influenced by the writing of a Belgian author, Robert de Wilde. His book *De Liége à L'Yser. Mon journal de Campagne* was published in 1918, the same year as Vidal's.[16] Very little mention of setting is made in Babel's story, less in fact than in the other three, but he does make reference to the Yser. The central protagonist, Ston, the Quaker of the title, is a curious figure, a man of God thrust into the turmoil of war, who shuns the company of human beings and cares only for animals. De Wilde had been at military school with a man called Martial Lekeux, a monk who underwent military training and served his country in the army. He was a remarkable, if eccentric figure who subsequently published his own memoirs, four years after de Wilde.[17] The two had been great friends and de Wilde mentions Lekeux in his own work. He was a man who loved animals, and they in their turn apparently returned this love; once, on patrol, his life was saved by his cat. Babel's hero, Ston, loses his life because of an animal: he is shot when he goes foraging for oats for an ill-treated horse. Is it perhaps too tenuous a theory to suggest that Ston is a free adaptation of Frère Martial Lekeux, as depicted by Robert de Wilde? The names of Babel's protagonists, Ston and Bekker, may also point to a Flemish connection; they are certainly dissimilar to the French names used in the first three stories.

A story with a French literary link published some twelve years later, but which dates from the same period as *Na pole chesti,* is Babel's 'Gyui de Mopassan'.[18] Although its setting is not that of war, but St Petersburg in the winter of 1916, it embodies certain themes and circumstances which link it with Babel's first cycle of war stories. Babel's love for Maupassant and French literature has been documented by others;[19] he in fact translated three Maupassant stories in the twenties for an edition of the author's collected works, including 'L'aveu' which is mentioned in his story 'Gyui de Mopassan'.[20] There he claims its hero to be 'le soleil de France',[21] that same sun which perversely illuminates his harsh backdrop of war in *Na pole chesti.*

Of himself in 1917 in St Petersburg, Babel wrote: 'In Petersburg in 1917 I understood how great was my lack of skill, and went off to make my way. I lived for six years among the people and in 1923 began my literary work anew.'[22] The comment occurs in a letter to Gorkiy, which also contains references to Kudryavtsev, a journalist friend of Babel, who was obsessed by anything Spanish, including collecting editions of *Don Quixote.* Cervantes' hero is alluded to in both cycles of war stories, and Kudryavtsev, it would seem, is a forerunner of Aleksey Kazantsev, the narrator's landlord and friend in 'Gyui de Mopassan'.[23] Babel's opinion of his literary ability at the time was somewhat harsh in view of the fact that both *Na pole chesti* and *Konarmiya* were taking shape in his mind and, in the case of the first cycle, had been written and published by 1920.

The story 'Gyui de Mopassan' treats, among other things, the narrator's improvement of another person's translation of a Maupassant short story. The situation of Babel's narrator resembles the author's own in his adaptations of Vidal's stories in *Na pole chesti.* Moreover, a reference in a hospital report at the end of 'Gyui de Mopassan' to the French author's mental condition in an asylum, 'Monsieur de Maupassant va s'animaliser', characterizes both the persecutors and the victims of Babel's cycle of war stories which he published at about the same time that this story was being written.[24] For Ratin and Bidu are each brutalized by the circumstances in which they find themselves, just as are Bozhi and Captain Zhem'e. Ston and Bekker exhibit respectively a capacity for cruelty, albeit mental in the former case and physical in the latter. Maresko and the lieutenant are also victims of war's cruelty but the brutalizing toll that it exacts is left unstated in their case and is consequently more affective.

EXPOSITIONS OF IRONY

I propose to examine aspects of the four *Lava* stories and to show the change in focus and emphasis that Babel builds into the three that he adapted from Vidal.[25] In doing so, one not only sees signs of an embryonic *Konarmiya* and the economy of Babel's literary technique, but one also gains insight into his use of tropes.

Two of Babel's stories represent a reduction in length from Vidal's versions,[26] a fact which is hardly surprising in view of the verbose nature of Vidal's writing and Babel's renowned predilection for paring verbiage, his 'hard labour' of which Paustovskiy writes.[27] The first story of his cycle, however, represents an expansion of a Vidal anecdote;[28] Babel, it would seem untypically, has added, when he normally prefers to take away. However, omission and addition recur repeatedly in each of Babel's adaptations and are not peculiar to one story alone. It is this selective treatment of the French raw material and a comparison of it with Babel's finished cycle that make this a rewarding study.

'Dezertir'

The plot of 'Dezertir' which is the second of Babel's cycle, corresponds exactly to that of the first part of Vidal's 'Deux actes devant une conscience'. A young French soldier has been found unarmed between enemy lines and has been brought back to his officer for retribution following his undoubted and admitted attempt at desertion. In both the French and Russian stories the same fate awaits the young man in the same circumstances. He pleads in vain for mercy in order to protect the honour of his mother, family and friends. The officer, while wishing him to be spared the ignominy of execution for cowardice, cannot spare his life. He offers the soldier the opportunity of shooting himself, which he is unable to do; the officer then kills him.

While the essential events of the narrative remain identical, there is much that is different in Babel's treatment of the story. The length of the French story is almost three times that of the Russian.[29] Vidal's story has a narrator, a Captain V., but he is not the primary narrator. One presumes the latter to be the author, who tells of meeting Captain V. by chance in a Paris café while on leave. The French story is told in the first person, while 'Dezertir' is related in the third person, with no narrator. In isolation, this fact seems of little significance, but as each story is read and compared it is noticeable how much the first person narrator, Captain V., dictates the viewpoint and conveys his own feelings while the officer in the Russian story does not.

It is apparent from the beginning that Babel has omitted much, both of Vidal's setting and of his description of his chief protagonist. In the French, some fourteen lines are devoted to a description of Captain V., extolling his virtues as a man of war and peace and glorifying him with trite metaphors: 'C'est à la guerre un lion qui rugit, au repos un aigle qui médite.' Approximately half this descriptive passage recounts his leadership qualities in war and the rest tells of his reasonable nature when encountered elsewhere as a civilian. Evident throughout is the author's admiration for the patriotic, courageous Captain.

Babel's story begins in different vein. His description of the Captain is condensed roughly to a third of the French version and is flavoured with irony. The two facets of the Captain's nature, his fervent patriotism and bravery together with his quiet home loving disposition, are juxtaposed in such a way that the officer loses credibility and becomes at once a figure of derision. Babel's opening sentences are uncharacteristic for the explicit praise that they convey and therefore have only ironic interpretation: 'Captain Zhem'ye[30] was a most excellent man, a philosopher besides. On the field of battle he knew no hesitation, in private life he could forgive small wrongs.' (ll.1–3 'Dezertir') These final words recur at the end of the story, after the deserter has been shot by the officer, and contribute to a framework of irony that is both astringent and ambivalent. The seemingly innocent inspiration in the French text for 'small wrongs' is taken from the phrase: 'oublieux des petits torts qu'on put avoir envers lui', which occurs in a sentence depicting the Captain's magnanimity. Babel's irony continues with a description of the officer's love for his country: 'He loved France with a tenderness that devoured his heart.' (ll.3–4 'Dezertir') The coupling of 'tenderness' with the forceful verb 'to devour' destroys the image of tenderness and exemplifies a fossilized metaphor acquiring vitality through the incongruous juxtaposition of the abstract noun and active verb in question.

Babel moves from metaphor to simile, the only one in his version of the story, to depict the Captain's hatred of the enemy: 'That is why his hatred for the barbarians profaning her [i.e. France's] ancient soil, was as unquenchable, ruthless, prolonged as life.' (ll.4–5 'Dezertir') The effect of the tenor with its elaborate and grandiloquent composition is punctured by the monosyllabic vehicle. The comparison of the particular emotion 'hatred' to the abstract and generic 'life' deliberately leaves the reader dissatisfied and therefore unconvinced as to the officer's integrity.

A rhetorical question opens Babel's second paragraph of description of the Frenchman: 'What else is there to say about Zhem'ye?' (l.6 'Dezertir') as if anything is necessary. Nevertheless one is told of his exemplary record as a family man, the description ending with a flourish in a series of five substantives, the last of which draws our attention to the fact that he is a lover of beautiful things: 'He loved his wife, made good citizens of his children, was a Frenchman, a patriot, a bibliophile, a Parisian and a lover of beautiful things.' (ll.6–8 'Dezertir')

Babel is now ready to begin the narrative events of the story, but the French original is not. In a third paragraph of fifteen lines, Captain V. assumes the role of narrator, reiterating some of the material already given us by the author and adding information about himself. These additional details about the emotional stress which the war has brought the Captain, and which he will proceed to portray, may well constitute part of the attraction for Babel in choosing this and the other Vidal story for adaptation. Certain of the dilemmas and personal crises which confront Lyutov, the central protagonist and participatory narrator in *Konarmiya,* have affinities with the central issues of this cycle.

Captain V. tells of the 'deux hommes qui se trouvent en moi' during the war – that extraordinary period of his life when he was both the peace-loving man of culture receptive to the opinion of others, and also the man of action, ready to suppress emotion, to act 'avec un parti pris absolu'. It is Lyutov's inability to act in this way, his incapacity to suppress his feelings, that brings him anguish in 'Smert' Dolgushova' or 'Posle boya', at the end of which he implores fate to grant him 'the simplest of abilities – the ability to kill a man'.[31] Lyutov's ambivalent attitude to the brutal yet graceful Cossacks, his vacillation between horror and admiration for them, find an echo here in Vidal's Captain with his two men in his Faustian heart; that Lyutov and the Captain are very different, however, is clearly felt in Captain V.'s prefatory comment, before he embarks upon his account of the two episodes on which 'Dezertir' and 'Na pole chesti' are based: 'Et je n'en éprouve nul regret'. The fact that he says this, having been instrumental in the deaths of two young men, may have goaded Babel into his ironic treatment of the Captain. Yet there is also a relaxation of the irony as the tale progresses, possibly prompted by the fact that Vidal's Captain does relate 'Deux actes *devant une conscience*' (my stress), as 'une personne qui fait une confession'. The title itself belies the assertion that he has felt nothing in the execution of his duty. While Babel implies condemnation of the French officer by his ironic treatment of him, one nevertheless suspects a certain admiration on the author's part for the Captain's singlemindedness. The latter is at least able to act upon his convictions.

'Na pole chesti'

The note of irony apparent in the exposition of 'Dezertir' is registered in the very title of the cycle. 'Na pole chesti' is also the title of the first story and Babel saw fit to make this his opening story, even though it is taken from the second and slighter of the two incidents which Vidal's Captain V. relates in 'Deux actes devant une conscience'. This second anecdote in French is much shorter than the first and comprises 346 words compared with the 1,520 of the latter. Babel, who not only enhances its status in terms of position, also lengthens it slightly to 426 words, adding new details.

As with all four stories of the cycle, two protagonists are included. Babel omits altogether the subordinate and insignificant lieutenant of Vidal's version. As with 'Dezertir' there is confrontation between intransigent establishment and pathetic rebel. The former is represented by an army officer, Captain Ratin, the latter by a soldier of the lowest rank, Bidu. Like the deserter Bozhi, Bidu refuses to fight and is made to suffer the consequences. Babel's plot, however, while bearing similarities with the French version, differs significantly in places, and as with 'Dezertir' the characters in each story receive a different treatment from their respective authors. Babel achieves this in his longer version not only through addition but by omission and a subtle alteration of imagery and figure.

The French anecdote, in which no protagonist is named, opens with some playful remarks between Captain V. and the narrator, who made the initial introduction some one hundred and seventeen lines earlier. The exposition then proceeds swiftly with time, place and circumstance stated within a sentence. The narrator and a lieutenant are on their rounds of inspection near the trenches, before an attack. The action continues with the sighting by the officers of a soldier crouching in a shell crater. His appearance indicates distress, he is shivering and wild-eyed. Vidal's scene is set, his principal characters introduced, the confrontation about to commence.

For Babel, however, this second French anecdote is to assume more significant proportions. In its exposition one can trace links of theme and imagery with both his 'Plans and Sketches' of *Konarmiya* and the work itself.[32] His introduction is more gradual than Vidal's; he portrays the broad canvas of war before focusing on the two protagonists. The French peasantry is fleeing before heavy German bombardment. The horror of their plight is seen as they drag with them not only their chattels and livestock but also the crippled, the maimed and the women in childbirth. The presence of birth amidst death, the incongruous and gruesome juxtaposition of the former with the latter, is also found in *Konarmiya*'s opening story, 'Perekhod cherez Zbruch'. The narrator, Lyutov, is awakened from a nightmare by a woman whose belly is swollen by pregnancy, a woman whose father has recently been brutally murdered by the Poles and whose corpse proves to be Lyutov's bedfellow.

The association of spring, the season of rebirth and rejuvenation, with death is an ancient theme and one that reasserts itself in the poetry of Mandelstam and repeatedly in the war stories of Babel.[33] Spring sends forth its burgeoning shoots either amid rotting corpses or in the shadow of death in the four stories of this cycle, in the 'Plans and Sketches' and in *Konarmiya*.

The French stories from which 'Dezertir' is adapted mentions that the narrator and author meet on a spring morning. In the Russian, more is made of the setting. The events unfold 'on one shining pink spring morning'. (1.9 'Dezertir') The series of adjectives with which Babel qualifies the morning contrast with the black events that follow; the fulsomeness of burgeoning life is an incongruous setting for the anguish and death of a young man in the prime of life.

Babel alters Vidal's lyrical digression in 'Histoire Shakespearienne' in which the sun is personified and made the envy of the narrator for its indifference to war: 'Lui, là-haut, n'a cure des batailles, des haines. Il luit paisiblement, impassiblement, fait éclore les fleurs, enivre les papillons.' The precious thoughts of Vidal's lieutenant are hardly those of Babel in his version, 'Semeystvo papashi Maresko'. This whole paragraph is virtually omitted from the Russian, and the only reference to the weather is made in three adjectives, but among them he introduces a new element, the spring: 'And then it's a bright clear spring morning.' (ll.13–14 'Semeystvo papashi Maresko') Babel's fascination for the perverse association of spring and death again becomes apparent. Nature assumes an antithetical mood to the tragedy that is to unfold or to be revealed. Babel's lieutenant juxtaposes his reference to a bright, clear spring morning with his presence amid the dead: 'And then it's a bright clear spring morning. I am lying on the dead looking at the rich grass, thinking of Hamlet.' (ll.13–15 'Semeystvo papashi Maresko')

The incongruous effect is increased by the epithet 'rich'. The addition of this detail by Babel implies that the lushness of the grass is due to the decomposition of the bodies, on which the narrator, as he tells us in a piece of hyperbole, is lying.[34] The effect is unsettling. In 'Kvaker', Ston, the central protagonist, is a lugubrious, death-like figure, portrayed amid vernal revivification: 'The sight of the clear sky, the chirping of sparrows in the grass – everything flooded him with joy.' (ll.17–18 'Kvaker')

Use of incongruous settings is made in *Konarmiya*. While Babel operates the pathetic fallacy to enhance atmosphere, he also exploits the reverse situation, in which nature contrasts with the grim events described, to increase horror. An example occurs in 'Sashka Khristos'. Sashka and his stepfather Tarakanych return to their home after a winter away. As they make their way, 'The first flocks were streaming down from the tumuli, foals were playing in the blue expanses of the horizon.'[35] They catch Sashka's mother unawares, who tells them that the younger children have both died the week before. Babel's masterly use of litotes enhances the anguish of the woman: 'The children have gone out, – said the woman, all white, and ran up and down the yard again and fell to the ground. – Oh, Aleshen'ka, she began to shout wildly, our kids have gone out feet first …'[36]

The sun, spurned by Babel in 'Semeystvo papashi Maresko', is included by him as an ironic harbinger of death in *Konarmiya*, the 'Plans and Sketches' and 'Kvaker'. In the last-named story an image occurs which could well have been taken from the 'Plans and Sketches' of *Konarmiya*, had the latter preceded the former:

> Around him [Ston] people of different countries were promptly dying. Old generals, freshly washed, with swellings on their faces, stood on hillocks and examined the locality through field-glasses. The cannonade thundered ceaselessly, the earth gave off a stench, the sun rummaged in upturned corpses. (ll.80–4 'Kvaker')

The coupling of the sun with rotting corpses is a distasteful image, designed to shock and disturb. It recurs in Babel's thoughts, as his 'Plans and Sketches' of *Konarmiya* show. They open with notes on the Battle of Brody in which the sun's presence is mentioned in close proximity to references to wheat or rye: 'The dead, slashed to death, sun, wheat, soldiers' notebooks, leaves of the Gospel … I go out to relieve myself … A corpse. A sparkling day. Everything is strewn with corpses, completely inconspicuous amid the rye',[37] and a little further on: 'Straightway a description of the battle – dust, sun, details … A field strewn with the dead.'[38] The rich grass of the Picardy graveyard in 'Semeystvo papashi Maresko' compares with the arable landscape of the Brody battlefield for the proximity of death. Babel's predilection for the sun as a concomitant of death finds epic expression in *Konarmiya* where the former symbolizes a victim of the latter: 'An orange sun rolls across the sky, like a severed head.'[39]

Such ingredients are to be found in the work of Expressionist painters, who use primary colours to provoke strong, direct reactions. As Clyman states, 'To achieve a more forceful effect the Expressionist painter applies colours in feverish, violent motions. Similarly, to lend greater emotional expressiveness to his images, Babel uses bold dramatic colours … in strong, assertive motion, [which] vivify and lend immediacy to … scenes of bloodshed, violence and death [and] intensify the impact of … war scenes.' [40] A painter who foreshadowed such expressionistic tendencies is Henri Rousseau, a pacifist who served with the French army of 1870–1 and who depicted grotesque slaughter and pain in a framework of lurid colours, the reds and yellows of the sunset.

In *Na pole chesti,* however, it is the midday sun that witnesses the flight of the peasant refugees from the heavy German bombardment: 'The sun was at its zenith. From the neighbouring section news came that all the officers in the 4th company had fallen.' (ll.7–8 'Na pole chesti') As in the previous quotation from 'Perekhod cherez Zbruch' in *Konarmiya,* Babel is painting a broad canvas of war, but unlike the hope that is afforded the reader at the end of the story by the pregnant woman's awesome respect for her dead father's courage, there is no such hope evident in the backcloth of horror and death in the blistering heat of the noonday sun above the 'Field of Honour'. Here the sky changes colour from blue to crimson and in its 'swelling and misting over' heralds the spilling of blood and the approaching carnage: 'The sky, its dark blue intense heat shining, was slowly turning crimson, swelling and misting over.' (ll.3–4 'Na pole chesti') These lines foreshadow an image from *Konarmiya,* but there the battle has already taken place: 'The village was swimming and swelling, crimson clay ran from its sad wounds.' [41] Lyutov is wearily walking back to the village of Cheskniki. He has been taunted and exposed by Akinfiyev, a transport driver, for going into battle with an empty gun. Chesniki itself has suffered in the recent rout of the Red cavalry. The same association of colour and distortion obtains. Both parts of each image reinforce the other and combine to present a graphic and grotesquely unified picture of death on a mass scale. It is as if the very sky in 'Na pole chesti' and the village in 'Posle boya' are bleeding.

The sky plays its part elsewhere in *Konarmiya.* In 'Gedali', Zhitomir is shrouded in deathlike inactivity; the market is dead: 'Dumb locks hang on the stalls and the granite paving is clean, like the bald patch of a corpse.' [42] Gedali's little shop is full of bric-a-brac from a past age and its owner, in conversation with Lyutov, is troubled and confused by the violence, of which he has been a victim, and the death that the revolution brings: 'The sky changes colour. Blood of a delicate hue flows from an overturned bottle there, and a light odour of decay envelopes me.' [43]

The broad canvas of war that Babel creates in his opening paragraph of 'Na pole chesti' is the sole example of this in the cycle and it is also rare in *Konarmiya.* However, one such scene, also of fleeing peasantry, occurs in the earlier editions of 'Syn rabbi'. While Babel's inclination for vignette as opposed to portrayal on a grand scale may explain its later partial omission, censorship is more likely to blame:

The train of the political section started to crawl along the dead backbone of the fields. And a monstrous, improbable Russia swarming like clothes' lice, began to tramp in bast shoes along both sides of the carriages. The typhous peasantry rolled before itself the customary hump of a soldier's death.[44]

Such epic descriptions of the devastation of war also recall the artist Goya who, like Babel the diarist, had sketched in pen and ink his visual impressions of the horrors of the Napoleonic invasion as they happened and produced a series of pictures entitled *The Horrors of War*.

Babel proceeds from the general panorama in his first paragraph of 'Na pole chesti' to a more particular setting in his second. Factual details of a regiment, its position and circumstances are given and the first protagonist, Captain Ratin, is introduced. Unlike the French writer, Babel names both his protagonists, although he forges no link with the protagonists of *Dezertir*. Reference is also made to the heavy losses which the regiment and company have suffered and to the fortitude with which these have been borne. The addition of this detail not only demonstrates a desire on Babel's part to give some acknowledgement to the pressures that the officer, like everyone else, is under, but it also provides a link with the heroic side of the Cossack soldiers in *Konarmiya*.[45]

The third paragraph represents the final stage in the particularizing process of the exposition. The reader is taken to a certain point, three hundred metres from the trenches, where the second protagonist is seen. Departures from the French original are evident: '… un de nos types accroupi, frissonant, les yeux égarés'.[46] The Russian instead mentions a 'human figure', not a 'type', and immediately names him: 'It was Bidu the soldier.' (ll.9–10 'Na pole chesti') As well as these differences in his treatment of the soldier, Babel adds a new fact and alters another. Both these changes apparently create a more negative picture of Bidu than Vidal does of his soldier, as if Babel is at pains to counterbalance the human element which he has introduced and which Vidal has not.

Bidu, cowering like Vidal's soldier, is straight away dubbed a little idiot – 'durachok' – and, in an involved, and at first sight uncharacteristically clumsy allusion, is portrayed as masturbating. Such a base, primitive act repulses the reader. It is difficult to reconcile, either with the previously mentioned heroic fortitude of the soldiers in the face of heavy losses, or with Babel's reference to a 'human figure'. Nevertheless, this human figure is compared to others in the elaborately coy circumlocution which Babel uses to convey the grossness of Bidu's act: 'The soldier was engaged in what wretched old men seek comfort from in the villages and shameful boys in public lavatories. We'll not speak of this.' (ll.11–13 'Na pole chesti') The essential ambivalence that imbues so many of Babel's stories is at work here, for, repugnant as Bidu's act is, it is no different, Babel reminds us, from that of certain other human beings. This fact, coupled with the knowledge that Bidu is of low intelligence, suffices for the reader not to condemn him totally. The use of diminutives to describe fellow perpetrators, plus the earlier diminutive 'Bidu the little idiot' serve both to soften the impact of Bidu's crime and to place him on the same pathetic level as the 'old men' and the 'boys'. While the French version has told the reader only of the distress of its fugitive, the Russian makes him relate to the pathetic figure at the bottom of the damp hole. Revulsion has been aroused by Bidu, but both the reader's curiosity and possible indulgence for him have also been engendered.

'Semeystvo papashi Maresko'

Babel's espousal of that Russian stock figure 'the little man' is again in evidence in the third story that he adapted from the French, 'Semeystvo papashi Maresko'. Unlike the previous two, the narrator is one of the protagonists. Babel follows Vidal's example and in doing so may have laid the foundation in his own mind of a participatory narrator for his major work, *Konarmiya*. In 'Kvaker' too, mention, albeit fleeting, is made of the narrator encountering Ston near the end of the story, although the narrator's role in this case is peripheral.

The French story 'Histoire Shakespearienne', the fifteenth of Vidal's cycle, like 'Deux actes devant une conscience', loses its title in the Russian. This accords with trends in the other stories. Vidal's narrator, or secondary narrator, inevitably allows himself greater focus. The respective officers who relate the stories centre events on themselves. The title 'Histoire Shakespearienne' emanates from the narrator's musings about Hamlet, while Babel's narrator is not evident in his title; it is the little man, the victim, who is immediately to the fore.

From the now familiar situation of two protagonists, one, the narrator, is an officer – a lieutenant, while the other, more unusually, is neither private nor soldier, but a civilian who has lost his whole family in a recent bombardment. Nor, unlike the 'little man' of 'Dezertir' and 'Na pole chesti', is he guilty of anything, but like them he is a victim of circumstance. His burden of grief, his incongruous and wretched appearance and his apologetic determination render him a pathetic and enigmatic figure. Here perhaps is the finest and most affecting of this short cycle of stories.

As in the case with 'Dezertir', Babel's story is much shorter than the French version, virtually half its length. Each comprises four sections: an exposition followed by Maresko (Marescot)'s entrance, a third section which is a flashback to the events which have befallen him, and a dénouement.[47] The first and third sections contain comments and musings by the narrator, the second and fourth the actions and dialogue of the protagonists.

'Especially close to the original is the story "The Family of Old Man Maresko", which is perceived for the most part as a translation.'[48] This statement by Smirin is erroneous. The structural proportions of the respective stories are different from the beginning. The proportions of the four sections are as follows:

Section	'Histoire Shakespearienne'	'Semeystvo papashi Maresko'
1. (Exposition)	38.6%	27.6%
2. (Development)	18.0%	20.4%
3. (Flashback)	12.5%	15.2%
4. (Dénouement)	30.9%	36.8%
	100%	100%

The three sections in which Maresko appears are each proportionally longer in Babel's version than in Vidal's. Indeed the widest discrepancy occurs in the section in which the narrator features alone, the exposition. It would seem that Vidal has given a disproportionate part to the narrator, in Babel's opinion, and he redresses the balance. There are many changes in the treatment of the subject matter and in the order in which things occur; that Babel's story is shorter is obvious at a glance; the parts that he has omitted are revealing in themselves.

Vidal's narrator establishes the time, the place and the circumstances in his opening paragraph. The setting is a pretty village in Picardy which has been recaptured from the enemy eight days earlier. The narrator is occupying the cemetery with his regiment. He contemplates his feelings of horror and fantasizes at being in a place of death at a time 'où la mort se multiplie'. In the second paragraph he describes the ravages of war which the graves around him have suffered. Images abound: in a simile he compares the damage to the flagstones to that caused by the hammer blows of some desecrating vampire; he adds vividness and irony to the details through metonymy: 'un grand christ qui gît à terre, fracassé, Dieu mort ainsi par deux fois'; he creates a macabre atmosphere with the following metaphor: 'des cercueils entr'ouverts laissant échapper des ossements'. The narrator's imagination is fired and the figurative language conveys the intensity of his impressions of a scene which he considers worthy of the brush of Michelangelo.

With this detail, the middle point of the French exposition is reached. Vidal has used 179 words. Babel employs 41 in his opening subsection, which represents 7 per cent of the story, while Vidal's amounts to 17 per cent. It is evident how much the French version is concerned with the feelings and imagination of its narrator, when the content of each story is compared. Babel's narrator invests less of himself in the text; his description is neutral and factual. For example, Vidal's lieutenant employs a mixture of both first person singular and plural pronouns in the course of his exposition. He acknowledges his own individual presence amid the collective one of his men: 'J'en occupe, avec ma section, le cimetière.' Babel's lieutenant acknowledges only the collective presence of the platoon: 'the cemetry fell to our regiment's lot'. (ll.2–3 'Semeystvo papashi Maresko')

It is clear from the figures given above that the 10 per cent structural discrepancy in the respective expositions occurs here at the very beginning. Vidal's narrator indulges himself and is accorded this section to portray himself. Babel's opening heralds that of many a *Konarmiya* story, in which factual description and detail are given in an objective manner.[49] Babel's opening sentences correspond closely to those of Vidal, setting forth the same facts concerning the village, although no mention is made of time. Equivalent epithets are used: 'charming and modest' (l.2 'Semeystvo papashi Maresko') and 'humble et charmant' ('Histoire Shakespearienne'). A description of the cemetery's desecration then follows, but no explicit reference is made by the narrator to his feelings of horror at being billeted in a cemetery. Instead, it is conveyed by the metaphors that Babel employs.

Vidal's debris of crucifixes, gravestones and flags is described but the French simile is replaced by a Russian metaphor. Babel's graves lie in ruins, 'played havoc with by the hammer of an unknown defiler'. (ll.4–5 'Semeystvo papashi Maresko') The metaphor is more direct than the simile; the linking of participle and instrumental substantive adds a sense of urgency and movement which is lacking in the French comparison: 'cassées comme à coups de marteau par on ne sait quel vampire profanateur'.

This replacement of one trope type by another is indicative of Babel's use of figure in *Konarmiya*. Metaphor outnumbers simile greatly there and it is the inherently vivid and direct nature of the former trope type that Babel exploits to the full. Here Babel moves directly from the 'hammer' metaphor to a second: 'Decayed corpses tumble out of the coffins, smashed by shells.' (ll.5–6 'Semeystvo papashi Maresko') Death is paradoxically invested with life – again one sees Babel's predilection for juxtaposing life with death – as the rotted corpses tumble out of the coffins. The image creates an intensity of horror that is lacking in Vidal, whose threefold sequence of tropes concludes with a less dynamic figure in which the coffins, not the decaying corpses, are animated: 'des cercueils entr'ouverts laissant échapper des ossements …'

Desecration is a theme that recurs in *Konarmiya*. There, the narrator laments the destruction which his fellow countrymen inflict, whether it be on churches, graveyards or even beehives: 'The chronicle of daily offences oppresses me without respite, like a disease of the heart.'[50] Having acknowledged his own presence to be that of a violent intruder in the church of Novograd, Lyutov witnesses a scene reminiscent of the one described by the French lieutenant in the graveyard: 'to meet me two silver skulls gleam on the lid of a broken coffin'.[51] Like other themes in *Konarmiya*, that of desecration receives ambivalent treatment: it is both deplored and celebrated by Lyutov. The latter is particularly true concerning the Catholic church, which is derided in stories such as 'Kostyol v Novograde' and 'U svyatogo Valenta' for its decadence and religious artefacts. Pan Apolek is a Babellian hero whose renown rests on his ability to paint sacrilegious paintings. In 'Pan Apolek', Lyutov compares the hero's skill as an artist with that of Michelangelo, whom both Vidal and Babel cite as being worthy of painting the desecrated graveyard in Picardy. Vidal's catalogue of desecration includes a reference to Christ, where, as noted above, he employs metonymy and an ironic metaphor. Babel shuns this; indeed further references in the French text to the Resurrection may have forced him to exclude all such details from his text, for Christ in his works is generally a figure at which the Jewish finger of derision is pointed most vehemently.

Following the reference to Michelangelo, Vidal's narrator continues immediately to describe the changes that war has brought about in the use of the cemetery. But there is no alteration in tone, and the abstract philosophizing continues: 'Et pourtant, la Guerre a mis sa marque et ramène aux réalités.' In Babel's version, there is a paragraph break and the blunt, terse language of the soldier-narrator becomes more assertive: 'A soldier can't be a mystic.' (l.7 'Semeystvo papashi Maresko') The abstract substantive 'war' of the French version becomes the personalized, concrete substantive 'soldier' of the Russian. Vidal's 'field of the departed', a politely conventional term, is transformed through synecdoche by Babel into the stark and forceful image, 'a field of skulls': 'Car tout ce champ des trépassés est bouleversé, retourné par nos tranchées. Vaste et nécessaire sacrilège!' ("Histoire Shakespearienne') 'The field of skulls is turned into trenches. But that's war.' (ll.7–8 'Semeystvo papashi Maresko')

The comment by each narrator on the digging of the trenches further reveals their different characters. Vidal's vapid exclamation is far removed from Babel's verbal shrugging of the shoulders. In these few lines, Babel's mastery of the technique of *skaz* is indeed visible.[52] His narrator assumes a credibility that Vidal's lacks, because of the direct nature of the language that he utters. The latter, by contrast, employs unctuous clichés and grandiloquent words which are intended to ennoble his steadfastness for the cause, but which in fact do not ring true: 'Nous nous sentons des vivants, âpres à la lutte, décidés à la défense.' Babel reduces this to the simple: 'We are still alive.' (l.8 'Semeystvo papashi Maresko') The final sentence of the respective paragraphs of each version further illustrates these points. Vidal's exclamatory, self-glorifying tone ends with a hackneyed metaphor: 'Et s'il nous faut mourir, ajouter nos cadavres à ces cadavres, nous voulons que ce ne soit pas sans avoir chèrement vendu notre peau!' This is the contrived language of bravado, possibly of a general addressing his troops before going into battle, not the self-musing of a lieutenant, holed up in a cemetery waiting for an enemy attack.

The lack of credibility that Vidal's narrator embodies supports an opinion on the author himself by Jean Norton Cru, in which he states that Vidal's memoirs, claimed as personal, cannot be so and should be treated as semi-historic tales.[53] For example, Vidal gives accounts of one battalion when he was no longer in it and of another in which he had not yet served. He also claims to be, among other things, a pacifist, yet glorifies violence in braggart fashion. Cru declares: 'ce pacifism ne m'émeut pas, ne m'intéresse pas. Il est illogique. L'auteur ne se rend pas compte de ce qu'il écrit.' He concludes by adjuring the reader to look elsewhere for true witnesses, for Vidal is not a witness, but a journalist who has seen copy among the 'chasseurs' and has exploited this to the full.

In Babel's text, the grim humour of the officer is audible as he contemplates his men dying for their country. 'If we are destined to increase the population of this chilly corner, well we've made the rotting old men dance to the march of our machine guns.' (ll.8–10 'Semeystvo papashi Maresko') Babel's officer emerges from the exposition with a personality. His individuality is stamped on the concluding metaphor of the second paragraph. The satisfaction that he feels in his men having at least done their duty is conveyed in the ironic image of the corpses dancing to the tune of their machine guns. Irony precedes irony, in fact, with the euphemism that the officer employs for 'dying'.

Vidal's original is colourless by comparison. His officer is not an individual but merely a mouthpiece of military ostentation, uttering hollow clichés. In the figurative language of Babel's lieutenant, the raciness of some of *Konarmiya*'s fighting men is perceptible; protagonists such as Konkin, Pavlichenko and Balmashov, whose personalities, individualistic and yet part of a collective 'Cossack' whole, are allowed to emerge strongly in their respective stories by displacing the primary narrator, Lyutov.

Babel's third and final paragraph of the exposition combines elements of the three paragraphs which Vidal employs to conclude his. The latter imparts the final details of the narrator's circumstances: he has installed himself in a niche that has been opened by a flagstone dislodged by a shell. Babel begins his paragraph with the same detail but also continues the irony embodied in the tropes of the previous one. His narrator ponders ruefully his discovery of the dislodged gravestone: 'This has been done to offer me shelter no doubt. (ll.11–12 'Semeystvo papashi Maresko') Babel also allows him to lapse into French, a device which he uses occasionally in the first three stories of this cycle, though generally in dialogue. This forms part of Babel's technique of maintaining authenticity and creating atmosphere of which Rothschild speaks.[54] It seems indeed to be an extension of his technique of using *skaz*, but it is a device which he employs sparingly. His French is close to that of Vidal, but it is of little surprise that he alters the content or position according to his own needs: 'I have installed myself on this hole, que voulez-vous, on loge où on peut. (ll.12–13 'Semeystvo papashi Maresko')

Babel's first attempts at writing were in French. We are told of the appetite his French teacher gave him as a child for authors such as de Maupassant and Flaubert. In *Konarmiya*, he includes material in Polish and French. The former occurs in the speech of Polish soldiers, where it is interspersed with bad Russian, and the latter occurs in the fragments of a note, written in Napoleonic times by an unknown hand, which the narrator chances upon in 'Berestechko'. The effect of such occurrences is to augment authenticity and to remind us, particularly in the first three stories of *Na pole chesti,* of the French setting and French protagonists.

Vidal's narrator, having defined his position more exactly, now comments in a lyrical digression on the indifference of the sun to man's predicament: 'Lui, là-haut, n'a cure des batailles, des haines. Il luit paisiblement, impassiblement, fait éclore les fleurs, enivre les papillons.' Such precious thoughts are hardly those of Babel's narrator. This whole paragraph is missing in the Russian. His reference to the weather is made in three adjectives, yet he is still able to introduce a new element 'the spring', and coupled with the next sentence in which he refers to the rich grass of the graves on which he is lying, Babel's narrator is able to affect us more deeply in two lines than Vidal does in seven. The latter's 'ces horreurs' and 'l'acharnement de cette sombre tuerie' are pallid compared with 'And it's a bright, clear, spring morning. I lie on the dead men, look at the rich grass, think of Hamlet.' (ll.13–15 'Semeystvo papashi Maresko') The incongruous effect of spring amid death is increased by Babel's addition of the epithet 'rich'. Vidal's narrator merely states: 'Je regarde les herbes.'

The reference to Hamlet precedes the lieutenant's final ironic thought in the exposition, namely that the tragic prince's ability to communicate with the dead would stand him in good stead now. In a terse figure reminiscent of the one which had the corpses tumbling from their coffins, Babel has the skulls answering Hamlet in human words. Alliteration and assonance increase the prominence of the figure. The consonant 'ch' commences and recurs in each half of the symmetrically balanced figure: 'The skulls answered him with human words. This skill would have been useful to a lieutenant of the French army.' (ll.16–17 'Semeystvo papashi Maresko') The full irony of these remarks concerning the eloquence of the skulls is not apparent to the reader until he learns, with the lieutenant, of the contents of the peasant Maresko's bag at the end of the story. It is the sharp crack of his deceased family's bones inside the bag that strikes the horrific note of realization upon lieutenant and reader alike.

Vidal, whose story bears the title 'Histoire Shakespearienne', does little more than allude to Hamlet before he reflects on the cruelty of the past, endowing history, in a clumsy image, with the ferocity of a beast of prey that possesses a violent disregard for moral laws. The French author's elaborate exposition thus ends on a vague and irrelevant note and it is difficult to catch sight of the narrator's presence in this last paragraph. We are reassured, however, that he is there in the opening of the next: 'Soudain, quelqu'un m'interpelle. Un caporal me dit ...' These remarks also signal the beginning of the second narrative section, the arrival of Marescot.

The control that Babel exercises in his portrayal of the narrator and his circumstances has been evident throughout. The use of *skaz*, the ironic soldier's humour of the narrator, has often been apparent; the extravagant philosophizing of Vidal's protagonist is never encountered. The flaccidity of the latter's writing is cruelly exposed when compared with Babel's sinew; nowhere is this more evident that in the imagery and figures. Indeed, the metaphor quoted above of the skulls talking to Hamlet with human speech exemplifies this. Vidal creates no opportunity to give a forewarning of the story's macabre dénouement.

DILEMMAS

Babel's choice of the two particular Vidal stories was, I assume, a deliberate one. That he rejected the other thirty-three in the cycle is, I believe, because he saw no hint of a dilemma amid their vainglorious jingoism. Babel's mission is apocalyptic; he wishes to exploit the awkward situations that war creates, the effect it has on the inadequate (Bozhi, Bidu and the defenceless Maresko), that is to say the 'little man', and also to demonstrate the respective dilemmas with which these men confront the so-called strong and adequate, i.e. the officers.

'Dezertir'

That Babel intends celebrating a *cause célèbre* of Russian literature, namely the cause of the little man, is evident from the shift in focus which he embodies in his three adaptations. He can both fashion tropes to this end and reject them, as in 'Dezertir'. Vidal uses a simile and a metaphor to describe the young soldier's reaction when he is confronted by the officer: 'Pâle comme une serviette' and 'tremblant, vrai chien battu'. Both these images serve to alienate the boy from the reader; they emphasize his cowardice and his wretchedness and the use of the animal image reduces him in status, if only momentarily. Babel uses no such imagery, rejecting both the trite figures which Vidal employs. The only detail given is the age of the youth, a fact that gains in prominence by the brevity both of the sentences and the paragraph: 'The escort moved off. Zhem'ye locked the door. The soldier was twenty.' (ll.18–19 'Dezertir')

The soldier's youthfulness is accorded no such prominence in the French version. The reader is told the youth's age only after the narrator's claim that he no longer merits being called a soldier – 'ce beau nom'. The reader is, however, made aware in the French version of a past history of insubordination on the part of the young man and the indulgence which had been shown him by the officer on these occasions. The latter is eager to play his part to the full: 'Tu comprends ce que tu as fait et ce que tu mérites cette fois, n'est-ce pas? Voyons, en deux mots, dis-moi franchement ce que tu fichais entre les lignes.' The French version continues with a summary of the soldier's reasons for deserting and Captain V.'s generosity is appealed to by the youth who both recognizes and regrets the criminal act which he has committed.

No mention is made in Babel's version of any history of insubordination on the youth's part, and the officer is taciturn by comparison with Vidal's. 'Do you know what is in store for you? – Voyons, explain yourself.' (l.20 'Dezertir') No summary of the youth's reasons for deserting is given and no appeal is made yet to the Captain's good nature. The youth retains a dignity that is lacking in the French. We are told simply of his tiredness, a result of six nights disturbed by shells. Babel's sympathetic attitude towards the youth is also evident from his repeated references to him by name: four times in fifteen lines one reads phrases like 'this little Bozhi' (ll.24–5

'Dezertir') and 'in front of this twenty-year-old Bozhi'. (l.26 'Dezertir')
Vidal's officer never uses the boy's name once in the forty lines of reported
and direct speech that are devoted to the latter's pleading and the former's
eloquent refusals. We are told the soldier's name, Bridoux, once only in the
French. Babel changes the name of the soldier and comments on his use of
names at the end of the story in a short paragraph. He claims that the name
Bozhi is the correct one, although he gives no evidence for this. Babel's
choice of names is generally significant and often ironic, as the name of his
participatory narrator, Lyutov – 'the fierce one' – testifies in *Konarmiya*.

In only one of the three stories adapted from Vidal's work does a victim
protagonist bear the same name in both versions (Marescot/Maresko). While
my explanation as to why Babel saw fit to retain this name but to alter or
create names for the two other 'little men' is largely hypothetical, it can be
partly furnished by Babel's transformation of Vidal's men of inferior rank
into figures of human dignity and worth. The heroic mould which Vidal is
at pains to create for his officers is transferred, albeit perversely, to their
'inferiors' in Babel's work.

Marescot's name may have appealed to Babel for its already Slavonic
ring; the implication is that Vidal's tragically bereaved Frenchman from
Picardy might just as well have been a war-widower from Petrograd. The
process of 'Russification' may also be at work in Babel's dispensing with
the name Bridoux in favour of Bozhi. Its similarity with the vocative case of
the Russian noun for 'god' ('bozhe') also indicates ironic purpose in Babel's
choice. Three times Vidal's Bridoux is disparagingly portrayed as betraying
not only himself, but also his family, fellows and country by not doing the
decent thing and shooting himself. Bozhi also fails the three opportunities
that he is given to do likewise, but Babel carefully contrives that our sympathy lies with the young private who has neglected to do his duty. It may
be stretching analogy too far to see a link with the figure of Christ, three
times disowned by one disciple and betrayed by another, but the analogy
does elevate Bozhi to the status of the *Konarmiya* figure Sashka Khristos,
who as saint and syphilitic, is equally an embodiment of Babellian irony.

Bidu of 'Na pole chesti' also engenders speculation. Vidal does not even
name the demented figure crouching at the bottom of the hole; Babel affords
him that dignity, among others, and in his choice of name again evokes
questions of affinity with a *Konarmiya* figure, namely the like-sounding
Afon'ka Bida. There would seem to be both ironic disparity and similarity
between Bidu's circumstances in 'Na pole chesti' and those in which Bida
encounters Lyutov in 'Smert' Dolgushova' and 'Afon'ka Bida'. In 'Smert'
Dolgushova' Lyutov is exposed as a coward (Bidu's role in 'Na pole chesti')
for not killing the mortally wounded Dolgushov, while Bida is the person
who has to rectify the situation and in so doing condemns the central narrator. Bida is thus both aggressor and victim, hero and villain. He has to act
in order to kill a man, to do his duty, forced upon him by Luytov's unfinished business. War thus renders him both hero and victim. Bidu, in 'Na
pole chesti', is likewise both: he is a victim of war, unable to cope with its

demands on him, while the sacrifice of his own life, forced upon him by the persecution of others, is his act of heroism.

In 'Afon'ka Bida', the peasant army led by a young Jew is mocked by Bida and his Cossacks (Bidu suffers mockery in 'Na pole chesti'), yet later the situation is reversed: Bida is grief stricken at the loss of his horse – a Cossack aggressor or purveyor of war becomes its victim. He even resembles the idiot Bidu – at least in his sleep – in his loneliness and grief: 'The clotted head of the platoon commander with its twisted lifeless mouth lay as if crucified on the bend of the saddle.'[55] 'The idiot laid his head on his knees, put his two arms around it and started to cry.' (ll.23–4 'Na pole chesti') Thus, Babel's circular symmetry is at work – heroes become victims and *vice versa*.

The officer's name also provides a point of interest in 'Dezertir'. Babel uses Zhem'ye, which is that of the Frenchman to whom Vidal has dedicated his story: 'A Firmin Gémier, en témoignage de vive admiration.' For Babel, this dedication is enough to indicate that Vidal's hero-narrator, Captain V., is in fact Gémier. Babel is thus able to strengthen his irony by dispensing with the presumably fictitious Captain V. in favour of Captain Zhem'ye, who does not receive from him the heroic portrayal of Vidal's Captain.

Nevertheless, Babel is not wholly unsympathetic to the Captain. While he has consciously altered the imbalance that exists between officer and youth in terms of their treatment by Vidal, the focus on both protagonists is in more or less equal proportion. The seventeen lines of paragraphs eleven to seventeen in the Russian contrast with the 34 lines of paragraphs fourteen to twenty one in the French. Captain V. himself speaks for 19 of these, whereas Bridoux speaks directly for two and is reported in eight. Zhem'ye, however, speaks for five lines, Bozhi for three and is reported in five and a half.

Captain V.'s oratory flows unchecked with frequent allusions to honour, dishonour, duty and himself: 'Mais il ne fallait pas que je me laisse séduire, je ne le pouvais, ni pour moi, ni pour ses [i.e. Bridoux's] compagnons.' Bridoux, also more frequently than Bozhi, pleads his cause. On three occasions he cites either his despair or his fear, his youthfulness or the shame that his family will feel as he attempts to shake the officer's resolve. Bozhi too refers to his age and his family but does not specify despair or fear as reasons for his being spared. His anguish is nonetheless affecting: 'Captain, what will my mother say when she finds out that I have been shot like the worst kind of villain? The soldier fell to his knees.' (ll.30–2 'Dezertir') Bozhi, however, is able to maintain a dignity that Bridoux has never had. As the narrative approaches its climax with the youth being led into the wood, Bozhi's reaction to the proffered gun is one of silence. Silence is indeed the reaction of both Lyutov and Babel in moments of crisis in their lives: the former in 'Smert' Dolgushova' and 'Posle boya' as he turns his back on Bida's gun and Akinfiyev's taunts, and the latter with the celebrated 'genre of silence' that he claimed to have cultivated in the thirties. Silence had also been Bozhi's reaction in the opening stage when confronted by Zhem'ye's ironic enquiry as to why he had been between the lines: 'You've availed yourself of the dawn to get some fresh air? Silence.' (ll.15–16 'Dezertir')

Bridoux's histrionics are also the same on each occasion: 'Oh! mon capitaine ...', he exclaims. Vidal's narrator's pejorative treatment of him continues with the repeated return of the Captain to the wood. The youth remains vacant and inert. 'Je n'ai pas le courage, bêle-t-il ... non, je n'ai pas le courage.' Sobbing, he repeats the pleas for mercy that he has already made.

Bozhi's fear is evident too; Zhem'ye finds him huddled up, but the youth does not 'bleat' about his failure to kill himself, he whispers: 'I can't Captain, – the soldier whispered – I haven't the strength left.' (ll.44–5 'Dezertir') Again Babel has omitted a trite animal metaphor, but he is also not averse to adding detail. He postpones the sobbing of the youth to the second return of the officer, who finds him lying on the ground: 'His fingers, lying on the revolver, stirred feebly.' ('Pal'tsy yego, lezhavshiye na revol'vere, slabo shevelilis.') (l.51 'Dezertir') Vidal's equivalent comment does not include the adverb, nor is there Babel's attention to assonance, with the liquid 'l' sounds blending with the youth's sobs: 'Il est toujours à la même place, tournant l'arme dans ses doigts.'

Babel exploits the repeated returns of the Captain to the wood to increase tension. His portrayal of Bozhi's fear develops gradually and this enhances the poignancy of the situation to a level that is missing in the French, where no sign of Bridoux's emotion is given. While his feelings are ignored, those of the narrator are not. The self-aggrandisement reaches a crescendo: 'Je compris l'impossibilité d'obtenir le geste de bravoure et de repentir. Je compris aussi qu'il était douloureux pour la mère, là-bas, de savoir la vérité. Je sauvai de la catastrophe ce qui pouvait en être sauvé: le nom du malhereux.' At the moment of climax, the focus is thus directed at the narrator and not at the boy; this continues with another comment on the officer's feelings, which Vidal has italicised: 'et, froidement, *sûr de faire un acte juste et bon*, je lui brûlai la cervelle ...' The resolve which Captain V. demonstrates by this act has failed him, however, at the time of narration, for he immediately asks his companion for his opinion.

Babel's Zhem'ye neither glorifies nor doubts his course of action. He returns to the prostrate, sobbing Bozhi and picks him up, a gesture of empathy lacking in the French. He addresses the youth in a quiet, sincere voice, looking him in the eyes, as he takes the revolver from the boy's wet hands. The officer accords him the dignity of a human being. The addition of the detail 'wet hands' (l.55 'Dezertir') by Babel enhances the pathos and complements the earlier 'stirred feebly' (l.51 'Dezertir') of Bozhi's fingers on the revolver butt; it also signals the culmination of the gradational portrayal of the tension and the youth's anguish.

The very words used to describe the breaking of the tension, namely the shooting of the youth by the officer, are indicative of the different standpoints of the respective authors. Captain V. blew out his brains while Zhem'ye shot him through the skull. The French, 'brûlai la cervelle', expresses the sense of satisfaction that the officer felt as he squeezed the trigger, the Russian 'shot him through the skull', (l.56 'Dezertir') reflects in subdued tone the sense of duty from which the officer does not flinch, and about which, unlike Captain V., Zhem'ye has nowhere seen fit to tell us. Indeed, Vidal's expression for the shooting foreshadows a comment by Balmashov in 'Sol', when he rids Soviet Russia of a black marketress: 'And taking a trusty rifle from the wall I washed this shame from the face of the workers' land and the Republic.'[57] Here too the narrator and his fellow soldiers had been deceived and Balmashov was as 'sûr de faire un acte juste et bon' as Captain V. had been.

Babel adds an epilogue, not only to state the source of the material for the story, but also to redirect the reader's attention to the initial irony which so flavours the opening description of Captain Zhem'ye. The virtues of the good captain are again expounded, not least of which, the reader is told for the second time, is his ability to forgive small wrongs: 'And then, Vidal testifies that the Captain really was a patriot, a soldier, a good father and a man who knew how to forgive small wrongs. And it's no small thing for a man – to forgive small wrongs.' (ll.61–4 'Dezertir') Babel, it would appear, does not forgive the Captain his vainglorious egotism in Vidal's version, for his dominant attitude towards him in his own is ironic. The good family man who knows no hesitation on the battlefield kills a twenty-year-old battle weary deserter: '… he is only twenty years old, mon Dieu, c'est naturel, at twenty you can make a mistake'. (ll.26–7 'Dezertir': these lines are the reported words of the youth, Bozhi.)

Yet Babel's voice is ambivalent. The Captain is both villain and hero, for he is shown to act with compassion, while remaining decisive in his actions and unwavering in his sense of duty. This is something to which Lyutov aspires in *Konarmiya* and generally fails to achieve. War repeatedly creates situations which expose the inadequacies of the central protagonist, and it is this theme, in *Konarmiya* and *Na pole chesti* to which Babel returns again and again. While the balance of his portrayal tilts in favour of the inadequate, the little man, his focus is indeed a dual one. The two protagonists of 'Dezertir' are portrayed as human beings. Babel both derides and ennobles Zhem'ye and while he portrays the wretchedness of Bozhi, he allows him the dignity and status of a human being. This is not the case in Vidal's story. The narrator, Captain V., glorifies himself, justifies his motives, monopolizes the centre of events, while the youth represents a hapless wretch, an object of contempt to be wiped away at the end.

'Na pole chesti'

The cause of the outcast, the inadequate, is again taken up in 'Na pole chesti' and the outcome is similar to 'Dezertir': the central protagonist is shot. It would seem, however, that the inadequacies he shows are too great for any sympathetic portrayal to be created, yet this is what Babel achieves. Although the Russian story is longer than Vidal's by some eighty words, it is testimony to Babel's mastery of dialogue that the questioning of Bidu, the central figure, is a third less in length. The inclusion of the masturbation detail in the final phase of the exposition facilitates this brevity. In the French, the equivalent detail is delayed.

More significant than its transposition, however, is the fact that Babel has altered the substance of it. Vidal's soldier cannot move from the hollow because of fear: fear which he cannot conquer and which has caused him to defecate in his trousers. This animal function which the soldier has involuntarily performed is less shocking than the physiological act which Babel introduces. It is nevertheless distasteful and, coupled with his wheedling manner, Vidal's soldier arouses nothing but antipathy: 'Je vous jure, mon capitaine, je ne peux pas … j'ai essayé tout … de me raisonner, de m'engueuler, de boire de la gniole … Rien n'y fait … J'ai le trac … J'en ai fait dans mon pantalon … Excusez que je dise ça … C'est pour que vous compreniez … Y a pas moyen, quoi …' Bidu, it may be argued however, is guilty on two counts. He has not only turned coward, but is also indulging in a gross act. By the introduction of sexual self-abuse, Babel has compounded the soldier's guilt. What then is his purpose in rendering Bidu doubly guilty and, notwithstanding this, how does he still embody the cause of the 'little man'?

Babel's soldier, unlike Vidal's, has the standing of a village idiot. This fact is referred to more than once in the story, for example, 'the hard head of a village idiot', (l.31 'Na pole chesti') and is registered by Babel at the first mention of his name, 'It was Bidu the soldier, Bidu the idiot.' (ll.9–10 'Na pole chesti') While the inclusion and stressing of this fact render the youth pathetic, they also assist in his portrayal as a fallible, feeling human being. Vidal's soldier, who has no claim to idiocy, consequently has this neither as an excuse nor as a redeeming factor and is not invested in any way with the dignity or status of a human being.

Babel's focus is, however, not monocular. His portrayal of the officer, Ratin, reveals his mastery of psychological insight. Ratin leaves us in no doubt as to his feelings. He expresses his loathing for Bidu in terms of bitter irony. Babel exploits the sexual theme further through hyperbolic metaphor: 'You have found a wife here, you swine!' (l.17 'Na pole chesti') In this section of dialogue a gradational development of Ratin's character is seen. He reacts firstly as a person, subsequently as an institutional representative. After the remark quoted above, the affronted dignity of Ratin the man yields immediately to that of the institution which he represents, as he adds: 'You have dared to tell me to my face that you are a coward, Bidu.' (ll.17–18 'Na pole chesti') His final comment indicates that he has regained the conventional stance of an officer and a superior: 'You have abandoned your comrades at the very hour the regiment is attacking. Ben, mon cochon! …'[58] (ll.18–19 'Na pole chesti') Thomas Rothschild quotes this speech by Ratin as an example of Babel's artistry in constructing the smallest of compositional details, creating thereby the psychology of his protagonist.[59] The soldier, in both versions of the story, speaks twice, relating his fear and his attempts to overcome it. (His only other utterance is his death yell at the end.) His final words in 'Na pole chesti' are a pathetic reiteration of his first: 'Je peux pas, capitaine … I'm afraid, Captain! …'(l.22 'Na pole chesti') Symmetry is thus achieved.

In the French version, because the soldier is more articulate, there is a lack of both symmetry and tension, which is reinforced by an imbalance in treatment of the protagonists by Vidal. Babel's officer and soldier speak at the same length and for the same number of times, and it is not without significance that it is the latter who ends the only dialogue in the story. The last word, however, in the form of a threefold insult, is reserved for Vidal's Captain, who is afforded one more opportunity to speak than the soldier. As in the first anecdote of 'Deux actes devant une conscience', the focus returns quickly from the soldier to the officer, although in this case it is not one but two officers who continue to play the central part. The Captain's companion, a lieutenant, takes the lead, amidst praise from the narrator. He abuses the youth further with more virulent invective, and when this is to no avail, temper grips him as he seeks a more satisfying way of venting his disgust. Vidal includes an observation open to both literal and figurative interpretation: 'Pas moyen d'obtenir qu'il sorte de son trou.' The soldier is crouching at the bottom of a hole, yet there is a trite figurative implication in the use of this substantive which further belittles him. The word 'hole' evokes the image of an animal and, coupled with the possessive adjective 'his', implies a comparison of the soldier with an animal that has gone to ground and is being baited.

The corresponding paragraphs in Russian are far removed from the French version. With the soldier's second declaration of fear terminating the dialogue, the focus remains with him and does not transfer to the officer. His reaction at being discovered and chastised is both pathetic and human. Again he is referred to as 'the idiot': 'The idiot laid his head on his knees, put his two arms around it and started to cry.' (ll.23–4 'Na pole chesti') Indeed he may be compared to old Shloyme, the chief protagonist in the eponymous story, which is Babel's earliest published work.[60] Old Shloyme is a wretched figure, who thinks little and feels so much more. 'Through a skilful use of the tragic ... Babel understands how to excite compassion, in spite of all the repulsiveness.'[61] Yet the reader's gaze and compassion are allowed to dwell only briefly on the hapless youth. Both are interrupted by the following sentence: 'Then he looked at the Captain, and in the chinks of his piggy little eyes a timid, tender hope was reflected.' (ll.24–5 'Na pole chesti') The focus is now transferring to the Captain; the narrative bridge which enables Babel to maintain his balance between protagonists is the glance from one to the other. The statement is made, however, not simply to expedite the action but, with the use of the epithet 'piggy', reminds the reader of the base conduct of the boy. Yet it is these very 'piggy little eyes', portrayed, as is the youth himself, by a diminutive, that register the human emotion of hope. One is aware in this sentence, not only of Babel's mastery of the narrative linking device and his maintenance of the balance of focus between protagonists, but also of his essential ambivalence at work, his inclusion of one seemingly irreconcilable viewpoint with another. The emotive quality of the sentence is enhanced by Babel's use of sound: the harsh sibilants and gutterals in the words used to portray the boy's animalism – 'shcholkakh

35

yego svinnykh glazok' ('the chinks of his piggy little eyes') (ll.24–5 'Na pole chesti') – cede to a softer assonant flourish at the end to portray the youth's essential human fallibility – 'otrazilas' robkaya i nezhnaya nadeshda' ('a timid, tender hope was reflected'). (l.25 'Na pole chesti')

In her work on Babel's metaphors, Danuta Mendelsohn misquotes these lines and creates a metaphor which Babel never intended.[62] She renders it thus: 'i v sholkakh yego sinikh glazok' ('in the silks of his little blue eyes'), thereby destroying the ambivalence that the line embodies, which Babel's contrasting sounds accentuate. Indeed, at various points in this story, in this cycle and elsewhere in his works, particularly *Konarmiya*, Babel exploits both assonance and alliteration to create emotive effects.[63]

One's admiration for Babel's craftsmanship and the subtlety of the last sentence are diminished somewhat by the next two: 'Ratin was quick tempered. He had lost two brothers in the war, and the wound on his neck had not healed.' (ll.25–6 'Na pole chesti') The change of focus from boy to officer is completed abruptly. These explicit statements on the misfortunes of war which have befallen Ratin are intended, one assumes, to justify the man's anger in the reader's eyes. He has suffered because of the war, so why should he tolerate this cowardly and obscene fool, is the implicit question that Babel is asking. Yet the explicitness of these details is not in keeping with the stories of *Konarmiya* where a more subtle presentation generally obtains. Babel's intention is clumsily transparent here and detracts from an otherwise successful psychological portrayal.

There is, however, a tenuous similarity between Ratin and a *Konarmiya* protagonist. In 'Eskadronnyy Trunov', a story with a confused origin, we are told that the central figure, Trunov, has been wounded.[64] The fact is stressed by two references to this at different points in the story, when the same simile recurs: 'Blood was streaming down from it [a wound], like rain off a rick.'[65] Trunov is perhaps one of Babel's least convincing figures and one in which Babel's ambivalence is seen at its most extreme. Trunov commits acts of great brutality and heroism and his wound acts as a factor in Lyutov's counterbalancing of these two aspects of his nature. The squadron commander emerges as a desperate, fanatical individual while Ratin, at this point of 'Na pole chesti', seems but a pallid representative of an institution.

Ratin proceeds to vent his anger on the boy. The intensity of his wrath is felt in the succession of metaphors. While the sequence begins and ends with fossilized figures, a visual image of originality lies between them: 'Blasphemous abuse came down upon the soldier, an *arid hail fell on him of those repulsive, violent and senseless words*, at which the blood hammers in the temples'. (ll.26–9 'Na pole chesti') The middle figure, which I have stressed, prompted by Vidal's, 'Les mots les plus durs pleuvent sur le misérable' has been transformed into one of originality. The sting and senselessness of Ratin's venom is felt. Vidal's hard words raining down on the soldier become Babel's arid hail flying at him. In the onomatopoeic substantive 'grad', a tired image becomes one of freshness and vigour and one sees a hint of the final abuse to come.

36

Just as previously Bidu's look at Ratin had transferred our attention to the latter, so the torrent of abuse now redirects the focus to the former. Again his reaction is described in the Russian, but ignored in the French. Babel informs us that the degree of Ratin's insult is enough to provoke a man to murder, yet Bidu's reaction is scarcely that: 'Instead of an answer Bidu quietly rocked his shaggy, round ginger head, the hard head of a village idiot.' (ll.30–1 'Na pole chesti') The concentration of adjectives (round, ginger, shaggy/krugloy, ryzhey, lokhmatoy) to describe the boy's uncomprehending head again stresses his abtuseness, while their rhythmical quality evinces pathos and accords him the dignity of a response.

It is interesting to note the use Babel makes of 'ryzhiy' ('ginger') in *Konarmiya*. At the end of 'U svyatogo Valenta', Lyutov stumbles upon what proves to be an image of Christ: 'the man in the orange greatcoat was being pursued by hatred and overtaken by the chase'.[66] The scene affects Lyutov greatly for he calls it the most extraordinary image of Christ that he has seen in his life. Christ is depicted as putting out a hand to ward off the blows of his pursuers: 'and above eyes closed in pain curved delicate ginger eyebrows'.[67] With the use of 'ginger' there is perhaps a link in Babel's mind between Christ and the red-haired Bidu. Both men are the victims of persecution; they have each incurred the hatred of others. Bidu, the village idiot, has indulged in a gross sexual act which is comparable to the sexual misdemeanours that Babel attributes to Christ in such stories as 'Pan Apolek' *(Konarmiya)* and 'Iisusov grekh',[68] and Babel may well have been thinking of Bidu as he wrote of a persecuted Christ in 'U svyatogo Valenta'. In both instances, a prolonged cry is uttered which enhances the grotesque nature of the events portrayed amidst an atmosphere of pathos.

A further story in *Konarmiya* in which the grotesque and the pathetic are intermingled is 'Perekhod cheroz Zbruch'. Here Lyutov is billeted with some Jews who are described as 'two ginger Jews with delicate necks'.[69] They clean the place up at his bidding, 'like Japanese at the circus, their necks spin and swell'.[70] One can surmise that Babel's choice of 'ginger' *vis-à-vis* the Jews is to contribute to the grotesquely comical nature of their actions, for the Russian adjective also embodies the colloquial meaning of 'a clown'. Might there also not be a similar intention in Babel's description of the idiot Bidu's behaviour, since he has become an object of ridicule in his officer's eyes?

Vidal's lieutenant, having failed like the captain to extricate the soldier from his crater through verbal abuse, arrives finally at the idea of urinating on the boy: 'Lève-toi, bon Dieu! ou je te pisse dessus!', he exclaims. Vidal exploits the duality of his officers in the final section of the French anecdote: 'Et son geste me gagne! Et nous voilà l'un et l'autre inondant le malheureux de toute l'abjection possible.' The inclusion of a companion for his captain has a twofold purpose. It allows Captain V. a way of sharing any sense of guilt, for it is not he, after all, who thinks of urinating on the boy, and it emphasizes the unity of the army's representatives, in that the army's honour will be upheld come what may. Superior rank is seen to triumph, and justice, on Vidal's terms, to be served with the subsequent death of the soldier.

Whatever the author's purpose, the tension and intensity of the Russian version is lacking in the French because the standpoint of the officers alone is given. The reader is given insights only into the minds of the representatives of the oppressor, the institution, and is duly meant to savour the defeat of a rebel by the establishment. Babel has excluded the lieutenant; oppressor and oppressed are balanced numerically and in terms of psychological insight. There is no intermediary between Bidu and Ratin, whose confrontation is consequently more intense.

The shift of focus that Babel embodies, however, in his portrayal of the 'little man' is again evident in a comparison of the following lines. Babel's statement is neutral: 'It was impossible to make him get up by force.' (l.32 'Na pole chesti'); it contrasts with the depreciatory equivalent in Vidal, by omitting the last three words: 'Pas moyen d'obtenir qu'il sorte de son trou.' Babel then proceeds to reverse the situation, for it is Ratin, the officer, who merits imagery with animal connotations: 'Then the Captain approached the very edge of the hole and hissed especially quietly.' (ll.32–3 'Na pole chesti') Ratin's threat is delivered in a quiet voice of menace like the hiss of a snake, whereas Vidal's lieutenant shouts his in a frenzy of temper.

The climax of the respective narratives has now been reached, and although Babel fashions his differently in detail and in imagery, both versions begin their respective paragraphs with a similar statement: 'Et il fait comme il dit!'; 'He did as he said.' (l.35 'Na pole chesti') In the laconicism of the statement, one sees a hint of the subsequent underplaying of violent or distasteful actions or events that so characterizes *Konarmiya, Odesskiye rasskazy* and other works. The bald statement of narrative fact to describe a violent climax is frequently employed to skilful dramatic effect by Babel and it is seen at the end of 'Na pole chesti' as Bidu is killed: 'An enemy bullet pierced his breast.' (l.41 'Na pole chesti') The fetid stream of urine redirects our attention to the boy. The hissing sibilants and liquid 'l' sounds that Babel employs stress the degradation of the youth: 'A fetid stream spattered forcefully in the soldier's face.' (l.36 'Na pole chesti') Vidal's language is vapid by comparison: 'Et nous voilà l'un et l'autre inondant le malheureux de toute l'abjection possible …' His use of the euphemistic substantive 'l'abjection' conveys little of the physical horror which is inflicted on the soldier. The final moments of Bidu's life and of his existence as an object of derision have arrived; his response begins with a yell, 'an inhuman and prolonged yell' (l.38 'Na pole chesti'). The use of the epithet 'inhuman' is paradoxical. It contrasts with and heightens the pathos of the series of epithets which follows. These, in a cluster of three, express the sentiments, the human feelings which the idiot boy has: 'this yell, melancholy, lonely, diminishing …' (ll.38–9 'Na pole chesti')

Babel subsequently named the hero of his *Odesskiye rasskazy* Benya Krik (Benya the Yell). He is an underworld Jewish gangster, who sheds the shackles of ghetto oppression to lead a life of flamboyance and wealth. That he should be dubbed Benya Krik implies that his life represents a loud and, in his case, long and successful protest at the normal lot of the Jew. Bidu's 'inhuman and prolonged yell' (l.38 'Na pole chesti') is short lived by comparison, but it is no less resounding in the mind of the reader. Contained in the adjectives describing the yell is the frustration, sadness and loneliness of a lifetime. With its threefold attributive phrase, the yell precedes the passage of the boy across the fields to the enemy trenches, for he launches himself in headlong frenzy towards the German lines. Symmetry is maintained in his actions; like the yell they are three-dimensional: 'the soldier darted up, wrung his hands and took to his heels across the field to the German trenches'. (ll.39–41 'Na pole chesti')

In Babel's works one meets groups of three consecutive adjectives or verbs at significant points or climaxes; for example in 'Prishchepa' three descriptive phrases precede three verbs as the young Cossack's vengeance nears completion: 'Scorched and torn, shuffling his feet, he led the cow out of the shed, put his revolver in its mouth and fired.'[71] As I have noted, Bidu's death is conveyed tersely, but at the end of the paragraph Babel adds three sentences, the contents of which are lacking in the French version: 'Ratin finished him off with two shots from the revolver. The soldier's body did not even twitch. It remained halfway, between the opposing lines. (ll.41–3 'Na pole chesti') Ratin resumes the centre of the stage, if only for a moment. The two shots that he fires not only remind the reader of his presence at Bidu's death, which he has caused, but also expose both the fury and anguish which the officer has himself suffered. Bidu had disobeyed an order, was guilty of indecency and cowardice and has met his end. Ratin's two shots are the gesture of a bitter man, who salvages some satisfaction from a war which has robbed him of two brothers. His final act is one of vengeance rather than mercy.

Bidu's refusal to do the duty that is expected of him, and which Ratin and others fulfil unquestioningly, compounds the soldier's guilt. His is a dual guilt and his punishment emulates this. For his self-abuse he is paid in kind; one animal act begets another and he suffers Ratin's urinating upon him. For his cowardice he meets the ultimate punishment, as does Bozhi in 'Dezertir'. Bidu's position at the end of the story is that of Bozhi at the beginning of the second story, that is, in no man's land, halfway between the opposing lines. This physical limbo which both men occupy is a circumstantial, cyclical link which is developed further in the respective central protagonists of 'Semeystvo papashi Maresko', 'Kvaker', and subsequently *Konarmiya*. Maresko, Ston and Lyutov all find themselves in a psychological limbo, caused or exacerbated by war.

At the end of 'Na pole chesti', one's sympathy lies with Bidu. His final gesture is both heroic and hopeless. Vidal explicitly states the irony that Babel implies: 'Deux minutes après, une balle en pleine poitrine permettait de dire qu'il était mort en héros.' Vidal's penultimate paragraph is composed of anacolutha and indicates Captain V.'s delayed sense of guilt: "Celle-là, qu'en dites-vous? ... Sur le moment je fus ravi du résultat ... Et maintenant, voilà, je ne sais pas … Et pourtant …' The final paragraph consists of a single line: 'Nous nous tûmes, pensifs', and confirms this sense of guilt.

The additional facts which Babel includes, stress the humane standpoint of the Russian author. Not only has Ratin fired the final shots and left the body in no man's land, with the result that the reader is conscious of his being the main instrument in Bidu's death, but the short penultimate paragraph serves as an epitaph to the dead soldier and has no counterpart in the French: 'Thus Selestin Bidu died, a Norman peasant, native of Ory, 21 years of age – on the bloodstained fields of France.' (ll.44–5 'Na pole chesti') These brief details place Bidu's life in a context and stress his actuality: the wretched youth possessed a christian name, a birthplace, a country. The fact that his death was ignominious is beyond question, but the cruel circumstances of it enhance the pathos that surrounds him.

The use of the epithet 'stained' (l.45 'Na pole chesti') exemplifies the symmetrical structure of Babel's work. If the second paragraph of the introduction is re-examined, we recall how he had painted a broad canvas of the peasantry fleeing from the enemy bombardment: 'The sky … was slowly turning crimson, swelling and misting over.' (ll.3–4 'Na pole chesti')

The sky had symbolized the slaughter that was occurring below. Now, at the end of the story, the use of a further similarly poetic image 'on the bloodstained fields of France' (l.45 'Na pole chesti') reminds us that we have moved from a representation of human misery and suffering on a mass scale, 'the peasantry' (l.2 'Na pole chesti') to that of a single individual, 'a Norman peasant'. (l.44 'Na pole chesti') Bidu dies on the crimson fields of France below that same blood-red sky which had witnessed the deaths of so many. Both the transition from sky to earth, which stresses the peasant roots of Bidu, and the linking of the two images through a repetition of colour, have the epic ring of the *byliny* about them.

The final paragraph of Babel's version continues the symmetrical link with the introduction and one senses a parallel with the 'kol'tso' or 'ring' structure in prose-works of which formalist commentators, such as Propp and Seyfullina, write.[72] In the first paragraph, Babel gives a general introduction to the source and theme of the stories; in the last, this source is identified and Babel ends on the same note of irony that his title 'Na pole chesti' sounded at the beginning. Captain V., the narrator, and Captain Vidal, the author, are equated: 'He also defended France, Captain Vidal.' (l.48 'Na pole chesti') is preceded by the equivocal sentence 'He was a witness to this.' (ll.47–8 'Na pole chesti') – 'this' is left undefined.

The method of ending a story with a factual reference is one which Babel employs in *Konarmiya* to give his work authenticity;[73] it is as if he wishes to create the illusion of documentary actuality. This seal of authenticity, which he also gives the *Na pole chesti* cycle – 'What I have related here is the truth. It has been written about in Captain Vidal's book – Figures et anecdotes de la Grande Guerre. (ll.46–7 'Na pole chesti') – is designed to stress the reality of the respective deaths or tragedies of each of the main protagonists, and to focus on the senselessness and inevitability of the ultimate sacrifice which war demands of them.

'Semeystvo papashi Maresko'

Maresko is a unique figure in the cycle. Unlike the other three central protagonists (this includes the Quaker, Ston), he loses not his own life but those of his family, and unlike Bozhi, Bidu and Ston, he is a civilian. His status and his sacrifice are different from theirs, yet in the pathos that he evokes he is their equal, if not their superior. His civilian status is stressed from the first. A corporal informs the narrator that 'some civilian or other' wishes to see him. The former has time only to register surprise: 'What the devil is a civilian looking for in this nether world? (l.20 'Semeystvo papashi Maresko')

Vidal's lieutenant, however, is reluctant to share the centre of the stage. Marescot's entrance is delayed as the officer evinces both surprise and annoyance and attempts to re-establish his identity, which has been submerged in the verbose philosophizing of the exposition. He mentions his rank and his wrath and, having done so, then regrets his irritation and attempts to atone for it. All this occurs as his fellow protagonist is about to emerge. Babel's narrator includes no direct reference to himself.

Similar details of Maresko's appearance are given in both the French and Russian versions. He is dressed in mud-spattered Sunday clothes, a fact which exacerbates the incongruity of his civilian presence, and he brings with him a sack which, the narrator assumes, contains potatoes. The details which differ in the two versions are noteworthy. Vidal specifies a colour: 'Vêtu de noir, endimanché me semble-t-il, d'ailleurs maculé de boue.' Babel refers twice to a garment: 'The character makes his entrance. A worn, faded creature. Got up in a Sunday frock-coat. The frock-coat is bespattered with mud.' (ll.21–2 'Semeystvo papashi Maresko') Babel's Maresko is the more wretched figure. He is a haggard, threadbare creature. The epithet 'faded', (l.21 'Semeystvo papashi Maresko') foreshadows the repetition of 'the frock-coat'. (l.22) The use of the dehumanizing substantive 'creature', (l.21) – the second of three with which Babel refers to Maresko – effects a transition from the first, 'the character', (l.21) to the third, 'the frock-coat'. (l.22) It is as if the coat, doubly incongruous in this setting, becomes Maresko. These references indeed foreshadow a final humiliation of the civilian in the closing section of the story, a humiliation which allows the reader a glimpse of Babel's genius in the use of metonymy.[74] There is no such pejorative gradation in Vidal's description. The single explicit detail indicative of wretchedness is the word 'pauvre'.

The second half of the respective paragraphs is devoted to the sack which the civilian has brought with him. Babel again alters details. Vidal's Marescot is pushing a wheelbarrow with a large sack placed in it. The sack, the narrator assumes, is half full of potatoes and makes 'un bruit singulier' when the old man lowers the barrow. Babel's Maresko is allowed no such luxury: 'A sack dangles over timid shoulders'. (ll.22–3 'Semeystvo papashi Maresko') The physical burden that the sack imposes upon him increases the horror of

41

realization experienced by the reader at the end, when the contents of the sack become apparent. The pathos of Maresko's emotional burden is thus also enhanced. The transfer from barrow to back is effective since the noise that comes from the crack, onomatopoeically portrayed as 'cracks' ('treshchit'), (l.25 'Semeystvo papashi Maresko') occurs every time the man moves, unlike Vidal's 'bruit singulier', which is heard only once as the barrow is lowered.

It is only with hindsight, perhaps, that the reader appreciates how every detail in Babel's description is significant, no matter how small; and it is through such a unique opportunity of comparison as this that one is able to evaluate each word. Vidal's sack is described as 'à moitié *plein*', Babel's as 'half *empty*'. (l.23 'Semeystvo papashi Maresko')[75] The different perspective of the latter, coupled with his addition of the adjective 'frozen' ('morozhennyy') (l.24) to describe the alleged potatoes, lends a sharpness to the cracking together of the sack's contents and to the subsequent poignancy of the situation that is entirely lacking in Vidal.

This section of the story concludes with the first brief dialogue between the two protagonists.[76] Maresko gives his name and declares his wish to bury his family. Babel adds details which cause Maresko to appear more hesitant, more pathetic. He whispers and bows and subsequently raises his hat to reveal a grey forehead:

> My surname, you see, is Monsieur Maresko, – the civilian whispers and bows. – The reason why I've come …
> – Well?
> – I should like to bury Madam Maresko and all the family, monsieur lieutenant!… (ll.27–31 'Semeystvo papashi Maresko')

Vidal's Marescot simply stammers and no other descriptive items are given: 'Qu'est-ce-que c'est? Voilà, bafouille-t-il … je viens, par rapport que je suis M. Marescot … et que je voudrais enterrer ma famille …' The latter conveys his name and request in one uninterrupted sentence, although he pauses midway; he also omits any reference to his wife when mentioning his family. In the Russian version, Maresko not only includes her, but uses her official title, the title that strangers would use when addressing her. This indicates a humility and self-effacing quality on the civilian's part which is supplemented by his mode of address to the lieutenant. 'Monsieur lieutenant' is in fact used in consecutive speeches by Maresko. The loss that he has suffered, and his humility, are felt more keenly in the Russian because of these extra details. Both writers, however, exploit the irony of the situation in Marescot (Maresko)'s remark which concludes the second narrative section. (Vidal) '… vous avez peut-être entendu parler …'; (Babel) 'Perhaps you've heard, monsieur lieutenant!..' (ll.34–5 'Semeystvo papashi Maresko'), he asks, as if his appearance and circumstances are perfectly normal.

The action of the narrative is then interrupted by the third section, a flashback to the events that ensued before the opening of the story. Both authors use the musings of the lieutenant as a device to inform the reader of the civilian's circumstances. We learn of the resolve of the people in the village to stay in their homes despite the bombardment, also of the death and injury of many as courage and stone walls proved an insufficient defence, and finally we are told the fate of one family, the Mareskos, who were crushed in their cellar.

Babel's version follows Vidal's closely in content and detail, apart from his *skaz* style which asserts itself in the succession of shorter sentences that constitute his lieutenant's reminiscing: 'Old man Maresko? I had heard these words. Of course I had heard them. Here's the whole story.' (ll.36–7 'Semeystvo papashi Maresko') compared with: 'C'est vrai, je me souviens du nom.'

The enumeration of the composition of Maresko's family, which is slightly more prolonged in the Russian version, and follows the stressing by both authors that the family was a true French one, evokes pathos: 'Their surname had stayed in my memory – a real French surname. *There were four of them* – father, mother and two daughters. Only the father escaped.' (ll.42–4 'Semeystvo papashi Maresko') 'Le nom m'est resté dans la mémoire, un nom bien français. Il y avait le père, la mère, deux filles. Le père seul est sorti sain et sauf de la catastrophe.' Babel's addition of the phrase which I have italicized stresses the decimation of Maresko's family. Vidal's hackneyed verbosity in his last sentence partially destroys the pathos that he has just created. Indeed the addition by Babel of small details, such as the one above or the earlier reference by Maresko to his wife, creates a far more affective picture. The cumulative emotional effect of such tiny embellishments is a powerful one.

The dénouement, which occupies a larger proportion of Babel's story (36 per cent of the total compared to 30 percent of Vidal's version), embodies for both narrator and reader the sudden realization of truth. Maresko's presence and purpose are explained. The apocalyptic nature of the story's climax furnishes an early glimpse of Babel's use of epiphany as a literary device.[77] The climactic section comprises four subsections, the first of which functions as a short link with, and continuation of, the dialogue which the intervening flashback had interrupted. In each version, the respective narrator offers sympathy but queries the Mareskos' presence in their fateful cellar. The corporal who had announced the civilian's arrival now warns of an enemy attack. His warning takes the reader into the second and larger subsection of the climax. Vidal's narrator reacts in exclamatory fashion: 'Il fallait s'y attendre! On a vu notre remue-ménage. Une salve à droite. Une en arrière. Mille dieux! Tout le monde dans les trous!' Babel's lieutenant is, however, less excitable. He reports the action apparently without emotion, his subdued tone foreshadows that of Lyutov in *Konarmiya*, who portrays conflicts and moments of crisis in a monotone, seemingly devoid of emotion, yet full of menace:[78] 'This was to be expected. The Germans had noticed the movement in our trenches. A volley on the right flank, then to the left. I grabbed old man Maresko by the collar and dragged him down.' (ll.49–51 'Semeystvo papashi Maresko')

A difference in imagery occurs at the end of this subsection. Babel has condensed the content of the attack, the protection afforded Maresko and the position of the men, into one paragraph. Vidal, having allowed his narrator the customary opportunity for verbosity with an extra paragraph, concludes the subsection with a double figure which depicts Marescot's fear at the sound of the guns: 'Il reste, immobile, abruti, replié sur lui-même comme une bête traquée.' The combined image is a graphic one with the metaphorical phrase 'coiled up on himself' forming part of the tenor which leads into the animal vehicle of the simile, 'like a hunted-down beast'. Babel moves directly into a metonymy which significantly avoids a pejorative animal comparison. The frock-coat, which had been a dominant feature in his portrayal of Maresko before, now assumes the actions of the old man. It turns pale and huddles in on itself: 'The Sunday frock-coat turned pale and huddled up.' ('Voskresnyy syurtuk blednel i yozhilsya.') (l.53 'Semeystvo papashi Maresko') With the verb 'huddled up' ('yozhilsya'), Babel may himself be hinting at an animal reference, for ' yozh', ('a hedgehog'), vividly conveys an image of fear and vulnerability. However, the reference is a veiled one, for the Russian verb is normally deprived of its literal associations, although it may be argued that Babel has revived them and thereby revitalized the verb as a metaphor. Instances of revitalized metaphor occur in almost every story of *Konarmiya*. The following sequence of six metaphors opens with two that in isolation seem trite but in sequence help invest the bullets with animation and fiendishness: 'Bullets whine and scream. Their plaintiveness grows intolerably. Bullets wound the earth and swarm in it, trembling with impatience.'[79]

There is no intention on Babel's part, however, of reducing Maresko's status to that of an animal through an explicitly pejorative image, as Vidal has done. With the now metonymic 'frock-coat' Babel not only achieves a consistency of imagery that is lacking in Vidal's version, but he also avoids brutalizing the figure of Maresko. His image stresses, rather, the pathetic nature of a piece of human flotsam cruelly buffeted by the fortunes of war. Maresko's wretchedness is as exposed to us as the shabbiness of his incongruous frock-coat.

The use of animal imagery on Vidal's part to focus attention on the unseemly behaviour of the protagonists of 'Deux actes devant une conscience' has been noted earlier, just as Babel's avoidance of this has been. The latter is at pains in the cycle to stress the hapless lot of the little man *vis-à-vis* the establishment, the ordinary, often inadequate individual against the ascendant, so-called adequate, officer class. Babel indeed portrays the predicament or dilemma for both sides of this divide and strives generally not to distance one from the other in terms of human status by divisive animal reference. Ratin, in 'Na pole chesti', however, receives pejorative treatment at times, and at one point through animal imagery, namely his hissed threat of urinating on Bidu which has the quiet menace of a snake: 'Then the Captain approached the very edge of the hole and hissed especially quietly: Get up, Bidu, or I'll soak you from head to foot'. (ll.32–4 'Na pole chesti'). But generally, animal reference is reserved for the instruments of war itself: 'Not far from us a 12-centimetre 'cat' mewed.' (ll.53–4 'Semeystvo papashi Maresko')

Instances of metonymies similar to that of the frock-coat are to be found in *Konarmiya*; in 'Kostyol v Novograde', for example, the cassock of the treacherous priest's assistant, Pan Romual'd, assumes the personality of its wearer: 'But that evening his narrow cassock stirred at every curtain, swept furiously along all the passages and smiled at all who wanted to drink vodka.' [80] The success of metonymy or synecdoche rests on whether the part which has been selected to represent the whole is that which most strikes the eye. This is the case with both Romual'd and Maresko. Both images are visually arresting, forcefully characterizing their respective protagonists. Just as he did in the exposition of 'Semeystvo papashi Maresko' with the 'hammer' metaphor, Babel is able to avoid using a simile, this time through metonymy. Compare: 'Around us broken crucifixes, bits of monuments, slabs, played havoc with by the hammer of an unknown defiler.' (ll.3–5 'Semeystvo papashi Maresko') with Vidal's: 'Autour de nous, des croix brisées, des fragments de couronnes, des dalles cassées comme à coups de marteau par on ne sait quel vampire profanateur.' Metonymy and synecdoche are tropes often used by Babel'. In *Konarmiya,* there are 1,331 instances of metaphor, 381 of metonymy and 200 of synecdoche compared with 210 examples of simile. Metonymy and synecdoche present in succinct terms the very kernel of an idea and concentrate the reader's attention, thereby heightening the effect. Vidal's sequence of metaphor and simile conveys Marescot's fear but does not approach Babel's sequence of metonymy and revitalized metaphor for power of effect. The latter evokes pathos, the former none.

Dialogue resumes as we move into the final two subsections of the dénouement. The revelations, firstly of the gruesome contents of the sack and secondly of the lieutenant's prevention of Maresko from carrying out his wish by occupying the family tomb, are approached in similar ways by both authors. Babel's terseness, however, leaves the reader in a greater state of shock. He relies almost solely on dialogue, whereas Vidal includes a six-line narrative paragraph to indicate the thoughts and feelings of his narrator. Instead of merely pointing to the sack as he does in Vidal's version, Babel's Maresko first tells the officer that the bodies are with him; his tone of courteous humility enhances the drama underlying the statement:

– The bodies are with me, monsieur lieutenant!
– What's that?
He pointed at the bag. The meagre remains of the family of old man Maresko were found to be in it.
I trembled with horror. (ll.60–4 'Semeystvo papashi Maresko')

Vidal's narrator is, as ever, more concerned with himself – with his error, his feelings, his self-control:

45

– Ils sont là, mon lieutenant.

– Où ça?

Il me montre le sac. Ce que j'avais pris pour des tubercules, c'étaient les restes, les pauvres restes des trois victimes. Le bruit singulier que j'avais entendu, c'était le heurt de leurs os. J'eus un bref sursaut de stupéfaction, de pitié, mais je me reconquis vite …

Babel's narrator omits any reference to his earlier erroneous assumption about the sack's contents. His single-line paragraph, which denotes his reaction to his realization, is sufficient pause for us also to grasp the horror of reality. Our recall, like the lieutenant's, of the 'frozen potatoes' (1.24 'Semeystvo papashi Maresko') and the crack that was heard each time Maresko moved, is involuntary and implicit.

In the French, the reverse is true. Vidal's narrator states explicitly the mistake that he has made and in doing so repeats the earlier, weak, generalized image of a 'bruit singulier', which is reinforced by a second and specific auditory image, 'le heurt des os'. The narrator's reaction is laboured and the final point that he makes of regaining his self-composure is unconvincing. He does not carry us with him as Babel's lieutenant does. Babel's reader is totally involved. Vidal's is not allowed to be. It is through terseness and omission that Babel tightens the screw of horror, whereas Vidal quickly dissipates any such effect through verbosity and a narrator who lacks veracity.

With the reactions of the respective narrators to Maresko's first revelation we move into the final subsection of each story. Again, the final jolt of embarrassment and horror is more forcefully made in the Russian. Babel follows Vidal closely in these final lines as the lieutenant promises to have a grave dug for Maresko's family as soon as the battle has abated. Maresko's reaction is one of seeming incredulity which further confuses the narrator, who precipitates the second shock by demanding to know the whereabouts of the Maresko vault. Vidal's Marescot delivers the final blow in an exclamatory last line: 'C'est que, mon lieutenant, nous sommes déjà dedans!' Babel's Maresko does so with apparent calm, consistent with his previous self-effacement: 'But, mon lieutenant, we have been sitting in it all the time.' (1.75 'Semeystvo papashi Maresko') The situation approaches black comedy; it is both horrific and absurd, and, in consequence, doubly disturbing. Maresko conducts himself as a person engaged in mundane, everyday matters, and it is this heroically absurd self-control and humility, especially in Babel's version, which create the situation that both authors exploit.

We can but surmise the volume of grief in the little man's heart. The pathos increases as we approach the awful double truth of the climax. As with *Konarmiya*, it is the underplaying of emotions, the understatement or omission of references to feelings which create the most powerfully emotive effects. As with *Konarmiya* too, we have a participatory narrator who acts as our filter. In Babel's version, we, the readers, identify with him; in Vidal's we do not. The latter's narrator is both obstructive and damaging to

the effectiveness of the story, although at the end, at least, he is not allowed
the last word. His composure, we may assume, has been finally destroyed.

'Kvaker'

'Kvaker', the fourth story of the cycle, does not afford us the ready insights
into Babel's literary method of the other three, since it is not a reworking of
another's material. As I have suggested, its chief protagonist, Ston, may be
a free adaptation on Babel's part of de Wilde's literary and wartime colleague, the monk Lekeux.[81] The content of 'Kvaker' would therefore seem
to be invention on Babel's part. What is of interest are the features which
link or disassociate it with the first three stories and with *Konarmiya*.

There are two protagonists, each of whom has a military role, albeit
a peripheral one. Ston is a driver and Bekker a groom. Both represent
polarized standpoints. Ston is an incongruous figure. While Maresko's
incongruity is transient, due to his appearance and civilian presence in the
besieged cemetery, Ston's incongruity is more extreme, both in a physical
and spiritual sense. He is incompatible with life; his incongruity is per-
manent. Babel's portrayal of him is consistently ironic, at times farcical. He
creates a central protagonist who is generally antipathetic. Irony distances
the reader from him and seldom do we experience the empathy that Bozhi,
Bidu, Maresko or Lyutov generate.

However, it is with the latter figure, Lyutov, that some comparisons can
be drawn. Ston is an isolate; both his conscience and his religious beliefs
render him different from his fellows. He has enlisted as a driver to avoid
killing his fellow men, but inevitably has to make compromises in the
consequent company that he is forced to keep.

> He was helping his fatherland without committing the terrible sin of mur-
> der. Upbringing and wealth permitted him to occupy a higher position
> but a slave to his conscience he meekly accepted the unenviable work
> and the society of people who to him appeared coarse. (ll.2–6 'Kvaker')

Ston's ubiquitous bible, together with his doggedness in his mission to save
the ill-treated horse, make him an eccentric figure. Like Lyutov, he is on the
periphery of the war both in function and in his social involvement with his
fellows. Unlike Bozhi and Bidu, he has not arrived at this periphery through
crisis but through a conscience which permanently enslaves him; but unlike
Lyutov he does not strive to break free, to get on terms – he is content with
his isolation.

At home, Ston is a member of a society for the protection of animals:
'People, through their sins, seemed less worthy of respect to him; but for
animals he felt an indescribable compassion.' (ll.49–51 'Kvaker') Affection
and concern for a horse is a recurrent theme in *Konarmiya*; many a Cossack
suffers a sense of loss over the animal.[82] For Lyutov too the horse
symbolizes an aspect of the challenge that he faces in gaining the respect
of the Cossacks. Horsemanship constitutes an important element in his
struggle to be treated as an equal.[83] Lyutov and Ston differ in many respects,

not the least of which is the former's vacillation between admiration for his Cossack associates coupled with a desire to emulate them, and the repugnance that he experiences for them on witnessing and suffering their callous and violent ways. Ston, however, is a single-minded missionary. He has no doubts, his purpose in life is clear and as such we are allowed no glimpses into his soul. Despite his piety he appears to have no humanity. His compassion for the horse and his disregard for his fellow men approach the unfeeling boorishness of the illiterate Kurdyukov in 'Pis'mo'. The latter relates without emotion to his mother the destruction of their family by one or other of its members, yet ironically the only tender note to appear in the letter is when Kurdyukov mentions his horse, voicing his fears as to its well-being.

Ston represents Babel's contempt for religion. The author ironically portrays him as a man of deeply religious convictions, a Quaker, who has no regard for his fellow men, preferring the company of animals. In *Konarmiya,* Lyutov's disdain for Catholicism and his own Judaism is made readily apparent, although the latter fills him with nostalgia, again exemplifying his vacillant disposition.[84] Babel skilfully employs metaphor to deride Ston's religiosity. Having been portrayed as a lifeless figure when carrying out his duty as a driver, it is his immobility, the figure's stimulant, which is ridiculed by a religious image. The man of God is described by means of a purveyor of God, a priest. Religion belittles itself: 'At the wheel of his vehicle, no matter how threatening circumstances were, he behaved with the wooden immobility of a priest at the pulpit.' (ll.10–12 'Kvaker')

A quality which both Ston and Lyutov have in common is their inability to kill. The former, however, experiences no dilemma in his situation. The opening words of the story, 'It is commanded – though shalt not kill.' (l.1 'Kvaker') remind the reader of the Ten Commandments. But for Ston the war presents no problem: he enlists as a driver in order not to disobey this command. For the irreligious Lyutov, who equally cannot commit this sin, the dilemma repeatedly poses itself in situations with which war confronts him. His oscillation between the desire not to kill his fellow beings and the craving for an opportunity not to appear a coward is exemplified in 'Smert' Dolgushova' and 'Posle boya'. In the latter, Lyutov is discovered with an empty revolver on the battlefield and is humiliated for this; in the former he cannot administer the 'coup de grâce' to a man who is mortally wounded.

The physical appearances of Lyutov and Ston do not help their respective causes. Lyutov is condemned for the spectacles on his nose and his intellectual background: 'You're one of these swots, – he shouted, laughing, – and specs on your nose, what a little wretch … They send you without asking, here they kill you for having specs. Think you'll survive with us?'[85] These are a Cossack commander's words to Lyutov in a story which ironically proclaims the narrator's first and only 'killing', that of a goose, and his faltering steps towards acceptance by the Cossacks. Ston's outward appearance is hideous in the extreme. His exterior complements his eccentric behaviour. Various figures are employed to create a grotesque effect: 'What was Ston? a bald brow at the top of a pole ...' (l.7 'Kvaker') Alliteration and assonance combine to enhance the irony of the phrase as synecdoche ('brow' for 'head') cedes to metaphor ('pole' for 'body'). Babel elaborates on Ston's most dominant physical feature, his head, through hyperbolic metaphor, and in doing so, employs biblical phraseology which resumes the note of derision registered in the opening words and stresses Ston's physical and spiritual isolation: 'The Lord had bestowed a body on him merely to elevate his thoughts above the terrible sorrows of this world.' (ll.7–9 'Kvaker') A fossilized image then follows in a simile which increases the effect of caricature: 'His every movement was no less than a victory won by mind over matter.' (ll.9–10 'Kvaker')

In ascribing seemingly positive traits to Ston, such as love of nature and God and concern for the horse, Babel continues with hyperbolic imagery or employs a triteness which negates any positive effect. Ston decides to go for a walk one morning when he is off duty: '... to bow down before the Creator in his creation ... The sight of the clear sky, the twittering of sparrows in the grass – all flooded him with joy.' (ll.15–16 and ll.17–18 'Kvaker') When he sees the emaciated horse, its ribs projecting: 'Immediately the voice of duty addressed him vehemently, – at home Ston was a member of the society for the protection of animals.' (ll.20–2 'Kvaker')

Hyperbole later cedes to bombast as Ston's sense of superiority and lack of feeling for his fellow men are further exposed: 'From this day Ston considered himself invested by Providence with a special mission – concern for the fate of the badly treated quadruped.' (ll.48–9 'Kvaker') The last word, an example of fossilized synecdoche, leads into the earlier quoted comment on Ston's lack of respect for sinful humanity and his indescribable compassion for animals, and stresses the gulf that exists between him and other mortals.[86] In berating Bekker, the groom, for his ill-treatment of the animal, Ston alludes to Bekker's right to destroy his own soul, and enhances the grandiloquent effect with a concluding metaphor of absurd triteness: 'The Almighty has perhaps permitted you to destroy your own soul, but your sins must not fall with all their weight upon an innocent horse.' (ll.41–2 'Kvaker') A similar effect is achieved a little further on with a delightful balance between bombast and banality. Ston's arduous duties do not prevent him from maintaining his promise to God and his protection of the horse:

Arduous chores did not prevent him from keeping inviolable his promise to God. Often at night the Quaker would crawl out of his vehicle – he used to sleep in it, bent up on the seat – to satisfy himself that the horse was at a proper distance from the hobnailed Bekker boot. (ll.51–6 'Kvaker')

The pomposity of the first sentence contrasts with the prosaic nature of the next statement about Ston's sleeping habits, which, in turn, is concluded with a similar juxtaposition of grandiloquence and mundanity. Epithets such as 'inviolable' (l.52) and 'proper' (l.55) make a crucial contribution to the overall balance, as does the final trite metonymy 'the Bekker boot' (l.55). Ston's promise to God is not to be violated.

Bekker, the second protagonist and Ston's antagonist, is as single-minded as the latter, but his *raison d'être* is far removed from that of Ston. The groom possesses a brutish nature which takes pleasure in sins of the flesh and the terrorizing of an animal. Ston's enormous dome of a head, symbolic of his spiritually inspired isolationism, is confronted, as the dominant feature of Bekker, by a square, jutting chin, testimony to his stubbornness, determination and profanity: 'The square jutting chin of the youth testified convincingly to an unconquerable stubbornness.' (ll.35–7 'Kvaker') Bekker foreshadows the sexual promiscuity and brutality of the Cossacks of *Konarmiya* and the Jewish gangsters of *Odesskiye rasskazy*, most of whom, however, direct their violence at human beings, not animals.

The wretchedness of the animal that Bekker ill-treats is complemented by the emaciation of its would-be saviour. Ston's quadruped, his 'pet jade' (l.57) self-importantly bears the long, meagre body of its lugubrious rider over the verdant fields. It is this mournful spectacle, its incongruity enhanced by the spring setting, which Babel compares with that of Don Quixote, riding his steed in the fertile countryside: 'With his insipid yellow face, pale compressed lips, Ston recalled the immortal and amusing figure of the knight of mournful appearance, trotting on Rosinante amid the flowers and cultivated fields.' (ll.58–61 'Kvaker') The lofty but impracticable ideals of Cervantes' hero, coupled with his funereal being and emaciated physique, find their equal in Ston.

While the allusion is itself not startling, its significance lies in the links that it has with a similar reference in the *Konarmiya* story, 'Eskadronnyy Trunov'. Lyutov is grieving over the loss of Trunov, the squadron commander, and has gone into the main square of Sokal, having just taken his leave of the dead man. There he mingles with different Jewish factions vehemently extolling their respective ideologies. He joins in the shouting in order to relieve his own suffering, but stops at the sight of a Galician crossing the square. It is an enigmatic and incongruous episode in what is one of the most complex stories in *Konarmiya*:[87] 'I caught sight of a Galician in front of me, tall and deathly like Don Quixote.'[88] The Galician appears as an embodiment of death. He is clad in a long, white, canvas shirt, like a shroud: 'He was dressed as if for burial or for communion ...'[89] He is leading a small, dishevelled cow. His body is huge, but his head is that of a snake, pierced and diminutive. The man is a vision of death to Lyutov, who, we learn subsequently, is guilt-stricken at having had a dispute with Trunov shortly before the latter's heroic demise. The enigma deepens as Lyutov describes how the Galician reaches a blacksmith's forge and gives the smith twelve baked potatoes before turning back. The significance of this incident is never explained, for a Cossack prevents the narrator from following the Galician. The first edition of the story refers to Lyutov's great curiosity for the Galician but this was omitted from later editions:[90] 'I started to follow him, because I could not understand what sort of a man he was and what sort of life he had here in Sokal ...'[91] Lyutov, who, as I have stated, is suffering from a sense of guilt, seems to interpret the episode of the Galician as a presentiment of, or desire for, his own death. He feels

50

that he has betrayed Trunov and, consequently, the cause of the Revolution. Earlier, at Trunov's burial, the regimental commander had spoken about the dead warriors of the first Cavalry Army, about his proud phalanx, beating with the hammer of history upon the anvil of future ages. Now it is the blacksmith, symbolic both of the Revolution, 'beating with the hammer of history upon the anvil of future ages',[92] and of Trunov, who receives the mark of Death.

There are many affinities between Ston and the Galician. Not only are both compared to Don Quixote, both are also grotesque in appearance.[93] Lyutov describes the Galician thus: 'On his gigantic body was set the mobile, diminutive shaven head of a snake ...'[94] Ston, we recall, is 'a bald brow at the top of a pole' (l.7 'Kvaker'). His wretched jade is portrayed as 'hopping importantly' (l.57 'Kvaker') when bearing aloft its master's long, lean body; the Galician is leading a wretched cow across the square 'importantly'.[95] Ston walks away 'with a solemn step' (l.34 'Kvaker') from his first confrontation with Bekker; the Galician 'with a solemn step crossed the square'.[96] On a spring morning, Ston 'with his long legs crossed (peresekal) the lawns, regenerated by spring.' (ll.16–17 'Kvaker'). The sky is referred to in the next sentence, 'the sight of the clear sky' (ll.17–18), whereas in 'Eskadronnyy Trunov' it is the Galician's long frame which cuts the sky like a gallows, as Babel employs the same verb figuratively: 'and with his long gibbet of a frame he cut (peresekal) the burning lustre of the skies'.[97] This powerful image is typical of many trope sequences in *Konarmiya*, which are largely lacking in the *Na pole chesti* cycle, thus marking a development in Babel's style. While the latter has many thematic links, rarely does it match the finely wrought imagery of Babel's masterpiece.

Most significant, however, is the embodiment of death that both Ston and the Galician represent. There are four references to it in ten lines of 'Eskadronnyy Trunov'.[98] Ston, 'with his insipid, yellow face, pale, compressed lips' (ll.58–9 'Kvaker') also bespeaks coldness and death with his very name, which conjures up the Russian 'ston' (a groan) and, incidentally, the English substantive 'stone'. Death is the leitmotiv of both 'Kvaker' and 'Eskadronnyy Trunov', with the violent death of the respective chief protagonists forming the outcome of each. Just as 'Kvaker' is thus linked thematically with the other three stories of the *Na pole chesti* cycle, for violent death occurs or has occurred there, so too are there broader thematic links with the *Konarmiya* cycle: the similarities between Ston and Lyutov, for example, which I have already indicated, and the association of spring and death which recalls a phrase from Babel's plans and sketches to *Konarmiya*.[99] However, it is only in 'Kvaker' and 'Eskadronnyy Trunov' that one encounters such a concentration of similar language and imagery, which creates the impression that 'Kvaker' represents a transitional phase or bridge between the two cycles.

This impression is strengthened at the end of the story. Ston, along with his division, is transferred to a more dangerous area. Returning after a week's absence to see the horse, he finds Bekker's negligence has been wilful. The animal is starving and Ston goes off to find the oats that the groom has not bothered to obtain: 'He looked at the sky shining through a hole in the ceiling, and left.' (l.94 'Kvaker') This detail recalls an image that occurs at the end of 'Moy pervyy gus''. Lyutov has gained a temporary acceptance among the Cossacks with whom he has been billeted and is lying in a hay loft alongside them 'beneath a roof full of holes, that let in the stars'.[100] His newly won acceptance has been gained at considerable cost to his own conscience. He had killed an old woman's goose and ordered her to cook it for him. His triumph is a hollow one. The moon, often a symbol of maternal comfort to Lyutov, now resembles the trappings of a whore and 'was already hanging over the yard, like a cheap earring'.[101] The stars shine in through the holes of the roof, 'and only my heart, stained with murder, grated and overflowed'.[102] The verb 'potekla' (overflowed) is used earlier by Babel to describe the blood flowing from the bird's crushed head, thus graphically linking the killing with Lyutov's feelings.

However, Lyutov, with his blood-stained conscience, does not pay as high a price as Ston. Of the latter, Babel reiterates, 'His religious beliefs did not permit him to kill, but allowed him to be killed.' (ll.78–9 'Kvaker') It is food for the animal and not for himself that brings about his death; his glimpse of the stars shining through the roof is a presentiment of this. Ston's death at the wheel of his vehicle is a violent one: 'A bullet had pierced the skull.' (l.103 'Kvaker') As with Bozhi in 'Dezertir' and Bidu in 'Na pole chesti' a similar physiological detail is given: 'he shot him through the skull'(l.56 'Dezertir') and 'a bullet pierced his chest' (l.41 'Na pole chesti') and like the Norman peasant in the first story of the cycle, Babel's final line commemorates Ston's demise:[103] 'So died Ston the Quaker on account of love for a horse.' (l.115 'Kvaker')

While the futility of Ston's death is charged with pathos, nearly everything else concerning him evokes antipathy. Through the extent of his love for animals to the exclusion of his fellow men, he has brought about his death in two ways. Firstly, he goes to forage for oats in a dangerous area and, secondly, it is his treatment of Bekker that reduces the animal to its final, pitiful state. We are told how Bekker feels an inexplicable fear in the presence of Ston and while he improves his attitude towards the horse whenever Ston is in evidence, he vents his savagery on the animal in acts of vengeance when the latter's back is turned: 'Feeling an inexplicable fear of the taciturn Quaker – he hated Ston for this fear and despised himself. He had no other means of advancing himself in his own eyes, than by taunting the horse, which Ston was protecting.' (ll.65–9 'Kvaker') Ston robs Bekker of the capacity for self-respect and is as guilty of the groom's actions as the latter is himself. Before outlining the vile acts of cruelty that the groom commits on the horse, Babel concludes the passage, quoted above, with the following phrase: 'Such is the contemptible pride of man.' (l.69 'Kvaker') While this ostensibly refers to Bekker, it applies equally to Ston. Both men refuse to temper their respective dispositions. The phrase is a pivotal one which condemns both, yet it is the unbending man of religion, the Quaker, who practices no philanthropy and who pays the ultimate penalty.

The futility of death in war is exposed in the tragedy of Maresko's family and through Bozhi and Bidu; both the latter figures are mental casualties before they become physical ones. They are inadequate and cannot cope with the demands that life makes of them in the context of war. Ston condemns himself to death because of his religiosity. He, too, is inadequate, unable to relate to his fellow beings. But whereas the cowardice of Bozhi and Bidu is a condition which the reader can understand and with which he can associate himself, he can neither understand nor relate to Ston's frigidity. The weakness displayed by Bozhi and Bidu, like the fallibilities of Lyutov in *Konarmiya*, are those of many men; Ston's inadequacy is his alone.

Only at the very end of the story is there a hint of pathos, intermingled with irony. Here too an unidentified, participatory narrator appears:[104] 'I met him some hours later and asked whether the road was dangerous. He seemed more tense than usual. The last bloody days had left a terrible mark on him, it was as if he were in mourning for himself.'[105] (ll.95–8 'Kvaker') As ever, it is with himself that the Quaker is concerned. The aura of death is more marked now, and the very phrase, 'it was as if he were in mourning for himself', ('on kak budto nosim [nosil] traur po samom sebe') (ll.97–8 'Kvaker') resembles the one used to describe the white shrouded Galician in 'Eskadronnyy Trunov', 'he was dressed as if for burial'.[106] Ston, too, is a man of death. His acts of compassion for an animal are not enough to rescue him, to render him a viable human being; in fact they condemn him. The reader, together with the unknown narrator, hardly mourns this ironic figure, whose death is as futile as his life: 'So died Ston the Quaker on account of love for a horse.' (l.105 'Kvaker')

CONCLUSION

My expository analysis of this small cycle of stories reveals an author who, in 1920, had virtually reached maturity as a writer. The touch of the master is evident, as are the germinating seeds of the masterpiece to come. The cycle is imbued with the pathos and horror, the ambivalence and irony, with which Babel's *Konarmiya* confronts us.

Babel's 'little men' enact the ultimate agony of their lives because of the unrelenting context of the wars in which they find themselves. Bozhi, the young battle-weary deserter; Bidu, the idiot-coward; Maresko, the pathetic, self-appointed undertaker of his own family – all three, despite their circumstances, retain their dignity as human beings; and with them on 'the field of honour', is Ston, religiose and lugubrious, who dies a martyr's death. Babel's title is indeed a wicked indictment of the violence and disruption that war represents. His aim in writing these stories is as apocalyptic as in any that he has written, but the physical and psychological limbo in which each of his central protagonists finds himself considerably foreshadows the circumstances of Lyutov in *Konarmiya*.

The imagery and the use of figure, while neither as rich nor as abundant as in *Konarmiya*, nevertheless reveal the stamp of the craftsman. Babel's use of vivid, visual imagery draws comparison with the work of painters, such as Goya or Rousseau and the later Expressionist school. However, the 'chiaroscuro' imagery, in which light and dark shades interplay in *Konarmiya* (e.g. 'Solntse Italii' *inter alia*), is lacking in this cycle and marks another development in the imagery of Babel's major work. His figures also frequently rely on both alliteration and assonance to enhance their effect. Occasional auditory images occur, but the synaesthetic imagery of *Konarmiya* does not. However, considerable emotive energy is generated by the tiny affective embellishments with which he imbues his work, and which are lacking in Vidal's original versions. This is exemplified in the revitalization of fossilized figure which is glimpsed here and which is a feature of *Konarmiya*.[107]

The literary merit of Vidal pales beside that of Babel, yet we owe a unique vote of thanks to the Frenchman, for without his work we should never be in a position to compare 'sentence by sentence, word for word'[108] the work of the 'Russian master of the short story'.[109]

That Babel is the truer witness of the misery of these French soldiers than their self-styled chronicler, Vidal, is indubitable. As J. Norton Cru states of the latter, one needs to look elsewhere for veracity:[110] 'L'auteur ne se rend pas compte de ce qu'il écrit!' I suggest that one should look no further than the work of Isaak Babel, whose short cycle of stories is epic in grandeur, if miniature in scale.

Part Two

NA PUTI K KONARMII[1]
(On the Way to Konarmiya)

INTRODUCTION

Since little is available of Babel's manuscripts and rough drafts, the opportunity that the adaptation of Vidal's stories represents in terms of insight into Babel's viewpoint and his literary method is a unique one. However, he did leave portions of a diary which he wrote in 1920, when serving as a war correspondent with the journal *Krasnyy kavalerist* in Budyonnyy's first cavalry regiment in Galicia.[2] This, together with what plans and sketches there are of his *Konarmiya* stories,[3] serve both to enhance our knowledge of Babel's preoccupation with war, whether it be imperialist, civil or revolutionary, and help us, in the words of Smirin: 'to penetrate the creative laboratory of the author, allowing us to compare the various stages of the project's development'.[4]

1920 saw both the publication of the cycle *Na pole chesti,* and the writing of Babel's diary. The seeds of the masterpiece to come, *Konarmiya*, were being sown, slowly at first, in the revision and adaptation of Vidal's stories, then more abundantly as Babel jotted down in his diary his reflections on the Polish campaign. The fruits of these labours became apparent three or more years later with the publication of the first *Konarmiya* stories. Their appearance, however, differs greatly at times from the original diary entries and indicates a period of considerable reworking by the author. The dates at the end of the stories signify when the events took place, not when the stories were written. 'Perekhod cherez Zbruch' for example was published in *Pravda* on 3 August 1924[5] and is dated by the author as July 1920. One of the story's themes – 'I sleep opposite a pregnant woman' – was jotted on the back of a sheet of paper on which notes from newspapers about a government loan of the 2 October 1921 had been made.[6]

From the plans, Sokal 1 and Sokal 2,[7] we can see motifs which were later included in 'Istoriya odnoy loshadi', 'Prodolzheniye istorii odnoy loshadi' and 'Eskadronnyy Trunov' respectively. The first named is dated by Babel, Radzivillov, July 1920; the second, its sequel, Galicia, September 1920.[8] Yet in the plans Babel refers to the Constitution of the USSR in a speech made by the military commissar.[9] The text of the USSR's Constitution was indeed only finalized on 6 July 1923. Thus the plans for these three novellas cannot have been defined until after this date.

Babel's 'bol' za cheloveka'[10] or his anxiety for his fellow man, had been to the fore in his first cycle of war stories as well as in earlier stories such as 'Il'ya Isaakovich i Margarita Prokof'yevna' and 'Dom Materinstva' and it is a theme which is manifest in his diary entries of 1920 and one which brought him into disfavour with Soviet critics of the day who complained of an author content to celebrate the negative aspects of life in the immediate post-revolutionary years: '[Babel] sees nothing, except countless suffering. At times he does not even want to understand the reason for it: it's enough for him that it exists. You see his wish is that one fine morning it will have just disappeared.'[11] The same critic then focuses on the cycle *Na pole chesti* and declares that Babel's 'demand for actuality'[12] is consolidated in the tales by his system of narration which is deprived of any shadow of pathos, even the pathos of terror and suffering. He claims that the stories represent a bill of indictment to war which is hateful not only because it destroys people physically, but also because it kills a man in the moral sense, awakening in him the worst instincts, defiling the very concept of humanity. Livshits concludes that Babel gives no hint of a possibility of finding a way out of war's power to corrupt and to destroy: 'Physiological excesses – fatal outcome of a chaos engendered by the fact that "man is killing man".'[13]

That pathos abounds, that the concept of humanity underlies the cycle, we have seen and do not need to dwell upon here. The Babel whom Livshits states was ready to embark upon his Cavalry diary, is indeed a different figure from the pejorative image that he paints of him. Babel's 'bol' za cheloveka' was in no way diminished or invisible. An image from the early part of his diary testifies to his concern for the men whom war has engulfed: 'The battle begins, they give me a horse. I see the columns forming up, they file on to the attack … they aren't people, only columns.' 'Nachinayetsya boy, mne dayut loshad. Vizhu, kak stroyatsya v kolonny, tsepi idut v ataka … net lyudey, yest' Kolonny.' (3 August)[14] The hyperbole that Babel employs to portray the collective regimentation of the army is preceded by an expression of feeling which is excluded in the Russian extract: 'I feel sorry for them, these unfortunates, they aren't people, only columns.'[15] (3 August, Mierau, p.195). The explicit nature of Babel's sentiments, here one of regret for the suppression of individuality amid the collective whole, is a recurring feature in the diary which represents an outpouring of impressions and feelings recorded by Babel as he moved from place to place. *Konarmiya*, on the other hand, contains little explicit declaration of feeling; the reader infers emotion mostly from the tropes which abound there. Babel's diary and his plans and sketches contain few figures by comparison with *Na pole chesti*, although the figure quoted above recalls a motif from this cycle, namely the will of the establishment prevailing over that of the individual.

Gorkiy, unlike Livshits, maintains that the attention Babel paid to the individual in *Konarmiya* allowed the psychology of the collective mass, the Red Cavalry itself, to be understood.

> Another such vivid and colourful portrayal of individual fighting men, which would clearly represent for me the psychology of the collective whole, the collective mass of the 'Red Cavalry' and help me to understand the strength which has permitted it to complete its astounding, historic campaign, – I don't know of in Russian literature.[16]

Whatever view one takes of the value of Babel's portrayals, the vignettes of the heroes and victims of both cycles of war stories are separated in time not only by three or more years but also by a creative period which saw the emergence of the *Odesskiye rasskazy*[17] on the one hand and journalistic prose of an intense nature on the other. It is to the imagery and use of tropes in the latter, and its contribution to the creation of *Konarmiya* that I now turn, since my brief and previous scholarship forestall reiteration of analysis of the former, and because Babel's journalistic writing has by contrast received little attention.

ZARYA VOSTOKA (DAWN OF THE EAST)

Having served with Budyonny at the front in 1920 and 1921, Babel severed his ties with *Krasnyy kavalerist* and became a journalist for *Zarya Vostoka* based at Tiflis in the Caucasus. The experience was to give him valuable ideas for his creative work; his newspaper articles contain some of the density and intensity of imagery and figures that so characterize *Konarmiya* and *Odesskiye rasskazy* and he was able to increase his mastery of the techniques of *skaz* writing. The region had adapted slowly to the Revolution, its acceptance delayed by the Mensheviks who had retained power there. In a metaphor that foreshadows the harsh, depreciatory imagery of *Konarmiya,* Babel calls them 'this variety of inert lice whose traces of creative genius are manifest here'.[18] Such pejorative use of entomic imagery is found in Lyutov's equally disparaging image of the fleeing, typhus-ridden peasantry in 'Syn Rabbi': 'And a monstrous, improbable Russia swarming like clothes' lice, began to tramp in bast shoes along both sides of the carriages.'[19]

A description that he had written a couple of months earlier of two ships which had been illegally seized and then reappropriated by the authorities suggests links with two *Konarmiya* stories, while recalling the expressionistic flavour of *Na pole chesti*. Nearly all his Tiflis newspaper articles, moreover, bore the pseudonym 'Lyutov'.

> The red water-lines of the 'Kamo' and 'Shaumyan' bloom on the blue water with the fire of the sunset. Around them sway the graceful silhouettes of Turkish feluccas, on the skows red fezzes burn like ships' lanterns, smoke from the steamers rises languorously to the dazzling Batum skies. Amidst this bright small-fry the mighty hulls of the 'Kamo' and 'Shaumyan' seem giant-like, their snow-white decks gleam and shine, and the incline of their masts cuts the horizon in a slender, powerful line. [20]

The concentration of metaphors and similes creates a vivid visual picture, an intensity of light whose brilliance is reinforced by contrasting colours[21] and alternating images of gentleness and power. Red fezzes burn like lanterns, smoke rises languorously, the ships' masts cut the skies, while below, their hulls blossom on the blue water.

The dazzling quality of the scene foreshadows episodes from *Konarmiya*. In particular Lyutov's impression of the Commander of the Sixth Division, Savitskiy in 'Moy pervyy gus'. There, he wonders at the beauty and power of his 'gigantic body';[22] here, the ships' hulls resemble 'giants'. There, Savitskiy rises and, in his dazzling purple and crimson, cuts the hut in two, as a standard cuts the sky; here, the snow-white decks gleam as the incline of their masts cuts the horizon in a slender, powerful line.[23] There is also a similar alternation between images of power and gentleness. Savitskiy's body emits a sweet, fresh smell and 'His long legs resembled girls, sheathed to the shoulders in shining boots.'[24] The powerful hulls of the ships receive a similar softening or feminization of imagery. They blossom on the blue water, 'amidst this bright small-fry'[25] while the smoke from other funnels 'languorously rises to the dazzling Batum skies'.[26] Each colossus is framed in a background of brilliance. Moreover a curious parallel exists between the fortunes of the Soviet ships and Savitskiy. The Divisional Commander's position fluctuates from one of glory and power in 'Moy pervyy gus' to dismissal and disgrace in 'Istoriya odnoy loshadi' and back to favour and reinstatement in 'Prodolzheniye istorii odnoy loshadi'. The Batum-based ships, originally called 'Rossiya' and 'Mariya', had been illicitly seized by interventionists and taken abroad where, refitted and renamed, they had brought goods back to Soviet ports. Here the authorities had triumphantly reappropriated them.

A second *Konarmiya* story, 'Konkin', also contains links with this piece of journalism. Konkin, a commissar, has captured a Polish general whom he describes to his audience as 'A crimson big-shot lads, with a little gold chain and a gold watch.'[27] Brightness of colour is coupled with a sense of bountiful nature: 'The little farm was all apple and cherry blossom.'[28] Again we recall the flowering hulls of the ships, but it is a simile that Babel employed in his article which more closely associates these two pieces of writing: 'on the skows red fezzes burn like ships' lanterns'.[29] Konkin's Polish general obstinately refuses to surrender to him, a fact which greatly angers him: 'In front of me the general's eyes blinked like lanterns. In front of me a Red Sea opened.'[30] The raciness of Konkin's manner of narration, embodied in this imagery, indicates that Babel had perhaps not only borrowed details from his journalistic seascape but had also used his journalism to perfect his technique of *skaz* writing. In the extract from *Zarya Vostoka* he had been celebrating the triumphant return of the two ships. The writing is propagandist, written from a particular standpoint that was not necessarily the author's own, just as, in *Konarmiya,* he employs *skaz* to reflect the viewpoints of numerous representatives of Civil War factions. A major difference, however, between his journalism and his creative work, is that the latter is concerned with the portrayal of individuals and allows insight to be gained from a cross-section of viewpoints, while the former represents a general celebration of Soviet success which has been written to order.

Another example of imagery harnessed to the Soviet cause but unmistakably Babelesque in its intensity occurs in an article published on the 24 June:

An indefatigable rain patrols the lilac clefts of the mountains, the grey rustling silk of its watery walls hangs over the chill, menacing dusk of the gorges. Amid the tireless murmur of the swirling water the blue flame of our candle twinkles like a distant star and flickers indistinctly on wrinkled faces hewn by labour's harsh, expressive chisel … Oh, this inimitable gesture of a worker's hand at rest, grudging in its purity and embroidered with wisdom.[31]

Foretastes of *Konarmiya*'s imagery occur in the alliteration and theme employed by Babel in the mixed metaphor of the rain's silken, watery walls: for example, the twilight sheets of evening in 'Moy pervyy gus': 'Evening wrapped me in the life-giving moisture of its sheets',[32] or the linen of enmity in 'Pan Apolek': 'He hangs before us the faded linen of silence and hostility.'[33] and the uncertainty in Gedali's unseeing eyes as he fumbles for reassurance from the Revolution: 'The Revolution – we'll say "yes" to it, but are we then to say "no" to the sabbath? – thus begins Gedali and entwines me in the silken straps of his smoke-coloured eyes.'[43] But in each of these quotations, the imagery applies to an individual in a particular situation, whereas in *Zarya Vostoka*, it portrays in bombastic tones the relaxation from their labours of tailors and metalworkers. Bombast cedes to farce as the workers' faces are reflected in the twinkling candlelight, faces whose wrinkles are hewn by toil, which is represented by a chisel. Metonymy is thus employed to ludicrous effect while in *Konarmiya* its use ranges from the farcical to extreme subtlety. The final apostrophe to the workers' hands, chaste in their thrift and wise in their purposefulness, compares with the opening of 'Vecher', in which the regulations of the Russian Communist Party are apostrophized: 'Oh regulations of the RCP! Through the sour pastry of Russian tales you have laid headlong rails.'[35]

It has been the Soviet boast that what Babel witnessed in his time in the Caucasus 'undoubtedly exerted indirectly the most significant influence on the formation of the mature Babel's style, the author of *Red Cavalry*'.[36] Indeed Livshits considered that it was in his journalistic writing for *Zarya Vostoka* that Babel developed the ability to create pathos and to be original: 'This is the very point that Babelesque pathos has its beginning, the striving to speak in uncommon ways about the "commonplace".'[37] These fundamental traits of Babel's writing are apparent in his earliest works and certainly in the *Na pole chesti* cycle. The 'reality' that Babel portrayed in his articles, which proved so pleasing to Soviet appetites, did indeed clash, in Livshits' words, 'with those impressions and that understanding of life that are characteristic of the diary'.[38] But as Babel, the journalist was absorbing 'facts precious for creative work',[39] the artist was developing further his techniques of *skaz* writing and his mastery of figure. As he himself declared some years later in 1932:

My reporting work gave me an unusual amount in the way of material and brought together a huge quantity of facts precious for creative work … *Spurning this material* I then began writing features and embarked on a series which subsequently became popular in newspaper and magazine feature-writing.[40]

Babel's journalism represents neither the advent of some new 'reality' for him, nor the beginning of an ability to create pathos or startlingly fresh imagery. It was a stage in his development but more importantly, it afforded him the means to practise, to experiment with a new diction and to indulge in effusive, intense imagery while allowing material for creative work to lie fallow in the fertile bed of his mind. The notes in his diary of the 1920 campaign, notes that revealed very different impressions and an understanding of life, were also serving a similar function. It is to an examination of these and the available plans and sketches of *Konarmiya* that I now turn, with particular attention paid to their development in or exclusion from the cycle.[41]

THE DIARY AND THE PLANS

The available part of Babel's diary, which covers some three months between June and September 1920,[42] was written in indelible pencil in a notebook; the extant portion has been commented upon by the author's daughter, Nathalie Babel-Brown: 'The text written on horseback is a sometimes almost indecipherable record of personal observations and reactions; names of places and people, striking details and associations of ideas alternate with reminiscences, snatches of conversation, descriptions of things seen.'[43] The plans that are available bear similar characteristics of disjointedness:

> The 'plans and sketches' have been preserved on assorted sheets; partially covered on both sides. They contain short summaries of plots, rough drafts of the composition of some stories, separate important details, and also indications to [Babel] himself for future work on the text.[44]

But they also demonstrate greater order than the diary, often supplying or making more definite details of character, such as the Lambert family in 'Demidovka', or the order of events in 'Labunya', 'Priyezd zheny' or 'Govinskiy'.

An examination of both diary and plans reveals that only thirteen published *Konarmiya* novellas have direct links with either one or the other. Two novellas, 'Grishchuk' and 'Ikh bylo devyat'', have roots in the same material but have never appeared in any edition of *Konarmiya*.[45] It is not true to conclude, however, that the remaining twenty two *Konarmiya* stories have no connection with the extant diary or plans material, nor that their roots lie solely in Babel's missing diary entries and unpublished plans. As I subsequently show in this section, there are many similarities between, on the one hand, either diary entries or plans or both, and some of these twenty-two stories on the other. Equally, it cannot be disputed that some stories have no foundation in either diary or plans, while some material in both of the latter is subsequently never exploited in a published story. Perhaps the missing material would indeed shed new light on Babel's creation of parts of *Konarmiya*, just as the fifteen or so stories that he originally intended to publish with the other thirty-five of the cycle would demonstrate direct links with the supposedly unused material of the diary and plans.[46] As Smirin writes in his article 'Na puti k *Konarmii*', when commenting on Babel's life in general and the early period of his creative activity in particular, 'numerous "blank spaces" are encountered, confusing points, unresolved riddles concerning both work that has been started but not completed, and at times the creation of separate works, and much else'.[47] Whatever the truth, both diary and plans reward analysis.

The diary is in fact a 'potok vpechatleniy'[48] or 'stream of impressions', which has little interest for war historian or biographer; what it does represent is of considerable interest for the literary scholar, however, for it consists of a series of explicit personal observations made by Babel on a variety of events captured in a private shorthand of a few words. The welter of material that falls into his field of vision is recorded in incoherent fashion but it possesses a rawness and spontaneity which the majority of *Konarmiya* does not. It reveals themes that recur in Babel's works, his predilections, as Smirin states, 'for "strange" people and confused destinies, attention to the seamy side of life, to its prosaic, everyday trifles, to the "fantasy" of existence etc'.[49] Several such motifs are realized in the desperate circumstances, tangled destinies and eccentricities of the protagonists of *Na pole chesti*. Yet the diary reveals the 'tortured musing'[50] of the writer himself, who now experiences things at first hand and records a genuine urge to make sense of what is occurring before his own eyes: 'Life flows before me, but what does it signify? ... Everything needs to be thought over: Galisia, the world war, and one's own destiny.[51]

The self-injunction 'to think everything over' is one of a number which occur in both diary and plans. In the former, the recurring keynote is to describe:

The end, describe (5 June)
Let Rovno breathe ... Describe the evening (6 June)
Describe the forests (23 June)
Convey the spirit of ravaged Leshnyuv, the cachectic, dismal semi-foreign filth (25 July)
Describe the day – reflection on the battle (28 July)
Describe the horseman's feeling (18 August)
Describe the aerial attack (20 August) (Livshits, pp.122–3)

The fact that each of the above refers to future action on his part is an indication of the value that Babel placed on what he was witnessing. Only once, as Livshits points out, does the present tense supersede the future: 'I'm writing – everything about pipes, about long forgotten things.' (12 August, Livshits, p.123)

An example of Babel carrying out one such injunction can be seen in the novella 'Berestechko'. Part of the diary entry of the 7 August reads: 'Before evening I go to the castle of the counts Ratsiborskiy. A 70-year old bachelor and his mother of 90. There were only those two, they'd lost their minds, the people say. Describe this couple.' (Smirin, p.476) The couple duly appear in the novella, their madness now exemplified: 'In the castle an insane ninety year old countess used to live with her son. She would jeer at her son because he had given their dying line no heirs, and – the peasants would swear to me – the countess would beat her son with a coachman's whip.'[52] Much more occurs in the same diary entry of 7 August and also appears in 'Berestechko'[53] but such comprehensive use of material from the diary is unusual. What is consistent between diary and novellas, however, is Babel's resolution to describe. The quantity of imagery that was to come in the cycle is not a surprise, but its quality can hardly be imagined from the hurried catalogue of jottings that he made as he rode round the countryside:

> Describe the soldiers, the fat, satisfied, sleepy, women. (3rd June, Mierau, 183)
> the new army, divisional commander and squadron – one body ... Describe (16 July, Mierau, p.188)
> We lose our way for a long time (describe the wounded man) under fire over the fields, nothing to see. (2 August, Mierau, p.194)
> Describe above all on this day – the Red Army and the air. (3 August, Mierau, p.195)

This recurring self-injunction to describe is continued in the plans, but as Babel shuffled and regrouped his ideas the admonitions that he gave himself became more elaborate and frequent. While at times they are merely reminders to describe something at a certain point, the immediacy and prominence that Babel attached to descriptive passages is evident from the respective opening words:

> At once a description of the battle – dust, sun, details, a picture of the action of Budyonnyy. (Boy pod Brodami II, p.491)
> At once a description of the monastery. (Milyatyn, p.494)
> Beginning – a description of the family, an analysis of its feelings and belief. (Demidovka, p.495)

Frequent directives are made by the author to himself over selection of language, precision and brevity and confirm the self-discipline that Babel imposed:

> No discourse – Caref(ul)[54] choice of words. (Boy pod Br(odami), p.490)
> Brief. – Straightway – the fire, Ap(anasenko) Galicians, Cossacks. (Pozhar v Lashkove, p.494)
> Simple. Brief. Description of a damp evening – Description of the little town. (Demidovka, p.496)

Brevity was to be concomitant with, if not generative of, drama: 'Daytime. Brief. Dramatic. – Include – the Polish airforce. Milyatin – Zaburdze. (Boy pod L'vovom, p.492)

Babel's preoccupation with the length and shape of his stories runs throughout the plans. The uncertainty that he felt over their final form is seen from the question marks that accompany his self-injunctions as well as from the different juxtapositions that occur in various plans:

The form of the episodes – on half a page. (Boy pod Br(odami), p.490)
1 page. Miniature. (Pozhar v Lashkove, p.494)
Chapters? (Boy pod Brodami II, p.490)
Form? (Demidovka, p.495)
Themes? – Dialogues. (Boy pod Brodami, p.491)
A chapter about Brody – separate passages. – Dialogues. (Boy pod Brodami, p.492)

The doubts that Babel felt over form, subject matter and order of episodes are as evident as the need that he felt for economy and a style of precision and pith:

Economy (Boy pod Br(odami), 490 and Boy pod Brodami II, p.491)
Style – 'In Belev'. Brief chapters, saturated with content – Dialogues. (Boy pod Brodami, p.492)
Very simple, *factual account*,[55] without any superfluous description – (Sokal' 2, p.493)

It is noticeable, in both cycles of war stories and indeed in Babel's works generally, how drama is created and enhanced by a low-key, documentary style. Many critics have commented on this facet of Babel's writing. Smirin writes, for example, of the dissonances between the content and intonation in the *Na pole chesti* stories, of the expressive restraint of the author's speech and how this is developed in *Konarmiya*.[56] The diary, by contrast, represents an explicit outpouring of Babel's feelings, which are for the most part unhappy. 'Ineradicable human cruelty. I hate the war. What a troubled life!' (1 August, Smirin, p.477) He bemoans his own emotional state and his awakening sense of isolation:

Nothing to eat, no hope, war, everybody is equally bad, equally alien, hostile, dreadful, previously a quiet life was the tradition (30 July, Mierau, p.193)
Damned soldier's life, damned war, a concentration of young, tormented, brutal and even younger people. (9 September, Mierau, p.202)

Gereben sums up such passages from the diary thus:

Meditative passages, outbursts of despair at the sight of bloodshed and human cruelty, remarks jotted down in moments of lost heart and

sorrow, and even renderings of incidents themselves, reflect, in an unam-
biguous and direct way that is inconceivable in the short stories, the
personal attitude of the writer.[57]

An unfinished letter found beside the diary entry of 13 August confirms the
private despair that Babel felt at the violence that he witnessed: 'I have
endured two weeks here full of despair, this has stemmed from the violent
cruelty which does not subside here for a minute and from my clear realisation of h[o]w[58] unsuited I am to the business of destruction.' (Livshits, p.123)

When his mood alters and he does express a sense of happiness at rare
moments of leisure, he fosters a romantic attachment for the past, for history,
for European and Western culture, or indulges in nostalgia for his Jewish
roots. 'I am happy', he writes of the 'wonderful evening' (Mierau, pp.184–5)
that he spent with Podolski, a Jewish shopkeeper in Zhitomir.[59] But a cup of
tea denied him reminds him of the unhappiness of his circumstances: 'In
this whole story I most regret the tea left behind, so much so that it sounds
queer. I think about it the whole night and hate the war.' (2 August, Mierau,
pp.194–5)

A few days later in Berestechko, a place 'enriched with the bloody history of European Polish ghettos', (7 August, Mierau, p.196) he gazes at old
books and precious Latin manuscripts in the ruined house of the priest. The
volumes evoke history and Western civilization for him, just as the synagogues evoke memories of his childhood. On 26 August he wrote: 'A
synagogue, as it was 200 years ago, the same figures in broad garments ...
The synagogue of Bels – a vision of the past ...' (Mierau, p.200) In Brody,
Lezniov, on 31 July, he spent an hour or two in a German owned bookshop:
'All magnificent books, uncut volumes, the West there it is, the West and the
Poland of the age of chivalry, reading books, the history of all Boleslavs,
and I don't know why it seems nice to me, Poland, her old body, decked out
in shining clothes.' (Mierau, p.193) As Gereben points out, Babel resembled
many of the fellow travellers and intellectual participants of revolutions
throughout Europe in his regret at the decline of bourgeois, or European
values.[60]

On 14 July 1920, in Belev, he encountered 'the West' in person: 'A
shot-down American pilot ... Oh how one could smell Europe, coffee,
civilisation, strong, ancient culture,' (Sicher, p.385). Babel savours such
hours spent away from the battlefield: 'Then away from the battle, golden
hours'. (The plans. Boy pod Brodami, p.492) Yet he acknowledges that war
can have a different aspect to its backdrop of violence, destruction and
misery, although for him its pejorative aspects predominate:

Above us captivating skies, a warm sun, nearby a pine sighs, hundreds of
steppe horses snort, one could live here, but all our thoughts are bent on
killing. My words sound foolish, but war is actually like this, at times
beautiful, yet always harmful. (An unfinished letter, 13 August, Livshits,
p.123)

> Two phases of the war. – Our victories, our fruitless attempts, but war's
> failure isn't apparent. (The plans. Boy pod L'vovom, p.492)

Likewise, the Jewish contacts that he makes bring him both nostalgic pleasure
and a loathing for their degradation. Thus Gereben notes in her discussion
of what Babel gave Lyutov of himself in *Konarmiya*, namely the essential
ambivalence with which Babel viewed his surroundings: '[He] "lent" his
narrator the sense of strangeness he so often experienced in that strange
milieu, as well as his ambivalent feelings of identification and rejection.'[61]

But it is the ugliness and abject degradation of the Jews which prevail
over nostalgia in both diary and plans. Of Brody he writes, 'I haven't
witnessed a sadder town. Jews' origins, their stamp on all life … Talmudists.
– Hasidism with oozing eye-sockets.' (The plans, Brody, p.492). Previously
in the diary Brody had been referred to as 'destroyed, plundered … 96
synagogues, all half destroyed … a wilderness, an endless wilderness.
Nothing to eat, no hope, war, everybody is equally bad, equally alien, hostile, inhuman …' (30 July, Mierau, p.193) Elsewhere, the scene is equally
depressing:

> In Galicia it is unbearably wretched, churches and crucifixes destroyed,
> an overcast sky … (29 July, Mierau, p.192)
> The synagogues of Dubno. Everything destroyed. …. The synagogues
> mean, old, small green and blue houses, hassidic, inside no architecture
> of any sort. …. What small, crippled figures, what emaciated faces,
> everything is resurrected for me as it was 300 years ago, …. Probably the
> ugliest Jews of Dubno have gathered here. (23 July, Mierau, p.190)

The effusive quality and explicit tone that Babel adopts in the diary, and
to a lesser extent in the plans, where declaration and description are reduced,
are tempered however by glimpses of the documentary style which is evident in both cycles of war stories. Comments in successive diary entries hint
at the low-key approach and controlled style: 'Ivan and I go back, mortal
danger, what I feel is not fear, it is passivity, he is openly afraid.' (2 August,
Mierau, p.194) In a description of carnage he gives a catalogue of details:
'a terrible field, strewn with the mutilated, inhuman horror, monstrous
wounds, skulls staved in, young, white naked bodies gleam in the sun,
notebooks scattered, loose leaves, pay-books, bibles, bodies in the corn'. (3
August, Mierau, p.195) In the same entry, he adds the remark: 'I take in the
impressions more with my mind', and then proceeds to enumerate further
events without any change in tone or pause to reflect on the horror that he
had witnessed: 'The battle begins, they give me a horse. I see the columns
forming up, they file on to the attack …' The apparent lack of emotional
response on the part of the narrator is a device Babel uses in *Konarmiya* to
enhance the impact of horror on the reader. Here, the author, even amidst the
emotional descriptions which his diary entries largely represent, manages to
foreshadow the terse, matter-of-fact style which, in its very understatement,
bristles with pent-up emotion.

PAST VERSUS PRESENT

The mixture of East and West that Galicia represents for Babel is a source of fascination for him: 'What is so special in the Galician towns? The mixture of the viscous, heavy Orient (Byzantium and Jews) and the German beer West.' (18 August, Mierau, p.200) Yet it is the West, with its modern technology, and despite its history, culture and civilization that sharply reminds Babel of the present, the changing times and the break with the past. In the plans, for example, the cavalry army retreats in some disarray: 'The cavalry retreats. From whom? From twenty aeroplanes ... The aeroplanes have a demoralising effect. ... A first time encounter with West[ern] European technology.' (The plans. Boy pod L'vovom, p.492) Babel's regard for western culture is now temporarily displaced by rueful admiration for its technology. While the present thus intrudes upon Babel it is the past which he likes to escape to and at times feels that he cannot escape from.[62] In his unfinished letter he reveals how clearly he understands his dilemma: 'H[o]w unsuited I am to the business of destruction, h[o]w difficult it is to tear myself away from olden times, from [indeciph.][63] from what was perhaps bad, but breathed of poetry for me, like the hive does of honey ...' (13 August, Livshits, p.123).

But it is the present which reasserts itself, and, as much as he likes to seek refuge in synagogues or churches, bookshops or castles, its brashness constantly jolts his love of history and his nostalgia. Such 'collisions' between past and present and the blurring of one with the other recur in diary, plans and *Konarmiya*. An example is seen in the diary entry 'Zhitomir' of 3 June; its central episode, the Sabbath eve that Babel spends with the old Jew Podolski, is the basis of the story, 'Gedali': 'The synagogues, old architecture, how it all grips my heart.' (Mierau, p.183) The philosophy of the Jewish shopkeeper Podolski, his 'old curiosity shop', the words of the tsaddik, as grim as they are, form an oasis of nostalgia, a conjuring of the past for Babel. 'Wonderful evening' (3 June, Mierau, p.185) he calls it, yet it is an episode in a day which begins and ends with the harsh and distasteful presence of the modern world:[64] 'Morning on the train ... it is dirty, the piercing morning sun, dirt in the carriage. Lanky Shukov, greedy Topolnik, the whole editorial staff – unimaginably repugnant people.' (3 June, Mierau, p.183) The catalogue of sordid details accumulates as Babel describes his surroundings in the propaganda train on which he works and sleeps. The absence of finite verbs creates a prevailing sense of stasis and apathy:

Wretched tea in borrowed kettles, letters home, parcels for Yugrosta,[65] interview with Pollak, ... Polish White Guard literature, a little book made of cigarette paper ... Ukrainian Jews, commissars; everybody is stupid, crazy, feeble, untalented ... The kitchen on the train, fat soldiers with red faces, gutted pigs, sticky heat in the kitchen, broth, midday sweat, washerwomen with fat legs, apathetic women ... Describe the soldiers, the fat, satisfied, sleepy women. Love in the kitchen. (3 June, Mierau, p.183)

The 'Jewish interlude', Babel's sortie into Zhitomir and his meeting with Podolski then occurs only to be put into perspective by the author's return. Even as he walks back to his quarters the brash, technological present reasserts itself.

> I walk, ponder, the quiet, alien streets. ... Then the night, the train, the painted slogans of Communism (contrast with what I saw at the old Jew's.) Noise of machinery, own electricity station, own newspaper, the cinema performance is on, the train radiates, blusters, thick lipped soldiers queue up at the washerwomens' ... (3 June, Mierau, p.185)

From Zhitomir to Klevan, in the next extant diary entry, he is still wondering a month later at the incompatibility of the old with the new: 'Klevan, its paths, streets, peasants and Communism – how far apart they are one from the other.' (11 July, Mierau, p.185)

But it is in the *Konarmiya* story, 'Berestechko' that past and present are most evocatively juxtaposed. In the diary, Babel writes of Berestechko's cosmopolitan population, resilient to a conflict-ridden past, in whose town 'everything breathes of the old times, of tradition'. (7 July, Mierau, p.196) He concludes the diary entry with two paragraphs of the story. Local Jews at a meeting in the castle grounds are electing a revolutionary committee, their women 'listen to speeches about a Russian paradise' while the 'children run around'. (7 August, Mierau, p.197) Babel meanwhile, leaves the castle, with its history and former occupants very much in his mind. Just as earlier, on the same day in Berestechko, he had witnessed the aftermath of the destruction of the priest's house and deplored the plundering of the church and the damage to its contents, so he found the ruined furnishings of the castle, the excrement on the floor, eloquent testimony to a break with the past. Moreover a tangible shred of history presents itself to him as he chances upon the 1820 French letters of a Countess, which had been trampled underfoot. The novella develops this detail from the diary and imbues it with poignancy by allowing Lyutov the discovery of only one fragment which it quotes:

> Berestechko, 1820. Paul, my beloved, they say that the emperor Napoleon is dead, is this true? As for me I'm fine, the confinement was easy, our little hero has reached seven weeks ...[66]
> Berestetchko, 1820. Paul, mon bien aimé, on dit que l'empéreur Napoléon est mort, est-ce vrai? Moi, je me sens bien, les couches on été faciles, notre petit héros achève sept semaines ...

In these few words, the history of nations is juxtaposed with that of one family through the balanced antithesis of Napoleon, whose death is spoken of, and the writer's baby son whose recent birth is mentioned. Thus one generation succeeded another all that time ago, and people's lives were inextricably bound up with the great events of history.

Now, as Babel leaves the castle and hears the meeting below in the park, he is conscious of an historical parallel. A new system, Communism, is in the process of establishing itself; the children run about oblivious to the events around them while their parents listen to the talk of a new 'paradise'; and a past that has been conflict-ridden is now being ousted by a present no different in its violence. 'And above all, everything repeats itself', (7 August, Mierau, p.196) writes Babel in Berestechko. The irony of historical parallel is a feature of the diary entry and plans of Demidovka and is something to which I shall return later.[67] It is also exemplified in events and protagonists of the different theatres of war that Babel portrays in his two cycles.

A PROCESS OF DISTORTION

Detailed examination reveals how much Babel reworked, regrouped, omitted and added, in his progression from diary notes, through the plans and sketches, to the finished stories. We have seen how, in *Na pole chesti,* he also altered details by omission and addition, thereby significantly changing the narrator's stance and the effect the respective stories have on the reader. Here, in material that he had engendered himself, it is nevertheless notice-able how frequently an opposite or reverse effect is obtained in *Konarmiya* from that created in the original diary entry or entries. It is as if a process of distortion, similar to that which occurred between Vidal's *Figures et anec-dotes de la Grande Guerre* and Babel's *Na pole chesti*, has been at work in the interim.

Babel himself hints at his creative process and, in doing so, explains how his diary notes may appear to conflict with finished stories. He describes his creative path as an unnatural one, since in allowing his imagination to work upon a theme which occurs to him in a seemingly arbitrary way, he claims that he does not have recourse to memory:

> Impressions obtained from reality, images and colours I forget. And then one thought appears, devoid of artistic flesh, one naked theme ... I start to develop this theme, to give free rein to my imagination, clothing it in flesh and blood, but not resorting to memory's help ... But the surprising thing is that what seems to be a dream, an invention often turns out afterwards to be reality, long forgotten and straightway recalled by this forced and difficult path. Thus was *Red Cavalry* created.[68]

It is hardly surprising therefore that the 'reality' which he now claims the finished work to embody differs from the 'reality' as he portrayed it previously in his diary, to which he states he did not even have recourse. Vidal's 'reality', similarly, had been Babel's in *Na pole chesti*: the former had bequeathed the 'naked theme' which the latter had transformed with his own 'flesh and blood'.

By contrast, however, in 1938 Babel is reported to have said that he had made use of his memoirs in his writing and that he regretted the loss of the greater part of the diary, a fact which, he suggests, accounts for any absence of unity or plot: 'During the campaign I wrote a diary, unfortunately the greater part of it was lost. Subsequently I would write, using this diary now more from memory, and the absence of unity or plot is perhaps explained by the absence of this diary.'[69] Just how much of the diary Babel did use, and whether the 'greater' part had been lost before or after the writing of *Konarmiya,* is a matter of conjecture. However, close examination of the extant portion of the diary tends to support his earlier statement that it was not followed closely. Nevertheless, knowledge of the diarist helps us to understand and appreciate the creative artist, and allows us to compare spontaneous impressions with finished stories via the transitional stage of the plans and sketches.

While the plans often contain the seeds of three, four, or even as many as eight stories together, it is occasionally possible to find whole episodes in the diary which have undergone little alteration. Apart from 'Berestechko', mentioned earlier,[70] one such passage occurs in the consecutive diary entry of 9 August and the novella 'Pis'mo'. Babel's predilection for stylized dialogue with its Yiddish rhythms is evident in his early works and is present here in the diary.[71] He had heard from a divisional commander's orderly how a neighbour, Stepan, had been tortured to death for serving under the rebel leader Denikin:

> They didn't allow his 'throat to be slit', they beat him in prison, they cut his back up, jumped about on him, danced: You alright, Stepan? Bad. But then who did you hurt, – was it alright? It was bad. But did you think that it would be bad for you? No, I didn't think so. But you should have thought, Stepan, here's us thinking that if we're caught, then you'll cut our throats … and now, Stepan, we'll kill you. They left him barely warm. (9 August, Livshits, p.128)

The impression that this 'epic conversation' made on Babel, must indeed have been profound for he reproduces it almost verbatim in 'Pis'mo'. There, Stepan's role is transferred to the father of the Kurdyukov family who has been serving Denikin, in whose cause he has killed Fedya, one of his own sons. In the story, the father falls into the hands of Semyon, the eldest son, and Lyutov asserts that the report he gives of their conversation is exactly what was told him by the eldest Kurdyukov brother. The diary entry gives the lie to this, but it does not clarify for us how much Babel the diarist had contributed of himself in the first place. We can surmise, however, that the Yiddish rhythms that he builds into it indicate manipulation of his material even as a diarist:

> – Are you alright in my hands, dad?
> – No, – said dad, – feel awful.

Then Sen'ka asked:

– And Fedya, when you were cutting him up, did he feel alright in your hands?

– No, said dad, it was awful for Fedya.

Then Sen'ka asked:

– But did you think, dad, that it would be awful for you?

– No, – said dad, – I didn't think that it would be awful for me.

Then Sen'ka turned to the people and said:

– And here's me thinking that if I get caught by your men, then I'll get no mercy. And now, dad, we'll finish you off ...[72]

The bland chorusing of 'awful' by interrogator and interrogated is as relentless as the blows inflicted. A link with another *Konarmiya* story, 'Zhizneopisaniye Pavlichenki, Matveya Rodionycha', is apparent in the lines of the diary preceding the conversation. The Kurdyukov brothers of *Konarmiya* served in Pavlichenko's regiment, and it is this former herdsman, turned Red general, who echoes the entry in Babel's diary: 'They didn't allow his throat to be slit, they beat him in prison, cut his back up, jumped about on him, danced ...' (9 August, Livshits, p.128), as he tramples his master, Nikitinskiy to death, declaring that shooting is too rapid a means of killing:

And then I trampled on my master Nikitinskiy. I trampled him down for an hour or more and during this time really got to know life. With shooting, – I'll put it this way – you only get rid of a man, shooting's – a pardon for him, and a despicable let off for yourself, with shooting you'll never get to the soul, to where it is in a man and how it reveals itself. But I, as a matter of fact, don't spare myself, I'll trample an enemy down in fact for an hour or more, I need to get to know life, what it's like with us ...[73]

The nonchalant recounting of violence is all pervasive in *Konarmiya* and is seen in *Na pole chesti*. There can be no relenting on the part of men like Pavlichenko, Kurdyukov, Zhem'ye or Ratin; the inadequate must be purged, the enemy destroyed whether it is one's own flesh and blood or a defenceless fool. Yet vulnerability can become apparent in such purveyors of violence, as we shall see in Part Three.

DIFFERENT PERSPECTIVES

Women

Apart from areas of similarity, there are a number of themes, episodes and in the case of 'Grishchuk', a protagonist, which remain undeveloped or receive a totally different perspective between the diary and *Konarmiya*. One such example is the role of the nurses attached to the cavalry army. While women feature in a number of stories in *Konarmiya*, their role is little

72

more than passive, their appearances fleeting. They are almost always portrayed in a pejorative light: old, widowed and persecuted, as in 'Moy pervyy gus' and 'Pesnya'; pathetic, as Tanakanych's wife in "Sashka Khristos'; deceitful, as the women in 'Sol' and 'Zhizneopisaniye Palichenki, Matveya Rodionycha' respectively; dull, as the two typists in 'Syn Rabbi'; or, most frequently, whorish, as the respective peasant women in 'Sashka Khristos', 'Pesnya' or Savitskiy's mistress in 'Istoriya odnoy loshadi'.

This last quality is the dominant trait of the only woman to appear in more than one story, the nurse Sashka.[74] She would seem to be untypical when compared with the nurses that Babel encountered from day to day, for his diary entries repeatedly speak of their heroism: 'A nurse is staying with the platoon. Heroine." (5 September, Livshits, p.131) 'They're trying to gather the brigade for a second attack .... Nurse-heroines.' (31 August, Livshits, p.131) Elsewhere Babel is even more fulsome in his praise. The plan entitled 'Budyatichi', based on the diary entry of 6 September, contains the following: 'Meet up with the 44th div[ision]. A doctor, a nurse ... proud nurse, med[ical] service well organised, order in the brigade ... The nurse, like getting greetings from Russia, there's something new there, if such women are going into the army. A new army, genuine.' (p.496) Thus, in progression from diary entry to plan, the nurses still rate highly. It is with a sense of irony, therefore, that one reads Babel's diary statement of 18 August: 'A volume could be written about the Red Cavalry women.' (Livshits, p.131)

Whether the balance would have been redressed in the fifteen additional stories that Babel had originally intended to write, we can only surmise. A fragment of a rough draft of a story is to be found in the plans entitled 'Arrival of a woman' (p.482) and may have been an attempt to allot a major and positive role to a woman. Other unfulfilled attempts are also visible in the plans and the diary: 'Nurse Ap[anasenko]. Story of a Russian woman. The story to be recounted day by day. Moral?' (p.481) On a sheet entitled 'The Woman of Bakhtur' we find the thrice repeated: 'The beginning – on the Red Cavalry women.' (p.481). Not only was Babel's admiration aroused by the women that he encountered in the army but his conscience was stricken too: 'I think to myself, the women now hear all manner of cursing, they live like soldiers, where are the kind words?' (24 July, Smirin, p.481)

A short piece of writing about a woman that did materialize is one of the few surviving examples of Babel's journalism of the time.[75] Entitled 'Her Day', it describes in sentimental terms the goodness, courage and patience with which a nurse goes about her duties, despite the hardship and suffering that war brings. The propagandist tone recalls the effusive grandiloquence of his Caucasian journalism and contrasts sharply with the astringent, pejorative imagery of *Konarmiya*. In his description of the uplifting effect that her morally pure character has on those surrounding her we hear the fanfare of socialist realism: 'There they are! – our heroic nurses! Hats off to the nurses! Officers and men, respect the nurses! A distinction needs to be made at the end of the day between the wagon-fairies defaming our army, and the martyrs of nurses who embellish it.'[76]

73

The exhortation that Babel the journalist makes to distinguish between the two types of women in the army is one that the creative writer largely ignores in *Konarmiya*. For there are only two instances in the cycle in which women are portrayed in a positive way. The first occurs in the conclusion to the opening story 'Perkhod cherez Zbruch': 'And now I want to know, – the woman suddenly said with frightening force, – I want to know, where on all the earth you would find such a father as my father …' The question is framed by a heavily pregnant woman who, amid her wretchedness, with her murdered father lying at her side, manages to sound a note of triumph as she recalls how he had died thinking only of her.

The vehemence of the woman's awesome question is matched by the tone of the nurse Sashka in 'Posle boya'. This second instance of a positive portrayal of a woman by Babel is ironic. Elsewhere in the cycle, Sashka's whorish qualities are to the fore. Yet her words in the story originate from the nurse in the diary who rails against the very nurses who are promiscuous: 'story of a nurse – there are nurses, who only give sympathy, we're helping the soldier, all the burden is on him, you'd shoot such people, but what will you shoot with, … nothing .' (31August, Livshits, p.131) The personification of what the nurse in the diary berates is Sashka. However, in 'Posle boya' it is her turn to chide the soldiers who have failed at Cheskniki: 'I saw you heroes today and I saw your villainy, commander …'[77] When the commander retorts that she should have joined in the battle, she tears off her hospital armband, declaiming in a tone of angry despair which recalls the language of the nurse in the diary: 'Shoot, … What am I to shoot with, this?'[78] Sashka's role in *Konarmiya* as 'the lady of every squadron'[79] is allegedly described thus by Babel': 'Stout Sashka with her pig's snout, she eats contentedly, she knows why she's here, and doesn't understand why she still has to carry out all kinds of other duties.'[80] This disparity between the nurses of the diary entries and the plans, and the women of *Konarmiya*, exemplifies the distorting filter through which Babel's raw impressions of his diary passed, impressions which, heavily pejorated, later emerged to confront Lyutov. The heroic, stoically dutiful nurses of 1920 subsequently became a whore who is willing to 'run round every squadron',[81] or flirtatious, young things, as giddy and playful as puppies:

Two plump nurses in aprons were packing things up there on the grass. They were pushing each other, jostling their young bosoms. They were laughing with the low, short laugh that women have and winking up at me with unblinking eyes. Thus do bare-legged country wenches wink at a dried up fellow, country wenches, yelping like overfondled pups whose night time is spent on troubled beds of hay.[82]

Bida, Pavlichenko, Kolesnikov

Such transformations of character between diary, plans and *Konarmiya* may not be as radical as that of the nurses of 1920 and Sashka, but it is rewarding to trace the development of protagonists between raw material and finished story, where this is possible. The former may contain hints, but there is often little inkling of how, or indeed whether, a character will emerge in *Konarmiya*. Afon'ka Bida exemplifies this. He features in four novellas,[83] but is afforded a single fleeting reference in the plans where he appears in connection with a captured Polish deserter, Govinskiy (The plans. Govinskiy, p.494). The latter, although in a state of shock and at first threatened with death, sets about his task as Lyutov's driver with panache. The plan continues with a self-injunction to write a 'revolutionary chapter' linking Afon'ka Bida with the enlisting of Govinskiy. The diary too mentions Govinskiy but there is no reference to Bida: 'I have a new driver – A Pole Govinskiy, a tall, agile, garrulous, fussy and of course impudent fellow. (29 July, Smirin, p.498)

The episode is never developed in *Konarmiya*, but there is an echo of the story 'Na pole chesti' from the eponymous cycle, in the name 'Bidu', which Babel gives to the young Frenchman, who is found cowering at the bottom of a hole by his superior officer. The proximity of the names 'Bidu' and 'Bida'[84] is indeed strange and one wonders whether Babel had had previous acquaintance with the name 'Bida' before 1920. Whatever the truth, Bida of *Konarmiya* largely typifies the reverse of the vulnerable, inadequate Bidu of 'Na pole chesti', both in the eponymous story, 'Afon'ka Bida' and elsewhere, although he too displays a vulnerability that nearly leads to his demise, when his horse is killed and he seeks a replacement. The 'rev[olutionary] chapter' (Govinskiy, p.494) mentioned above from the plans also does not materialize in connection with Bida, for it is the latter's Cossack traits that Babel celebrates, rather than his revolutionary fervour.

A story of similar celebratory theme, which affords greater insight into a character's psychological development and which underlines a shift of emphasis between diary and plans on the one hand and finished story on the other, is 'Zhizneopisaniye Pavlichenki, Matveya Rodionycha'. Its chief protagonist, Pavlichenko, is based on the Red general, Apanasenko, whose brutality and motives the diary entries of 9 and 11 August describe. The first entry, linking the emergent character of the Red general with the half-wit Kurdyukov of 'Pis'mo', has been quoted earlier. It tells of an epic conversation which took place between Apanasenko and a Denikin traitor, a conversation remarkable for its clinical relishing of brutality, which was later reproduced in *Konarmiya*'s 'Pis'mo'.[85]

The second entry outlines Apanasenko's motives. It opens with the comment: 'Apanasenko is thirsty for glory, – the new class is.' (11 August, Mierau, p.198) and enumerates Apanasenko's career, his rise to fame, his lack of respect for officers, his sense of unwavering purpose, his professionalism and the honours that he received. It concludes with further comment on his motivation: 'That is no Marxist revolution, but a Cossack rebellion, which would like to win everything and lose nothing. Apanasenko's hatred for the rich, the intellectuals, unquenchable hatred. (11 August, Mierau, p.198) The plans reiterate a few details but are noticeably lacking in comparison with the diary entries: 'A non-commissioned officer. 4 George Crosses. Son of a swine-herd. – Assembled the village. Acted at his own hazard or risk. –

Joined up with Budyonnyy. Astrakhan campaign.' (The plans. Zhizneopisaniye Apanasenki, p.495)

The initial impulse for the writing of the story, 'Zhizneopisaniye Pavlichenki, Matveya Rodionycha', came, however, as Smirin points out,[86] from a biography on I. R. Apasenko which appeared in *Krasnyy kavalerist*. Babel, who worked as a correspondent on the journal, was interested in the life-stories of the new war commanders, men who had been: 'yesterday's workers or herdsmen, elevated by the revolution'.[87] His diary testifies to this: 'Write the biography of a divisional commander, the military commissar Kniga etc.' (28 June, Smirin, p.478). Iosif Rodionovich Apanasenko, native of the Stavropol province, was one such:

> [H]e was born into a poor peasant family, and until he was called up had to work for landowners and local kulaks: grazing sheep, horses etc., enduring all sorts of insults, even beating, hearing the vilest, most repulsive of foul language from the landlord's overseers and other servants. Thus passed the youthful years of com. Apanasenko.[88]

The summary of Apanasenko's revolutionary career, which Babel's diary entry of 11 August gives, represents a shift in emphasis, Smirin argues, when one examines the story, 'Zhizneopisaniye Pavlichenki, Matveya Rodionycha'. He claims with some justification that the deeds of valour in war to which the diary and plans refer, are replaced in *Konarmiya* by an analysis of the circumstances which caused Apanasenko's hatred for his oppressors. What Smirin neglects to demonstrate, however, is that the germ of this analysis is clearly evident in the opening and concluding remarks on Apanasenko's motives in the diary entry of 11 August, which I have quoted above. Babel's diary would seem to have left both options open to the author, to portray either the man's wartime career and, or, his temperament. That he chose to give us an insight into the psyche of Pavlichenko/Apanasenko, through a depiction of his reactions to the changing circumstances of his life, both reflects the Babel of *Na pole chesti* and represents the author's development in psychological portrayal. Vidal's emphasis had been reversed by Babel, and the 'little man' had emerged to a perverse glory from his crater of humiliation or his tomb of despair. Here, another 'little man', a tender of sheep and cattle, emerges to tell his own story, with the difference that he becomes the agent and not the victim of violence and oppression. The satisfaction of revenge which Apanasenko experiences as he tramples his former master Nikitinskiy to death, coupled with his rise to renown and high office, emulates that of Benya Krik, the Jewish gangster-hero of *Odesskiye rasskazy* who has risen above the confines of the ghetto to become a powerful and successful leader of the underworld.

The hero of 'Kombrig dva', Kolesnikov, is an example of Babel's elevation of a protagonist between diary, plans and story. Like Apanasenko, Kolesnikov has achieved rapid promotion, and the story makes reference to this, unlike the portrayal of Pavlichenko. But it focuses largely on the isolation and tension of the youthful brigade commander directly before he leads his men into battle, and portrays him in the successful aftermath of this. Two rare examples of transfer of imagery between diary, plan and story are also apparent. In the plans Kolesnikov is an anonymous figure; we are told only of a retreat, a battle and the casualties: 'Retreat from Brody. A corpse. A field sown with corpses. Pil'sudskiy's proclamation. The battle, Kolesnikov and Grishin.' (The plans. Boy pod Br[odami], p.490) The diary offers a few more details:

> The battle-field, I meet the divisional commander, where the staff is, they've lost Zholnarkevich. The battle begins, the artillery hems us in, explosions nearby, a terrible hour – will we stop the Polish attack or not. Budyonnyy – to Kolesnikov or Grishin – I'll shoot you down, they walk off pale. (3 August, Smirin, p.498)

But there is no mention of Kolesnikov's heroism, indeed Babel is unsure in his diary as to which man Budyonnyy issues his threat of 'win or die'. That Babel chose to base his story on Kolesnikov rather than Grishin and to elevate the former from anonymity to renown may well stem from the fact that Kolesnikov's name readily lends itself to a pun. 'Katis', Koleso,' 'Roll on, Wheel',[89] shouts a Cossack bystander, linking the brigade commander's name with the Russian for 'a wheel' ('koleso') and drawing attention to his rapid promotion and relentless path to victory. We have seen elsewhere how significant Babel's choice of names is for his protagonists;[90] he probably could not resist here the appeal that Kolesnikov's name held.

Imagery encapsulates the development of Kolesnikov's status between diary and story. In the former we read: 'The battle begins, they give me a horse. I see the columns forming up, they file on to the attack … they aren't people, only columns.' (3 August, Smirin, p.498) No such dehumanization of Kolesnikov's men occurs in *Konarmiya*. We merely hear their response to their new commander, a response signifying both fear and support:

> An orderly led up a horse for him.
> He leapt into the saddle and without turning round galloped off to his brigade. The squadrons were waiting for him at the main road, the Brody highroad.
> A groaning 'hurrah' reached us, torn by the wind.[91]

The image of 'columns' is transferred to the story, but there it does not detract from the heroism of the brigade but rather enhances the heroism of its commander by creating an elevatory, visual image of bravado: 'Pointing my binoculars I glimpsed the brigade commander, spinning on his horse in *columns* of blue dust.'[92] The image complements the eleven lines of the story that Babel had earlier devoted to stressing Kolesnikov's isolation in his task. The long descriptive passage of his path across the fields enhances the tension of the moment, culminating in the brigade commander adapting a larger than life pose, in which he becomes the dominant feature of both the landscape and the minds of the onlookers, a true hero in the making: 'And suddenly on the earth stretching out, on the ravaged and yellow nakedness of the fields we could see only Kolesnikov's narrow back with its dangling arms and sunken grey-capped head.'[93]

By comparison, the description of the battle is scant indeed, but it is here that a second, rare instance of image transfer to the story from both the plans and the diary occurs: 'The hurrah ceased. The cannonade died away. Futile shrapnel burst over the wood. *And we heard the pregnant silence of the charge.*'[94] The portrayal of unseen slaughter through the paradoxical image of an audible silence further heightens tension. In the diary we read: 'the firing reaches its peak, the charge occurs in silence'. (3 August, Smirin, p.498) The image is repeated in the plans: 'The battle, the charge in silence.' (Boy pod Br[odami], p.490). It can be argued that its terseness merely reflects the notated form that Babel generally adopted there but it also conveys the tension that he himself had felt, for he continues: 'The divisional commander. – I move away. Why? Haven't the strength to endure it.' (Boy pod Br[odami]. p.490). Whatever Babel's reasoning, the impression of the moment must have been powerful, for it is rare to glimpse an image recurring in three stages of his work. The fact that it is only in the final stage however, that Babel's genius is fully appreciable, with the replacement of the banal 'proishkhodit' ('occurs') by the taut 'uslyshali' ('we heard'), testifies to the self-inflicted process of 'hard labour' that Babel endured in his quest for perfection.[95]

'Kombrig dva' exemplifies Babel's predilection for symmetrical structure and complementary detail. The references to the battle intervene in the portrayal of Kolesnikov before and after his triumph. The post-battle description is virtually identical in length to the pre-battle aggrandizement of the brigade commander. Again, he is alone on horseback but this time at the head of his victorious brigade; again, his arm dangles down but this time in a sling.[96] The inertness of the brigade in the diary's metaphor, 'columns', contrasts with the relaxed and colourful animation of the story's final simile: 'The brigade stretched out dusty and never ending, like peasants' carts bound for the fair',[97] while the forced cry of welcome that the brigade had given their new commander before going into battle is now replaced by the indolent singing of the first squadron.

TOWARDS THE PEJORATIVE

The development that is evident between diary, plans and story in the elevation of Kolesnikov is in fact the exception when one examines the rest of Babel's diary and plans' material. The trend is noticeably towards the pejorative, the ugly, the shocking and the violent. In the interim between diary entries and the shaping and writing of the stories, Babel's lens selects and filters mostly visual messages of pain, suffering, brutality and death, as we have seen in the *Na pole chesti* cycle and which I shall exemplify subsequently in my examination of the tropes of *Konarmiya*.

The first extant diary entry of 3 June 1920, which contains elements of 'Gedali' and 'Rabbi', typifies this in part. A list of Babel's impressions of a morning spent in his depressing billet on the propaganda train is followed without a break by his move to Zhitomir in the afternoon. There he makes the acquaintance of Podolski, an old Jew, whose philosophy and way of life are the basis of the character, Gedali, in *Konarmiya*. Babel records the latter's ironic view of life thus: 'all say they struggle for truth and all steal'. (3 June, Mierau, p.183), and he has both an eager ear for his companion and a keen eye for the town with its Jewish inhabitants, its old architecture and synagogues: 'Old Jews bathing with long, thin, grey haired legs. Young Jews. Women rinsing washing in the Teterev. A family, beautiful woman, the husband has the child ... The synagogues, old architecture, how it all grips my heart.' (3 June, Mierau, p.183). He adjures himself to describe the bazaar: 'an old shoemaker, washing blue, chalk, twine ... baskets full of cherries, inside an eating house ... Then weak tea, I devour life, farewell you dead.' (3 June, Mierau, pp.183–4).

Despite the acknowledgement by Babel in the diary of the subdued and defeated nature of Zhitomir,[98] and the news from Podolski of earlier pogroms inflicted by both Poles and Cossacks, an animation, an assertion of life, persists in Babel's diary account of Zhitomir, which contrasts both with the world of the propaganda train that he had left that morning and with the picture of the town and its Jewish inhabitants in the story, 'Gedali': 'At the ancient synagogue, at its yellow and indifferent walls old Jews sell chalk, wicks and blueing – Jews with prophets' beards, with passionate rags on hollow chests ...'[99] The marketplace is lifeless: 'There before me is the market and the death of the market. Finished is the fatted soul of plenty. Dumb padlocks hang on the stalls, and the granite pavement is as clean as the bald pate of a corpse.'[100] Nor is the eating-house any source of comfort: 'and good people used to run it, but people don't eat there any more, they cry ...'[101] Even Gedali himself, with the animation of a brightly coloured bird, is surrounded by the inert and inanimate in his little shop, and by desolation outside it: 'Everyone had left the market, Gedali had stayed. And he hovers over a labyrinth of globes, skulls and dead flowers, waves a brightly coloured brush of cock's feathers and blows dust from the dead flowers.'[102] As day becomes night, the odour of death and decay is all-pervasive: 'The sky changes colour. Up above a subtle shade of blood pours from an overturned phial, and a light odour of decay envelopes me.'[103]

'Gedali' also provides an example of Babel's transfer of details from one setting to another.[104] From a section of the plans that Babel's wrote with the heading 'Brody', a number of features are transferred to the Zhitomir setting of both 'Gedali' and 'Rabbi'. In the latter, Gedali speaks of the durability of Hasidism despite the violence that it has suffered: 'With eye-sockets oozing Hasidism still stands at the crossroads of the winds of history'.[105] The same image appeared in the 'Brody' plans: 'Hasidism with eye-sockets oozing'. (p.492) and other details occur there which resemble those of the cycle's Zhitomir setting: 'I haven't seen a sadder town ... Friday evening. The town – quickly pass round the centre, destroyed. The outskirts, a Jewish town. – The main thing is a description of the synagogues.' (Brody, p.492)

The misery that Babel witnesses on a Sabbath eve in Brody compares with what Lyutov sees in Zhitomir, and in a diary entry of 30 July written about Brody, Babel notes details which again recur in the Zhitomir of 'Gedali':

> 30 July Brody ... The town is destroyed, ravaged. A town of great inter-
> est. Polish culture. Ancient prosperous original Jew(ish) settlement. These
> awful markets, dwarves in hooded hats and plaits, ancient old men, school
> street, 96 (?) synagogues, all half destroyed ... (30 July, Smirin, p.498)

Here are the lifeless market and the wretched Jewish traders of Zhitomir of which the diary entry of 3 June makes no mention, and here too in the phrase 'hooded hats and plaits' is a glimpse of Babel's use of metonymy and synecdoche for pejorative effect, which recurs in *Konarmiya* and of which we have seen an instance in the first cycle: 'The Sunday frock-coat turned pale and huddled up' (l.53, 'Semeystvo papashi Maresko'). This entry of 30 July reveals that Babel did witness and record details of degradation, and that when he subsequently wrote the *Konarmiya* stories such details were not merely facets of his imagination. However, the grimness which pervades *Konarmiya* does not dominate to the same degree the impressions and feelings which are recorded in the diary.

The final paragraph of the entry of 3 June, on which the novella 'Rabbi' is based, exemplifies this. As Babel spends the last part of his day with Podolski at a Tsaddik's house, his feelings are buoyant, despite the conspic-uous presence of death and decay:

> An extraordinary image for me, although dying and utter decay are unmis-
> takable. The Tsaddik, his small, haggard, narrow-shouldered figure. The
> son – a well educated boy in a little hooded cap, you look into prim but
> spacious rooms. Everything is particular ... I am happy ... I think about
> a lot of things, farewell you dead ... I go deeply moved. Podolski, pale
> and sad gives me his address, wonderful evening. (3 June, Mierau,
> pp.184–5)

The story 'Rabbi' omits any such feelings on the part of Lyutov as he endures the sabbath at Motale's. The house is unwelcoming, its inhabitants alien: 'We entered a room – stony and empty, like a morgue. Rabbi Motale was sitting at a table, surrounded by liars and the possessed.'[106] Lyutov witnes-ses the madness of Reb Mordkhe, the Rabbi's assistant, and is then disturbed at the sight of Motale's son: 'He was smoking and shuddering, like a fugi-tive brought into prison after a chase.'[107] The effect is such that Lyutov comments on his anxiety to leave, and his relief at returning to his unfin-ished work on the propaganda train with its noise and glare is apparent:

When the supper was finished, I arose first ... I went off to my quarters at the station. At the station, in the propaganda train of the First Cavalry Army, there awaited me the glare of hundreds of lights, the magical glitter of the radio station, the persistent running of the machines in the printing press and an unfinished article to the *Red Cavalryman* newspaper.[108]

The diary makes similar references to the noise and glare of the train and explicitly mentions the contrast there with what had been witnessed at the Jews', yet no sign of pleasure at returning is apparent on the author's part. The concentration of images, including references to soldiers queueing for sexual favours, invests the concluding episode with a brashness and vulgarity that is absent in the story. In the diary, the old, Jewish world, even with its drawbacks, had seemed the more attractive; now, by contrast, in *Konarmiya* it is the brash, new world of communism that appears so.

The frontier town of Berestechko also reflects a change of emphasis with a worsening of its image between diary and story. Like Zhitomir, it is the Jewish inhabitants who suffer the thrust of this depreciatory trend. In the diary entry of 7 August, Babel describes what he sees as he wanders through Berestechko, commenting generally on the history, architecture and mixed population, all once zealous and prosperous, and on the Jews in particular: 'The Jews are less fanatical here, more elegant, stronger, almost happier too, ancient old men, hooded hats, little old women, everything breathes of the old times, tradition, the place is enriched with the bloody history of the European-Polish ghettos ... (7 August, Mierau, p.196) Yet in 'Berestechko' an image is attributed to the Jews which implies a fanaticism that the diary has explicitly contradicted; the severity of the Hasidic faith is also alluded to:

Here the Jews have tied with threads of gain the Russian peasant to the Polish landowner, the Czech colonist to the Lodz factory. They were smugglers, the best on the frontier, and almost always defenders of the faith. Hasidism kept that bustling population of hawkers, dealers and inn-keepers in stifling captivity.[109]

In a subsequent description of the town's population of whom Jews form the majority it is difficult to recognize the happier, more elegant tones of the diary: 'Berestechko reeks inviolably even now, a smell of rotten herring emanates from all the people. The small town reeks on in expectation of a new era, and instead of people faded outlines of frontier misfortunes go about in it.'[110] The homes of the Jews are also disparagingly portrayed in comparison with the small, smart, suburban houses of the clean-living Russians. Jewish architecture, deemed the most important feature by Babel in the diary,[111] embodies a 'traditional wretchedness'[112] in the story, which portrays the secret passages and catacombs linking the gloomy rear sheds of the Jews' houses. There, human excrement and cattle dung accumulate as the inhabitants seek refuge from Berestechko's many conflicts: 'Dejection and horror fill the catacombs with an acrid stench and the putrid acidity of faeces.'[113] The diary also mentions the 'long, narrow, covered and stinking yards' (7 August, Mierau, p.196) but does not designate them as specifically Jewish, nor is it disparaging of Berestechko's population, depicting it as 'more resistant than in other places', even deserving of optimism: 'Life is gradually setting itself right again'.

The story not only paints a picture of wretchedness, depression and decay that is largely absent in the diary entry, but it also focuses on images of death and violence. As Lyutov enters the shuttered and hostile town with the cavalry army he sees grotesque corpses lying on ancient burial mounds; his billet is with a woman 'reeking of a widow's grief'[114] and under his window an old Jew has his throat cut by a Cossack who takes care not to splash himself in the blood. The diary is not without references to death either; at the beginning of the entry, Babel writes of his horror at seeing the 'bloated, naked corpse' of a murdered Pole, (7 August, Mierau, p.196); he mentions Cossacks' graves and the freshly dug graves of Polish officers, but the references are random details among a catalogue of others. In no way do they create the funereal image of the Berestechko of *Konarmiya*.

Catholicism too provides a focus for pejorative treatment. The depreciatory trend between diary and *Konarmiya* is in evidence in a story which gives insight into Babel's development of irony and whose basis is at least partially seen in the same diary entry of 7 August, 1920. 'U svyatogo Valenta' is placed twenty-fourth in the cycle, four places after 'Berestechko', with which it shares both a geographical and historical setting. The events of each occur in the same place on the same day; a further link is furnished by Babel's change of tone from neutrality to pejoration between diary and story as Lyutov moves from one wretched world to another, and the plundering of the Catholic church and the priest's house at Berestechko is described.[115] The diary records what Babel finds in the latter and supplies information about its former occupant:

> [T]he priest's house is destroyed, I find old books, precious Latin manuscripts. Priest Tuzinkevich – I find his dwelling, cluttered and small, he has worked here for 45 years, lived in one place, a scholar, the books, much Latin, publications of 1860, Tuzinkevich lived there like that, an old, spacious room, darkened pictures, photos of the prelates' assemblies in Zhitomir, portraits of Pius X, a good face, a magnificent picture of Sinkevich – there he is, the essence of the nation. (7 August, Mierau, p.196)

In the story it is not the priest's possessions that are recounted, but parts of his life. The possessions have been translated into events and give a psychological portrayal of the priest. In this transition the neutral tone of the diary is replaced by an anti-Catholic stance.

Tuzinkevich's house serves as the Staff's quarters and it is there that Lyutov learns about the former occupant. He had fled Berestechko, ignominiously disguised as a peasant woman before the troops' arrival. Lyutov replaces the neutral verb in the diary statement: 'has worked here for 45 years' (7 August, Mierau, p.196) with the derisive remark: 'Of him I know that he *busied himself with God* for forty years in Berestechko ...'[116] Apparent praise becomes ironic insult: 'and he was a good priest. When the inhabitants want us to understand this, they say: the Jews loved him'.[117] We recall that in 'Berestechko' Lyutov had described these same inhabitants, of whom Jews form the majority, as sub-human, 'mere faded outlines of frontier misfortunes'.[118]

The pejorative tone is then extended to the Zhitomir prelates of the Catholic church as the darkened photos of their assembly in the diary become, in 'U svyatogo Valenta', the double celebration of the third centenary of the church and of its restoration. This imaginative transformation by Babel permits him to create more irony by employing simile and hyperbole to ridicule the dignitaries of the Church and their celebrations. The effeteness of the episcopacy is felt in Babel's image of incongruity and impotence: 'Pot-bellied and benign – they stood like bells in the dewy grass.'[119] The heavens too participate in an exaggerated scene of celebration as the collective peasantry dutifully attends: 'From the neighbouring villages flowed submissive streams. The peasantry bent its knee, kissed hands, and clouds without precedent blazed in the heavens that day. The heavenly flags were flying in honour of the ancient church.'[120] The final glory is accorded Tuzinkevich, however: 'The bishop himself kissed Tuzinkevich on the brow and called him father of Berestechko, pater Beresteckae.'[121]

Directly following the section on Tuzinkevich's possessions, the diary lists the damage committed in the church, a catalogue which is prefaced by the words: 'Terrible event – plundering of the church' (7 August, Sicher, pp.381–2). In the story, reference to the damage occurs as an afterthought to Lyutov and it is not until two-thirds of the way through that he comments on it at all: 'Driven mad by my dream of Apolek,[122] I did not notice the traces of destruction in the church or they did not seem great to me'.[123] The sentiment is repeated a few lines further on: 'I listened, looked about and the traces of destruction did not seem great to me.'[124] The only details that the narrator finds amiss are the crazed playing of the organ by Afon'ka Bida and the broken shrine of St Valentine, which affords Lyutov another opportunity for a simile of anti-Catholic derision: 'Lumps of decayed wadding lay around beneath it and, resembling chicken bones more than anything, the absurd bones of the saint.'[125] Yet the damage recorded in the diary incorporates eight acts of sacrilege and was Babel's prime impression as he entered the church: 'chasubles rent, gleaming bejeweled materials lacerated on the floor, a sister of mercy dragging off three bales, lining torn, candles taken, trunks broken open, bulls discarded, money stolen, a magnificent church – 200 years old, what it was seeing ...' (7 August, Sicher, p.382)

By contrast, the relative absence in the story of comment or expressions of regret at any damage is in keeping with the pejorative, anti-Catholic trend that is apparent in the changing tone from Babel to Lyutov. The opulent decadence of the church's interior is what preoccupies the latter, not what damage has occurred. More than one of his senses are assailed as he moves from an ante-chamber into the main body of the church. Olfactive, auditory and visual images envelop him. Sashka the nurse is rummaging among scattered silks, amid a cadaverous odour of brocade, flowers and aromatic decomposition. A wild, drunken Afon'ka Bida is playing the organ and Lyutov's attention is arrested by the heresies of Apolek's 'intoxicating brush'.[126] Among his paintings a distastefully fat infant Christ is depicted surrounded by pot-bellied Apostles whose faces bear a deathly, blue sheen[127] and double chins festooned with fiery red warts. Catholic saints are portrayed meeting death in ostentatious fashion and John the Baptist's image is one of seduction: 'In this portrayal the Baptist's beauty was of that reticent, equivocal kind, for the sake of which the concubines of kings lose their already half-lost honour and their luxuriant life style.'[128]

Such sexual innuendo is reminiscent of Lyutov's description of another Catholic church's interior in an earlier *Konarmiya* story, 'Kostyol v Novo-grade'. Many links in circumstance and ethos are apparent. The priest has fled, his house is being used as quarters by the Army Commissar, the bells peal out in crazed fashion like the wild organ playing of Bida in St Valentine's and the atmosphere is seductive to the narrator with the impedimenta of Catholicism suggesting eroticism and sexual promise:

Madonnas, studded with precious stones follow our path with pupils pink like those of mice.[129]
Oh, crucifixes, tiny like the talismen of courtesans, the parchment of papal bulls and the satin of women's letters decaying in the blue silk of waistcoats!
I see you now, perfidious monk in a violet cassock, the plumpness of your hands, your soul soft and ruthless, like the soul of a cat, I see the wounds of your god oozing semen, a fragrant poison to intoxicate virgins.[130]

The diary entry of 7 August alludes to the works of art in the church at Beresechko but in no way concentrates on negative aspects as Lyutov does in 'U svyatogo Valenta': 'magnificent Italian painting, rosy mothers, rocking the infant Christ, a magnificent dark Christ, a Rembrandt, Madonna in imitation of Murillo or perhaps a Murillo', (7 August, Sicher, p.382). A hint of a critical attitude on Babel's part is apparent in the next diary phrase: 'and the main thing is the holy well-fed Jesuits', (7 August, Sicher, p.382), but there is no extensive pejorative treatment of the Catholic Church's representatives nor of the figure of Christ.

THE TRUNOV COMPLEX

Changes in authorial stance can also be monitored in the complex pedigree of 'Eskadronnyy Trunov', but a word needs to be said first on the maze of sources from which the novella developed. Its roots lie in three diary entries:

14 July, 26 and 30 August 1920; parts or the whole of various plans: Polish airforce, Battle of L'vov, Brody, Sokal 1 and 2 and the Death of Trunov;[131] and in two fragments, 'Ikh bylo devyat'' and 'Ikh bylo desyat''.[132] The story, 'Prodolzheniye istorii odnoy loshadi', also developed from the plans of which 'Eskadronnyy Trunov' is the nucleus. The reason for such a difficult conception and period of gestation lies in Babel's wish to portray the diverse facets of a Cossack leader's personality, hence the juxtaposition of two antithetical episodes concerning the main protagonist, Trunov, namely his callous murder of Polish prisoners and his heroic stance against the might of the enemy airforce. The fragment, 'Ikh bylo devyat'' testifies to Babel's original intention of keeping the prisoner episode separate from the aerial battle, but he chose finally to combine it with the latter in a complex exposé of Lyutov's struggle with his conscience. For the purpose of my analysis, it is necessary to examine all available source materials to appreciate the changing tone of the authorial voice.

The first diary entry of 14 July recounts Babel's admiration for the Polish airforce and for one of the American pilots who has been shot down. Although the latter has a dishevelled appearance, he is a symbol of culture, civilization and elegance: 'A good system – Frank Mosher. Shot down American pilot, barefoot but elegant, neck like a column, dazzlingly white teeth, suit full of oil and dirt … Oh, how one could smell Europe, coffee, civilization, strong, ancient culture.' (14 July, Sicher, p.385). Despite his display of earnestness in trying to ascertain what Bolshevism is, Mosher represents western impressions of Russian 'imperialism' and its lack of understanding of Bolshevism: 'What are they telling the W[est] Euro[pean] soldiers? Russian imperialism, they want to destroy nationality, customs, that's the main concern, preserve all Slavonic lands, what ancient words.' (14 July, Sicher, p.385) These sentiments are expressed in a letter that Mosher has in his possession from a major Font-le-Ro, and it is this name that Babel uses in 'Eskadronnyy Trunov' for the combat squadron leader of the four bomber planes which cut Trunov and his companion to pieces near Sokal at the end of the story.[133] No adulatory comment is given by Lyutov in *Konarmiya* for these representatives of the West, nor of their technology. Indeed the inequality of the battle, four bombers against two men, is a cause for irony:

> There in the forest we awaited the end of the unequal battle between Pashka Trunov and the major from the American forces, Reginald Faunt-Le-Ro. The major and his three bombers showed skill in this battle. They dropped to three hundred metres and shot up Andryushka first then Trunov.[134]

A plan that makes direct reference to Mosher and an aerial attack – 'Polish airforce. Battle of L'vov' – also gives no appreciative sign of western culture nor of Babel's attraction to its representatives. The emphasis is very much to the contrary, describing the demoralization and pain that the new methods of warfare bring, methods which the diary entry of 14 July had stated 'should be studied':

The Red Cavalry retreat. From whom? From twenty aeroplanes.
The secret is discovered, the remedy found. Mosher was right. The aeroplanes have a demoralising effect ... The letters of major Font-Le-Ro to headquarters in New York – For the first time an encounter with West[ern] Euro[pean] technology – They take off in the morning.
Battle of L'vov – Describe the battle with the aeroplanes. ... Battle. A squadron reels round us, pursues us, we rush about, moving from place to place. (p.492)

The diary entry of 30 August [135] contributes to both 'Eskadronnyy Trunov' and the fragment 'Ikh bylo devyat'' in its description of the handling of some prisoners. Smirin states that the diary entry recounts the fate of ten prisoners taken at Zavoda station, one of whom is a young, stately Pole, with sidewhiskers, in a knitted jumper. A worker-soldier who is present gives vent to his feelings of hatred for the enemy: 'I'll cut the swine down and not answer for it!' (30 August, Smirin, p.478) Sicher provides further details from the same diary entry, some of which recur in 'Eskadronnyy Trunov', at times in amended form, and in conflict with Smirin's. The prisoners have taken off their uniforms so that it is difficult to ascertain which are officers. Two command attention: an old man, who limps and whines (in the diary he is a Jew) and whom Babel surmises is an officer, and the 'stately Pole' who is described thus: 'stately, calm, with sidewhiskers, in a knitted jumper, behaves with dignity', (30 August, Sicher, p.383). But he is not described as young; Smirin had drawn this conclusion himself, perhaps from the description in the story: 'This ninth one was a youth, similar to a German gymnast from a good circus, a youth with a proud [136] German breast and sidewhiskers, in a knitted jumper and soft woolly pants.' [137] Nor is there mention of ten prisoners, indeed the phrase 'There were nine of them' is included in the diary entry (30 August, Sicher, p.383). It also describes the collective fear of the prisoners, a detail which is lacking in the story, and which recalls Bozhi and Bidu, 'prisoners' themselves, albeit of circumstance, in 'Na pole chesti': 'all displayed a brute fear, wretched, unhappy people'. (30 August, Sicher, p.383).

Significantly, however, in the diary entry there is no murder of any prisoner; the old Jew and the dignified Pole survive. Both are easily recognizable as Trunov's victims in the story: the former has his throat cut, the latter his skull shattered by Trunov's bullet. In the diary, all the prisoners are dragged away and handed over to an escort, whereupon the worker-soldier, or 'Putilov worker', gives vent to his wrath: 'The fury of the Putilov worker, foams at the mouth, a sword, I'll cut the swine down and not answer for it'. (30 August, Sicher, p.383)

It is the figure of the Putilov worker and the subsequent use Babel made of him in the story which present the greatest interest from this diary entry. He is recognisable as Andryushka Burak in the fragment 'Ikh bylo devyat'', a pink-faced Cossack who takes a prisoner's coat from Golov, the main protagonist, but his role in 'Eskadronnyy Trunov' is shared by both Trunov and Andrey Vosmiletov. The latter, like Burak, helps himself to some Polish prisoners' uniforms, including the trousers of the old man whom Trunov has just struck down. When Trunov forces him to return the clothes by firing at him, his anger matches that of the 'worker' of the diary: 'Listen, countryman ... on your mother's life I've a good mind to strike you down, countryman ... You pick up ten Poles and make a hell of a fuss, we've picked up hundreds each – and not called for you ... If you're a worker – get your own job sorted ...[138] Trunov's earlier taunt to Andrey that he should not go sharing out the Soviet republic for personal gain by taking clothes, is thus turned back on him as Andrey reminds him of his 'worker's' duty. Yet it is Trunov who in fact carries out the vicious threats of the 'worker' of the diary by the murder of the two prisoners.

Events between diary, fragment and story have thus intensified. The increased visual horror that the *Konarmiya* story embodies is reminiscent of a scene depicted by Goya, 'Se aprovechan' ('They avail themselves'), in which the clothing of dying soldiers is removed by their enemies.[139] Goya's sharply drawn scenes compare with Babel's depiction of war in the brevity and vigour of their statements. Implicit in the telling visual reports of both men is a sense of the tragic and a denunciation of war. Babel's prose embodies the technique of chiaroscuro, the interplay of light and shade which Goya chose to depict human vices.[140] Like Goya's series, too, one not only witnesses the aftermath of violence in Babel's work but also the cold-blooded slaughter of victims, a slaughter at which his diary only hints. The pejorative trend between diary and cycle, noted earlier, becomes here an intensification of horror.

But what of the plans? Their contribution is significant for they develop a third strand – Lyutov's stricken conscience – by focusing on a third narrative event, the burial of Trunov. They also sketch in a Jewish backdrop to the Sokal setting, which features prominently in another diary entry of 26 August. Moreover, while they refer more than once to the threatening presence of enemy aeroplanes and give a hint of material subsequently used in 'Prodolzheniye istorii odnoy loshadi', they exclude any mention of the 'prisoner episode', which I have just described from the diary entry of 30 August, a fact which indicates that Babel had still not linked this episode with his central protagonist Trunov by the time that he wrote these plans.

A synagogue stands on the square in Sokal and representatives of Jewish factions are arguing amongst themselves. The diary of 26 August supplies more information on the factions as well as descriptions of their respective synagogues.[141] The plan, 'Sokal 1', alludes to one synagogue only but mention of the eighteenth-century Jewish leaders makes Babel think that he has stepped back into the past: 'A vision of olden times' (Brody, p.492); 'Religious slaughter, you'd think it was the eighteenth century' (Sokal 1, p.493); 'And I would have believed in Iliya's resurrection'.[142] (Smert' Trunova, p.493) The illusion is fleeting however, and the present intrudes: Cossacks are digging a grave for Trunov and an enemy plane is visible in the sky. The corpse lies prepared for burial, its presence merely referred to in 'Sokal 1', but in 'Sokal 2' description is added: 'The body of Trunov with legs set together, boots polished. Head on the saddle, stirrups round his chest.' (p.493). The story contains a similar detail: 'polished boots, heels set together, as if drilling'.[143] But the short vehicle of the simile creates a macabre irony, for the corpse in the story is 'shot-riddled', its face 'peppered with wounds, the tongue torn out' and its mouth 'stuffed with broken teeth', – hardly presentable for drill.[144] The absence of similar gruesome description in the plans is made more apparent by the frequency with which Babel mentions Trunov's burial honours. 'Trunov's funeral, the salute' (Sokal 1, p.492); 'We're burying Pavel Trunov' (Sokal 2, p.493); 'We're burying Pavel Trunov, world hero' (Sokal 2, p.493); 'We're burying Trunov, world hero, the military commissar has a word to express'. (Smert' Trunova, p.494).

That Babel attached importance to the ceremony and felt affection for Trunov and regret at his death is indeed evident from both the plans and Lyutov's comments in the story. 'I have lost you, Sasha/Pava', he writes twice in the plans (Sokal 1 and 2, p.493); 'and I, tormented with grief for Trunov, I also pushed in amongst them, yelling out along with them to relieve my own pain.'[145] Yet it is noticeable how grandiloquence is juxtaposed with solemnity in the plans and allays the sense of loss and extreme grief. The military commissar's speech at the burial is one of vacuous propaganda: 'And the military commissar uttered a speech about the power of the soviets, the constitution of the USSR and the blockade.' (Sokal 2, p.493) Babel hints at the irony to come with his repeated references to Trunov as a 'world hero'[146] and in his wry injunction to the commissar: 'We're burying Pavel Trunov, world hero. Military commissar, say a word … mention the hero in front of the men.' (Sokal 2, p.493) That the commissar ignores this is evident from his words, which Babel's plan gives in detail: 'Com[rades], – the comm[unist] party is an iron rank, countlessly giving of its blood in the front line. And when blood flows from iron, then it's no joking matter for you, comrades, but victory or death.' (Smert' Trunova, p.494)

Babel's skill in creating bathos, in juxtaposing the noble with the comic has been commented on by Smirin: 'But the tendency to combine the elevated with the comic, so peculiar to Babel, is already in evidence here. Hence the reference to Trunov as a "world hero" and the military commissar's speech which has been composed according to all the rules of newspaper rhetoric.'[147] Babel's experience as a war correspondent and his ability in *skaz* technique is turned to ironic effect, yet the above speech is not included in 'Eskadronnyy Trunov' but transferred to 'Prodolzheniye istorii odnoy loshadi' where it is used by Savitskiy in his reply to Khlebnikov's letter. The former had taken the latter's prized white stallion in the earlier story 'Istoriya odnoy loshadi'. Both men feature in the 'Trunov collection' of plans, as Timoshenko and Mel'nikov respectively, and Babel uses unaltered expressions from these plans in the story 'Prodolzheniye istorii odnoy loshadi'. Khlebnikov accords Trunov's title 'universal hero' to Savitskiy in his conciliatory letter, which exonerates the army for his troubles: 'I understand my sufferings within that army … And to you, comrade Savitskiy, a world hero.'[148] The first phrase Babel has taken directly from his plan Sokal 1 (p.492), a phrase which he had noted in Mel'nikov's (Khlebnikov) letter: 'One phrase from Mel'nikov's letter – And I understand my sufferings within that army.' (Sokal 1, p.492)

Savitskiy's reply of bluster and bombast uses almost identically the words of the military commissar's funeral oration to Trunov to remind Khlebnikov of his earlier foolishness at resigning from the Communist Party: 'Our communist party, comrade Savitsky, is an iron rank of fighting men, giving of their blood in the front line, and when blood flows from iron, then it's no joking matter for you comrades, but victory or death.'[149] The sufferings experienced by Mel'nikov (Khlebnikov) and expressed by him in a letter, as we have seen noted in the plans, struck a chord with Babel who had Lyutov record his affection for the commander of the first squadron: 'So we lost Khlebnikov. I was terribly saddened by this, because Khlebnikov was a quiet fellow, similar to me in character … we were both shaken by the same passions.'[150] Khlebnikov's quiet disposition had allowed contact between himself and the diffident Lyutov, contact of a type which the latter could never forge with a Savitskiy or a Trunov, men that he could view but at a distance. The fact that Babel accords the words of Trunov's funeral oration to Savitskiy, a speech 'composed according to all the rules of newspaper rhetoric',[151] exposes the latter in a pejorative way and redresses the awe-struck impression that Lyutov had gained of him in 'Moy pervyy gus'.[152] As is usual with Babel's protagonists, fallibilities are exposed and the narrator's essentially ambivalent view is evident; Savitskiy may be god-like in one respect but he is an unbending man of little feeling and outrageous vanity in another. The letter that he writes in reply to Khlebnikov demonstrates Babel's skill in *skaz* technique, for it captures the gauche rhetoric of clichés and crudity of which Savitskiy and his ilk are capable. Lyutov's ambivalent view of Savitskiy which emerges from three *Konarmiya* stories,[153] has affinities with the relationship that he forms with Trunov except that Babel has striven to contain all facets of the protagonist and the narrator's different reactions to him within the one story.

The plans contain the seeds of this embryonic ambivalence. The author's cries of 'I have lost you, Pavel', (Sokal 1 and 2, p.493) and references to his burial honours, betoken affection; the ironic juxtaposition in the funeral oration's shallow rhetoric indicates disaffection. The ambivalence is fully exploited in the story where the two antithetical episodes concerning the prisoners and the aerial attack are juxtaposed, the one incomprehensible and repugnant to the narrator, the other equally incomprehensible yet admirable. Lyutov's lens filters a series of equivocal details. Trunov's body, we are told, lies in a place of honour: 'and we removed Trunov, our late commander, to gothic Sokal and buried him there in a place of honour …',[154] a flower bed in a public garden, no less. His body lies on display in an open coffin, his polished boots placed together as if back on the parade ground, yet his face is disfigured with wounds, his tongue torn out, his mouth stuffed full with broken teeth. The band play The Internationale, Cossacks bid him farewell in spectacular fashion, firing at full gallop and scattering red flowers on his coffin, while earlier: 'Our decrepit little cannon gave the first shot. It saluted the dead commander with all of its three inches.'[155]

The speech of the military commander, Pugachov, is as unimpressive as the cannon's salute, though, unlike the commissar's speech of the plans, it does mention Trunov by name and renders the irony there more subtle:

> – Men, Pugachov, regimental commander, said then, standing at the edge of the hole and looking at the deceased, – men, – he said, trembling and tugging at his seams, – we are burying Pasha Trunov, world hero, we are paying Pasha our last respects ...
> And raising to the sky eyes inflamed through lack of sleep, Pugachov shouted forth his speech about the dead soldiers of the First Cavalry Army, about this proud phalanx beating with the hammer of history upon the anvil of future ages.[156]

The last part of this speech, which Lyutov reports to us, contains an image similar both in theme and epic tone to the commissar's 'iron rank' image in the plans. Here the army is 'beating the hammer of history upon the anvil of future ages'. The unyielding determination of the Communist Party, to which the military commissar absurdly alludes in the plans, is replaced in 'Eskadronnyy Trunov' by the historic mission of the army to forge communism from a malleable world. Pugachov's image, like the sound of the hammer on the anvil, rings as hollow as that of the commissar of the plans; it forms a link with an image that occurs in the 'Galician episode' of 'Eskadronnyy Trunov', an episode of which there is no trace in diary or plans. Trunov, as a representative of that 'proud phalanx'[157] beating its hammer, would seem to be the blacksmith in an allegorical portrayal which has Lyutov as a funereal Galician, an embodiment of death, leading his stricken conscience, in the form of a cow, upon his act of betrayal.[158]

Babel thus in one story contains the extremes of Lyutov's ambivalence, the focal point of which, Trunov, emerges as a character both repugnant and resplendent. The complex birth of the central protagonist and the shaping of the story undoubtedly caused Babel considerable 'hard labour'.[159] Diary entries and plans contribute to our knowledge of Babel's complex 'creative laboratory'[160] as does the fragment 'Ikh bylo devyat''. The fact that the latter was never published by Babel indicates dissatisfaction.[161] Its portrayal of Cossack brutality and callousness is completely one-dimensional; the unequivocal message perhaps provides a clue to Babel's similar rejection of the 'Demidovka' episode of which his plans, unusually for once, give a full outline. The misdemeanours of Prishchepa, its central protagonist, are equally callous, unatoned and most significantly unatonable. Babel prefers to develop the story of his vengeance in the *Konarmiya* story 'Prishchepa', where his ruthless, savage acts are to some degree expiable. In a diary entry of 21 July, Babel asks: 'What is our Cossack then?' (Smirin, p.477) Smirin argues that Babel is halted in bewilderment at the conflicting features: 'Strata:

a ragamuffin, a dare-devil, a professional, a revolutionary, a brutish barbarian.' (21 July, Smirin, p.477)

Babel's portrayal of Trunov is one attempt to encapsulate the diversity of Cossack traits and to rationalize his bewilderment. One feels that, although he still remains bewildered, Babel is endeavouring throughout *Konarmiya* to give a more detailed answer to the fundamental questions of the meaning of violence and war than is the case in *Na pole chesti*. The 'Trunov plans' reveal at least partially the ambivalence with which Babel invests his 'world hero';[162] the diary does not. But what is again exposed in the transition between diary, plans and finished story, is an intensification of horror and Babel's obsession with violence and death, with those that are their inflictors and their victims. Babel's *Konarmiya* is 'an artistic attempt at understanding all of this multicoloured current of impressions'.[163] 'Ikh bylo devyat'' and 'Demidovka'[164] are, by contrast, monochrome and thus rejected.

GRISHCHUK

Another protagonist who makes fleeting appearance in *Konarmiya*, and whose story was subsequently excluded from the cycle is Grishchuk.[165] He features in seven diary entries[166] and examination of these, and his eponymous story, facilitates comprehension of the peripheral figure that he remains in the cycle, and leads to a discovery of a double reversal of roles between Grishchuk and Lyutov in the transition from diary to cycle. Moreover, unlike Trunov, Grishchuk is essentially a victim, one of the 'inflicted', who resembles in his suffering the victims of the *Na pole chesti* cycle in general, and Ston and Lyutov himself in particular.

The first reference to him in the diary reads, 'I have a coachman, 39 years old Grishchuk. Five years in captivity in Germany, 50 versts from home (he is from the Kremenets district) they don't set him free, he is silent.' (14 July, Livshits, p.115) It is Grishchuk's taciturnity, his apparent utter lack of emotional response to his circumstances which intrigue Babel: 'What is Grishchuk then, endless silence, limitless languor. 50 versts from home, hasn't been home for 6 y[ears], doesn't run away.' (19 July, Livshits, p.115) He repeatedly mentions Grishchuk's plight and apparent indifference to returning home. 'Why doesn't Grishchuk run away?' (21 July, Livshits, p.115) 'Grishchuk is 50 versts from home. He doesn't run away.' (23 July, Livshits, p.115) His silence provokes curiosity in Babel, who refers to him as 'mysterious Grishchuk',[167] and anger in Lyutov: 'You're always silent, Grishchuk, – I said to him, gasping for breath, – how will I understand you, wearisome Grishchuk?'[168] His conduct in a moment of danger does nothing to assuage the author's annoyance or inquisitiveness. The diary entry of 22 July describes an encounter with a group of Polish soldiers in which Babel and Grishchuk come under fire. The author remarks, 'Sometimes Grishchuk behaves with a morose, taciturn energy, then in moments of danger – he's incomprehensible, listless ...' (22 July, Livshits, p.115) He does permit himself one remark, however: 'Grishchuk abruptly seizes the reins – in his unexpected ringing tenor – we're done for, the Pole will catch us up.' (22 July, Livshits, p.115)

The isolation with which Grishchuk surrounds himself reminds us of the respective situations of the 'little men' of *Na pole chesti*. The four protagonists are the victims of circumstances which war has created. Isolation represents their response to situations with which they cannot cope. Grishchuk's sombreness and taciturnity are particularly reminiscent of the Quaker Ston, also a driver, who shunned his fellow men, preferring the company of animals.[169] Grishchuk in his world of silence appears equally self-sufficient, needing neither to break free, to find companionship, nor to visit his family whom he has not seen for a considerable time. Lyutov is provoked by Grishchuk's detachment, not merely because he wishes to break through the latter's wall of silence to discover his motives, but also because he feels an affinity with his isolation. The central protagonist of *Konarmiya* frequently experiences situations in which he himself is isolated, at times ostracized by those around him. In the very manner of his recording of events, Lyutov displays a predilection for understatement. His taciturnity resembles that of Grishchuk, but in the primary narrator's case we are able to infer his emotions from the imagery, from the tropes that he employs. Seldom is there an outpouring of feeling, particularly when emotional reaction of a pejorative nature is expected. The 'naked prose'[170] of *Na pole chesti*, which is replaced by a more finely constructed and ornate prose in *Konarmiya,* springs from the same psyche that has respectively created a Ston, a Lyutov and a Grishchuk.

It is to the subsequently excluded story, 'Grishchuk', that we must look for an explanation of Grishchuk's behaviour, an explanation which clarifies some of the remarks which appear in the two *Konarmiya* stories in which he does feature.[171] 'Grishchuk' is dated 16 July 1920, a day when the diary entry bears no mention of him. Lyutov and Grishchuk return at noon in their wagon from a foraging expedition. The latter faints from hunger as he is driving into a village, but does not lose total consciousness for he very deliberately gathers the reins together as he slides from his seat: 'His chill head rocked slightly, the horses were at walking pace, and a yellowing fabric of repose settled on Grishchuk's face, like a shroud. Not eaten, – he courteously answered my cry of alarm and wearily lowered his lids.'[172] Lyutov fills him with bread and potatoes; Grishchuk prostrates himself on the ground, 'face upwards',[173] but does not break his silence at this point when pressed to declare himself by the narrator. 'And only at night when we lay on the hay, warming each other, did I get to know one chapter of his mute tale.'[174]

The circumstances of Grishchuk's revelations to Lyutov, are reminiscent of the latter's celebration of his hard won acceptance among the Cossacks in 'Moy pervyy gus'. There, in a hay loft, Lyutov reflects on his overcoming the earlier isolation that he had experienced: 'and then we went to sleep in the hayloft. We slept there six of us, warming each other, legs intertwined, beneath a roof full of holes that let in the stars.'[175] The latter part of this quotation also resembles an image which occurs in 'Kvaker'. Ston has returned after a week's absence to find his horse badly neglected in a dilapidated shed. The groom Bekker says defiantly that he has been unable to obtain food for the animal: 'Very well – answered Ston – I'll get some oats. He looked *at the sky shining through a hole in the ceiling*, and left.' (ll.93–4, 'Kvaker')[176] The imagery employed links the three protagonists, Ston, Lyutov and Grishchuk, in the physical circumstances of their isolation, which in the case of at least the latter two is temporarily dispelled. Lyutov has gained an acceptance on the one hand in 'Moy pervyy gus' from the Cossacks, his earlier persecutors, and on the other in 'Grishchuk' from a man who had seemed to need no human contact at all.

Grishchuk recounts to Lyutov how, as a prisoner of war, he had been taken on by a mad, solitary German farmer to help with the harvest and how he had stayed four years with him. The farmer's madness had consisted of maintaining an unbroken silence. Grishchuk was taught by blows, privation and signs what was required of him. The diary entry of 29 July speaks of this: 'At times he exclaims – I was tortured, he couldn't learn German, [be]cause his master was a sober man, they would only quarrel with one another, never converse. It also seems – he went hungry for seven months, since his master stinted on his food.' (29 July Livshits, p.116) The story also relates how no words were spoken at Grishchuk's parting from his master, although a bond had developed between them. Having arrived at the edge of the village, 'the German pointed at the church, at his heart, at the limitless, empty blue of the horizon. He inclined his grey dishevelled insane head to Grishchuk's shoulder. They stood thus for a while in silent embrace.'[177]

The three-fold description of the madman's head recalls that of Bidu, the idiot-boy in 'Na pole chesti': 'Instead of an answer Bidu quietly rocked his shaggy round ginger head … of a village idiot'. (ll.30–1, 'Na pole chesti') Both depictions evoke pathos, and while the German's part is that of an oppressor and Bidu's that of a victim, the similarity of description confirms a blurring of these roles throughout Babel's ambivalent portrayals.

Lyutov's curiosity has thus been satisfied. He has learnt of the sufferings of Grishchuk and of the reasons for his gloominess and taciturnity. The latter's silent, passive acceptance of being refused a visit home had seemed an enigmatic response to the narrator, but it now becomes, in the light of what he has heard, a comprehensible and heroic example of stoicism and of the human capacity for suffering. Again, a link with *Na pole chesti* is apparent: Grishchuk here resembles in degree of pathos the old man Maresko – the latter had lost his family through an act of war, the former had likewise been lost to his. 'Grishchuk' extends the bridge or link, of which I have already spoken with particular reference to 'Kvaker',[178] between Babel's two cycles of war stories, although paradoxically it appeared in neither. Its exclusion from *Konarmiya* may stem from the sketchiness of characterization. With no access to the diary notes, Grishchuk and his German master remain vague characters; it is only through analysis of the story with the diary material that a clearer picture of the two men emerges.

Grishchuk's extant role in *Konarmiya* is limited; while he is not lost to the cycle, he makes an enigmatic impression particularly in view of a monologue that he utters and his probable saving of the narrator's life in 'Smert' Dolgushova'. Again, it is only through scrutiny of the diary entries and his eponymous story that one is better able to put Grishchuk into context in the two *Konarmiya* stories in which he appears, 'Ucheniye o tachanke' and 'Smert' Dolgushova'. Although they are placed together in the cycle, 'Grishchuk' itself was published with the former and not with 'Smert' Dolgushova', which was published some two months later.[179] In 'Ucheniye o tachanke', Lyutov celebrates receiving a driver and outlines his background, not only repeating information that appears in the diary but also elaborating on his escape from Germany:

> A driver has been sent me from headquarters, or as it is customary among us to say, a coachman. His name is Grishchuk. He is thirty nine years old. His story is a terrible one.
> Grishchuk remained in German captivity for five years, some months ago he escaped, crossed Lithuania, north west Russia, reached Volhynia and in Belyev was caught by the most brainless mobilisation commission in the world and made to do military service. There were only fifty versts left to Grishchuk's native district of Kremenets. He had a wife and children in the district of Kremenets. He had not been at home for five years and two months. The mobilisation commission made him my coachman, and I ceased to be a pariah among the Cossacks.[180]

What is excluded is any reference to Grishchuk's taciturnity. Indeed there is no attempt to characterize him at all, each reference is factual: 'Grishchuk leads the horses from the stable … Grishchuk sits sideways on the coachbox'.[181] Some characterization occurs however, in the following story, 'Smert' Dolgushova'. The first reference to Grishchuk is disparaging and betokens annoyance on Lyutov's part: 'Grishchuk with his stupid cart and I'.[182] Lyutov's anger may be understandable from the discourse on the carts that he gives in the preceding story, for there he ironically depicts the new found role that they played in the armies of Makhno and Budyonnyy.[183] But one also senses an annoyance akin to that expressed by the primary narrator in 'Grishchuk', which stems from the driver's continued, unbroken silence and from his introverted, sullen nature of which the diary makes much.[184]

Another reference to Grishchuk occurs in an episode of 'Smert' Dolgushova' that has been roughly transposed from the diary entry of 22 July. There, Grishchuk and Babel retreat under fire from Khotin, where their regiments are based. Imagery recurs between diary and story: 'The bullets hum, whistle.' (22 July, Mierau, p.189) 'The bullets whine and scream.'[185] In the story, the action is around Brody, and Grishchuk and Lyutov are ambushed at the city cemetery by a Polish scout. Grishchuk turns the cart round, wheels screaming, and proceeds to give a soliloquy, more gloomy with each utterance, on the pointlessness of life:

– It's a joke, – he answered gloomily …

– Why do women take such pains, – he answered even more gloomily, why the proposals, the nuptials, why do the god-parents revel at the weddings …

– Makes me laugh, – Grishchuk said sadly and pointed with his whip at a man sitting at the side of the road, – makes me laugh, why women take such pains …[186]

The monologue comes as a surprise in 'Smert' Dolgushova', a sudden outburst for which the reader is unprepared. The sombre import of his speech is in keeping with the sullenness of his nature as exposed in the diary and the story, 'Grishchuk'; indeed it supports a statement written about him in the diary on 22 July: 'then in moments of danger – he's incomprehensible, listless …', (Livshits, p.115) but it also breaks the silence with which the diary has associated him.

Evidence suggests that Babel was preparing a different monologue for Grishchuk, and one in which the author's predilection for ambivalence may have been to the fore. On a separate sheet of preparatory observations, Babel had written under the heading 'Two Russias': 'Had left six years ago. Arrived back – what he saw. Grishchuk's monologue – style.'[187] The implication is that Grishchuk was to recount the differences that he saw between the Russia that he had left and the one to which he returned after six years in captivity. As far as we know, the speech was never written and may have been another factor in Babel's exclusion of 'Grishchuk' from *Konarmiya*, since Grishchuk's character was thus never as fully developed as he would have liked.

'Smert' Dolgushova' contains a double reversal of roles between Lyutov and Grishchuk. The diary reports how Grishchuk broke his silence with a cry of panic when he and Babel came under fire: 'in his unexpected ringing tenor – we're done for, the Pole will catch us up'. (22 July, Livshits, p.115). But in the story the cry is uttered by Lyutov prior to Grishchuk's unsignalled and bitter soliloquy: 'We're done for, – I exclaimed, seized with calamitous frenzy, – we're done for, old man!'[188] The transfer of role has a dual explanation. Firstly, explicit emotional reaction is not usually part of Grishchuk's disposition, as we have seen from the diary entries which tell of his silence at not being allowed home. Secondly, Lyutov's curiosity at Grishchuk's behaviour is founded on a sharing by the narrator of the latter's sense of isolation and suffering. Lyutov suspects experiences in Grishchuk which in one way or another he himself has undergone. Babel thus transfers part of Grishchuk's role to Lyutov; the latter subsumes the former, just as he represents in different ways the sufferings of Ston and all the victims of the two cycles of war stories.

The second and more significant reversal of roles in 'Smert' Dolgushova' is a reciprocal humanitarian act made by Grishchuk towards Lyutov, an act which goes some way towards redressing the pejorative image of the former that his monologue had created. Babel's balancing of characteristics, his creation of an ambivalent picture is thus once more apparent. Grishchuk's character undergoes a partial redemption which the inclusion of the eponymous story would have completed.

I have already described how Lyutov in 'Grishchuk' had given his driver some food when he had collapsed at the wheel of the cart. The imagery used implies that the latter's death had been thwarted by Lyutov's action: 'His chill head rocked slightly, the horses were at walking pace, and a yellowing fabric of repose settled on Grishchuk's face, like a shroud. – Not eaten, – he courteously answered my cry of alarm and wearily lowered his lids.'[189] A full reciprocation of Lyutov's act is made by Grishchuk in 'Smert' Dolgushova'. The narrator has failed to administer the *coup de grâce* to Dolgushov, a telephonist, lying mortally wounded at the roadside, despite being urged to do so by the wounded man. The consequence of his inaction is that he is threatened with death himself by an indignant Afon'ka Bida, who has carried out the shooting:

> – Go away, – he answered turning pale, I'll kill you! You four-eyes pity our brother as much as a cat does a mouse …
> And he cocked his gun.
> I rode off at walking pace, without turning round feeling the chill of death in my back.[190]

Grishchuk intervenes by seizing Bida's arm and preventing him firing. The latter rides off, threatening revenge. When Grishchuk catches Lyutov up, the narrator merely bemoans his loss of Bida's friendship. Grishchuk's response is to proffer him a shrivelled apple which he had kept hidden away: 'Grishchuk extracted a shrivelled apple from his seat. – Eat it, – he said to me, – please eat it.'[191] The gesture is the obverse of Lyutov's action in 'Grishchuk'.[192] Grishchuk had probably saved Lyutov's life by his intervention in 'Smert' Dolgushova'; the offering of the shrivelled apple is a symbol which engenders both pathos and hope. It complements the food that Lyutov had given Grishchuk by representing a spiritual sustenance, a tangible if humble symbol of the promise of new friendship which for Lyutov is a means to going on, to survival: 'And I accepted this act of kindness from Grishchuk and ate his apple with sorrow and awe.'[193]

This final act by Grishchuk in 'Smert' Dolgushova' counterbalances the monologue that he had uttered earlier, in which he had cynically condemned life, declaiming as to why women inflict such toil upon themselves by marrying and having children when war can undo their work in a minute. Here, at the end of the story, he has intervened both to save life and to promote it by offering sustenance and help to the disconsolate Lyutov. Babel's balancing of the pejorative with the praiseworthy thus produces an equivocal characterization of Grishchuk and once again indicates the author's essential ambivalence: an ambivalence which is only seen at its most complete from an examination of the diary entries and the three stories,[194] 'Grishchuk', 'Smert' Dolgushova' and 'Ucheniye o tachanke'. Ultimately, by excluding 'Grishchuk' from his *Konarmiya* cycle Babel may have indicated a desire to retain its central protagonist as the 'mysterious Grishchuk' (26 July, Livshits, p.115) of the diary.[195]

DEMIDOVKA

Just as the content of many plans is altered considerably in the finished cycle, so are the plans of other stories unused in *Konarmiya*. Examples include 'The Day of a Divisional Commander' (p.496) about a 'collective day';[196] 'Lepin', (p.495) a fragment which cryptically mentions 'a mutiny of the soul';[197] 'Govinskiy', (p.494) concerning a Polish deserter; and 'Budyatichi' (p.496) which, as I have already mentioned, indicates Babel's original intention to allow women a greater, more positive role in *Konarmiya*.[198]

However, an episode centred on one protagonist, Prishchepa, like Grishchuk a driver of Lyutov in *Konarmiya*, affords an extensive example of Babel's selective use of his raw materials, his diary notes and his plans, and contains narrative strands and tensions realized in other stories of the cycle. The *Konarmiya* story, 'Prishchepa', was published twice in 1923,[199] the second time with a date and place added: 'Demidovka, July 1920', which was subsequently removed by Babel. The diary notes correspond with this date, for the three consecutive entries in which Prishchepa features are 23, 24 and 25 July. In the plans, the 'Prishchepa episode' bears the heading 'Demidovka' (pp.495–6) and is afforded more space than most of the other headings respectively.[200] Such extensive treatment might therefore be assumed to signal equivalent significance in the finished cycle, but this is hardly the case.

Prishchepa is first referred to in the diary as: 'a new acquaintance, a caftan, a white hood, an illiterate communist …' (23 July, Smirin, p.499). His description and circumstances are then developed in the next day's entry:

> Prishchepa's soul – an illiterate boy, a communist, cadets killed his parents, recounts how he gathered his property from round the village. Decorative, hood, as simple as the grass, he'll be a rag-and-bone man, despises Grishchuk for not liking or understanding horses. (24 July, Smirin, p.499)

The description of Prishchepa in *Konarmiya* includes elements of the diary's portrayal, but it adds to it with a series of attributive phrases. The fact that Prishchepa merits such a catalogue of description indicates that Babel originally envisaged a more extensive role for him in the cycle than he is finally given:[201] 'a youth from the Kuban region, a tireless boor, a washed out communist, a budding rag-and-bone man, a happy-go-lucky syphilitic, a calculating liar'.[202] His colourful dress is also added to: 'He has on a crimson Circassian coat of fine cloth with a hood of down thrown behind his back.'[203] The 'white' of the diary is omitted and reference is made to his crimson coat, symbolic of the 'bloody imprint of his soles'[204] made as he goes about his murderous business of revenge in the cycle. There is too, in the story, little hint of his artless naïveté; he is 'as simple as the grass', proclaims a simile in the diary,[205] (24 July, Smirin, p.499) with a fierce love for horses, yet the descriptive catalogue of the story is a highly critical one.

The plans relate more to *Konarmiya*'s portrayal of Prishchepa, although paradoxically they contain little direct description of him, merely the cryptic statement: 'Prishchepa exposed. – blood-stained swine'. (p.495) The animal image of the plans' metaphor is a far cry from the simile of the diary, 'as simple as the grass', (24 July, Smirin, p.499) but it is indeed justified by the events which the plans then recount. The narrator[206] and Prishchepa are billeted in a house of a Polish Jewish settlement in Demidovka on the eve of a Jewish religious festival, the 9 Ava, a day of fasting in mourning at the memory of the fall of Jerusalem and the destruction of the temple. The Jewish element is all-pervasive both in diary entries and plans and creates a dual ambience of nostalgia and suffering. The entry for the 23 July reads:

> The synagogues of Dubno. Everything is in ruins. Two small entrances have remained intact, centuries, two little rooms, full of memories … The synagogues mean, old, small, green and blue houses, Hasidic, inside no architecture. I enter an Hasidic one. It is Friday. What small, stunted figures, what emaciated faces, everything has risen up before me as it was 300 years ago, old men run through the synagogues – no wailing, for some reason they always run from one corner to the other, quite unconstrained praying. Probably the ugliest Jews of Dubno have gathered here. … A quiet evening in the synagogue – that always has an inexpressible effect on me. (23 July, Mierau, p.190)

Here one can discern the Lyutov of 'Gedali', 'Rabbi', 'Berestechko', and 'Ucheniye o tachanke', in which his words of anguish are heard – anguish at the tragic lives of the emaciated Jews of the barren, Galician region; nostalgia for the bubbling Jews of his childhood, the Jews of the South:

> Lifeless small Jewish towns cling to the feet of Polish landowners' estates. … concealed among scattered hovels, a synagogue squatted on the barren earth, eyeless, pitted, round like an Hasidic hat. Narrow-shouldered Jews loiter at the crossroads. And the image of the Jews of the south, jovial bellied and bubbling like cheap wine burns in my memory. The bitter disdain of these long, bony backs and these tragic, yellow beards cannot compare with them. In their features, etched with passion and anguish, there is no fat, no warm pulsing of blood.[207]

In the diary entry of 24 July, Babel spends little time generalizing on the plight of the Jews, preferring to focus on the individual members of the Jewish household in which he and Prishchepa are billeted: 'The Jews have vanished, everything is destroyed. We are in a house with many women.' (24 July, Mierau, p.190) The plans indicate how important it was for Babel to portray the members of the family as well as other individuals who were present: 'Beginning – description of the family, analysis of its feelings and belief. – How will I learn all this? General phenomenon. (Their) political ideology.' (Demidovka, p.495) The individuals to be portrayed include an orphan; a youth; a girl from Kremenets who is a prospective daughter-in-law; the father – a respected Jew of the old school; the daughters, about whom Babel adjures himself, 'describe each sister separately' (p.495); and the mother, whose role is that of an intermediary between the generations, the younger of which is described metaphorically: 'new shoots, ... she heeds what's new, doesn't interfere, mother is a mediator, the children go their own way'. (p.496) Family tensions, the conflict between generations, was thus a theme which Babel envisaged in this episode, as well as in stories in which it was finally realized, such as 'Sashka Khristos' and 'Syn Rabbi'.

A narrative theme on which I have already commented, and which was largely unrealized in *Konarmiya* – the role and plight of women in war[208] – appears from the Demidovka plans to have preoccupied the narrator, for his impressions of the various daughters are individual and definite, and his descriptions are elaborate in comparison with elsewhere: 'there's a hunch-back, there's a proud one (a dentist), there's a magnificent (marr[ied] one), one devoting herself to the family and keeping house, another is a midwife helping the peasant women, she'll grow old in Demidovka'. (p.496) His observations are developed further and illustrate the importance of the potentially different roles of each girl, the hunchback whose life is one of service, the 'proud one' and the 'beauty' for each of whom one senses the narrator's keen sense of pathos at the situation which is developing:

> Into this family, as yet still undivided, Prishchepa and I came. – The hunchback serves us, then towards morning Dora Aronovna bestirred herself, how difficult it is to look at broken feminine pride. A beautiful girl, the only beautiful one, that's why it's such a complicated thing for her to marry – in her is a mixture of parochial well-being, Jew[ish], very black, liquid eyes, Polish cunning and Warsaw slippers, these ever anxious parents had conceived her in a moment of simple abandon ...

The elaborate nature of the comments on the daughters may have contributed to Babel's subsequent exclusion of the 'Demidovka episode' from *Konarmiya*, where women are portrayed in a subordinate, and usually negative role. To have included a story with such extensive and positive treatment of them may well have seemed incongruous to the author.

The narrator's stress on the unity and Jewishness of the Polish family – 'they live suffused with tradition' (p.496) – is a major factor in creating pathos. These features, together with the occasion, render the family a prime target for Cossack animalism and brutality. The Jewish religious festival, 9 Ava, and the presence of the extended, closely-knit Jewish family, are circumstances ripe for archetypal Babelesque victims, vulnerable to the violent intrusion of a Cossack oppressor. The guilt which Babel's narrator feels is that of an outsider who intrudes and is reminiscent of Lyutov's in 'Kostyol v Novograde': 'A foreign aggressor, I spread out a lousy mattress in a church abandoned by its priest.'[209] But it is also guilt by association.

The apparent triviality of the narrative events heightens the deeply wounding nature of the violent outcome. In the diary we are told that Prishchepa orders potatoes to be roasted, but the Jewesses refuse since it is the eve of the religious festival and the sabbath. The proud girl, the dentist, reacts thus: 'the dentist, turning pale with pride and self respect, declares that no one will dig up potatoes, [be]cause it's a holiday'. (24 July, Smirin, p.499)

Babel's comment on his own role at first acknowledges the polarization of Pole and Russian that war has caused: 'and I am silent, because I am indeed a Russian'. (24 July, Mierau, p.191) In the Novograd temple, Lyutov, who, as we have seen, had acknowledged his intrusion as a member of an occupying force, also comments on the suffering of the Polish nation: 'Here is Poland, here is the proud sorrow of the Republic of Poland!'[210] Here it is the distress of a family that Babel has become a party to, a family whose Jewishness he feels only too keenly: 'Prishchepa, long restrained by me, breaks loose … they all hate both of us, they dig up potatoes, fearful, in someone's kitchen-garden, prostrate themselves on crosses, Prishchepa is indignant. How painful it all is. (24 July, Smirin, p.499)

The author feels that the situation results from his impotence, an impotence which links him with Lyutov's inability to act at times of crisis in *Konarmiya*. He blames his inaction and helplessness at the Jews' fate on his being Russian; he feels the pain and suffering for the anguished family the more keenly for his Jewishness. An ironic parallel can be drawn with Maresko who foreshadows the pathos, if not the complete circumstances of these Jews. His pathetic burden, the alleged sack of potatoes, is the remains of his family destroyed by war. Here the Jews' family honour is forced upon a path of destruction with the very potatoes that they are made to prepare to satisfy the animal hunger of their oppressors. 'Like wolves we devour the roast potatoes and 5 glass[es] of coffee each … 9 Aba. The old woman sobs, sitting on the floor …' (24 July, Smirin, p.499)[211]

Babel's inaction, like Lyutov's, is prompted by fear. The latter is afraid to kill a man in battle or as an act of mercy, as is seen for example in 'Posle boya' or 'Smert' Dolgushova' respectively. The author/narrator's failure to respond is of the same brand in Demidovka; he is afraid not only of Prishchepa but also of weakening the affinities that he covets and cultivates with the Cossacks as he witnesses Prishchepa's base acts in the early morning. The story, 'Moy pervyy gus', depicts Lyutov's acceptance by Cossacks after he has slaughtered an old woman's goose which he then orders her to cook for him in a manner as brutal as Prishchepa's: 'For the love of God, – I muttered then, irritably and punched the old woman in the chest, – I've had enough of you … – For the love of God, I said, digging into the goose with my sword, – roast it for me, landlady.'[212] While the assumption by Lyutov, however fleetingly, of a Prishchepa-like mantle of violence, brings him an entrée into the Cossacks' circle, his feelings are full of anguish. His triumph is a hollow one: 'We slept there six of us, warming each other, legs inter-twined, beneath a roof full of holes that let in the stars. I dreamt and saw women in my dreams and only my heart, stained with killing, grated and overflowed.'[213]

The extremes of Prishchepa's violence, the pursuit and rape of the prospective daughter-in-law, are foreshadowed by Babel in the diary in a parallel that he draws between events in the past and present. Babel's regard for the past and for his Jewish roots, well to the fore in the diary entries seen above, and witnessed a little later in a letter found amid the pages of his diary – 'h[o]w difficult it is to tear myself away from olden times' (13 August, Livshits, p.123) – is further aroused by the song sung by the Jewish youth, a future son-in-law of the family, who, to comfort the sobbing mother, sings in commemoration of the destruction of the temple in Jerusalem.[214] The same youth had already been provoked by Prishchepa into an argument about religion which had demonstrated the latter's ignorance: 'Prishchepa is outrageously stupid, he talks about religion in ancient times, confusing christ[ianity] with paganism,' (24 July, Smirin, p.499). The youth's words ring out melodiously amid the sounds of the satisfying of voracious Cossack appetites and the sobbing of the old lady:

> The terrible words of the prophets – excrement is eaten, the girls defiled, the men killed, Israel in ruins, angry words of grief. The little lamp smokes, the old woman wails, the youth sings melodiously, the girls in white stockings, beyond the window Demidovka, night time, Cossacks, every-thing is as then, when the temple was destroyed … (24 July, Smirin, p.499).

Past had become present for Babel as he stepped into the Hasidic synagogue the previous day. Here the mood is continued; the merging of past and present effectively makes time stand still. The blurring of events creates a timelessness, a limbo similar to that felt by Lyutov in 'Berestechko': 'A way of life had vanished in Berestechko, but it still had a firm base here. Shoots, which were over three centuries old, were still sprouting in Volhynia with the warm mould of olden times … The little town reeks on in expectation of a new era.'[215]

The words of the youth's song assume a particular and personal poignancy for their Jewish audience. The destruction of the temple in Jerusalem resem-bles the desecration of this Jewish household in Demidovka. The events of long ago find particular parallels with these of 1920. The potatoes that the Jews of Demidovka have been forced to prepare represent the excrement eaten in Jerusalem, the girls who were dishonoured there are paralleled in the final act of brutality performed by Prishchepa: 'The girls half naked and dishevelled run up and down the wet kitchen gardens, lust relentlessly enslaves Prishchepa, he assaults the betrothed of the one-eyed old woman's son …' (25 July, Smirin, p.499) As the soldiers eat the meat out of the pans, and the wagons are prepared, Babel comments further on his growing sense of despair and guilt, which reaches a climax as Prishchepa's brutality and lust reach theirs: 'Two tortuous hours, awoke the Jewish women at 4 in the morning and they're forced to cook Russian meat and it's the 9 Aba ... she – I shall cry out, her face ... he presses her against the wall, repugnant scene ...[216] (25 July, Mierau, p.192) The explicitness of the author/narrator's feelings indicates the depth of the personal dilemma that he himself experiences: 'how difficult it is to look at broken feminine pride'. (Demidovka, p.496) Babel is indeed stranded in a limbo; as a member of a Russian army of brutal oppressors, his inaction is seen as tacit approval by the Jewish victims for whose religion and beliefs he has respect and sympathy. Such is also the limbo or 'no-man's-land' which the respective *Na pole chesti* victims had occupied in another theatre of war two years previously. Here, Babel is as much an inadequate figure and victim as a Bozhi, Bidu or Ston had been, and as Lyutov was to become.

The plans of the 'Demidovka episode' develop the content of the diary entries. At one point Babel has the narrator turn story-teller, entrancing the whole family with his tale, even the proud and haughty daughter, Dora Aronovna, thus perhaps easing the narrator's burden of guilt.[217] As with other plans, Babel shuffled details and facts round, adding and omitting, but in the final reckoning he chose to ignore almost the total dramatic potential of the 'Demidovka episode', merely utilizing in *Konarmiya* what amounts to two lines in the diary and two words in the plans: 'cadets killed his parents, recounts how he gathered his property from round the village'. (24 July, Smirin, p.499). This brief reference is alluded to in the plans merely by the words 'Prishchepa's story' (Smirin, p.495). The result is the story entitled 'Prishchepa', which recounts the bloody revenge that the returning Prishchepa wreaked on the villagers who had looted his murdered parents' home. The brutality that he displays in this story is indeed on a greater scale than that recorded in the diary, yet it is a brutality with an appreciable motive, while that displayed in Demidovka is gratuitous, and consequently more shocking. The story is slight even by *Konarmiya* standards, yet the string of six attributive phrases, which are reserved for Prishchepa as the story opens, seem excessive in comparison with Babel's usual style of understatement. With our 'privileged' view of the events of Demidovka, they assume fresh justification, just as Grishchuk's personality is more explicable from a knowledge of the content of the diary and plans: 'My companion as previously is Prishchepa – a youth from the Kuban, a tireless boor, a washed out communist, a budding rag-and-bone man, a happy-go-lucky syphilitic, a calculating liar.'[218]

Yet the question remains as to why Babel should not include this material in *Konarmiya*. Perhaps he felt that the various elements were more effectively portrayed elsewhere, that the role of the women conflicted with that of other women in the rest of the cycle, or that the proximity of his personal role portrayed in the diary was so indistinguishable from that of his narrator in the plans as to make him ashamed. Alternatively, perhaps it is simply that the manuscript has been lost or destroyed. Whatever the reason or reasons, the exclusion of 'Demidovka' from *Konarmiya* remains an enigma. It may well indicate a creative process that can only be surmised; it certainly points to the frequent gulf between Babel's diary and plans on the one hand and his finished cycle on the other, and underlines again the value of comparing Vidal's original stories with Babel's *Na pole chesti* in order to 'penetrate the creative laboratory'[219] of the latter. The exclusion also partly belies the claim of his second wife Tamara Vladimirovna Ivanova, who commented that, 'reflection and memory ... were [Babel's] creative laboratory'.[220] Memory was certainly discarded in the case of Demidovka and memories were much distorted in the re-working of material between diary, plans and cycle, as Babel himself acknowledged: 'Impressions obtained from reality, images and colours I forget. And then one thought appears devoid of artistic flesh, one naked theme ... I start to develop this theme, to give free rein to my imagination, clothing it in flesh and blood, but not resorting to memory's help ...'[221]

What I hope my exegesis of Grishchuk's and Prishchepa's respective characters has achieved is to illuminate what Babel held dear, namely an exposé of the 'how' and the 'why' of his protagonists. It is with the answers to these questions and with the place of himself or his primary narrator, Lyutov, in relation to those around him that Babel is concerned. As he is reported to have said when giving reasons for his slowness in working: 'By disposition the 'how' and the 'why' always interest me. One needs to think a great deal and study a great deal concerning these questions and to treat literature with great integrity in order to answer them in an artistic form.'[222] It is to a study of the 'how and 'why' of the protagonists of *Konarmiya* through their formation and use of figurative language that I now turn.

Part Three

THE TROPES OF WAR

INTRODUCTION

> ... a book is a world seen through a man.[1]

In my study of Babel's use of tropes in *Konarmiya* and *Na pole chesti* I have taken account of the protagonists associated with each figure, for Babel's cycles of stories are elaborate fabrics of *skaz*. Kvyatkovskiy foreshadows Rice's interpretation of *skaz* when he calls it: '... a special form of authorial speech pursued throughout the whole artistic production in the spirit of the language and nature of the characters in whose name the story is conducted'.[2] *Konarmiya* presents not one language register but a whole range of authorial speech. The richness of the 'linguistic document'[3] that it constitutes has been commented upon since the first publication of the stories and has continued to excite comment subsequently:[4] '... – every character appearing on its pages speaks in a way fully consistent with his or her social and cultural background – be it Russian, Polish, Ukrainian or Jewish, literary or crude, revolutionary or philosophical, military or lyrical.'[5] The reader is caught up in the stances and interplay of the various protagonists, and becomes almost the plaything of the author. Carden likens Babel's characters to 'verbal masks [who] manipulate the reader in a profoundly psychological way'.[6] Babel himself admits to such licence: 'I set myself a reader who is clever, educated, of sound and austere taste. ... and then I think of ways to deceive, to stun this clever reader.'[7] It is as if he sees himself toying with his reader with a heartlessness approaching that of one of his Cossack or bandit protagonists. But, like Dvoyra – the late-married sister of Benya Krik, the hero of *Odesskiye rasskazy* – Babel is merely anxious that his reader participates as fully as possible in what is to ensue. His rich tapestry of language reflecting a multiplicity of perceptions – cultural, moral and philosophical, is analogous to the urgent hands of the aforementioned 'King's'[8] hideous sister, while the reader plays the role of her reluctant husband: 'Pushing her timorous husband with both hands towards the doors of their nuptial chamber she was gazing at him carnivorously like a cat that bears a mouse in its mouth and gently tests it with its teeth.'[9]

Carden notes three types of narrator in *Konarmiya*: the Cossack hero, the author-narrator and common mortals.[10] Lyutov, the author-narrator, is the predominant one. His proportion of the cycle which I have designated 'Lyutov-based' or 'Lyutov-narrated' amounts to 66.9 per cent, with fourteen stories exceeding 80 and four 100 percent.[11] Yet we are given few explicit details of the man whom Babel chooses to present in his cycle. Biographically he resembles Babel in that he was Jewish, a graduate, wore spectacles and worked as a reporter for the military newspaper *Krasnyy kavalerist*. We learn also that Lyutov's wife had left him, but very little else is volunteered. The two-thirds of the cycle that Lyutov narrates includes what direct speech he utters. This comprises a mere 1.1 per cent and helps create an impression of him as a taciturn introvert who wishes to share with us in writing his subsequent recording and interpretation of events, events which are not, however, his sole preserve to interpret.

Stories such as 'Konkin' and 'Zhizneopisaniye Pavlichenki, Matveya Rodionycha' give an oral account of a 'Cossack hero's'[12] perception of life in the Red Cavalry or in pre- and post-revolutionary Russia, others such as 'Pis'mo', 'Prodolzheniye istorii odnoy loshadi', 'Sol'', 'Izmena' and 'Solntse Italii' (in part) present aspects of the same epistolary form. I have categorized the language of the Cossack protagonists under the heading 'Cossacks' in my tables of analysis, abandoning Carden's term 'hero' since many of these men are portrayed in a pejorative light, for example the syphilitic Tarakanych in 'Sashka Khristos' or Kurdyukov in 'Pis'mo' and 'U svyatogo Valenta'. Although the whole cycle is presented to us by Babel's central persona, Lyutov, who comprises its sentient centre and who, it might therefore be argued, is the source of all the language used, Babel is at pains in an early story of the cycle, 'Pis'mo', to stress that the language employed there is not that of his primary narrator. Both at the beginning and the end of the story Lyutov states that the words which he records are indeed not his own but those of an illiterate Cossack, who has dictated a letter to him: 'I have transcribed it without embellishment and pass it on word for word in accordance with the truth ... That is Kurdyukov's letter, not altered in a single word.'[13] Nowhere else does Lyutov make such an explicit declaration. Babel has made the point early and does not need to repeat it; the style, tone and lexis of the Cossacks' tropes, their brash hyperbole and colloquialisms are but some of the features which for the most part, as we shall see, clearly demarcate their language from that of the primary narrator.

The third *skaz* category is the speech of 'common mortals';[14] while it occurs in more than half of the Lyutov-narrated stories, it amounts only to 5.4 per cent of the cycle. Again, I prefer to attach a different label to that of Carden, and designate this category as simply the speech of 'others'. While this may seem nondescript, I feel that men such as Apolek and Gedali should not be dubbed mere 'common mortals'. They represent significant alternative Weltanschauungen to Lyutov's and give him, if not a fleeting sense of triumph, some cause for optimism amid his adverse circumstances and personal dilemmas. This category also includes a number of people diverse in nationality, creed or status, from peasants to Polish officers, from Jewesses to commissars, and thus seems not to fit Carden's term.

Why in fact did Babel create not one narrator, but a variety of them? *Odesskiye rasskazy* saw the emergence of a first-person narrator, whose function was to provide a framework to the stories' events and to act as a link between the number of scenes that each comprises. Yet as we have seen, the pattern had been set, if only tentatively, in the first cycle of war stories, *Na pole chesti*. The first, second and fourth stories are related almost entirely in the third person. Do we assume that it is simply the voice of the author, Babel, that we are hearing? I think not. Apart from the elaborate circumstances concerning the narrator in Babel's source material, Vidal's 'Deux actes devant une conscience',[15] in which the author retells a story related to him by a Captain V., Babel's narrative tone is frequently hyperbolic and often resembles that of his soldier protagonists. Is the narrator himself then a soldier participant? Certainly, in 'Semeystvo papashi Maresko', the only story told in the first person and whose narrator is identifiable, the events are portrayed through the eyes of a French lieutenant. Further confirmation of the presence of a participatory, and therefore possibly military narrator, is furnished at the end of the cycle in 'Kvaker', when the author-narrator suddenly mentions his own meeting with the chief protagonist, Ston: 'I met him after several hours and asked whether the road was dangerous? (l.95, 'Kvaker'). However, we are given less information as to the identity of the narrative voice of *Na pole chesti* than we receive concerning Lyutov in *Konarmiya*. For purposes of categorization I have followed the *skaz* patterns that I have set for *Konarmiya*; the greatest portion of the cycle is designated as belonging to the 'author-narrator' (62 per cent), the second category is labelled 'soldiers' (32.1 per cent) and is thus the equivalent of the 'Cossacks' of *Konarmiya*, while the third category, the language of other protagonists, bears the same name as it does for the major cycle, namely 'others' (15.9 per cent) and only occurs in one story, 'Kvaker', where it refers to the language of Ston and his groom, Bekker.

It is the major cycle, however, that contains the most varied and complex system of 'author-narrators', with at times a double or triple narrative device at work. In 'Pis'mo', as I have mentioned, the facts are related by Kurdyukov to Lyutov, thus a secondary narrator temporarily displaces the primary one. The acts of cruelty that the former recounts are thus 'at a double distance from the reader. Vassiliy's indifference becomes a strategy whereby Babel can present acts of cruelty without having to fall back upon conventional responses.'[16] The absence of any explicit reaction of horror or dismay is explained partly through Babel's wish to involve the reader as fully as possible in the events and also by the author's avowed desire to stun him. The reader compensates for the apparent authorial lack of emotion and in so doing is more deeply affected.

Instances also occur of a triple narrative device at work. In a number of stories – 'Put' v Brody', 'Zhizneopisaniye Pavlichenki, Matveya Rodionycha', 'Konkin', 'Eskadronnyy Trunov', 'Sol'', 'Izmena' and 'Pis'mo' – a secondary narrator reports or records, in speech or writing, the words of another or others to the primary narrator who reproduces them. The effect of this is to distance the reader even further from the events described, yet the authenticity with which Babel imbues the varied speech of his protagonists allows an understanding of the events which enhances their impact, increases tension and heightens emotional response. Such 'distancing' of the reader is countered, however, by Lyutov's narrative voice changing from the first person singular to the first person plural. The opening story, 'Perekhod cherez Zbruch', which depicts the contrast between the calm of Volhynia and the chaos to come in Poland exemplifies this: 'Purple poppy fields flower around us ... Volhynia recedes from us ... in flowery knolls ... The blackened Zbruch roars and twists the foaming knots of its rapids. The bridges are destroyed, and we wade across the river.'[17] The collective first person pronouns cede to the singular as Lyutov reaches his billet: 'They put a disembowelled feather-bed down for me, and I lie down against the wall, beside the third Jew who is asleep. Timorous destitution closes in over my couch.'[18] Such transfer of number, apart from allowing the collective whole to obscure the individual viewpoint and thus, when coupled with the use of the third person and its epic flavour, to vary the mode of perception, also 'has the advantage of encompassing the reader as a common participant, thus adding the impression of immediacy as well as of universality to what is being presented'.[19]

But how does Babel ensure that the reader will understand how to play his part? His confidence in the latter seemed unbounded when in 1924 he declaimed to his contemporary, Furmanov: 'And remember one more thing then, Dmitriy Andreyevich: do not explain. Please there's no need for any explanations – just portray things, and the reader will work them out for himself.'[20] Babel's ability to cajole his audience into such participation and comprehension, to make them aware of the conflicting perceptions of his secondary protagonists and of the tensions within his central narrator, Lyutov, lies in his use of tropes, in particular metaphor, which predominates. He relies on his reader's appreciation and interpretation of tropes. It is well documented how the childhood development of language in a person and his perception of reality is based on the use of metaphor.[21] Babel was undoubtedly aware that an appreciation of creative and artistic metaphor rests on this and is something that all articulate and literate people possess. His exploitation of the latent 'metaphoric mode of perception'[22] is brilliantly realized in the tropes of *Konarmiya*.

Critics such as Tomashevskiy and Leondar have pointed to the importance of context in the study of creative metaphor, whether this is the immediate situation of a particular figure or the whole work in question.[23] Mendelsohn also focuses on the interaction of both reader and context in the interpretation of Babel's metaphors when she argues that in metaphoric expression:

> the words do not act as one would expect them to within a given syntactic structure, but as separate entities with a tendency towards multiplicity of associations. The process of the release of semantic and emotional associations occurs simultaneously for all the words in a given phrase. Its interpretation is the role of the reader with the reference to the context as a controlling factor.[24]

She compares this introduction of the reader into the action with Ricœur's term for metaphor as:

> a 'semantic event', where through contextual interaction a new word meaning is created ... The reader has to make an effort to create a 'network of interactions' of all the words in the text and then make

a choice as to the selection of the appropriate associations and connotations, thus re-interpreting both the metaphoric expression and the context.[25]

Babel's predilection for metaphor, as well as for metonymy, synecdoche and, to a lesser extent, simile, hyperbole and litotes, as vehicles for various shades of expression and modes of perception, rests on the unique properties of these tropes. They convey not only information on the viewed object but also the feelings of the viewing subject. As Mendelsohn states:

> the metaphor always projects the personal vision of the person to whom it belongs and thus has an 'affective value', that is, it indicates the feelings and attitudes of the person, as well as having a 'referential' or 'informative value' – it usually contains some concrete information about the object (and subject) of perception ... As such it is an excellent medium of psychological portrayal ... [and] it is important to note that the ability of metaphor to reflect and project human perception makes it an excellent indicator of the extent to which the narration expresses the subjective perceptions of the author, the narrator or the characters. In other words, the examination of the metaphoric expressions in the literary discourse may help to define whether the narrator projects the point of view of the author, the narrator, or the characters.[26]

However, before moving to my analysis of metaphor *vis-à-vis* the protagonists and narrators of Babel's two cycles of war stories, I shall examine the nature and form of metaphor *per se* and, in doing so, outline the terminology that I employ.

METAPHOR

> 'To attempt a fundamental expression of metaphor would be nothing less than an investigation of the genesis of thought itself.'[27]

Imagery is the vehicle that allows a writer's innermost thoughts and emotions to be vividly released to view: 'si l'idée a créé l'image, l'image à son tour a singulièrement aidé l'idée à se préciser et à développer toute sa richesse'.[28] What constitutes figurative language, however – '... a using of objects belonging to one order of being to explain, represent, picture forth objects belonging to another order'?[29] or 'an intermediate region wherein the world of visible things seems to blend with the world of thought'?[30] Brown observes that every object has a significance of itself, as a 'fragment of reality and a significance as symbol, emblem or image of something other than itself'.[31] He cites a 'star' as an example, which can interest the astronomer, physicist, navigator as well as the poet. For the latter it evokes a world of association and imagery. Indeed the same example is chosen by Tomashevskiy to demonstrate the function of figure.

111

He writes of the necessity to distinguish between the first or straightforward meaning of a word, which is the usual meaning, and the secondary or transferred meaning of the word, which is determined by the given context. In tropes the basic meaning of a word is destroyed, he claims, and it is usually on account of this destruction of the basic meaning that its secondary one enters into perception. By calling eyes 'stars' we sense the indication of a shining or lustrous appearance, an indication which cannot appear in the use of the word in the first or straightforward meaning. An emotional colouring also arises because of the image; 'stars' are an elevated concept imbued with the emotions of enthusiasm and admiration: 'Tropes have the capacity to evoke an emotional response to a subject, to inspire feelings of one sort or another, their purpose is both sensuous and evaluative.' [32]

With a figure, the involuntary reaction of audience or readers is to ask themselves how the given concept is denoted by the word in question. A swift mental search follows to find the secondary signs or indications which play a linking role between the primary and the transferred meanings. As Tomashevskiy states the greater these signs are and the more naturally that they arise, the clearer and more effective the trope is, the stronger the emotional saturation becomes, and the more actively the imagination is aroused. Metaphor involves this process but one must add that, to be both vivid and effective, the image needs to be fresh or newly minted.

Language itself can be described simplistically as a mere device: 'a more or less imperfect and clumsy device – "for words, like Nature, half reveal and half conceal the Soul within" – whereby we seek to convey to other minds the ideas that have had their origin in our own'. [33] It can indeed be argued that figures in general, and metaphor in particular, exemplify this. Metaphor, like other tropes, treads a narrow divide between illumination and obfuscation. One has to follow the thought processes of the metaphor-maker if one is to appreciate the significance of his figure. Notwithstanding the inherent dangers of unintelligibility which metaphor embodies, it cannot be denied that it is the prime agent of the evolution of language: 'The process of language is a great metaphor … The evolution of the meaning of words, nay the very life of language is a continual metaphor.' [34] Man has felt the need to express his innermost thoughts from time immemorial and metaphor has been the most commonly used means to do it: 'Metaphor represents in its origin an attempt to express in terms of experience thoughts lying beyond experience, to express the abstract in terms of the concrete, to picture forth the unfamiliar by means of the familiar, to express insensuous thoughts by sensuous terms.' [35]

Whether metaphor is successful in this attempt depends on the effectiveness of the chosen image. Metaphor is not the preserve of the creative writer alone, but that of all men, however humble. Nevertheless, in my analysis I have found it necessary to distinguish between the figure that is new and original and that which has either been long absorbed within the language or is becoming so. For my own purposes I have designated the former type as 'living' and the latter as 'fossilized'. [36] The latter may be uninteresting

112

individually, but collectively can be revelatory of attitude or thought on the part of their respective spokesmen and I have paid due attention to them in my study of Babel's war cycles. Others have used alternative labels for these respective types. Brinkmann calls the fossilized variety 'incarnate', which he defines as those that have been 'completely absorbed into the blood of the language so as no longer to be felt as metaphor'.[37] Müller uses the terms 'radical' for fossilized, and 'poetical' for living,[38] while Brown, who similarly dubs the former type as 'fossil', defines it as representing a state 'when the users of it are no longer conscious that it is not literal ... From being a mere label or token standing for a given object of sense-perception it has come to be a mere label or token standing for some other object of quite a different nature.'[39]

I have already given an indication of the processes involved in the formation of metaphor in my references to the Russian formalist writer Tomashevskiy. Yet whether one looks to Russian, to French, or to commentators of any nationality, makes little difference, for metaphor is common to all tongues, to all men and to all epochs. A definition of it has preoccupied philosophers, philologists, writers and critics alike from early to modern times. A definitive explanation and definition of metaphor, its function and its effects have proved to be as elusive as its brilliance can be fleeting. The Greek word from which it is derived is itself a metaphor for it embodies the meaning of 'bearing' or 'carrying between' or 'among', similar to the transfer from the primary to a secondary meaning of which Tomashevskiy speaks. Aristotle defines metaphor as 'the transference of a word to a sense different from its proper signification',[40] while Quintilian, including metaphor in a general statement on tropes, says that it is 'an expression turned from its natural and primitive signification to another for the purpose of adorning style'.[41] Cicero does not help much more with: 'Similitudinis ad verbum unum contracta brevitas.'[42] A Russian definition includes the concept of transfer: 'A phrase which includes the use of words and expressions in a transferential sense on the basis of some or other analogy, resemblance, comparison.'[43] The *Oxford English Dictionary* is similar in its definition: '[Metaphor is] the figure of speech in which a name or descriptive term is transferred to some object different from, but analogous to, that to which it is properly applicable.'[44] Other definitions approximate to this but can also be applied to figures such as simile, metonymy or synecdoche. Metaphor is 'the form of trope which is founded on a resemblance of relations'[45] or 'the instantaneous perception of a likeness between two objects or acts',[46] 'a figure of speech by which a word or phrase is lifted to a meaning to which it is not literally entitled.'[47] The words 'likeness', 'resemblance', 'transfer' or their variations, recur. Some attempts at definition fail to shed much light: 'when a word is translated from its proper and genuine signification to another less proper ...'[48] Some resort to metaphor itself: '– a blossom of one tree on the branch of another',[49] while others hint at the function of metaphor: 'a transference of the relation between one set of objects to another for the purpose of brief explanation',[50] or at its manner of transfer: 'a figure of speech whereby the word which properly belongs to one set of phenomena is transferred to another, not arbitrarily, but in accordance with some natural and obvious analogy'.[51]

The last definition redirects us more or less to those quoted above from the *Slovar' russkogo yazyka* and the *Oxford English Dictionary* respectively. These prove the most apt of those cited. They make no exaggerated claims which is often the failing of the others. Such assumptions that metaphor is formed for the purpose of 'brief explanation'[52] and 'in accordance with some natural and obvious analogy'[53] can be false. Indeed metaphor may well embody a facility to obscure, to darken thought rather than the reverse, and the analogies drawn may be far from obvious. A metaphor taken from Babel's 'Moy pervyy gus' supports this argument: 'I rejoiced as I read, spying out exultantly the secret curve of Lenin's straight line.'[54] It is wise, however, to examine the elements of metaphor and the thought processes inherent in its formation if one is to investigate its facility for illumination or obfuscation.

In every metaphor there is a 'main idea'[55] or 'stimulant', the concept which engenders the metaphor and which is usually implicit. There is also an image which is introduced to express this concept or idea, the 'imported image'.[56] Between the two there is a perceived resemblance which leads to a 'momentary and tacit identification'[57] of the latter with the former, to the extent that language which applies to the imported image is used of the main idea. It is how this momentary and tacit identification is made by the reader or listener, that is, how readily or whether it is made at all, which determines a metaphor's degree of originality, illumination and effectiveness. Babel's metaphor quoted above from 'Moy pervyy gus' has an enigmatic quality which is understandably enhanced by its removal from its context. One might indeed claim that the figure is unsuccessful if ready comprehension is a criterion of effectiveness. The image is original however, and what the figure indicates above all is that an author's metaphors need to be studied in context and *in toto* if their respective messages and value are to be understood and appreciated. While a metaphor like 'The wheel of a gun-carriage groaned round a corner'[58] communicates a readily comprehensible message, there is a lack of originality compared with the metaphor from 'Moy pervyy gus'. Whether Babel's metaphors need to be enigmatic or obfuscatory in order to maintain originality is a matter for later discussion, however.

Obscuration is indeed an aspect of metaphor which simile, for example, can more easily avoid. In a discussion in which greater pleasure is attributed to the former trope type when compared with the latter, Whateley indicates the essential difference between the two: 'All men are more gratified at catching the resemblance for themselves than in having it pointed out to them.'[59] Simile points out the resemblance explicitly, whereas metaphor sets the reader the task of doing so: 'The figure does not turn over into the reader's mind the finished, pigeon-holed, cut-and-dried concept which the mind of the writer has formulated; but it simply begins the formulative process, leaving the mind of the reader to complete it for itself.'[60] This completion of the task that is set by the author can remain unimplemented if the imagery employed is so dazzling or ornate that it obscures the main idea. As Brown states: 'Indeed, the imaginative writer is apt to deck his idea in trappings so gorgeous that our thought when not actually dazzled by the gems and the brocade, lingers curiously over the embroidery, admires the folds of the drapery with scarce a thought for the figure behind.'[61]

One remembers Quintilian's statement concerning the function of tropes – 'for the purpose of adorning style'[62] – in this warning. If the imported and adventitious image which comes before our mental vision so vividly causes the real subject of the discourse to fade into the background, there is a danger for the discourse to be spoken of for a time in the terms of the image, and for it to be forgotten or obscured. Buck also writes of the 'conflict' and 'concussion' which images can bring if they are too ornate and extensive.[63]

Another cause of obscuration may be the esoteric nature of an imported image. Again Brown sounds a warning: '[The writer] may draw upon experiences peculiar to himself, or at least not shared by the reader or hearer, images drawn from his country which is not ours, or from the technicalities of his calling'.[64] But what writer is it, one may well ask, who does not 'draw upon experiences peculiar to himself',[65] which spring from his milieu and upbringing? Babel's Lyutov is unmistakably a Jew as well as an intellectual, thrust into circumstances which are favourable to neither condition. Yet these experiences, unfamiliar to many a reader, are shared and appreciated because of his writing, because of his imagery. What Brown intends in the remarks which I have quoted is to indicate that an author's choice of images should not be based upon specialist knowledge which is the preserve of a small minority but that it should be intelligible to the majority. However, he does stress that even the most perfectly known image can still produce uncertainty and here he exposes the central nerve of metaphor's obscurative facility: '... every concrete object, even the simplest, possesses a number of different qualities or properties ... Consequently even when both the main notion and the imported image are known, the scope of the comparison may still remain uncertain or obscure.'[66] If the metaphor is one that is in some degree of fossilization, that is to say in frequent and universal use, then the identification of image with idea is confined for us within definite limits, but if the metaphor is new:

> [T]he reader or hearer must trust to the context or to his own keenness of insight. It is of the very nature of metaphor not to explain itself. It will not state in express terms wherein lies the resemblance, real or fancied, between main idea and imported image and often to grasp its significance there is needed an imagination equal in intensity and vividness to that which first evoked it.[67]

The last few words point to the effort which a writer like Babel asks his readers to make; we must follow the paths that his imagination has taken if we are to comprehend and appreciate his viewpoint or those of his

115

protagonists. The very density of his metaphors coupled with their originality make this a demanding task.

One cannot neglect a third factor which contributes to the impression of metaphor as an obscurative trope. In Babel's work there is seldom a direct statement of emotion, yet the affective capacity of both war cycles is great. The emotional intensity is pent up in the imagery of the tropes, of metaphor in particular. It is this very emotional intensity, necessary to the creation of living metaphor, that can obscure the point of identification and the main idea or stimulant which lies behind it. Ready-made metaphors, however, are the current coin of speech and no special effort of the mind is made either to formulate or to comprehend them. 'There is a mutual relationship between affective states and the creative or constructive imagination ... An emotional frame of mind in seeking self-expression produces original metaphor.'[68] Indeed, it is living metaphor which:

> Would seem to be, very commonly at least, the outcome of an emotional mood reacting as such a mood generally does on the imagination. Such a mood, when it achieves adequate expression, 'issues forth' in poetry. Now metaphor is the natural language of poetry. The mind, possessed by the imaginative and emotional realization of some idea, ranges in search of images wherewith to picture it forth in an outward expression which shall be in keeping with the inward state, that is to say, not in terms of the intellect, but in terms of the imagination, in concrete pictures rather than in abstract propositions ... In this state of heightened emotion and imagination objects from different spheres or orders of being are brought within the sweep of one mental glance. They are seen in the light of the idea which for the moment possesses the mind. In this light differences are ignored, some point of resemblance stands out in relief, is seized upon and realized so vividly that the two objects – the idea already in the mind and the newly found image – appear for the moment identical, and can be spoken of as such without any consciousness of falsehood.
>
> When an idea has taken strong possession of the mind, aroused the emotions, caught the imagination, analogies and resemblances start into view on all sides in the most unlooked for places, and a thought thus vehemently felt, particularly if scarce expressible in proper terms, is prone to break forth in image. It seeks expression in terms adequate not merely to the intellectual concept, but to one's emotional possession of it. Indeed, the primary aim in such moods is not clearness of logical statement, but force, vigour, intensity, so that the outward expression may bear some resemblance and proportion to the inner frame of mind.[69]

Brown's delineation of the process of creation of living metaphor and his warning that such a process may involve a clouding of logical thought through concern for adequate expression of emotions reminds us of observations made on Babel's work, that there is a sense of the distorted, an opaqueness, an enigmatic quality in his writing: '[Babel] is an extremely self-conscious and cerebral writer, often to the point of opaqueness ... 'My

First Goose' is particularly dense in texture and on first reading may even mystify the reader as regards its meaning.' [70] Beneath the surface of his dense texture one feels the heartbeat of intense emotion, however. Babel is at pains to convey an intensity of feelings to his reader, and a principal aid in his achievement of this is metaphor; hence its profusion. [71] There are instances, indeed, where concern for emotional intensity has obscured the scope of the comparison, with the consequent sense of opaqueness or mystery spoken of above: 'My soul, suffused with the oppressive intoxication of reverie, was smiling mysteriously at someone, and my imagination, a blind happy peasant woman, was swirling ahead like July mist.' [72] The main ideas lie obscured behind the imported images: Lyutov's imagination swirls like mist and yet is a blind peasant woman; his soul uplifted in reverie is smiling mysteriously. The three contributory factors to obscuration which metaphor possesses – ornate language, esoteric imagery and the expression of emotional intensity – may well overlap in a sequence such as this, [73] but it is rare in Babel's case for them either to detract from his writing or to obscure his main idea. These factors are overwhelmingly exploited by him to enhance his work and make more vivid and appreciable the moral dilemmas with which his narrator is faced.

It may nevertheless be argued that a trope, like metaphor, which possesses potentially obscurative qualities, detracts from or conceals the truth, and that an author whose use of such a figure is considerable is thereby consciously attempting to darken or conceal the pith of his message: 'In metaphor the object spoken of disappears behind another which resembles it. Comparison illuminates discourse, metaphor darkens it.' [74] Is the simile thus the trope of the honest writer, who will resort to imagery which is more readily accessible and which, while permitting colour and intensity, also embodies clarity? Is Babel who is a prolific user of both trope types, [75] deliberately obscurative because of his pronounced predilection for metaphor? 'In the case of simile the introducing word "like" or "as" puts the illustration in the clearest light, whereas in the metaphor, the illustration is decidedly, if not deliberately obscured.' [76] These questions are best answered at the end of my analysis, but such disparagement of metaphor and of Babel's motives in his prolific use of it would seem misplaced if only, at present, for the following reasons: seldom does simile match the emotional intensity that metaphor can muster; the delay which is brought about by an explicit and consequently more laboured comparison detracts from the overall truth and vigour with which the analogy has been first perceived by its formulator; the author who can convey emotion implicitly to a reader through his imagery will live long in the memory – metaphor is the most effective and versatile instrument that he possesses in this quest:

The use of metaphor involves no sacrifice of truth … it may express a portion, or at least an aspect, of the truth which would not otherwise find expression … By means of it … an imaginative and emotional element … is put into the expression of that mood. Without the element the expression would be inadequate, that is, less completely expressive of the object of thought as affected by the mood or frame of mind, and so less completely true.[77]

Babel's prose may appear terse, his language as honed and tempered as pressed steel, yet this very impression does not take account of the vibrancy of his metaphors which, more than any other figure, inject a sense of pathos or poignancy, humour or horror that is singularly his. Imagery as a whole presents truth more concisely, vividly, memorably and emotionally than literal statement, but it is 'metaphor, indeed of all the figures [which] comes nearest to painting, enabling us to clothe at will the most abstract ideas with life, form, colour and motion.'[78] Tropes in general and metaphor in particular enable a writer 'to lay hold of the reader's or hearer's whole mind and bring him not merely to understand with the point of the intellect but to realize and bring home to himself'[79] the writer's thoughts or those of his narrators and protagonists. Metaphor represents an appeal to the imagination; to be successful it uses concrete more often than abstract terms, particular and individual rather than general terms; it speaks in pictures.

Babel's figures generally bear testimony to this statement. Those of his main protagonists and Lyutov embody the concrete and the particular more than the abstract and the general. It is true also of his similes where, for example, there are a number of references to different types of animal, but few are the occasions when the generic term 'zhivotnoye' ('animal') appears.[80] 'Metaphor is the unique expression of a writer's individual vision', states Murray.[81] Babel's vision is indeed individualistic. The saturation of his work with metaphor and other tropes helps create his singularity. His work, the result of painstaking mental rehearsal, revision and rewriting[82] represents an attempt not only to convey his ideas but also his feelings and it is largely through the figures which his protagonists use that he is able to do this. Babel has a genius for the formulation of fresh or living metaphor. His figures embody what Brown calls 'this unlooked for bringing together of unlikes'.[83] The preponderance of living figure invests his prose with the flavour of poetry with all its 'multitudinous connotations [and] infinite suggestiveness'.[84] Richards speaks of a comprehensive truth that metaphor can bring:

> Metaphor is the supreme agent by which disparate and hitherto unconnected things are brought together in poetry for the sake of the effects upon attitude and impulse which spring from them … Metaphor is a semi-surreptitious method by which a greater variety of elements can be brought into the fabric of the experience.[85]

Babel had, in his labours of rewriting, calculated the effects of his metaphors, foreseen their manipulation of readers' impulses and attitudes. To him, metaphor was a means to a realization of his unique vision, and to the depiction of this to others. His awareness that 'prose that would be an expression of human personality cannot remain wholly alien to the spirit of poetry'[86] is as profound as his knowledge that, as such, prose 'draws near, whether through the emotions or through the imagination, to the expression of the spirit, so will the role of imagery gain an ever greater importance'.[87]

SIMILE

Nihil est in rerum natura unde simile duci non possit.[88]

Similes or literal comparisons can be indistinguishable. Indeed, Russian employs the term 'sravneniye/simile, comparison' for a comparison of any sort. For purposes of my analysis I have included all explicit comparisons under the term 'simile'. Most are figurative similes in which 'the original object (the tenor) and the one used as the illustration (the vehicle)'[89] are of different orders of being. Whether other comparisons are literal or figurative is debatable. While an example such as 'Blood was streaming down from the squadron commander's head, like rain off a rick'[90] has figurative claims, with the profuse flow of Trunov's blood being compared to the action of rain, can one state with conviction that the following are literal comparisons, merely because tenor and vehicle contain images from the same order of being? – 'a Galician, tall and deathly like Don Quixote';[91] or 'In charred little houses, in mean kitchens, Jewish women resembling ancient negresses were busying themselves …'[92] What is clear, however, is that two basic conditions have to be met for a simile or comparison to be created. Firstly, both sides, tenor and vehicle, of the comparison have to be stated explicitly; secondly, 'the fact that there is *some kind* of similarity (though not necessarily the exact area and nature of the similarity) between the tenor and the vehicle must be pointed out by the speaker or writer'.[93]

Simile is thus an explicit form of comparison, metaphor an implicit one. Simile includes a 'pointing' word or device, most commonly 'like' or 'as' in English, 'kak' ('like/as') and combinations such as 'kak budto' ('as if') in Russian. Russian also includes a hybrid or transitional form of comparison, which lies between metaphor and simile, in its use of the instrumental case: 'when he [the enemy] hangs like/with a weight on our legs and binds our arms like/with snakes'.[94]

'… the language of passion will not admit simile which is always the result of study and deliberation.'[95] This observation embodies the dangers of overstatement inherent in generalizations, but it also contains an element of truth. Babel's similes are indeed 'the result of study and deliberation'[96] but so is every trope in the two cycles. Simile may not, however, be so easily invested with emotional intensity, although Babel's vehicles often embody an affective capacity. The fear which Lyutov experiences in the similar calm of the road to Brody is captured in the following sequence: 'The earth lay like a cat's back, overgrown with the shimmering fur of crops.'[97] While Brown would consider Babel's prolific use of metaphor to be an indication of his desire to thread emotion throughout the fabric of his cycles, he

119

considers simile to be an agent for the suppression of emotion: 'Emotion so fuses thought and image that they appear as one and we have metaphor ... simile deliberately holds them apart and views them separately. The formal nature of the "as" or "like" brings a pause, a slackening and a certain coldness.'[98] It is fallacious, however, to think of Babel's similes as being less intense or affective in general than his metaphors. They are certainly less frequent but are most often an integral part of a sequence of metaphor, metonymy or synecdoche in which they play a key role in terms of emotive effect.[99] Babel's choice of vehicular form and content is as significant and indicative of his protagonists' frame of mind as that of his metaphors. The 'coldness' or 'slackening' and consequent loss of intensity of which Brown writes is minimized in the similes of Babel's two cycles, for the majority of them are extremely brief, possessing unelaborate vehicles of minimal length, with two, three or four words at most.[100] It is rare to find the elaborate, digressive vehicle peculiar to such as Homer, Virgil or even Gogol. Babel seldom indulges in comparison for the sake of ornament, although I consider the following Lyutov-based simile to be a rare example of this: 'The prisoners were howling and running from Andryushka, he pursued them scooping them up in one arm like a hunter does the reeds in order to survey a flight of birds making its way to the river at dawn.'[101]

Babel's more usually terse vehicles arrest the attention through stark, unexpected imagery: 'An orange sun rolls across the sky like a severed head ...'[102] Earle's generalization on the motives of those who formulate literary similes and metaphors is as dangerously fallacious as the one attributed to Goldsmith, which I quoted earlier: 'Similes are sought out for the sake of ornament, but metaphor is a resource of expression that starts up instinctively by affinity with the process of sincere meditation.'[103] All tropes in Babel's work stem from the process of 'sincere meditation' and, polished as they are, smack rarely of the ornate. Like his metaphors, Babel's similes have an aesthetic appeal; they embody a likeness between objects which are often widely different, the discovery of which gives a shock of surprise. They heighten the emotional effect, most frequently imparting humour, irony or pathos: 'The moon was already hanging over the yard like a cheap earring'[104] is Lyutov's perception of the moon after his self-demeaning slaughter of a goose. Babel's metaphors and similes frequently embody personification in their imported images or vehicles. Human personality invests the inanimate with life, and animation is a common device in his tropes. The moon in the above quotation becomes a symbol of human ostentation and is an example of how Babel creates settings to reflect the moods of his respective narrators, an aspect which I shall discuss later.[105]

METONYMY AND SYNECDOCHE

Two trope types which Babel employs throughout his cycles are metonymy and synecdoche.[106] Both are branches of metaphor and often engender subtly striking effects. The sinister nature and brooding presence of the priest's assistant, Pan Romual'd is enhanced through metonymy in 'Kostyol v Novograde': 'But that evening his narrow cassock stirred at every curtain, swept furiously along all the passages and smiled at all who wanted to drink vodka.'[107] In 'Syn rabbi', synecdoche evokes the grim horror of death and destitution that war brings: 'The typhous peasantry rolled before itself the customary hump of a soldier's death.'[108]

Metaphor represents the substitution of a given idea by a term taken from a different sphere of things. In the case of metonymy and synecdoche, the imported image is closely linked with the main idea, which it replaces. The difference between these two tropes lies in the relationship of the imported image to the main idea. In the case of synecdoche, the imported image is part of the main idea which it replaces – for example, 'all hands on deck', where 'hands' has replaced 'men' or 'crew'; or where 'gorb' or 'hump' has replaced 'corpse' in the quotation above, and in which the singular number also stands for the plural. In the case of metonymy, the imported image has one or various connections with the main idea, but is not part of it – for example, 'to rely on the bottle'. Here the container has replaced the contents which we assume to be alcoholic liquor. Metonymy has various categories, such as cause and effect, container and contents, possessor and possession, an office and its sign or symbol (Romual'd's cassock replaces its owner) and so forth, whereas synecdoche is most commonly the physical part for the whole, the genus for the species, the material for the thing made of it, or vice-versa.

Like metaphor, metonymy and synecdoche quickly become fossilized, so embedded in language that they hardly present a picture any more. Babel's works contain living and fossilized examples of these tropes of which many prove a stimulus to the imagination:

> They economize attention by fixing it upon the serviceable part of the idea to the exclusion of the rest ... Their force lies in the more powerful effect both as regards the understanding and the feelings, of the concrete and the particular, as compared with the general and the abstract ... They often lend forcefulness and suggestiveness ...[109]

– and, as part of tropes' sequences in *Konarmiya* and *Na pole chesti*, they often play a significant part in the engendering of emotions.

THE TABLES OF ANALYSIS

Such sentiments are echoed by W. G. Weststeijn, when he writes of figurative language providing 'a deeper insight into reality than literal language ever can [since] it is precisely in metaphors that an author expresses the essentials of his personality and of his vision of the world'.[110] Meylakh had earlier stressed the special power that metaphor possesses to bring this about: 'An individual perception of reality, exactly characteristic of a given author, makes itself apparent with a special strength in metaphors'.[111] Babel's individualistic perception of reality is fragmented among his protagonists: each represents a strand which combines or conflicts with others. His central persona, Lyutov, is a tangle of contradictions, as are his Cossacks and French soldiers. Through an investigation of the respective figurative language of each, insight is gained not only into the protagonists themselves but also into Babel's perception of the world. But I would first like to comment on the composition of the respective *skaz* categories which I have outlined.[112]

The middle or second category of Table 1, which shows the proportions of *skaz* in the two cycles of war stories, posed problems of eligibility concerning the Cossacks of *Konarmiya*. It is generally obvious which protagonists are Cossacks but at times I have had to make a distinction. For example, Tarakanych, Sashka's stepfather in 'Sashka Khristos' is manifestly a Cossack, but I have not classed his wife, Sashka's mother, as such. I have included her in the third category because Lyutov draws a distinction between the men and women of Sashka's village: 'The women still pottered in the kitchen-gardens, and the Cossacks sprawled among the lilac, drinking vodka and singing.'[113] Conversely, Pavla the sensual mistress of Savitskiy in 'Istoriya odnoy loshadi' is deemed a Cossack: 'The Cossack woman put aside her comb and taking her hair in her hands tossed it over her back.'[114] Sashka, 'the lady of every squadron',[115] while displaying much of the toughness of the Cossack fighting men, is never once called a Cossack and is consequently included in the third category of other protagonists.

Of interest in Table 1 is the comparison that it affords between the two cycles of war stories. Both divide into similar broad categories, with a large section of each cycle related by an author-narrator, a second section by an assortment of fighting men – Cossacks and French soldiers respectively – and a third section by a variety of other figures who vary from a central, if fleeting, role, such as the artist Apolek, Gedali the Jewish shopkeeper and Ston the Quaker, to a peripheral and subordinate one such as the peasant women who deny Lyutov food in *Konarmiya*[116] and Bekker the groom in 'Na pole chesti'.

What is of greater interest, however, is the similarity of *skaz* proportions between each cycle. Lyutov narrates 66.9 per cent of *Konarmiya* with 62 per cent of *Na pole chesti* attributable to the author-narrator. The soldier protagonists of the latter cycle account for some 32.1 per cent, the Cossacks for 27.7 per cent of *Konarmiya*. Lyutov, who is clearly the more developed and identifiable narrator, thus holds greater sway than his counterpart in the French-based cycle, while the Cossacks relative to the French soldiers of 1918 have a lesser role. The two-third categories of other protagonists are almost identical in their proportions: 5.4 per cent in *Konarmiya* and 5.9 per cent in *Na pole chesti*. The relatively greater proportion of the major cycle that is allotted to its primary narrator, Lyutov, helps the reader quickly to gain the view that Babel has centred his masterpiece on the perceptions of his central persona. Lyutov is indeed the lynchpin, the hub around which all else revolves and through whom everything, or almost everything, is viewed.

In *Na pole chesti,* the narrator is largely anonymous and our focus is directed beyond him to the officers and men, to the 'establishment oppressors' and rank and file victims of war, both military and civilian.

Table 2 shows both the density and the number of tropes occurring in the three *skaz* categories. It is clear from a comparison of the average densities of the two cycles that *Konarmiya* is nearly twice as rich in tropes. This supports the view that Mendelsohn holds, namely that Babel's work became notably more figurative after 1920.[117] Both the stories of *Odesskiye rasskazy* and *Konarmiya* show a marked increase in the occurrence of tropes compared with earlier works. The average density in *Konarmiya* of one trope to 13.3 words is indeed high, but what is significant is how closely the respective proportions of tropes match those of the three *skaz* categories in the major cycle. Lyutov, with 66.9 per cent of the cycle, has 64.6 per cent of the tropes; the Cossacks, who account for 27.7 per cent, are responsible for 29.1 per cent of the tropes; while the 5.4 per cent of the cycle attributable to other protagonists is matched by 6.3 per cent of the tropes. This demonstrates a uniformity of approach on the part of Babel in the creation of his characters, for figurative language is not the sole preserve of his primary narrator but is an important feature in the language of all his protagonists. Indeed, the average trope density for Lyutov is a little lower than either of the other two *skaz* categories, with the Cossacks and other protagonists using one trope to 12.6 and 11.5 words respectively, and Lyutov one to every 13.7 words.

There is not such an even and close correlation between *skaz* and tropes' proportions in *Na pole chesti*. The narrator, who accounts for 62 per cent of the cycle, is allotted only 53.9 per cent of the tropes, while the soldiers are responsible for 40.5 per cent of the tropes compared with a *skaz* proportion of 32.1 per cent.[118] These results support the view stated earlier that the narrator is less distinct, less important a figure in his cycle, than Lyutov is in his. The language of the soldiers, however, embodies a proportionally greater amount of tropes and their role, relative to that of the minor cycle's narrator, is greater than the Cossacks' *vis-à-vis* Lyutov. The average trope density figures corroborate the view of a less dominant central persona in *Na pole chesti*: the author-narrator uses one trope to 29.8 words, other protagonists one to 27 words and the soldiers one to every 20.5 words.

What early conclusions can be drawn from these statistics? Firstly, the figurative language of each *skaz* category merits analysis, not simply that of the respective primary narrators, for stories with little or no central narrator participation, such as 'Zhizneopisaniye Pavlichenki, Matveya Rodionycha', 'Konkin', 'Sol'', 'Prodolzheniye istorii odnoy loshadi' and 'Semeystvo papashi Maresko', are richer in tropes than those in which the primary narrator's prose predominates.[119] Secondly, the fact that Babel employed such a catholic abundance of tropes with such proportional uniformity, at least in *Konarmiya*, indicates the value that he placed in their powers of characterization and of conveying emotion. They enable us to view events through the eyes of a wide range of protagonists and to appreciate a diversity of perceptions and feelings about war and violence.

An example of Babel's portrayal of the absurdity and desperation of war is heard in the words of a Polish prisoner in 'Eskadronnyy Trunov'. The man, old and emaciated, had been captured in his underclothes together with nine of his fellows, their uniforms jettisoned so that the officers among them could not be distinguished from the men. In broken Russian he pleads his cause: 'This war limit, said the old man with incomprehensible enthusiasm – all officers gone, this war limit ... Five fingers ... with such five fingers I brought up my family ...' [120]

The absurdity of his appearance is increased by the mock-comic nature of his mutilated Russian. The repeated metaphoric use of 'kray' ('limit/edge') for 'zakonchena' ('finished'), and his use of 'utik' ('gone') about the supposedly absent officers, from the Russian verb 'utiknut'' ('cease/subside/fade away'), evoke an ominously prophetic image of their 'fading away' or 'dying', which as we discover is all too pertinent. His repeated use of metonymy to denote a lifetime of paternal devotion and hard work, by holding out the five fingers of his hand, each contributes to the creation of a scene that is at once amusing and disturbing. Its full pathos is indeed realized a little later when Trunov puts an officer's hat on the old prisoner's head, decides that it fits and thrusts a sword into his throat. Tropes have helped create both the comedy and the pathos and have contributed a sense of authenticity through the old man's pigeon language in his vain plea for life.

Table 3 shows the proportion of trope types that Babel uses in his two cycles. While I have distinguished between metonymy, synecdoche and metaphor, and have recorded their respective occurrences, I have not done so with epithets or prosopopoeia since I believe that they are types of metaphoric expression which can be narrowly defined, [121] unlike metonymy and synecdoche which can be found with a number of variations. [122] Thus, epithets such as 'the live, grumbling stove' in 'Solntse Italii'; [123] or Lyutov's use of prosopopoeia: 'and then the young sabbath ascended to her seat from out of the blue gloom'; [124] and Gedali's representation of the revolution – all have been included in the category of metaphor: 'Yes, I cry to the revolution, yes, I cry to it, but it hides from Gedali and sends forth nothing but shooting ...' [125] I am aware, however, of the close relationship between metonymy, synecdoche and metaphor, and indeed if the respective totals of these tropes are added together for each cycle, the dominance of metaphorically related tropes becomes even more pronounced with their accounting for some 79.4 per cent of *Konarmiya*'s tropes and 67.4 per cent of *Na pole chesti*'s. Nevertheless, the proportion of metaphors alone in each cycle is almost identical: 55.3 per cent and 53.9 per cent respectively, and while the smaller cycle has but half the density of metaphors of the larger one (one to 48 words, compared with one to 24 words) Babel displays a predilection for metaphor over other tropes that is equal to both cycles.

Given that metaphor is the most commonly used trope type, it still only accounts for just over half of the total tropes. The remainder, apart from metonymy in *Konarmiya,* is evenly divided, with synecdoche, simile and hyperbole each sharing some 8 per cent. Litotes, the reverse of hyperbole, plays a lesser role but it is interesting to note how, in a story such as 'Zhizneopisaniye Pavlichenki, Matveya Rodionycha' where the use of hyperbole is high, both *per se* and in the general metaphoric tone, litotes counterbalances the extravagance of the hyperbolic expressions. The most notable instance occurs near the end when Pavlichenko describes how he finally gains revenge over his master Nikitinskiy for all the wrongs that he has done him. His low-key comment, which equates the gaining of revenge with 'getting to know life' thoroughly by trampling his master to death, throws into sharp relief the violence and determination that possesses the narrator: 'I trampled him down for an hour or more and during this time I got to know life thoroughly.'[126] Litotes is similarly employed elsewhere, its function of understatement helping to characterize and emphasize both the violent nature of the times and the brashly jocular attitude to events of men like Pavlichenko. As the latter tells of the year of revolution and boasts of the deeds that were accomplished he says: 'It's not the chroniclers who flew about the Kuban in those days *releasing the souls of generals* at a distance of one pace'.[127] Instances occur in other stories where Lyutov has been replaced as central narrator, such as 'Konkin' and 'Sol''. Indeed, hyperbole and litotes are at their most frequent in the speech of Cossacks or other protagonists. In 'Vdova', the third of the story that is not attributable to Lyutov contains nearly all the hyperbole and litotes. Lyovka, the Cossack driver of the dying regimental commander, Shevelyov, is boasting of his exploits before the war in a small town called Temryuk: 'Of course the little town was tedious for a woman, the ladies would catch sight of me and storm the walls ...'[128] His exaggerated language of bravado is laced with the same themes as Pavlichenko: sexual conquest and violence.[129] Hyperbole is juxtaposed with litotes to portray his character. He humorously recounts how a drunk approached him and a woman companion in a tavern: 'I look – some gent or other is poking his nose in, dressed O.K., neat, *but I notice he's got a lot of imagination about him* and he's under the influence'.[130] Litotes often occurs in speech to denote sexual activity. As the helpless Shevelyov listens to the sounds of battle, Lyovka copulates with the commander's mistress, Sashka. Shevelyov registers both bitterness and hopelessness in his comment: 'You're warming yourselves ... and it looks as if he's routed the fourteenth division ...'[131]

Litotes occurs not only in the language of Cossacks but in the speech of other protagonists, such as Tarakanych's wife in 'Sashka Khristos'. On his return from working away, Tarakanych demands to see the children. '*The children have gone out*, said the woman all pale, again she ran up and down the yard and fell on the ground. Oh, Alyoshen'ka, – she cried wildly, – *our children have gone out feet first* ...'[132] Here, litotes becomes the vehicle of expression for another of life's taboos, death, and with its capacity for understated euphemism, Babel tugs at our emotions in a subtle and shocking way. Hyperbole is likewise not merely the preserve of the Cossacks, for Lyutov employs it too in his description of Lyovka. In the opening section of 'Vdova', as the Cossack concludes his recounting of the brawl in the tavern, Lyutov portrays him thus: 'Breathe your last, – Lyovka repeats excitedly, stretching his arms to the sky and surrounding himself with the night like a nimbus.' [133] The image of a dominant, larger than life Lyovka is punctured by a subsequent sequence of tropes which is both ironic and hyperbolic as Lyutov foreshadows the callousness and infidelity of Shevelyov's companions: 'Stars glow like wedding rings in the darkness, they fall on to Lyovka, become entangled in his hair and are eclipsed in his tousled head.' [134] The use of the image, 'wedding rings', renders the story's title, 'Vdova', both more poignant and ironic, for Sashka, never having been Shevelyov's bride, can scarcely be called 'widow'.

It is significant that in *Na pole chesti,* where the *skaz* proportion for the soldiers is greater by 4.4 per cent than the similar Cossack proportion of *Konarmiya,* the amount of hyperbole and litotes is greater by 5.1 and 4 per cent respectively. This indicates a predilection on Babel's part for employing these tropes to create a raciness of language which characterizes the soldiers and other protagonists. Again, sexual excesses or deviations are depicted: 'Bekker left inconsolable brides at every stop' (ll.28–9, 'Kvaker') is how the groom's amorous exploits are portrayed. But it is the captain, Ratin's, ironic jibe to a masturbating Bidu in 'Na pole chesti' that has a damning astringency: 'You've found a wife here, swine?'. (l.17, 'Na pole chesti') As in *Konarmiya,* hyperbole and litotes are employed not only as vehicles for sexual reference but also to reflect the brashness of war's exponents *vis-à-vis* violence and death. The lieutenant in 'Semeystvo papashi Maresko' portrays the burial ground, now a battlefield, thus: 'Decayed corpses tumble out of the coffins ... I lie on the dead men ...'(ll.5 and 14 respectively, 'Semeystvo papashi Maresko') In a sequence of litotes and hyperbole which contains the grim humour of black comedy and which foreshadows the tone of stories such as 'Sol'', the officer wryly acknowledges that he will fulfil his duty whatever the circumstances: 'If we are destined to increase the population of this chilly corner, well we've made the rotting old men dance first to the march of our machine-guns.' (ll.8–10, 'Semeystvo papashi Maresko')

ANALYSIS OF METAPHOR

It is to an analysis of metaphor, Babel's principle trope of war, that I now turn. As Table 3 indicates, it occurs in every story and in all three *skaz* categories of both cycles. The essential qualities and effects of metaphor and those of other figures have been discussed in general terms and some hypotheses made concerning Babel's reasons for employing metaphor so frequently.[135] I wish now to examine Babel's metaphors from a variety of aspects and to note general trends and particular features of their formation and use. I have looked first at their form by examining the grammatical categories of the words employed with particular reference to abstract or concrete transfer between stimulant and main idea. I have considered the links that metaphor often has, both with other metaphors and other tropes by examining how trope succeeds or, as is often the case, begets trope in sequences for which Babel is justly noted.[136] I have analysed the position of the main idea or stimulant relative to the imported image; the former is at least partially implicit in the latter but it is possible to distinguish whether the figurative element is pre- or post-positive. I have also addressed myself to the question of theme, examining the spheres from which Babel most commonly selects his imagery. I have then examined the metaphors from the standpoint of the transfer that is effected in them between their respective main ideas and imported images. I have conducted this, both on a sensuous basis, investigating whether for example a visual stimulant is realized in a visual image or whether a different sense is employed, and from the standpoint of animation. Is, for example, an animate imported image employed to portray an inanimate stimulant or vice-versa? Finally, I have evaluated the metaphors, firstly by analysing whether an imported image enhances the main idea or detracts from it, and secondly by judging whether a metaphor employs fresh or living imagery, or whether it is fossilized or trite. Connected with this final section is the use that Babel makes of 'revitalized' metaphor, a seemingly dead or moribund figure into which he has contrived to breathe fresh life, to re-endow with the spark of originality. My analysis embraces each of the *skaz* categories of Babel's two cycles of war stories and inevitably at times I have made recurring quotations of the same figures to show how they exemplify different aspects of particular points in relation to the analytical criteria that I have outlined above.

Form

A story in the major cycle which affords a useful starting point is 'Solntse Italii'. Here, an almost equal balance exists between Lyutov narrated prose and the written *skaz* of his Cossack neighbour, Sidorov. The story follows 'Pan Apolek' and, unusually for the cycle, the events of both are chronological. Apart from Lyutov's recounting how he was sitting again in the servant's room at Pani Eliza's, the room in which he had heard the artist's anti-Christ story, epithets are employed which reinforce the link between the setting of the two stories. In a paragraph in 'Pan Apolek' depicting Lyutov's expectation of hearing Apolek's heretical tale, the senses of sight, sound and smell are harnessed to create a concentration of imagery which betokens the narrator's sense of keen anticipation. The garden is hushed, night stands motionless, the earth lies in a shadowy radiance, necklaces of fruit gleam, while the powerful scent of lilies, '[this] fresh poison is sucked into the *seething, greasy* respiration of the stove'.[137] It even overrides the resinous exhalation of the fir logs which had been strewn about, symbolic of the paganism about to be revealed.[138] In 'Solntse Italii' the stove is again animated in an epithet coupling whose assonance echoes that of the previous occasion: 'I sat by the warm *live grumbling* stove'.[139] The stove which had sucked in the 'fresh poison' of a previous evening is reacting perhaps to Apolek's irreverence which had so affected the narrator.

Epithets which form some 26.2 per cent of all metaphors in *Konarmiya*,[140] are used elsewhere as linking devices, and as we shall see, together with other tropes, help forge a unity in the cycle which may not be apparent on first reading.[141] In 'Solntse Italii', as is the case generally, Lyutov is the prime user of epithets; 'Konkin', for example, in which Lyutov is replaced as narrator, includes only one instance of epithet. An example of the powerfully symbolic nature with which Babel at times invests the epithets of his primary narrator can be seen in the following reference: 'a *hunchbacked* candle – a *sinister* beacon of dreamers'.[142] But a word is necessary first on the ethos and themes of 'Solntse Italii'. It is a story of chiaroscuro, whose narrative moves through gradations of light and shade. The vagrant moon, which at the end of 'Pan Apolek' had accompanied Lyutov on his dreamer's path back to his billet, is here both an aid to his fantasy and a matriarchal symbol of deliverance.[143] It represents a symbolic antithesis to the Italian sunshine of the ironic title. Lyutov's moonlight is at least real in its presence; Sidorov's sunshine, his dream of a better life in a foreign country, is remote, unreal and unattainable. His world is lit by a miserable, 'hunchbacked candle – a sinister beacon'[144] whose guttering light, 'zadykhalas', 'gasped for breath'.[145] The candle is the link between the primary narrator and Sidorov and between their respective worlds; through it Lyutov is able to read his companion's letter and thereby penetrate the Cossack's dreams, to move from his own fantasies to those of someone alien to him. The candle represents both a wretched reality and acts as an intermediary between Sidorov's solar dream of paradise and Lyutov's lunar vision of mother comfort. The attributes which Babel bestows upon the candle ('sinister' and 'hunchbacked') betoken facets of the ugly and savage existence that Lyutov endures with Sidorov, aspects which Lyutov's tropes and Sidorov's letter exemplify. The latter's grotesque nature is graphically realized in Lyutov's metaphorical description: 'Returning home I dreaded meeting my neighbour, Sidorov, who nightly lowered upon me the hairy paw of his anguish.'[146] The Cossack's capacity for violence is taken a stage further in a sequence of tropes, as Lyutov recounts the effects upon him of Sidorov's anguish evident in the latter's abandoned letter to his girlfriend: 'Sidorov, anguished killer, tore into shreds the pink wadding of my imagination and dragged me into the corridors of his sane-minded madness.'[147] The oxymoron at the end is indicative of Lyutov's ambivalence, a trait which renders him ineffectual in situations such as those described in 'Posle boya' and 'Smert' Dolgushova'.[148] Here, despite the antipathy that Lyutov has for the Cossack, the suffering at his hands that he tolerates, and the tension that he feels as he reads the letter, he cannot help himself: 'A vague sense of intoxication fell away from me.'[149] His tropes indicate clearly his high state of tension and show that Sidorov's written word can have as violent an effect upon his sensibilities as the Cossack's physical presence does upon his person.

But what similarities or differences are discernible in the metaphors of the two men? Apart from the 25 per cent of metaphors that comprise an epithet, considerably more than half of both Lyutov's and Sidorov's metaphors involve the figurative use of a verb. Yet the two protagonists differ in the amount of verb-only figures that they include. Both narrators employ metaphors involving a verb and a substantive but Sidorov's total is double that of Lyutov, who shows a preference for verb-only figures, which occur often in sequences of tropes and which lend dynamism and a visual force to his imagery.[150] In a synaesthetic image that Babel abandoned in later editions, Lyutov's imagination is as all-encompassing as mist: 'and imagination, a blind, happy peasant woman, swirled ahead like July mist'.[151] The metaphorical verb 'swirled' forms the crucial part of the simile's tenor and allows the vehicle 'like July mist' to be realized. Lyutov's imagination again assumes a visual, concrete identity as he prepares to read Sidorov's words. He tells us firstly that the reverie which he had indulged in on the walk back to his billet is finally dispelled. Again, a visual image is conveyed by the use of a finite figurative verb which forms the tenor of a simile's vehicle: 'A vague sense of intoxication fell away from me, like a skin cast by a snake.'[152] Intoxication is thus shed in dramatic fashion. But the next sequence of metaphors, which comprises verb-noun phrases, illustrates the violent effect that Lyutov's companion has upon him: 'Sidorov, anguished killer, *tore into shreds* the pink wadding of my imagination and *dragged* me *into the corridors* of his sane-minded madness.'[153] It is the verbs in combination with the prepositional phrases which convey the forcefulness of the experience that Lyutov undergoes. The powerful effect of such imagery is seen in Sidorov's figurative use of verbs. In the paragraph in which he outlines his wish to be sent to carry the revolution to Italy, he writes: 'In Italy the earth is smouldering.'[154] Mentioning his story in a Moscow hospital after being wounded he portrays the nurses who brought him food: '*Bridled* with awe they would drag it on a big tray …'[155] The use of the participle 'bridled' betokens dumbness and obedience, qualities which Sidorov despised. But it is near the beginning of the letter's excerpt that he uses his most forcefully damning imagery: 'Volin rigs himself up in apostolic vestments and scrambles up to Leninism from anarchy.'[156] As with the two images quoted above, Sidorov, like Lyutov, employs visual imagery. Here his erstwhile colleague Volin is condemned for his loyalty to Makhno, a bandit leader with whom Sidorov had become disillusioned.[157] The assonantic, rhythmic symmetry of the two halves of the sentence betrays Babel's hand, but we also detect a jarring incongruity which is in keeping with the figurative powers of a literate, Cossack fighting man.[158]

Such visually powerful and dramatic images are also counterbalanced in *Konarmiya* by instances of metaphor in which a softer, more gentle, though equally active imagery obtains. In 'Solntse Italii', examples occur in which figurative verbs again play a crucial part in the formation of tenors, without which the similes' vehicles could not be realized: 'The damp mould of the ruins *flowered* like the marble of opera seating … Blue roads *flowed* past me, like streams of milk, spurting from many breasts ... dreams *leapt* about me like kittens.'[159] Such a contrasting blend of gentleness and force can also be seen in 'Perekhod cherez Zbruch'. Although this story was the twenty-seventh to be published, its position at the beginning of the cycle focuses attention on the symbolism of its title. The Cavalry Army is crossing into Poland. Two worlds are portrayed; their difference is manifest in the description of their natural phenomena. Volhynia, the one being left, recedes into effete tranquillity; the Zbruch, the boundary of the new world, reverberates in a frightening, cacophanous chasm. Lyutov's path to war, the transition from a tranquil paradise to a battle terrain is effected in eighteen lines of finely wrought imagery in which we detect the narrator's ambivalence: his regret at what he is leaving, yet his impatience to be gone; his pride in the military campaign, yet his horror at the events of war.

The passage begins with an affirmation of life; three active verbs are employed: poppy fields flower, virginal buckwheat rises on the horizon, while in a single verb metaphor: 'the midday wind *plays* in the yellowing rye ...'[160] Yet the stark note of death is struck as the tranquillity of an emasculated Volhynia is shattered by a simile of *ostraneniye*:[161] 'An orange sun rolls across the sky like a severed head ...'[162] Again, a metaphorical tenor formed from a verb paves the way for the ensuing vehicle.

Although the Lyutov-narrated section of this story is greater than it is in 'Solntse Italii', the same pattern emerges of a domination of other tropes by verb-bearing metaphors. Half contain verbs, with two-thirds of these formed from a verb alone. The figurative coupling of a verb with a concrete substantive creates an imagery which is epic in tone and visually dramatic. Again the contrast of the two worlds is visually juxtaposed: 'the standards of the sunset fly above our heads', while the blackened Zbruch roars 'and twists the foaming knots of its rapids'.[163] Concrete substantives alone are also employed figuratively but unlike the dual effect of gentleness and power which the verbs embody, they point only to a grandeur which is sinister and bespeaks the presence of death. The road, along which the Cavalry's wagon-train is spread, has been built: 'on the bones of peasants by Nicholas I'; the gentle pageantry of the sunset begins to change 'in the gorges of the storm-clouds', and the Zbruch full of the din of troops in transit becomes a river of 'snaking moon trails and gleaming hollows'.[164]

A story which contains a greater concentration of figurative substantives is 'Kladbishche v Kozine', where, for once, verbs are in the minority in terms of metaphor formation. The story, which is but a contemplative, descriptive passage, concerns the distasteful face of Judaism, a theme to which Lyutov returns at various points in the *Konarmiya* cycle. His nostalgia for his southern Jewish childhood and a yearning to savour the atmosphere of old Sabbath days, in 'Gedali' for instance, remains unsatisfied as he encounters the depressing picture of 'lifeless little Jewish towns',[165] such as Brody, Zhitomir and Berestechko. Of the inhabitants of the latter, he writes: 'and instead of people faded outlines of frontier misfortunes go about in it'.[166] In 'Ucheniye o tachanke', nostalgic images of Jews from another time and another place are evoked: 'And the image of the Jews of the south, jovial, bellied, bubbling like cheap wine burns in my memory. The bitter disdain of these long, bony backs, these tragic, yellow beards cannot compare with them.'[167] The comment stems directly from an observation made in his diary: 'The Jews – portraits, lanky, taciturn, long bearded, not our jovial ones.'[168] But his jovial Jews of the south are not to be found on the plains of Galicia and Volhynia: 'In their features etched with passion and anguish there is no fat, no warm pulsing of blood.'[169] In 'Gedali', the same image, 'net zhira/there is no fat', finds a metaphorical echo, as Lyutov describes the once bustling, now desolate market place. 'There before me is the market and the death of the market. Finished is the *fatted* soul of plenty. Dumb locks hang on the stalls and the granite pavement is as clean as the bald pate of a corpse.'[170]

The granite graveyard of commerce at Zhitomir finds a link with the Jewish cemetery at Kozin. 'Kladbishche v Kozine' is an expression of bitterness at the decay and stagnation of the East, a process to which the Jews have contributed and from which they have suffered. The story has no movement, few finite verbs occur. Tropes formed by substantives contribute to a language that is as heavy and ponderous as the granite of the gravestones that it describes. 'Smoothly ground grey stones with three hundred year old inscriptions. Crude impressions of high relief hewn in granite.'[171] Granite links the story with the deathful imagery of the Zhitomir market in 'Gedali'; the inscriptions and carvings on the tablets in the cemetery at Kozin employ ponderous synecdoche in Lyutov's description of Jewish hopelessness: 'Azriil, son of Ananias, *mouth* of Jehova. Iliya, son of Azriil, *brain* entering into single combat with oblivion.'[172] Jehovah's mouth and a brain indulging in single combat are florid images of ridicule which Lyutov filters to us. The second of the concrete substantives of synecdoche – 'mozg' ('brain') – evokes a visual, metaphoric image of absurdity as Iliya is depicted fighting with oblivion. A momentary relief from the stasis is afforded in Lyutov's introduction to the inscriptions, as he writes of the tablets singing, but the metaphoric verb is incongruously light in tone, lying as it does between two similes which further pejorate the resting place of the rabbis through the inert, leaden quality of their imagery. 'Four generations lie in this vault, as lowly as a water-carrier's dwelling, and the tablets, the greening tablets sing of them with the floridity of a bedouin's prayer ...'[173] At the end, death is reproached for its thieving qualities in a three-fold apostrophe. The personification of death is a device common to epic poetry, but the juxtaposition of 'Oh death, oh selfish one, oh greedy thief'[174] renders the prosopopoeia parodic. The bald, mundane image of death as a 'greedy thief', following the loftier epithet, 'o covetous one', sets up the final wail of egoism: 'why have you not spared us, if but once?'.[175]

While metaphors formed from verbs alone are the single most common type in Lyutov's prose,[176] those employing substantives, more usually concrete than abstract ones,[177] are also frequently used. In 'Solntse Italii', nine of Lyutov's metaphors which employ substantives comprise concrete nouns, three abstract. The Cossack's metaphorical substantives in the same story are seven concrete nouns and two abstract ones. Both Lyutov and Sidorov evince a tendency to 'concretize', to render an abstract concept both visual and tangible. 'Smert' Dolgushova' presents a similar picture. Half the primary narrator's metaphors employ a verb only, while less than a quarter of the Cossacks' figures do likewise. A succinctness and dynamism obtains in Lyutov's imagery, which is often diluted in the figurative language of other protagonists. The shocking image of physiological detail concerning Dolgushov's injuries is brought to us with chilling effect because of the finite verb that the primary narrator uses: 'his intestines were creeping on to his knees …'[178] Earlier, six metaphors are used in rapid succession by Lyutov to depict a bombardment by Polish machine-gunners. Each figure would have little effect in isolation, but the rapidity of the sequence, aptly suited to the subject matter, lends each image freshness and impact: 'Bullets whine and scream. Their plaintiveness grows unbearably. Bullets wound the earth and swarm in it quivering with impatience.'[179] Three of the metaphors are finite verbs, one a gerund, as the auditory and the visual are combined, with the effect of the former enhanced through onomatopoeia and sibilation. A sequence of figurative Cossack *skaz*, by comparison, loses impact through its lack of accessibility to the reader, due to the mixed nature of its metaphors: '– if he's replaced, then soap the withers and knock away the supports. Period.'[180] Afon'ka Bida's words concerning the possible replacement of his divisional commander comprise esoteric imagery peculiar to the lifestyle of a Cossack cavalryman. A wry mixing of metaphor is found elsewhere in the same story and betokens the colourful humour of the Cossacks. Its inclusion also indicates the affection that Lyutov held for the uncultured platoon commander. The latter is lecturing the regimental commander on taking his time in reaching the battle front: 'how will you cut them down when the horses are done for … There's no need to grab – there's time aplenty to taste a virgin's fruits …'[181] The lengthier, more obscure nature of the imagery, together with its greater tendency to embody 'verb–concrete noun' metaphors, contrasts with the pithy, concentrated sequences of Lyutov. Even when the latter employs concrete substantives figuratively, their effect is more striking, their message more coherent. Two such examples are encountered in the same story. In isolation they appear unremarkable, but when viewed together retrospectively they assume a greater significance.

The second instance, and the only example of a concrete noun as sole figurative element occurs halfway through the story: 'Grishchuk with his stupid cart and I stayed alone hanging around between two *walls* of fire.'[182] When linked with the opening, grandiose figure of the story, the image assumes an importance that is both thematic and structural: 'The *curtains* of battle were drawing towards the town.'[183] Both metaphors use a concrete noun as the main or sole figurative element and evoke tangible images which are antithetical. The position and thematic nature of each figure is significant. The first image of 'curtains' is an inclusive one, the narrator is part of the gathering storm, one of the expectant army awaiting the enemy. In the second image, which is placed exactly halfway through the story, he belongs nowhere, he is isolated once again.[184] Apart from Grishchuk, his driver, the battle has cut him off from the enemy and his division; the 'walls' image is one of exclusion. The 'curtains of battle' which were to envelop him now cede to a process of ostracism, the start of which is signalled by Babel's second concrete image, 'walls', and the culmination of which is the denunciation and rejection of him by both Dolgushov and Bida near the end of the story. 'The divisional staff had disappeared. Other units would not accept us',[185] writes Lyutov, and as the battle round Brody ebbs and flows, he and Grishchuk look for solace and shelter in a cemetery, but, as in Kozin, none is forthcoming. A Polish scout fires on them from behind a tombstone and they run, their cartwheels squealing. The appearance of evening signals the ultimate humiliation that Lyutov is to suffer. The stricken Dolgushov hoves into view as Grishchuk ironically bemoans the cheapness and pointlessness of life: 'In the sky a pink trail flared and died out.'[186] Lyutov's entanglement in circumstances that he cannot control is underway.

It is the Cossacks, however, who employ figurative concrete substantives more frequently than the primary narrator.[187] They are often used to convey insult. The language, as with Bida, is colloquial, the imagery trite. Playful insult is intended in Vytyagaychenko's order to his men, 'Girls, mount up!',[188] and malice in Dolgushov's 'Run, skunk ...' and Bida's 'Bloody groveller',[189] both of which are addressed to Lyutov. But it is in stories, such as 'Konkin' and 'Sol'', where the primary narrator has been displaced by a Cossack, that the process is most apparent. Indeed, it is noticeable how much the spoken figurative language of the Cossack commissar, Konkin, resembles the written language of Sidorov or another 'soldier of the revolution', Balmashov.[190] While Konkin has temporarily adopted the role of narrator, he rejects Lyutov's propensity for verb-only metaphors with just 4 or 13 per cent in this category. 40 per cent of his metaphors do, however, comprise a verb-substantive coupling, a proportion similar to that found in the Sidorov section of 'Solntse Italii' and in 'Sol''.[191] The clichéed colloquialism of a Sidorov or Bida is heard again in the metaphor that Konkin uses as he signals his killing of a Polish general's horse: '*I set the wheels in motion* and put two bullets into the little horse'.[192] The casual tone of the image strikes a discordant note with the regret that Konkin then expresses at his action, indicating an ambivalence that is reminiscent of Lyutov: 'Felt sorry for the stallion. A little Bolshevik the stallion, a real little Bolshevik'.[193] Konkin's brash manner belies a softer temperament which is seen later in his comparison of the captured Pole's tears to human milk: 'tears are flowing down his cheeks, white tears, human milk'.[194] Elsewhere Lyutov notes such signs of humanity with surprise and gratification, though the latter emotion is not stated explicitly: 'Tears started from his eyes. I stared at Afon'ka in utter amazement.'[195]

Of the substantives that are used figuratively by Konkin either as the sole metaphorical element or in combination with a verb, virtually all are concrete.

70 per cent of the story's metaphors consist of a concrete substantive, an amount which far exceeds the use that Lyutov makes of them.[196] There is a manifest desire to deal in basic concepts, in tangible images, in the tone and formation of the Cossack's figures. While some of Konkin's figures are repetitive and fossilized, for example, the Polish general that he pursues and captures is referred to four times as 'tuz' ('big shot/ace'),[197] others are crudely descriptive: 'His person's all of a lather, his eyes are hanging from his mug on threads',[198] or surprisingly affecting, as we have seen from his equation of tears with human milk. Konkin's dearth of abstract figurative substantives is noticeably more pronounced than is the case with Lyutov,[199] but a rare example occurs as he chances upon what may be the enemy's staff: 'we look – *the arithmetic's right* … About six hundred metres away, well no more, it's either their staff or their transport wagons stirring up the dust'.[200] However, Konkin's predilection for imagery of a tangible nature is seen more clearly in an analysis of the transfer that he makes between the stimulant or main idea and the imported image of his metaphors. 30 per cent involve a transfer from a concrete stimulant to a concrete imported image, while a further 26.7 per cent effect a synaesthetic or 'unlike' transfer from an abstract stimulant to a concrete imported image. 'Go to the Turk,' the equivalent to 'Go to the devil',[201] he says to his comrade Zabutyy who covets his high-ranking prisoner, and as Konkin endeavours to persuade the general to surrender to him, further synaesthetic transfer is encountered, in both metaphor and simile: 'A red sea opened before me. The insult felt like salt entering a wound, because I can see the old boy doesn't believe me.'[202] Rage becomes a red sea to him, the Pole's insult salt in a wound and when finally the general capitulates, breaking his sword in two, Konkin describes the look in his eyes thus: 'and two lampions light up in his eyes, two lanterns over the dark steppe'.[203]

When these results from 'Konkin' and other Cossack-narrated stories are compared with those in which the primary narrator is the major narrative voice, a difference is discernible. In 'Solntse Italii', more than half of Sidorov's metaphors comprise a concrete imported image, which in the majority of cases has been engendered by an abstract main idea, while less than half of Lyutov's fall into this category.[204] In 'Smert' Dolgushova', only 15.8 per cent of the primary narrator's metaphors embody a concrete imported image whereas 52.9 per cent of non-Lyutov metaphors do, of which all but one make the synaesthetic abstract to concrete transfer described above. This is not to say however that the Cossack narrators or other protagonists never employ abstract imported images which have been engendered by abstract stimulants.[205] Indeed, 'Konkin' embodies some 43 per cent of these, 'Sol'' 66 per cent; yet it is noticeable that the primary narrator has greater concentrations of abstract transfer, for example 80 per cent in 'Smert' Dolgushova', 60 per cent in 'Kombrig dva' and 70 per cent in 'Vecher', thus demonstrating that the man of intellect is happier to deal in abstraction than his Cossack contemporaries who rely more on the tangible and the concrete for their self-expression.

'Prodolzheniye istorii odnoy loshadi' provides an interesting example of the latter. Like 'Konkin', the story comprises a large section of Cossack *skaz*,[206] and although it has a lower than average density of metaphors,[207] their formation corroborates the trends noted elsewhere in non-Lyutov figures. No verb-only figures occur in the nine metaphors; the two that do comprise a verb also embody a figurative concrete substantive, while two more metaphors comprise a concrete substantive as the sole figurative element. Only one metaphor employs an abstract noun.[208] In terms of transfer between main idea and imported image, there is again a marked tendency to 'concretize', with five figures embodying a transfer from an abstract stimulant to a concrete imported image. This is exemplified in a sequence of tropes which includes such a synaesthetic figure and occurs in Savitskiy's reply to Khlebnikov's conciliatory letter.[209] In isolation, the metaphor contains a hackneyed image, one that Babel may well have culled from a source encountered in his work as a war correspondent, since it is one of the few metaphors included in his plans of *Konarmiya* and one that must have remained prominent in his memory.[210] In the story, however, the metaphor is the keystone or central pivot of a symmetrical sequence of tropes: 'Our Communist Party, comrade Khlebnikov, is an iron rank of fighting men, giving their blood in the front line, *and when blood flows from iron*, then it's no joking matter to you comrades, but victory or death.'[211]

Hyperbole both opens the sequence, with the epithet '(made of) iron' changing to the substantive 'iron', which itself forms the central metaphor, and also closes the sequences with the bathetic juxtaposition of 'then it's no joking matter to you comrades, but victory or death'.[212] In between, the central metaphor is flanked by synecdoches, identical in their use of the word 'blood', but not in their effect. 'Blood' used as a symbol of 'dying for a cause' is a trite image; the phrase with which it is coupled – 'men, giving their blood in the front line' – recalls a clichéd image that Galin, a fellow *Krasnyy kavalerist* journalist of Lyutov, employs in 'Vecher': 'the revolutionary curve has thrown into the front line the free Cossacks ...'[213] But when blood spurts from iron in the second synecdoche, an image of *ostraneniye* is created which is both disturbing and immediate in effect. The verb 'flows from' connects the two figurative substantives in a way that revitalizes both. The use of 'iron' as an image of resolution and strength in the Revolution's cause, is as trite as the use of 'blood'. Indeed, it is the hapless Galin again who employs it in the concluding part of the above quotation, with absurd results: 'the revolutionary curve has thrown into the front line the free Cossacks, steeped in many prejudices, but the CC in its manoeuvring will wear them down with a brush of iron ...'[214] Yet Savitskiy's sequence of tropes produces the elevatory effect that he desires. The central trope sequence 'and when blood flows from iron' is an image of ennoblement which revitalizes the trite hyperbole of the rest of the sequence. The reader's attention is arrested by the incongruity of the image. Two hackneyed, concrete figurative substantives are thus presented in a fresh and vital way.

Savitskiy's choice of 'iron' is by no means an arbitrary one; it exemplifies how Babel employs imagery to create cyclical unity, as I hinted earlier.[215] The subtle repetition of figure maintains and develops the image of a protagonist from one episode to another. 'Moy pervyy gus'' opens with a description of Savitskiy's physical beauty as Lyutov meets the divisional commander for the first time. A little later the primary narrator refers again to the admiration that he felt for the Cossack commander. Irony is created in the juxtaposition of Lyutov's admission of literacy and scholarship with his unvoiced, physical adulation for Savitskiy 'Literate, – I answered, envying *the iron and flower* of that youthfulness, – law graduate from Petersburg University …'[216] 'Iron' again has an incongruous figurative comparison in the substantive 'flower', as metaphor is employed twice to portray the extent of Lyutov's infatuation. In 'Prodolzheniye istorii odnoy loshadi', Savitskiy himself employs the same two figurative images, which, although not in such close proximity, gain in prominence because of the general dearth of metaphor in the story. This time the substantives are not applied to himself but to the revolutionary cause; the fortitude and beauty that Lyutov had noted in Savitskiy are transferred by the latter to the cause that he is supporting: 'and when blood flows from *iron*, then it's no joking matter to you comrades, but victory or death. It's the same concerning the common cause, whose *flowering* I do not expect to see …'[217] Just as the triteness of the first metaphorical coupling of 'blood' and 'iron' is allayed through the *ostraneniye* created by the linking verb 'flows from', so the banality of the image 'the flowering of the common cause' is alleviated when Lyutov's earlier coupling of 'iron' and 'flower' is recalled. A link is thus made by Babel between the Revolution and one of its more spectacular exponents. The former is ennobled in its direct association with the latter through the use of identical imagery.

A story which affords examples of Babel's use of figure for satirical purposes, and one which has already been mentioned in connection with a recurrence of the metaphorically fossilized substantive 'iron', is 'Vecher'. It was originally entitled 'Galin' and focuses on a fellow contributor of Lyutov to the army newspaper.[218] Hyperbole and bathos in particular are employed to depict the sorry figure that Galin represents. The opening images of *ostraneniye* set the derisory tone of the story: 'O, regulations of the RCP! Through the sour *pastry* of our Russian tales have you laid headlong *rails*.'[219] The initial apostrophe manifests Lyutov's satire; it is not even addressed to the Party but to its regulations personified in the second metaphor as giving firm directive to writers in their work. Again we see, from the substantives I have stressed, Babel's predilection for the concrete and for the synaesthetic transfer of abstract stimulants to concrete imported images. The absurdly mixed metaphors of dough intersected by a railway line reveal an author with his tongue fixed firmly in his cheek.[220] The mock aggrandizement continues. The same regulations have not only given a directive but have also created those who obey it: 'Three bachelor hearts with the passions of Ryazan Jesuses have you turned into contributors of the "Red Cavalryman"

136

newspaper.'[221] The pejorative use of the figure of Christ to depict someone of a weak-willed nature ready to succumb to the temptations of the flesh is a leitmotif in *Konarmiya* and elsewhere. Apolek's adulterous Christ; crucifixes in a Catholic church compared to the talismen of courtesans; and the figure of a crucified Christ, his wounds oozing seed, a poison fragrant enough to intoxicate virgins – all testify to Lyutov's sacrilegious fascination.[222]

Lyutov's fellow journalists are indeed hardly the advertisement that the Communist Party welcomes. The transformation has taken place 'in the barren dust of the rear';[223] their journalistic contributions are described thus: 'and the rebellion and fire of their leaflets wear down the ranks of the dashing Cossacks on leave ...'[224] The coupling of the trite figurative substantives, 'rebellion' and 'fire', together with the incongruous image of friction in the verb 'prodirayut' (wear down/tear holes), establish the derisory tone. Like Lyutov's pastry railway the images are visually such strange bedfellows that *ostraneniye* results.[225] The 'gallant' correspondents themselves enhance the farce. In keeping with many of the protagonists of the third *skaz* category, they represent the physically maimed, the defective and in particular the grotesque: 'Galin with his wall-eye, consumptive Slinkin, Sychov with his gnawed away guts ...'[226] Galin merits seven different attributes which focus on his physical inadequacies: he is in turn wall-eyed, narrow-shouldered, pale, purblind, round-shouldered, thin-wristed and with a chest like a chicken's breast. Such a catalogue is seldom found elsewhere about one man. Prishchepa, in the eponymous story, incurs a damning string of attributives, but, as we have seen, this is due to events in the diary and plans which do not reach *Konarmiya*.[227] Lyutov too is almost as sorry a figure: 'And facing the moon, on a slope by the sleeping pond, I was sitting bespectacled, with boils on my neck and my legs bandaged.'[228]

The association of such decrepitude with the ability to 'wear down' or to 'tear holes' in their audience through the fiery quality of their writing is indeed absurd. Galin's efforts are apparently so great that at the end of the story 'blood was flowing from his torn palms',[229] as Babel neatly ties both beginning and end together through a symmetrical use of imagery. Indeed, the participle 'razodrannykh' ('torn' or 'lacerated') provides a second link with the verb 'to wear down/tear holes', which recurs as Galin adopts Lyutov's earlier image, again in masterfully contrived mixed metaphors:

– The Cavalry Army, – Galin then said to me, – the Cavalry Army is a social focus brought about by the Central Committee of our party. The revolutionary curve has thrown into the front line the free Cossacks, steeped in many prejudices, but the CC in its manoeuvring *will wear them down* with a brush of iron ...[230]

The fact that Galin is then immediately portrayed in the final paragraph as having 'torn palms', a detail which initially appears gratuitous and which was omitted in later editions, indicates that he has himself been both an agent of such 'manoeuvring', such sleight of hand and also its victim, since

137

the 'brush of iron' has left him torn and bleeding. Like so many of the cycles' protagonists, he fulfils the role of hero and victim.

As elsewhere, Lyutov's metaphors employ more verbs as the sole figurative element. There are ten such examples in his prose while only two of the metaphors of the other protagonists are formed in this way. Succinctness and a rapid sequencing of figurative imagery are hallmarks of the primary narrator's prose: 'Night *comforted* us in our sorrows'[231] and the whispering sibilants, the assonantic symmetrical recurrence of 'ch, sh, sh, ch' usher in the next image: 'a light wind fanned us like a mother's skirt'.[232] Then, in a double metaphor, we see how a verb and a concrete substantive serve each other figuratively, how either would be ineffectual without the other. Galin is lecturing Irina, a washerwoman for whom he holds amorous but unrequited desires, on imperial Russian history: 'And raising a naked eye full of adoration to the washerwoman, Galin relentlessly *violates the vaults* of expired emperors.'[233] The coupling of images aptly illustrates the sensationalism of Galin's version of Tsarist Russia's monarchy.

Sequences of tropes are also found in Galin's speeches, the *skaz* of other protagonists, but the juxtaposition of the metaphors stresses the triteness of his thoughts, as he relies on clichés or clumsily gropes for words to convey his ideas: 'The whole party is going about in aprons smeared with blood and excrement, we're cleaning the kernel of its shell for you; a little time will pass, you'll see this kernel cleaned, then you'll take your finger out of your nose and glorify the new life in exceptional prose.'[234] His solace is to be found in the clichés of political cant. His bewildering succession of hyperbolic images renders him absurd, a condition which Lyutov's metaphors confirm. Although the primary narrator evinces a general predilection for concrete substantives, he is not averse to employing abstract imported images in his metaphors when ridicule is his prime objective:[235] 'And then towards midnight Galin emerges from the coach to shudder at the *bites* of unrequited love for Irina the washerwoman of the train.'[236] The choice of the abstract noun 'bites' is deliberately trite. Its application to Galin is indicative of Lyutov's view of him as a small-minded propagandist and its position after the hyperbolic 'to shudder' intensifies the ludicrous impression that he makes.

An equally skilful use of abstract figurative substantives is found in a story of the first cycle of war stories, 'Kvaker'. There too, Babel's purpose is one of ridicule. The narrator's figures combine, as they do in 'Vecher', with the unwittingly self-condemnatory ones of the central protagonist; Ston, like Galin, is also grotesque in appearance: 'What was Ston? A bald brow at the top of a pole.' (l.7, 'Kvaker') Hyperbole adds to the derision: 'The Lord had bestowed a body on him merely to elevate his thoughts above the terrible sorrows of this world.' (ll.7–9, 'Kvaker') Of the figurative use of substantives in the cycle *Na pole chesti,* there is almost an equal predilection for concrete and abstract nouns, unlike *Konarmiya* in which concrete substantives predominate.[237] However, by far the greatest figurative use of abstract substantives occurs in 'Kvaker', with seven, or 63.6 per cent, of the cycle's quota to be found in the story whose central protagonist is characterized and condemned for his unworldly and incompatible attitude to life. Babel's choice of form for his tropes is part of his process of characterization; the aloof man of God thinks, and is thought of, in abstract terms which render him ridiculous. Just as in the depressing cemetery at Kozin ponderous concrete substantives portray the barrenness and decay of Jewish life, so Babel employs here abstract images to reflect the unearthliness of his quaker protagonist: 'but a slave to his conscience' (1.4, 'Kvaker') 'Immediately the voice of duty addressed him vehemently ...' (ll.20–1, 'Kvaker'). Ston's own figures do nothing to dispel the impression of dullness and inflexibility: 'son of sin' (1.45, 'Kvaker') he calls the groom Bekker as he pompously berates him, 'but your sins must not fall with all their weight upon an innocent horse.' (ll.41–2, 'Kvaker'). Both the narrator's and Ston's choice of imagery is trite. It contains no spark of originality and presents to the reader a view of a man who is pretentiously religiose and inadequate.

A further illustration of Babel's use of form in his metaphors to characterize as well as to create mood or atmosphere occurs in 'Kombrig dva'. Here too we see how the form of his figures contributes to our impression of the central protagonist and also creates ambivalence. The story concerns the making of a hero. Lyutov is one of a group of onlookers who witness the promotion and departure into battle of a Cossack officer, Kolesnikov. In common with a number of stories on first publication, this one's original title bore the name of its central protagonist. The alteration of this to the office that he held focuses attention on the themes of the story, and on leit-motifs of both cycles, namely the fickleness of fortune in times of war and the expendibility of its hero-victims. Budyonnyy,[239] in terse, alliterative language, informs Kolesnikov of the consequences should the latter fail in his mission: 'We'll do or die. No way – otherwise. Understood? ... An hour ago Kolesnikov was commander of a regiment, a week ago he had been commander of a squadron.'[240] The use of anaphora is the first stage in the building of tension within the story, a tension that is created both through a mixing of elevatory, ennobling images with those denoting uncertainty and apprehension, as well as through an alternation of images which create stasis and movement. While Lyutov witnesses the forging of a hero he is also aware of the latter's vulnerability. The increasing tension of the moment is communicated to us as Lyutov focuses on Kolesnikov's lonely figure making its tedious way back to the brigade. The burden of office that he bears is seen in his slow, tense progress. There is indeed a long way to go before he can be acclaimed a 'Tartar Khan', Lyutov's accolade for him at the end of the story. 'And suddenly – on the expanse of earth, on the furrowed and yellow nakedness of the fields we could see only the narrow back of Kolesnikov with his dangling arms and sunken grey-capped head.'[241]

For a story that portrays the making of a hero, whose career reflects a rapid rise to success, there is a certain irony in the static nature of the imagery. The frequency of concrete substantives as the sole figurative element in a number of metaphors almost matches that of verbs, with the result that a mixture of stasis and movement is created, which mirrors the slow walk back of Kolesnikov followed by the rapid engagement of his troops with the enemy. 'Katis', Koleso' ('Roll, Wheel')[242] puns one of the Cossacks as the newly appointed brigade commander salutes and turns to go. The remorseless course of his expected success is conveyed in the double metaphor of verb and noun, but Kolesnikov's vulnerability, unlike the optimism of the Cossack bystander, is then reflected in the lines which follow Budyonnyy's parting salute to him: 'The latter spread out five youthful, red fingers at the peak of his cap, broke into a sweat and went off along the fields' furrowed boundary … He was walking with head bowed, his long, crooked legs moving with agonizing slowness.'[243] Lyutov's focus on Kolesnikov's 'five youthful, red fingers' recalls the wet, ineffectual fingers of the equally youthful Bozhi who is unable to shoot himself after he has been caught deserting.[244] The vulnerability of both men is poignantly realized in the gestures of their respective hands,[245] but it is significant that it is only Kolesnikov's that merits the adjective 'red', a colour that Babel generally employs to denote flamboyance and success.[246]

The ambivalent portrayal that Lyutov gives of Kolesnikov is clearly seen when the metaphors of 'Kombrig dva' are analysed. Half of those in both *skaz* categories – Lyutov- and Cossack-based respectively – possess images which elevate their respective stimulants and half depreciate their status. Six elevatory metaphors refer directly to Kolesnikov. At the end Lyutov depicts him thus: 'That evening in Kolesnikov's mounted posture I noticed the lordly indifference of a Tartàr Khan',[247] and, before the battle, Budyonnyy supposes that the brigade commander will 'extract' the honour that he seeks: 'He's looking for honour. You have to reckon on him getting it.'[248] The use of Kolesnikov's name to denote remorseless progress has already been commented on,[249] but in a rare instance of a trope which draws partly on imagery from Babel's diary,[250] the 'Wheel' is seen by Lyutov to spin round in columns of dust as he leads his men into battle: 'Pointing my binoculars I caught sight of the brigade commander spinning on his horse in columns of blue dust.'[251] The tension of the moment is felt in the polarity of the imagery. There is a revoking of the elevatory participle which continues the theme of Kolesnikov's unrelenting path to glory as the concrete substantive 'columns', still an image of glorification, a triumphal arch, cedes to the pejorative image of dust.

Other images of depreciation are in close proximity. A groaning hurrah which is distorted by the wind greets the new commander: 'A groaning hurrah reached us, torn by the wind.'[252] Elemental violence is thus recruited by Lyutov to enhance the tension that has mounted with every step of Kolesnikov's laborious walk across fields, against whose furrowed and yellow 'nakedness' his lone figure, with its stooping back and gangling legs, stands out. Does not a further reference to the elements, the sun, at least reflect the glory to come amid the barren landscape? – 'a blazing sunset flooded over him, as crimson and improbable as approaching death'.[253] The significance of the simile, for which the metaphor 'a blazing sunset flooded' acts as tenor, hinges on the epithet 'improbable'. The sequence of tropes exemplifies the enigmatic ambivalence that Babel so often likes to create. On first impression, the imagery is that of glory, the lone hero walking into the sunset, yet the luminary's brilliance is deemed to be as improbable as approaching death. Why should the former be any less improbable than the latter? Indeed sunsets often blaze brightly. Hence the sun, by its very presence, manifests the reverse, the likelihood of Kolesnikov's death and not the improbability of it. The sun, as we have seen elsewhere, is often associated with violent death by Babel. In the plans we read: 'Those slaugh-tered, hacked to death, sun, heat, soldiers' notebooks, leaves from the gospel … A corpse. Sparkling day. Everything is strewn with corpses.'[254] A story which matches 'Kombrig dva' for its changing mood brought about by the use of figure is 'Perekhod cherez Zbruch'. Here the sunset, together with other natural phenomena,[255] marks the transition from the peace and beauty of a familiar, daytime world to the chaos and violence of the night and the new world of Poland and war: 'An orange sun rolls across the sky, like a severed head.'[256] In 'Kombrig dva', the 'sunset' sequence of tropes sim-ultaneously reflects both triumph and disaster and adds to the mounting suspense. In 'Perekhod cherez Zbruch', the imagery of the sunset has a similar function – its role is both celebratory and sinister.

Tropes' sequences and series

What is at first striking and perhaps surprising when examining the statistics of Babel's trope sequences is the discovery that, in *Konarmiya* and to a lesser extent in *Na pole chesti,* the number of Lyutov- or narrator-based metaphors occurring in trope clusters is less than in the prose of the Cossacks and other protagonists of the major cycle or the French soldiers of the minor cycle. Indeed, in *Konarmiya* there is a marked difference, 38.8 per cent (Lyutov) compared with 56 per cent (Cossacks) and 52.6 per cent (others). Yet one gains an overriding impression of trope saturation within the cycle with passages abounding in metaphor and other tropes. Two observations need to be made in this respect. Firstly the percentages do not reveal the proportion of Lyutov's 38.8 per cent of adjacent metaphors that beget or are begotten sequentially by other tropes, whereas the adjacent metaphors of all other protagonists are generally without this capacity, merely being tropes juxtaposed with one another without mutual reference or involvement. This is not to say however, that the sequentially componential metaphor is entirely lacking in Cossack figurative language or that of other protagonists; the author's predilection for a sequencing of tropes is in evi-dence here, albeit in a minor way. The second observation concerns the fact that 61.2 per cent of Lyutov's metaphors are non-adjacent which points to their greater independence, prominence and therefore impact.

A third detail to emerge is the dominant role that metaphor plays in trope sequences or series in all *skaz* categories. While metaphor accounts for 55.3 per cent of *Konarmiya*'s tropes, 66.7 per cent of Lyutov's metaphors, 78.7 per cent of the Cossacks' and 83.3 per cent of others' metaphors are involved in trope clusters. A similar pattern emerges in *Na pole chesti*; although the narrator's prose embodies a greater contribution by metaphor to trope clusters than the soldiers' does, 73.3 per cent and 62.5 per cent respectively, metaphor as a trope-type constitutes but 53.9 per cent of the cycle's tropes. These statistics thus indicate that metaphor plays a disproportionately significant role in the formulation of tropes' series or sequences in both cycles.[257]

Examples have already been cited which embody clusters of Lyutov's tropes, such as the second paragraph of 'Perekhod cherez Zbruch', the densest passage of tropes in either cycle.[258] Further examples are found in almost all Lyutov based *Konarmiya* stories. In a passage from 'Sashka Khristos' we see how Babel depicts the return of spring. The rapid succession of visual, metaphorical images is interrupted by a simile whose power to disturb is enhanced by its different sensuous base. The whole series is a mixture of joyfulness and ugliness which both contrasts with and complements the return of the sexually tainted father and son:

> Tarakanych and Sashka went through the fields. The earth lay in April dampness. Emeralds shone in black hollows. Green shoots embroidered the earth in intricate stitching. And the dank earth smelt like a soldier's wife does at dawn. The first flocks were streaming down from the tumuli, foals were playing in the blue expanses of the horizon.[259]

Amid the sense of celebration are signs of menace and foreboding: jewels gleam from black holes, new shoots cover the ground in an artful way and the very smell of the earth suggests sexual encounter. Babel's ambivalence is at work here; forebodings of death blend with the reassertions of life.[260] The very animals gambol over tumuli as Sashka and Tarakanych cross rejuvenated fields to discover that the mother is mourning the recent deaths of her children. Such evocative series of tropes can be found in much of Lyutov's prose. In 'Berestechko' for example: 'A way of life had vanished in Berestechko, but it still had a firm base here. Shoots, which were over three centuries old, were still sprouting in Volhynia with the warm mould of olden times',[261] and in 'U svyatogo Valenta' hyperbole depicts Catholic celebration thus: 'The peasantry bent its knee, kissed hands, and clouds without precedent blazed in the heavens that day. The heavenly flags were flying in honour of the ancient church.'[262]

A feature of Babel's trope series concerns the engendering of one trope by another; such often short sequences, with one metaphorical image begetting another, are a hallmark of his artistry. This 'telescoping' or fusing of images intensifies their effect upon the reader. As the Cavalry army ride into Berestechko, their carefree mood evaporates: 'A song babbled like a brook running dry.'[263] The metaphoric verb 'babbled' forms the tenor of the simile's vehicle. In 'U svyatogo Valenta', the crazed bellringer Ludomirskiy is described thus: 'and his blue nose rose above him like a flag above a corpse'.[264] Hyperbolic metaphor here helps create simile. A number of metaphor-simile sequences occur in 'Solntse Italii'; they convey Lyutov's mood of fantasy

142

and foreboding as he returns at night to his billet. Each time metaphor forms the tenor of a simile: 'The damp mould of the ruins flowered like the marble of opera seating … Blue roads flowed past me like streams of milk spurting from many breasts … I sat apart dozing, dreams leapt about me like kittens.'[265] The 'milk' image of the second vehicle recurs in a subsequent combination of metaphors: 'Fortunately that night, *rent by the milk of the moon*, Sidorov did not utter a word.'[266] The violence which Lyutov felt that his companion might inflict upon him does not materialize, but his sense of apprehension is conveyed in the imagery of *ostraneniye*, (*making strange*), 'night rent by the milk of the moon'. The earlier comforting image of succour, of roads bathed in moonlight, now cedes momentarily to a night that is being savaged by the moon. Such proximity of tropes and recurrence of imagery, albeit with an altered effect, lends Lyutov's prose not only succinctness and saturation but above all a sense of ambivalence engendered by the wealth of metaphorical nuances which lurk beneath the surface.

Babel's ability to revitalize fossilized images through a concentration of tropes is exemplified in a series of metaphors in 'Smert' Dolgushova'. Six metaphors in symmetrical groups of three succeed each other with the speed and impact of their common theme: bullets. The first cluster contains three auditory images, the second three visual ones. The opening images are unremarkable in isolation but the aggregate impression as the sequence develops is vivid and frightening: 'Bullets whine and scream. Their plaintiveness grows unbearably. Bullets wound the earth and swarm in it, quivering with impatience.'[267] The imagery invests the bullets with human and animal behaviour and evokes an image of irresistible, demonic force. The opening verbs and following noun are onomatopoeic; in them in turn one hears the hiss of violence and the sense of wretchedness that the bullets embody for Lyutov: 'skulyat, vzvizgivayut, zhaloba' ('whine, scream, plaintiveness'). The auditory images do not possess, however, the degree of freshness which obtains in the more complex second cluster. The bullets, invested by Lyutov with the human faculties of distress, now pass into his line of vision as a target is reached. Three visual images complement the three auditory ones. The earth is likewise invested with human feeling, the bullets 'wound' it. The climax of the sequence is reached with the most startling and pejorative image of the six, the bullets fleetingly assume the identity of myriad insects as they infest the earth. They are like a plague destroying mankind, yet paradoxically they embody the feelings of men: 'Bullets wound the earth and swarm in it, quivering with impatience.'[268]

But it is not only metaphor and simile that occur in trope series. Babel also has Lyutov employ synecdoche and metonymy in close succession, as he describes the ascendancy of the Jews in Berestechko: 'The Jews have tied here with threads of gain the Russian peasant to the Polish *pan*, the Czech colonist to the Lodz factory.'[269] The contrast in the opening metaphor of the three plural references to the Jews and their activities with the threefold use of synecdoche in the singular references to the other nationalities culminates in a final metonymy ('factory' for 'work') and evokes a vivid image of the Jewish wrong-footing of others. Further in the same story Lyutov describes the squalor of Jewish refuges, their clandestine passage-ways and dark sheds which they presumably found it necessary to maintain in order to ensure their survival: 'Here after many days human waste and cattle dung accumulate. Dejection and horror fill the catacombs with an acrid stench and the putrid acidity of faeces.'[270] In the second sentence, metonymy is employed twice as emotions replace the people who feel them. The resulting prosopopoeia is made more effective through assonance as respective sounds in the opening substantives recur in the final noun 'faeces'. Their combination in the final word conjures more vividly the foulness and degradation of these places.

But it is metaphor nevertheless that Lyutov often employs for his most poignant effects. In 'U svyatogo Valenta', in the recently desecrated Catholic church, Lyutov encounters a blind old woman, the bellringer's wife, who is obviously distressed at the sacrilegious events: 'Zrachki yeyo byli nality beloy vlagoy slepoty i bryzgali slyozami.' ('Her pupils suffused with the white moisture of blindness spurted forth tears.')[271] The seven-fold use of the liquid 'l' sounds and the metaphoric substantive 'moisture' for blindness evoke pathos,[272] but it is the following sentence with its seemingly trite figure that reveals the subtlety of Babel's metaphoric sequences: 'Zvuki organa, to tyagostnyye, to pospeshnyye, *podplyvali* k nam.' 'The sounds of the organ, now anguished, now precipitate, *flooded across* to us.'[273] The 'liquid' imagery of the woman's eyes is continued in the verb whose figurative effect would be banal without the preceding metaphor. In her blindness she must have been even more conscious of Afonka Bida's crazed organ playing than the sighted Lyutov. Babel has thus given both primary narrator and reader her eyes – we visualize the sound of the notes and share in her anguish. The moisture of her tears is again evident as liquid 'l's continue to flow: 'Polyot ikh byl truden, sled ikh zvenel zhalobno i dolgo.' ('Their path was difficult, their passage prolonged and mournful.')[274]

Such linking of imagery focuses the reader's attention sharply and engen-ders a considerable emotional response from him. The tropes in question may be adjacent as in 'U svyatogo Valenta', or at some distance from each other. Two examples of the latter occur in 'Smert' Dolgushova' and 'Moy pervyy gus' respectively. The starkly unnerving sight of the mutilated Dolgushov is described thus as, propped up against a tree, his boots thrust apart, he peels back his shirt: 'His belly had been torn open, his guts *were creeping* on to his knees, and his heartbeats were visible.'[275] The same verb is used a few lines later to describe Lyutov's reaction to Dolgushov's taunt-ing of him once the narrator had refused to administer the *coup de grâce*: 'Sweat was creeping over my body.'[276] The image is unremarkable, but it regains a living quality because of the preceding figure. For a moment it paradoxically links Dolgushov and Lyutov. The former, lying mortally wounded, becomes the persecutor of the latter, who, because of the request made to him, assumes once more the role of the persecuted. Lyutov is thus victim, Dolgushov ironically the oppressor. Yet both men, we discover, share a similar fate. Dolgushov faces the prospect of certain and possibly tortuous death, Lyutov that of guilt, contempt and death also. For, as he moves away, having incurred the contempt firstly of Dolgushov, and subsequently of his friend Bida, whom he has recruited to carry out the shooting, the latter cocks a gun at the narrator: 'I rode off at walking pace, without turning round feeling the chill of death in my back.'[277]

Babel employs zeugma to convey Lyutov's sense of fear and despair, a trope type which is used sparingly by the author,[278] but a further instance occurs in 'Moy pervyy gus', another story depicting persecution of the primary narrator. Lyutov had made a defiant and successful gesture to rid himself of his Cossack persecutors and his own hunger pangs by killing an old woman's goose. The zeugma recalls in theme and in the pathos that it evokes, the distressed old woman of 'U svyatogo Valenta': 'The old woman, *her blindness and glasses glistening*, picked up the bird, wrapped it in her apron and began bearing it off to the kitchen. – Comrade, – she said to me, pausing, – I would like to hang myself, – and closed the door behind her.'[279] The old woman and her goose are the victims and Lyutov, for once, the oppressor, but the primary narrator's triumph is a transient one. The story depicts Lyutov as apparently successfully overcoming his isolation and rejection by the Cossacks with whom he is billeted. Their group, which had at first ostracized him, now includes him to the point that he eats and sleeps among them, 'warming each other, legs intertwined'.[280] Lyutov has compromised his ideals, however, in order to achieve this; he has shed blood and cannot be at peace with himself. 'I dreamt and saw women in my dreams, and only my heart, stained with murder, grated and overflowed.'[281] Just as in fact the goose's head had previously cracked and gushed forth beneath his boot: 'the goose's head cracked beneath my boot, cracked and began to leak'.[282] Babel links both events through a repetition of the verb 'to flow, begin to flow'; its second and figurative use would have been trite without the previous literal use. The final lines of the story unmistakably indicate that Lyutov is his own third and final victim. The same imagery renders the narrator both hero and victim; 'teklo, potekla' ('overflowed, began to leak') is a unifying image which denotes his role as both oppressor and oppressed.

Adjacent tropes in the language of Cossacks and other protagonists ——
Statistics in Section IB, Table 4, reveal that a clustering of tropes occurs more frequently in the language of the Cossacks and other protagonists than is the case with the language of the primary narrator.[283] However, such series of tropes are characterized, certainly in the speech of Cossacks, by repetition, incongruity of imagery, and often a crudity which portrays their purveyors in a pejorative light. The 'begetting' and linking qualities noted in Lyutov's sequences are largely lacking in the tropes' series of both Cossacks and others. In 'Nachal'nik konzapasa' we hear, framed in turgid hyperbole, Dyakov, the Remount Officer's, flippant reply to a peasant's charge of injustice at the exchange of horses: 'But as for the horse falling – that's not a fact. If a horse falls and gets up again, then it's a horse; if, to put it the other

way round, he doesn't get up again, then it's not a horse.'[284] The peasant's response likewise employs a series of figures including personification which lends some interest, but this is quickly dispelled by its immediate repetition: 'Oh Lord, merciful mother of mine ... how she's to get up, the orphan ... She'll snuff it, the orphan ...'[285]

In two adjacent metaphors in 'Solntse Italii', Sidorov writes of his ill-spent time fighting with the anarchist leader Makhno and condemns his colleague Volin for remaining with him: 'Volin rigs himself up in apostolic vestments and scrambles up to Leninism from anarchy.'[286] Although one metaphor directly succeeds the other, the imagery in each is discrete and, because of its juxtaposition, incongruous; in no way does the second metaphor emanate from the first as is so often the case in Lyutov's prose. Instead Babel presents us with the opportunity to appreciate the effusive gaucherie of a literate Cossack who is motivated, as Lyutov earlier encapsulates in an oxymoron, by a 'common-sense madness'.[287] In another series of tropes a few lines further on, a trite metaphor is succeeded by one of crudity before Sidorov finishes the sequence with a laboured series of puns: 'And now I don't know whether there isn't the foul seed of anarchy in all this and whether we'll wipe your prosperous noses for you, self-made members of the self-made CentCom made in Khar'kov, in the self-made capital.'[288] The intensity of a 'telescoped' Lyutov sequence is lacking both here and also on the occasions when Sidorov does employ a metaphor to form the tenor of a simile. The language is trite, the imagery banal in these consecutive examples: 'Italy has entered my heart like an obsession. The thought of that country I have never seen is sweet to me, like a woman's name, like your name, Victoria ...'[289]

In 'Moy pervyy gus', two Cossack speakers, Savitskiy and the quarter-master, combine crude, colloquial metaphor with metonymy as they outline to Lyutov the hard time that awaits him: 'and they cut specs down here ... It's a waste of time with specs here with us and you can't stop it.' ('Kanitel' literally means a 'thread' and has a figurative meaning of a 'long drawn-out proceedings' or a 'waste of time'.)[290] A third Cossack cruelly equates Lyutov's spectacles with the badge of a coward as metonymy, metaphor and simile combine in a rapid, yet discrete cluster of crude images: 'Guns number double zero ... slink away ...'[291] But it is not just to emphasize the derision and harshness of these men of violence that Babel supplies them with metaphor, it is also used to touchingly comic effect at the end of 'Moy pervyy gus'. Lyutov, having won his acceptance among the Cossacks, reads aloud a speech by Lenin from *Pravda*. Sincerity and simple peasant roots are evident in the series of figures which an admiring Cossack employs to show his appreciation of the leader of the revolution. 'Truth tickles everyone's nostril ... and how do you drag it from the heap, but he hits it straightway like a chicken does grain ...'[292] The comparison of Lenin's grasp of the truth to a chicken's successful discovery of grain is both laughable and endearing, and as such embodies the essence of Babel's ambivalent portrayal of the Cossacks. They are both deprecated and appreciated by his primary narrator; the opening prosopopoeia in which truth firstly resembles the tickling quality of smoke and then resides in a large heap, prepares us for the absurdity and delightfulness of the final simile.

While Lyutov's intensity and stunning quality of sequential metaphor is lacking in the farce and crudity of the figures quoted above, there are instances where tropes employed by Cossacks resemble those of the primary narrator. Babel's verbal mask would seem to have slipped and we glimpse instances of imagery comparable in originality and impact with that of Lyutov. Two instances occur consecutively in 'Solntse Italii'. Again Sidorov is writing about Makhno and Volin: 'And the old man listens to him, strokes the dusty wire of his curls and emits through rotten teeth the long snake of his peasant smile.'[293] The figurative use of the substantive 'wire' to describe Makhno's hair and the graphic encapsulation of treachery in the image of his smile reveal the touch of a literary master of which Sidorov is largely incapable elsewhere.[294] The second metaphor was in fact omitted in editions from the thirties onwards, the rest of the sentence reading simply as 'and emits through rotten teeth his peasant smile'. The omission cannot have been due to censorship, since Makhno was not thought of in kindly fashion by the Soviet authorities, but is the result of another earlier omission by Babel of a simile that he had originally attributed to Lyutov. As he bent over Sidorov's abandoned letter, Lyutov recounts his feelings of anguish at reading another man's private thoughts: 'Vague intoxication fell away from, like the scales of a snake casting its skin'.[295] The simile's metaphorical tenor 'vague intoxication fell away from me' is omitted from later editions, while the vehicle 'like the scales of a snake casting its skin' appears only in the first edition of the story. Apart from representing another instance of a trope sequence in Lyutov's prose, what affords us particular interest is the image of treachery that Babel selects to portray Lyutov's action. The 'snake' theme, we recall, was also the illustration for Makhno's treacherous nature. Babel would seem to be equating Lyutov in his act of betrayal with the Ukrainian anarchist. Indeed the link is not as tenuous as it may seem, for both men embodied an ambivalent attitude to the revolutionary cause. Makhno led the rebel revolutionary army of the Ukraine and fought against both the White Guards and the Red Army, while Lyutov, who ostensibly embraces the cause of the Red Cavalry, is sickened by many of its actions. Whether Babel in fact omitted the vehicle of the simile because he decided not to equate his primary narrator's action with the character of Makhno, or whether he felt that the phrase to describe the latter's smile was of too rich a literary pedigree for the pen of Sidorov, is a matter of conjecture. What is again exemplified, however, is the linking or unifying property of Babel's tropes. An early figurative reference finds an echo later on, thus affording the reader a sudden and heretofore unperceived insight or 'epiphany'.[296] No image is gratuitous; if one is subsequently removed, so is its sequel.

Babel also employs tropes to fashion his other protagonists. Here, amid images of crudity similar to the Cossacks', one meets few tropes' series and no examples of the 'telescoping' of figures. This is hardly surprising since it is largely the speech of peasants, old women and other briefly encountered people that he records. Nevertheless there is a colour and vitality which contributes both authenticity and interest. In 'Sashka Khristos', metaphor and hyperbole are juxtaposed in the language of the whoring beggar woman as Sashka's stepfather copulates with her: 'A little rain on an old woman, – she laughed, – I'll give twelve hundred kilos an acre ...'[297] The verb-less nature of the metaphor enhances the distastefulness of the act – it is as if two substantives collide. The grossness so graphically conveyed contrasts with the humility and grief of Sashka's mother, as she recounts later in the story the recent deaths of the younger children. Hyperbole is replaced by litotes: 'The children have left the yard ... our children have gone out feet first ...'[298]

But amidst the often crude metaphors of invective one can discern subtle links between distant figures which afford flashes of insight and the gaining of a new perspective on protagonists and events. In 'Smert' Dolgushova', the mutilated telephonist, to whom Lyutov refuses to give a mercy killing, calls the narrator a vile creature: 'You're running off – he muttered sliding down, – run, *skunk* ...'[299] The image is unremarkable, the banal parlance of insult, yet in an earlier instance of colloquial metaphor the regimental commander, Vytyagaychenko, employs the same image, 'skunk/foul creature', as an epithet to describe the prolonged Polish bombardment that they are facing: 'Son of a bitch ... what a foul waste of time.'[300] With Dolgushov's later taunt to him, Lyutov is equated in guilt and contempt with the enemy for the prolongation of a wretched situation; he is as much an enemy to Dolgushov, Bida and others, because of his inability to act, as the Poles are. With the repetition of 'foul/loathsome' and 'skunk/foul creature' Babel is informing us of Lyutov's realization of this. Vytyagaychenko's comment, directed at circumstances in general, applies equally well to Lyutov's behaviour in particular.

The richest source of tropes in the *skaz* of other protagonists is the Jewish shopkeeper, Gedali. In the eponymous story Gedali's confused thoughts on the Revolution are delivered in dramatic fashion, with tropes abounding. Prosopopoeia, litotes, synecdoche and metaphor are juxtaposed in a blend of tragi-comic phrases as Gedali wrestles with his conflicting opinions: 'The Revolution – we'll say yes to it, but do we say no to the sabbath? ... Yes, I shout to the Revolution, yes I shout to it, but it hides from Gedali and sends out ahead nothing but shooting ...'[301]

Like this personification of the Revolution, which is extended elsewhere in the story, so Gedali prolongs the animal theme of his references to the Poles. Synecdoche, litotes and metaphor combine in language whose crudity could easily be voiced by a Cossack: 'A Pole has closed my eyes ... the Pole is an evil dog. He takes the Jew and tears out his beard, ah, the cur! And now they're beating him, the evil dog.'[302] The enigmatic opening figure, together with the repeated singular references to the enemy, lend a dramatic, mock-epic quality to the Jew's words, which Lyutov himself adopts as he interrupts the old man's monologue: 'The sun doesn't enter closed eyes ... but we will tear open eyes that have closed ...'[303] Later, in reply to the old man's statement about the composition of 'The International' 'The International, comrade pan, you don't know how it is served up ...'[304], Lyutov adopts Gedali's metaphoric verb and like him extends his theme through a succession of other tropes. The rhetoric of the old shopkeeper, whose name in Hebrew means 'wisdom', strikes a chord with the primary narrator who emulates him. Lyutov's reply is a symmetrical pairing of metaphor and metonymy: 'It's served up with gunpowder ... and seasoned with the best blood ...'[305]

The allegorical mode that Gedali adopts is further developed in 'Rabbi' where he effuses about the immortality of mothers and of Hasidism, comparing the latter with the former: 'A mother's memory feeds compassion in us, as the ocean, the boundless ocean feeds the rivers dissecting the universe ...'[306] As elsewhere, a metaphor is repeated, the verb 'feeds', which then recurs in the vehicle of the simile lending the sentence an epic grandeur and the rhythm of Yiddish rhetoric. Cuckierman, writing about *Odesskiye rasskazy,* comments on the dynamically rising and falling intonation that is to be found in the language of Babel's Odessan gangsters. He states that this is typical of Jewish speech and that it 'can be felt in the frequent questions, and answers to them, which repeat the same words or phrases'.[307] He adds that 'the same effect is achieved in passages in which a character philosophically ponders two sides of an issue'.[308] Gedali's conflicting thoughts on the Revolution, previously voiced to Lyutov in 'Gedali', exemplify this just as the dramatic cadences of his intonation do in his second and longer allegorical statement in 'Rabbi': 'In the passionate edifice of Hasidism the doors and windows have been broken open, but it is immortal like a mother's soul ... Hasidism still stands with oozing orbits at the crossroads of the violent winds of history.'[309] In the welter of mixed metaphors, Gedali 'concretizes' and then animates the abstract. Hasidism is both a structure with the immortality of a mother's soul and a physical being buffeted by events around it. In Gedali's rhetoric we see the Lyutovian capacity for 'telescoped' tropes, one figure emanates from another and is rapidly succeeded by a third. Nine tropes in all occur and create a mixture of impressions. They are epic and absurd, comic and affecting. Babel develops the character of Podolskiy from his diary in his creation of Gedali;[310] indeed the old Jewish shopkeeper must have made a significant impression upon the author, for no protagonist other than Lyutov is afforded such trope-saturated language relative to their appearances in *Konarmiya.* Again an imagery link is perceptible: in 'Gedali' we learn how Gedali has been blinded – 'a Pole has closed my eyes'[311] he tells us; in 'Rabbi', the Hasidic faith stands with oozing orbits. So often in Lyutov's prose blindness is associated with moistness;[312] Gedali, like his faith, survives, but both badly need direction.

Adjacent tropes in Na pole chesti —— In the first cycle of war stories the proportion of the narrator's tropes that are adjacent to other tropes is higher than Lyutov's in *Konarmiya* by some 10 per cent.[313] There still exists, however, a higher proportion of adjacent metaphors in the language of the soldiers, although the difference is much less marked than is the case in the major cycle. 38.8 per cent of Lyutov's metaphors and 56 per cent of the Cossacks' are adjacent, while 48.4 per cent of *Na pole chesti*'s narrator's and 53.3 per cent of the soldiers' metaphors fall into this category. These figures reveal a close correlation between the two cycles in the incidence of tropes' series for both Cossacks and French soldiers. Metaphor too predominates as the trope type most likely to occur in such series. Indeed the narrator of the minor cycle shows an even more marked predilection for metaphor than Lyutov, 73.7 per cent compared with 66.7 per cent. Apart from a reduced variety of tropes generally in the lesser cycle, including a dearth of similes and a preference for hyperbole or litotes in the soldiers' tropes' series, an almost identical pattern obtains between the two cycles. [314]

The saturation and condensed nature of sequences of tropes similar to those of Lyutov are sought largely in vain in *Na pole chesti*. However, the narrator, in his exposure of the vainglorious Zhem'ye and the religiose Ston, deliberately couples trite images, thereby enhancing the pejorative impression of these men. In a coupling of epithet and simile in 'Dezertir' the officer's hatred for the barbarian invaders of his country is couched in precious, banal terms: 'his hatred … was as unquenchable … as life.' (ll.4–5, 'Dezertir'). Zhem'ye's contempt for the young deserter is felt in the empty grandiloquence of his comment on the soldier's excuses. Trite metaphor is succeeded by hyperbole: 'and he will redress [literally 'smooth over'] his wrong before France'. (ll.28–9, 'Dezertir') In 'Kvaker', similarly banal imagery is reserved for the dull, morose Ston: 'Ston forgot his horse. Within a week his conscience had set about its nagging [literally 'nibbling/ gnawing] task.' (ll.85–6, 'Kvaker') and later, similarly sterile language is used: 'The last bloody days had left a terrible mark on him.' (ll.96–7, 'Kvaker') There is no alleviation in the coldness of the narrator's tone, Ston's isolation and self-centredness are stressed to the end: 'it was as if he were in mourning for himself'. (ll.97–8, 'Kvaker')

However, fresh images are also encountered which can occur independently of other tropes or which can be mutually reinforcing agents in a trope sequence. An example of the former, which, significantly, does not apply to the central protagonist Ston, describes the horror of war: 'The earth gave off a stench, the sun rummaged in upturned corpses.' (ll.83–4, 'Kvaker'). In another instance in the first story, the uncompromising Ratin is given a sinister quality as he prepares to urinate on the idiot Bidu: 'Then the captain approached the very edge of the hole and *hissed* especially quietly …' (ll.32–3, 'Na pole chesti') [315] His comment resembles the hiss of a snake. Living imagery also occurs in tropes' series. In Kvaker synecdoche and metaphor combine to portray the grotesque physical spectacle that Ston presents: 'What was Ston? A bald brow on the top of a pole.' (l.7, 'Kvaker') The second image is developed in a second sequence a little later in the same story: 'he behaved with the wooden immobility of a priest at the pulpit'. (ll.11–12, 'Kvaker') The epithet 'wooden' complements in theme the metaphoric substantive 'pole' of the first series and also contributes to the tenor of the disguised simile's vehicle which follows.

In the first story of the cycle, a three-fold series of epithets renders the masturbating Bidu both culpable and worthy of compassion: 'Then he looked at the captain, and in the chinks of his *piggy* little eyes a *timid, tender* hope was reflected.' (ll.24–5, 'Na pole chesti')[316] But it is a little later in the same story that we meet one of the cycle's finest sequences of tropes. Before a determined Ratin resorts to urinating on the boy in the crater he tries to flush him out with verbal abuse: 'Blasphemous abuse came down upon the soldier, an arid hail fell on him of those repulsive, violent and senseless words ...' (ll.26–8, 'Na pole chesti') The epithet-substantive coupling of 'arid hail' constitutes an oxymoron which conjures vividly the hurtful and unproductive hatred of the officer's words. The sequence gives a rare glimpse of the 'telescoped' cataloguing of tropes which was to come in the language of Lyutov.

An equally skilful use of tropes occurs in the soldier-narrator's language of 'Semeystvo papashi Maresko'). The civilian's arrival is heralded by a three-fold figurative description, with two epithets preceding a single metaphoric substantive: 'A worn, faded creature.' (l.21, 'Semeystvo papashi Maresko') The series is complemented later by the portrayal of Maresko's reaction to renewed German fire: 'The Sunday frock-coat turned pale and huddled up.' (l.53, 'Semeystvo papashi Maresko'). The dual epithets of the first series, 'threadbare, faded', have prepared the reader for the subjugation of the civilian to the status of a frock-coat, while the substantive 'creature' is complemented by the metaphoric verb 'huddled up', whose Russian root lies in the noun 'yozh', a 'hedgehog'. The same story provides other examples of tropes' series which not only embody a living quality akin to Konarmiya's but which also characterize the soldier-protagonist who utters them. So often do we discern the grim humour of the soldier in the field of battle, a humour which foreshadows that of a Cossack narrator like Konkin or Pavlichenko: 'The field of skulls is turned into trenches', (l.7, 'Semeystvo papashi Maresko') and in a sequence of irony, litotes and metaphor: 'If we are destined to increase the population of this chilly corner, well we've made the rotting old men dance first to the march of our machine-guns.' (ll.8–10, 'Semeystvo papashi Maresko') The irony of these contemplative asides finds a counterpart in the speech of Ratin in 'Na pole chesti': 'You've found a wife here, swine!' (l.17, 'Na pole chesti') he asks Bidu. The crude final invective follows an ironic litotes and gives a foretaste of Cossack abuse in Konarmiya. Indeed while we do not meet the frequency and concentration of the tropes' sequences of the major cycle, we do encounter, at least in the speech and thoughts of the soldiers of the first cycle, a richness and intensity that matches and in places exceeds that of Konarmiya's Cossacks.

Pre- and post-positive metaphor

Section IC, Table 4, concerns the proportion of pre- and post-positive metaphors in the language of the protagonists of the two cycles. These terms refer to the position of the imported image in relation to the part of the trope's main idea or stimulant which is outside this image. This is more clearly seen in simile where the main idea, called the tenor, is distinct from the vehicle, the part which contains the imported image. In metaphor, although the stimulant is an intrinsic part of the figure, it is still possible to discern among the words surrounding the imported image those that relate to or convey the main idea. If we examine a fossilized metaphor such as 'the bus crawled through the fog' or one from Babel's 'Rabbi': 'The wheel of a gun carriage groaned round the corner',[317] the respective substantives 'bus' and 'wheel' are non-figurative; with their appearance, our expectations of what may logically follow such a subject are firstly established, only to be immediately dashed. The verb in each sentence deviates from the norm and, as such, constitutes the true figurative element, the element which deals us the shock of surprise. The bus or wheel assume the characteristics associated with the actions of crawling or groaning and, as a result, stimulant and imported image are fused. However, since the figurative element or imported image follows, and does not precede, the initial part of the stimulant, I would designate both these metaphors as post-positive. If, on the other hand, the true figurative element had occurred before the discernible part of the stimulant, they would have been termed pre-positive ones, since the reader has formed a narrow range of expectations from his reading of verbs like 'crawled' or 'groaned' and when these are contradicted, the shock of surprise is all the greater. Hence the seeming illogicality of the respective inanimate subjects freshens the figurative verbs: 'through the fog crawled the bus' or 'Round the corner groaned the wheel of a gun carriage.' The usual order in prose is, however, the reverse, that is to say the entity which is responsible by its actions, nature or appearance for the creation of the figurative image, precedes that image, yet there are many instances in Babel's tropes of war where this process is reversed and pre-positive metaphors are employed.

Indeed, in *Na pole chesti*, pre-positive metaphors predominate in both the narrator's and soldiers' categories. The effect is often to enhance a figure's impact, to lend it the flavour of poetry by making the unification of a number of incongruous elements more vivid. A sequence quoted earlier from 'Na pole chesti' exemplifies the arresting quality of pre-positive metaphor: 'an arid hail fell on him of those repulsive, violent and senseless words', (ll.27–8, 'Na pole chesti') although another directly preceding pre-positive metaphor gives the reader some initial preparation for what ensues: 'Blasphemous abuse came down upon the soldier.' (ll.26–7, 'Na pole chesti')[318] The 'blasphemous abuse' which falls upon Bidu becomes the 'arid hail' flying at him which in turn takes the place of the final reference to Ratin's 'furious words'. 'Sukhoy grad' ('arid hail') is a pivotal metaphor, it fulfils both a post-positive and pre-positive function and demonstrates that Babel's technique of 'telescoping' tropes was something that he possessed at this earlier stage of his literary career. Less striking examples of pre-positive metaphors occur in each of the four stories of the first cycle: 'and he will redress [literally 'smooth over'] his wrong before France', (ll.28–9, 'Dezertir') and in 'Kvaker' a substantive constitutes the figurative element: 'but a *slave to his conscience*'. (l.4, 'Kvaker')[319] But it is with epithets that we meet the most common form of pre-positive metaphor, for where a figurative adjective is employed attributively we may argue that the imported image precedes the stimulant or main idea, namely the substantive to which it applies. Examples abound,[320] often in series of two or three: 'and in the chinks of his piggy little eyes a timid, tender hope was reflected'; (ll.24–5, 'Na pole chesti') 'A worn, faded creature' and 'over timid shoulders dangles a sack'. (ll.21 and 22–3 respectively, 'Semeystvo papashi Maresko') The inversion of subject and verb is another common source of pre-positive metaphor: 'not far from us mewed a little 12-centimetre cat', (ll.53–4, 'Semeystvo papashi Maresko') and in another battle scene we sense keenly the hostile world in which Ston finds himself. The initial pre-positive metaphor has an ironically mellifluous ring to it, created by the inversion of subject and verb, but this is quickly dispelled by the concluding post-positive figure of the sun rummaging among corpses: 'Ceaselessly *thundered the cannonade*. The earth gave off a stench, the sun rummaged in upturned corpses.' (ll.82–4, 'Kvaker')[321]

While *Konarmiya* boasts a greater variety of pre-positive metaphor, there is similarity both in formation and effect with the pre-positive figures of *Na pole chesti*. In addition, Babel has developed pre-positive metaphor as a device which increases unwitting self-ridicule in the case of the Cossacks and achieves an aesthetically poetic effect in the tropes of his primary narrator. 'Kostyol v Novograde' affords frequent examples of Lyutov-based pre-positive metaphor, both through inversion of subject and verb, '*Howling* in the church next to the house were the *bells*',[322] and through the juxta-position of two substantives: 'he enumerated the wounds of his country ... the satin of feminine letters ... carpets of money'.[323] Lyutov, who admits to being seduced by what he sees and hears in the Catholic church,[324] transfers his feelings in a pre-positive metaphor of pathetic fallacy to the world out-side: 'and beyond the window in the garden beneath the *black passion* of the sky the path shimmers'.[325]

Similar examples are to be found in much of the primary narrator's lan-guage elsewhere in the cycle, but as with all tropes it is the quality of the imported image employed that determines the degree of originality and effectiveness, not simply the order of the stimulant and its image. What a reversal of these components does achieve in Lyutov's case, however, is to enhance the poetic quality and epic grandeur of his language. Kolesnikov's lonely walk back to his men, as he bears his burden of command and Budy-onnyy's hopes for victory, are portrayed in a series of short tropes, some of which are pre-positive metaphors that contribute to the significance and tension of the occasion: 'on the furrowed and *yellow nakedness of the fields* we could see only the narrow back of Kolesnikov';[326] the fields lie exposed and vulnerable like Kolesnikov whom Lyutov witnesses 'spinning on his horse in *columns of blue dust*'.[327] In 'Perekhod cherez Zbruch' we meet pre-positive images of a truly epic nature; as Lyutov leaves the tranquillity of Volhynia for a warring Poland, the sky registers the transition and re-introduces a militaristic note: 'a gentle light glows in the *gorges of the storm-clouds*, and the *standards of the sunset* fly above our heads'. [328] In this two-fold sequence of metaphors, a concrete substantive precedes a noun denoting a natural phenomenon. The freshness of each imported image is enhanced by its position relative to its respective stimulant. The visual shock that each image creates as the reader subsequently realigns his mental picture brings with it the pleasure of the poetic.

A clear trend is discernible in the pre-positive metaphors of the Cossacks and other protagonists. The tropes' function is often to belittle or humiliate the protagonist who utters them. The placing of a trite imported image before its stimulant focuses greater attention upon the image, and the exaggeration that a Cossack, like Balmashov for example, embodies in his imagery, is consequently more exposed. He depicts the men in his platoon as: 'And each, *boiling over with my truth*' and daybreak merits 'and red drummers had begun to play in the dawn on their red drums'. [329] The farcical nature of his imagery complements the gullibility that he displays, for he is deceived by a matronly black marketeer and suffers the condemnation of his men. Bombast abounds in the language of another Cossack narrator, Matvey Pavlichenko, who, in recounting his adventures, tells of his hunting down his master Nikitinskiy, who had made advances to his wife: 'and I grew in his doorway like a burr' [330] – the opening metaphoric verb is realized in the farcical vehicle of the simile for which it forms the tenor. The fustian nature of such figures, when they are mentally re-stated by the reader, amounts to anticlimax for him. The thrill of surprise that the pre-positive living imagery of Lyutov comprises is turned to satirical purposes by Babel in his portrayal of Cossack men in action. They are the unwitting mouthpieces of a self-ridicule which is based upon capricious language spiced with peasant imagery.

A story in which the imagery of Lyutov matches the farcical tone of a Balmashov, Konkin or Pavlichenko is 'Vecher'. Pre-positive figures likewise enhance the satirical effect. Lyutov is in a bad way; he is sick, confused and desperate. He portrays himself with boils on his neck, bandages on his legs and complains of his plight to Galin, one of a wretched trio of fellow-contributors to *Krasnyy kavalerist*: 'Galin, – I said, stricken with loneliness and pity, – I'm ill, it's evident to me the end has come. And I'm tired, Galin, of staying in our cavalry army ...' [331] Lyutov's distorted view of a world with which he is so out of sorts is reflected in pre-positive metaphor: 'In the sky the squint-eyed lantern of the provincial sun goes out', [332] and in a depiction of sordid love-making between Vasiliy, the cook, and Irina, the washerwoman, the world becomes inverted in Lyutov's lenses, the firmament reduced to the level of man: 'Irina listens to the absurd muffled muttering of love, above her *in the black seaweed of the sky drag the stars*'. [333] In Lyutov's confused eyes the earth, with its absurd mortals, is mirrored in a cloying, pejorative image of the sky which would not be out of place in the satirical writing of Ilf, a fellow Odessan of Babel's. Even the moon, elsewhere often a symbol of maternal comfort, is portrayed as 'sticking out up there, like a sore thumb' (literally 'a prickly, insolent character').[334]

Theme

Violence and the military —— It is perhaps surprising to reflect that in two cycles of war stories in which physical and mental violence and cruelty are portrayed, so few images are recruited from the thematic spheres of fighting and the military world.[335] In both cycles we are privy to very few battle scenes; in 'Syn rabbi' and the opening of 'Na pole chesti' we come closest to the epic backdrop of a battle-scene of Tolstoyan proportions, but such portrayal is fleeting. Violence on a mass scale is neither what preoccupied Babel nor what he sought to portray. His mission is to delineate as acutely and intensely as possible individual dilemmas, to portray the victims and the purveyors of violence and war or, as is often the case, the same protagonists in both roles.

The relative dearth of violent imagery in Babel's tropes stems from the author's desire to understate, to allow the reader to supply the emotions, the pain of reaction and thus to identify more closely with his protagonists. However, two stories with different narrators exemplify the disturbing use that Babel makes of what violent imagery he does include. Both stories, 'Perekhod cherez Zbruch' and 'Konkin', celebrate war and also portray murder and suffering; the first is narrated by Lyutov, the second by a Cossack. In the case of the primary narrator, only one metaphor includes an image of violence,[336] and Konkin only employs three (13 per cent of his metaphors). A startling synaesthetic figure concludes a four-fold sequence which signals the transition between the two worlds of peace and war in *Konarmiya*'s opening story: 'The smell of yesterday's blood and slaughtered horses drips into the cool of evening.'[337] More than one of our senses are assailed in rapid succession as Volhynia's serenity cedes to Poland's chaos. The sunset resembles a public execution amidst a military pageant, and in the image of heightened sensuous awareness quoted above the smell of recent slaughter pervades the evening air while the blackened Zbruch roars and foams.

Amid the hyperbole of 'Konkin' we meet the colloquial register of a Cossack's bravado: 'We were giving the Poles the chop down at Belaya Tserkov, giving it to them hot and strong.'[338] The use of 'kroshit'' (to 'crumble' or 'chop') is fossilized, as is a third figure of violence: 'Two we cut down with our rifles',[339] in which the last pair of words in Russian, 'na kornyu', compares the killing of Poles to cropping or destroying a root system. Thus, even in explicit statements of slaughter the Cossack resorts to images of peasant-based occupations. Indeed, the whole of 'Konkin' reverberates with colloquial euphemisms for violence and mayhem, yet it is rare to find an explicitly violent imported image in the metaphors. It is Lyutov's metaphors in fact which generally employ a slightly greater degree of violent imagery. 'Solntse Italii' affords evidence of this. Here, *skaz* proportions are fairly evenly divided between the language of Lyutov and the written word of the Cossack, Sidorov, whom the primary narrator describes as 'an anguished

155

killer' and who, like Konkin, looks to violence as a way of life: 'who nightly lowered upon me the hairy paw of his anguish'.[340] Yet the greater degree of violent images in Lyutov's metaphors indicates the tension that he feels and his inability to forget the violence that he both witnesses and suffers. Even a moonlit night is viewed thus: 'on this night rent by the milk of the moon'.[341] Sidorov's letter, by contrast, contains only one metaphor whose imported image is based on violence.

Even fewer figures are concerned with military imagery. As with violence, little use is made of what may seem an obvious sphere from which to recruit imagery. Where it does occur, as in the language of Balmashov in 'Sol'', it contributes to the satirical portrayal of the narrator: 'After some time had elapsed when the night had relinquished its post and red drummers had begun to play in the dawn on their red drums ...'[342] The bombast of Balmashov's figures concerning the dawn contrasts with the subtlety of Lyutov's portrayal of the sunset in a rare instance of military imagery from the primary narrator: 'the standards of the sunset fly above our heads'.[343]

In *Na pole chesti,* the proportion of explicitly violent and militaristic imported images in metaphor is also slight. The narrator employs three of violence and one of a military theme, while the soldiers use two. In his satirical exposure of Captain Zhem'ye, as with the self-condemnatory Balmashov in *Konarmiya*, the narrator deliberately juxtaposes an incongruously violent image with the abstract noun 'nezhnost' ('tenderness'): 'He loved France with a tenderness that devoured his heart', (ll.3–4, 'Dezertir') while at the beginning of 'Semeystvo papashi Maresko', as the soldier-narrator sets the scene and recounts the destruction all round him in the graveyard of the pretty Picardy village, the epic and serious note of a Lyutov is struck: 'Around us lie broken Crucifixes, fragments of monuments, gravestones, played havoc with by the hammer of some unknown defiler'. (ll.3–5, 'Semeystvo papashi Maresko')

Insult —— It may be argued that metaphors of insult are a variation of metaphors of violence, for insult is surely violence of the tongue. I have therefore juxtaposed them with 'violence' in Section ID, Table 4, placing their percentages in parentheses since insult constitutes a purpose rather than a metaphorical theme. What is significant is the monopoly of metaphors of insult held by the Cossacks and soldiers respectively. The central narrators are not concerned with insulting their fellow protagonists, at least not openly; whatever pejorative portrayal they wish to create is done implicitly, and generally in a subtle way. The hackneyed terms of abuse that the Cossacks adopt in their language rely mostly on the animal world for their imagery. We have seen the link that Babel forges between the seemingly casual remark on the status quo by a Cossack commander in 'Smert' Dolgushova' and its application to Lyutov at the end: 'Son of a bitch ... what a foul waste of time', and 'run, skunk/foul creature ...'[344] In the same story Bida addresses Lyutov with the fixed Cossack epithet of insult that is reserved for intellectuals – 'ochkastyy' ('four eyes') – but again it is allied with animal imagery, this time in a simile: 'You four eyes pity our brother like a cat does a mouse ...'[345] In written *skaz* the language of insult also employs animal imagery: firstly in 'Izmena', when describing a doctor who had sneered and provoked him and his comrades, Balmashov writes: 'And then, seeing before him a beast and not a human being';[346] earlier, in 'Sol'', the noxious citizen who had deceived Balmashov is described by the Cossack as an insidious flea: 'like a flea you can't be seen and you gnaw on and on and on ...'[347]

In 'Na pole chesti' Bidu receives the trite animal description 'svin'ya' from Ratin, whereas in 'Kvaker' the animal-loving Ston shuns such imagery for purposes of invective. Instead, he employs references to irreligious entities and practice. 'Satan's fiend ... son of sin', (ll.40 and 45 respectively, 'Kvaker') in his greetings to the groom, Bekker. The Cossack, Akinfiyev, in 'Posle boya', employs the reverse of Ston's imagery, equating Lyutov's alleged cowardice for not being prepared to kill in battle with proof of religious beliefs: 'You didn't put cartridges in ... you worship God, traitor ...'[348] But it is left to Sashka the nurse to have the last word, one of invective which again draws upon the animal world for its effect: 'Cocks only care about one thing ... smacking each other in the mouth.'[349]

With the relative dearth of overtly violent imagery in *Konarmiya* and *Na pole chesti*, from what themes does Babel import imagery to create an overriding impression of violence and suffering? We have seen how references to the animal world contribute to this in terms of metaphors of insult, but they also afford examples of Babel's techniques of understatement and pejoration. In the first cycle, the firing of the gun is depicted thus: 'Not far from us mewed a little 12-centimetre cat.' (ll.53–4, 'Semeystvo papashi Maresko') The French officer's words form a metaphor of understatement; a weapon of death paradoxically becomes a 'little cat' that 'mews', the incongruously affectionate terms, including the diminutive, are unexpected and assume both an absurd and sinister aspect. In *Konarmiya*, animal imagery is employed for pejorative purposes by Lyutov and especially by the Cossacks and other protagonists.[350] Sidorov depicts the nurses waiting on him as 'Bridled with awe' and in a plea to his fiancée he asks her to intercede for him: 'If you don't help – I'll *snuff* it without rhyme or reason. Who would want a worker to *peg out* in such a disorganised way, surely not you.'[351] The verbs that he uses for 'dying', 'izdokhnu, padokh', are normally reserved for animals; they not only suit the brash language of fighting men but also reflect the primary narrator's view of Sidorov as a man capable of animal savagery: 'I dreaded meeting my neighbour, Sidorov, who nightly lowered upon me the hairy paw of his anguish.'[352]

But the effect of Babel's animal imagery is not solely one of pejoration – humour is also present. In 'Ivany', a Cossack extols the virtues of Akinfiyev to the malingering deacon whom Akinfiyev is persecuting as he drives him to Rovno for medical tests: 'Understand what sort of man you're travelling with. Another would have stitched you up like a duck and not given a quack, but he's fishing the truth out of you and teaching you a lesson, unfrocked priest …'[353] In a rapid succession of tropes, three metaphors, a simile and hyperbole, we see Babel's revitalizing technique at work. The vehicle 'like a duck' is followed by a colloquial verb, 'kryaknul', which, when applied to human beings is the equivalent of 'gave a grunt' in English. Here its basic meaning re-emerges: 'gave a quack'. The opening and closing metaphors, 'stitched up' and 'fish the truth out of you', also reinforce the common theme as well as the grotesque humour. The sequence is a good example of the mutually reinforcing properties with which Babel invests his tropes. In isolation, each would be less effective than it is when in concert with others. The sequence also contains the essence of black comedy with which the whole of 'Ivany' is invested, the interplay between the hapless, malingering deacon Ageyev and his obsessively vengeful persecutor, the Cossack Akinfiyev. Similarly humorous notes are present in the imagery of Balmashov, which so often condemns its spokesman to the level of absurdity that one wonders whether Babel intended the name of this 'soldier of the revolution' to be associated with the noun 'balagan' or 'farce'. While he is capable of acts of brutality – 'I washed away this shame from the face of the workers' land and the Republic'[354] – he also displays compassion and, as such, represents the different facets of many of Babel's Cossack soldier-protagonists of whom he is the self-elected spokesman.[355] In 'Sol'' he reproaches his fellows for their coarseness towards a would-be female passenger: 'but it only surprises me to hear such *horseplay* from you'; the animal imagery continues as the woman, now safely ensconced, is adjured to go to her husband and raise more children to replace the fighting men: 'and we're relying on your conscience to raise replacements for us, because the old are getting older and there's few *offspring* about you see'.[356] Just as Cossack natures are likened to those of stallions, so are their offspring to the young of animals.[357]

In the minor cycle, there is a greater difference in the amount of imported animal imagery between the soldiers' *skaz* and that of the narrator, compared with the equivalent categories of the major cycle.[358] Animal references form the single most common theme of the soldiers' metaphors while only 6.4 per cent of the narrator's recruit from this sphere. In the latter's prose a pejorative effect is again created, however. Bidu's eyes are portrayed as 'svinnykh' ('piggy') while Ratin's threat to the idiot boy borders on the sinister for it is delivered with the quiet menace of a snake: 'Then the captain approached the very edge of the hole and hissed especially quietly.' (ll.24 and 32–3 respectively, 'Na pole chesti') In the imagery of the soldier-narrator, a blend of humour and pathos obtains when Maresko, 'A worn, faded creature … turned pale and huddled up' on hearing the 'mewing' of the little gun close by. (ll.21 and 53 respectively, 'Semeystvo papashi Maresko')

The human sphere —— The single most common theme from which Babel's protagonists import imagery is that which concerns human characteristics, functions and emotions, or physical, bodily parts. Each of the six *skaz* categories draws heavily on human imagery in their tropes.[359] Lyutov is the most frequent user, with half his tropes employing human-derived images.

And the inanimate or the inert are often invested with feelings or capabilities belonging to man. Bullets complain and tremble with impatience in 'Smert' Dolgushova'; the village of Chesniki wallows like a stricken soldier in 'Posle boya': 'The village was swimming and swelling, a crimson clay oozed from its dismal wounds';[360] while that frontier to chaos, the cacophonous Zbruch full of gleaming hollows and serpentine trails of the moon in the cycle's opening story, does not alter its sinister qualities even when its later mood is one of serenity: 'the noiseless Zbruch rolled a dark, glassy wave'.[361]

Herein lies the essence of Babel's power to alarm and disturb the reader. Nature, the surroundings, the artefacts of war – everything is invested with the sentiments of his central persona. So often is Lyutov's suffering or joy transferred to his environment. The moon is both whore and comforting mother, darkness and funereal garland,[362] and in another example of animal imagery engendering a sinister mood, the earth is portrayed as if lying in wait for him: 'The earth lay like a cat's back, overgrown with the gleaming fur of crops',[363] whereupon an ambush is sprung upon him and his companion at the top of a nearby hill on which even a village bespeaks hostility: 'On a hillock crouched the mud-walled hamlet of Klekotov.'[364]

Grotesque effects are also created through the use of human-derived imagery in synecdoche. In the depressing, weed-ridden cemetery at Kozin, Lyutov quotes from the inscriptions on a Jewish memorial stone which recalls four generations of rabbis. A physical feature is used to characterize the respective virtues or accomplishments of two of the deceased and in so doing renders them absurd in a way that is reminiscent of Gogol:[365] 'Azriil, son of Ananias, *mouth* of Jehovah. Iliya, son of Azriil, *brain*, entering into single combat with oblivion.'[366] While the Cossacks and other protagonists of *Konarmiya* only employ approximately half the amount of human-derived images that Lyutov does,[367] the imagery is likewise stamped with the personality and perception of the individual protagonist. I have already cited Gedali's passages of prosopopoeia concerning the Revolution, in which the old man voices his confusion over its identity and its exponents,[368] and it is again the Revolution which inspires further allegory in 'Zhizneopisaniye Pavlichenki, Matveya Rodionycha'. Here, Pavlichenko describes how it provided a timely intervention into the problems of his own aimless and oppressed existence. He allegorizes the year, rather than the events, in language which embodies the spirited rhythm of a ballad: 'pyat' propashchik godov propadal ya, pokuda ko kne, k propashchemu, ne pribyl v gosti vosemnadtsatyy godok. Na vesyolykh zherebtsakh pribyl on, na kabardinskikh svoikh loshadkakh. Bol'shoy oboz vyol on za soboy i vsyakiye pesni.' ('five wasteful years I wasted, until the little year eighteen came to visit me, a wastrel. On spirited stallions it arrived, on its Kabardin horses. In its wake it brought a large convoy of wagons and all manner of songs.')[369]

Amid the tautology and bluster, the Cossack's perception of what took place is couched in terms appropriate to the parade of a victorious warrior chieftain. The imagery adopts an epic and masculine tone in the second sentence, having firstly sounded a note of affection in the personified diminutive 'godok' ('little year'). The mood switches again as Pavlichenko's allegory takes a different turn, and rhyme is added to the insistent rhythm: 'I ekh, lyuba zhe ty moya, vosemnadtsatyy godok! I neuzheli ne pogulyat' nam s toboy yeshcho razok, krovinochka ty moya, vosemnadtsatyy godok?' ('And eh, little year eighteen, you sweet love of mine! Is it that we shan't walk out together just one more time, little year eighteen, you little drop of blood of mine?')[370] While his pleasure at what happened is evident from the rhythmically symmetrical diminutives, masculine imagery cedes to the feminine imagery of courtship. The Revolution assumes the role of a betrothed with whom one walks out and whom one cossets. A colloquial, feminine, adjectival substantive, 'lyuba' ('love/sweet'), is applied to the masculine 'godok' ('little year'), and while feminine images dominate where masculine had before, the tonal beat, providing an ethos of epic masculinity, is still very much in evidence. The courtship is brief and exciting and Pavlichenko remembers its fleeting pleasures with regret, his words resembling the songs that have been squandered: 'We've squandered your songs, drunk up your wine, established your credentials, only your chroniclers remain to us. Eh sweet love of mine!'[371] The Cossack's view of the momentous events reflects his personal interests. The Revolution for him was a swashbuckling, victorious general in whose wake one followed and a sweet girl to be wooed, won and savoured. However, the dominant interest for Pavlichenko, in his espousal of the revolutionary cause, is the opportunity it affords for bloodshed and violent revenge. Litotes and hyperbole testify to the pleasure that he gained: 'It's not the chroniclers who flew about the Kuban in those days releasing the souls of generals at a distance of one pace, and Matvey Rodionych was lying then in blood at Prikumsk …'[372] His parting words reveal even more the depth of his bitterness for he talks of discovering what life is about as he slowly tramples his master to death: 'I trampled him down for an hour or more and got to know life fully during this time.'[373] More than any other of the cycle, the story represents a uniquely bitter-sweet Cossack view of life.

All four stories of *Na pole chesti* include images imported from the human sphere of activities and, like *Konarmiya,* it is the narrator who monopolizes them. Moreover, despite the absence of a narrator as defined and participatory as Lyutov, signifying a less individualistic colouring of the imagery, there are links with the major cycle. Human sentiments are applied to abstract substantives as in *Konarmiya*; Bidu's eyes, for example, gleam with a 'timid, tender hope', (1.25, 'Na pole chesti') and in 'Kvaker' we encounter an early forerunner of the derisory synecdoches of 'Kladbishche v Kozine': 'What was Ston? A bald *brow* at the tope of a pole.' (1.7, 'Kvaker')[374] In the same story we meet another figure, whose import is as strongly sinister as those Lyutovian images of an alien world in which the inanimate assumes hostile, human or animal capabilities: 'the sun rummaged in upturned corpses'. (ll.83–4, 'Kvaker') The sinister effect of such imagery is also created by the soldiers of the cycle. Ratin's cutting comment on Bidu's masturbation pejoratively juxtaposes human and animal imagery: 'You've found a wife here, swine!' (l.17, 'Na pole chesti'), while the officer-narrator of 'Semeystvo papashi Maresko', in a grimly ironic sequence, contemplates the corpses of the rotting old men dancing to the tune of his men's machine-guns. [375] His reference later to the resumption of enemy fire, 'they bite here', (ll.55–6, 'Semeystvo papashi Maresko') embodying the tone of bravado so often audible in the imagery of *Konarmiya*'s Cossacks, reveals the utter normality for him of the violent events around them.

Natural phenomena —— My statistics show that the primary narrators of both cycles employ more imagery from the sphere of natural phenomena than any other protagonists or secondary narrators (indeed in *Na pole chesti* the narrator is its sole user), and I have already commented on the use that Lyutov makes of pathetic fallacy, whereby natural phenomena mirror or receive his feelings.[376] The moon for example is a frequent concomitant of the primary narrator. In 'Moy pervyy gus' it symbolizes his conscience, reminding Lyutov of his fleeting pleasure and shallow triumph,[377] while in 'Solntse Italii' its role is dynamic as it nurtures his fantasies: 'The naked brilliance of the moon streamed on to it with inexhaustible strength. The damp mould of the ruins flowered like the marble of opera seating.'[378] The flowering mould of Lyutov's imagination finds an echo in the imagery of Konkin, Cossack and political commissar, whose farcical manner of narration embodies images of natural phenomena which are reminiscent of the *byliny*:[379] 'We were giving the Poles the chop down at Belaya Tserkov'. We were giving it to them hot and strong, *even the trees bent low*'[380] and his Cossack assistant in the butchery is portrayed thus: 'But here's Spiridion before me like a leaf before grass.'[381] Cossack recruitment of natural phenomena in tropes is, however, generally similar to the use that other protagonists make of it in the cycle. It characterizes basic, peasant roots. Lenin's perspicacity merits this exclamation from a Cossack: 'and how do you drag it from the heap, but he hits it straightway like a chicken does grain …',[382] while Galin employs an equally homespun image to depict the work of the Communist Party: 'we're cleaning the kernel of its shell for you, a little time will pass, you'll see this kernel cleaned'.[383] Such imagery not only characterizes those who utter it but also exposes them and the respective stimulant of each image to ridicule, here Lenin and the Communist Party.

Of the six metaphors of the primary narrator in *Na pole chesti* whose images are imported from the sphere of natural phenomena, only one compares in originality with those of Lyutov. I refer to Babel's transformation of Vidal's 'les mots les plus durs pleuvent sur le misérable …',[384] in which the trite epithet 'durs' and the figurative verb 'pleuvent' are replaced by a living image from the same thematic category: '*an arid hail* fell on him of those … words …' (ll.27–8, *Na pole chesti*). Other metaphors which employ imagery from this category are deliberately trite; they stress, for example, the colourless lugubriosity of Ston: 'he behaved with *wooden* immobility … Ston's diligence *bore fruit*'. (ll.11–12 and 62 respectively, 'Kvaker')[385]

Fabric —— An equally fossilized image drawn from another sphere is also reserved for the dull Quaker: 'From this day Ston considered himself *invested* [literally '*clad in*'] by Providence with a special mission.' (ll.48–9, 'Kvaker')[386] The literal meaning of the participle, 'clad in', places this image in the thematic category which I have designated 'fabric'. While this sphere is but a minor source of Babel's themes, it does produce images of originality in both cycles. I refer in particular to the soldier-narrator's references to Maresko in *Na pole chesti* in which epithets and a metonymy so decry the incongruous civilian that our compassion is immediately aroused: 'The character makes his entrance. A worn, faded creature. Got up in a Sunday frock-coat. The frock-coat is bespattered with mud ... The Sunday frock-coat turned pale and huddled up.' (ll.21–2 and 53 respectively, 'Semeystvo papashi Maresko') Similarly, in *Konarmiya,* metonymy recruits from the same thematic sphere but with sinister results; the shadowy figure of Pan Romual'd, a priest's treacherous assistant is depicted thus: 'and somewhere in the snaky twilight a monk's cassock whirled ... But that evening his narrow cassock stirred at every curtain, swept furiously along all the passages and smiled at all who wanted to drink vodka.'[387] Curtains embody the threat of enveloping doom in 'Smert' Dolgushova', 'The curtains of battle were drawing towards the town',[388] and in 'Put' v Brody', 'Bullets extended along the road like threads.'[389] The use of everyday, domestic objects as images of war gives a chilling effect. A feeling of personal hostility emerges strongly in a metaphor in 'Pan Apolek'. The artist's wish to relate his heretical story of Christ to Lyutov is at first thwarted by the brooding presence of the warden of the Catholic church: 'He hangs before us the faded linen of silence and hostility.'[390]

But it is not just the pathetic or the sinister that is achieved by images from this thematic sphere; Babel's versatility is seen in metaphors of *ostraneniye* in which domestic imagery combines with natural phenomena to signal, albeit fleetingly, the primary narrator's sense of well-being in 'Moy pervyy gus': 'Evening wrapped me in the life-giving moisture of its twilight sheets'. The figure is the first half of a sequence of anaphora in which human derived imagery continues the domestic theme, as Lyutov alludes to the maternal nature of the comfort that he now feels: 'evening laid a mother's palms on my burning brow'.[391] The comfort registered by Lyutov in 'Moy pervyy gus'', however, is short lived; his tropes reveal an overwhelmingly depreciatory view[392] and this thematic category of imagery plays no less a role in this than any other. Comfort is replaced by anguish in 'Argamak' as he surveys the mess that he has made of a horse's back because of his lack of horsemanship: 'On his back ichor twisted like lace between the strips of torn flesh'.[393] The delicacy of the vehicle's image 'like lace', when applied to ichor oozing from the animal's torn back, has the reader wincing along with the narrator and is as disconcerting an image as any that can be found in either cycle.

Miscellaneous —— I have drawn up broad categories of theme from which Babel selects the majority of his figurative images; there are indeed tropes whose imported images do not belong in any of these categories. However, it is in the imagery of the Cossacks that we encounter the greatest proportion of what I have designated miscellaneous imported imagery.[394] I would suggest that the reason for this is the predilection of Babel's Cossack narrators to exaggerate. Lyutov indeed comments on Konkin's farcical mode of narration: 'Konkin related this story to us at a halt with his customary buffoonery.'[395] In their striving to portray their feats of savagery and their respective situation, men such as Balmashov, Pavlichenko and Konkin resort to hyperbolic tropes which recruit from a less conservative range of themes than those of the primary narrator. The result is a language that is rich in colour, humour, bombast, unwitting self-derision and, at times, pathos, as can be seen in the following quotations: 'The general's eyes blinked before me like lanterns. A red sea opened before me';[396] 'all three of us had a fever in our bones';[397] '… treason has abandoned its boots so that the floorboards in the plundered house don't creak'.[398] Konkin's anger is a red sea, Balmashov's ardour is heat in the bones and treason is an insidious, barefoot presence.

Transfer

Section II, Table 4, depends for its results on the process of restating a trope in literal terms. This affords the opportunity of determining whether the stimulant is complemented by an imported image of a like generic kind. Such an analysis enables us to gain a greater perception of the psyche of the respective protagonists and to develop an understanding of the author's Weltanschauung. I have examined Babel's process of figurative transfer between stimulant and imported image from aspects of both sense and animation.

In sensuous terms, Lyutov's metaphors appear to contain more visual imagery than the narrator of *Na pole chesti* – 36.8 per cent compared with 19.4 per cent. However, when one takes into account the amount of visual imagery employed by both narrators in metaphors of the most common synaesthetic type (namely, an abstract stimulant realizing an imported visual image), there is in fact a greater proportion of figurative visual imagery in the minor cycle – 74.2 per cent compared with Lyutov's 67 per cent. The difference is slight, however, and emphasizes how visual Babel's portrayal of war is in both cycles. It is synaesthetic transfer which creates imagery of the greatest interest and provides deeper insight into the creative thought processes of the author, for it represents the fusion of unlike generic entities and produces metaphors of startling originality. On one level it can be defined as a sensation experienced at a point distinct from that of stimulation. For example, an abstract concept, 'death', is visualized as a 'greedy thief' in 'Kladbishche v Kozine'.[399] My use of the term 'synaesthetic transfer' embraces, however, not only the interplay of sensuous planes but also that of animation and inanimation. Death in Lyutov's metaphor of inscription is personified, thus an abstract concept is not only perceived on a visual level but also in an animate form.

I return firstly, however, to the statistics of sensuous transfer. Lyutov's figures indicate that a greater range of metaphoric transfer is present in his prose compared with both the narrator of *Na pole chesti* and the other *skaz* categories of both cycles. 10 per cent of his metaphors comprise a like-auditory transfer,[400] while only three such figures occur in the whole of the minor cycle and none in the other *skaz* categories of *Konarmiya*. Lyutov's range of synaesthetic metaphors is also greater. He uses fewer of the type common to other protagonists, namely an abstract stimulant realizing an imported visual image, but employs 13.2 per cent of differently based syn-aesthetic transfer. The fact that the Cossacks and other protagonists of the major cycle also employ a range of synaesthetic imagery that is not found in *Na pole chesti* indicates development both in Babel's figurative formulation and in his *skaz* technique.[401] In the short period between the two war cycles, Babel's figurative range has undergone a considerable process of matura-tion. Apart from the seventeen instances (54.8 per cent) of abstract to visual transfer in the metaphors of *Na pole chesti*'s narrator, only one instance of another synaesthetic type is to be found, namely abstract to auditory transfer. In *Konarmiya,* the 13.2 per cent of Lyutov's metaphors, which are synaesthetically different from the common abstract to visual transfer, include the reverse variety – visual to abstract – of which none exists in *Na pole chesti*. The greater range of synaesthetic transfer in the major cycle is not, however, the sole preserve of the primary narrator. In common with their counterparts in *Na pole chesti*, Cossacks and others employ a consider-able amount of abstract to visual transfer but not to the exclusion of other synaesthetic types as happens in the first cycle. Together they employ slightly more of these rarer tropes than Lyutov.[402]

There is also a trend in Lyutov's prose away from like-abstract transfer in his metaphors. The narrator of *Na pole chesti* is closer to each of the other *skaz* categories in his degree of usage of this type,[403] while Lyutov's 9.4 per cent represents a reduction, which is explained by the author's desire to involve the reader mostly in visual, less frequently in auditory, or occa-sionally other sensuous perceptions of his central persona's distorted world, and in so doing to shock or stun him. Often an imported abstract image complementing an abstract stimulant constitutes the most banal of imagery and is thus chiefly the preserve of those whose language is hackneyed or whose perceptions are dulled and less individualistic.

As I have stated, Babel's imagery in both cycles appeals frequently to the visual mode of perception, less to the auditory and seldom to smell, taste or touch. The rare involvement of these last three senses is itself significant. Figurative tactile contact, as with smell and taste, would place the reader at once in the centre of Babel's scenarios but he prefers to keep him at a distance, mostly viewing through Lyutov's prism or listening either to his sound-track or, less frequently, to those of others. We thus remain apart from the events, observing and reacting from the outside rather than seeing and feeling from within.

Animation (i) —— The results of my analysis of the degree of animation in Babel's metaphors show a considerable degree of correlation between equivalent categories of the two cycles. Both primary narrators employ only 16 to 18 per cent of like-animate transfer while the Cossacks' and soldiers' imagery is far more prone to this, making up 53 and 46.7 per cent respectively. Moreover, since the *skaz* categories average only 20 per cent usage of like-inanimate transfer, the figures would seem to indicate, thus far, a greater degree of animation in the imagery of protagonists other than Lyutov and the narrator of *Na pole chesti*, with a possible consequent loss of interest and impact in the latters' tropes. This is not the case, however, since both narrators demonstrate a marked predilection for synaesthetic transfer, in which an *inanimate* stimulant realizes an imported *animate* image; thereby, as on a sensuous level, fusing unlikes, and creating images of freshness and vigour. The reverse synaesthetic process of an animate main idea leading to an inanimate imported image is far less common and indeed is virtually non-existent in the prose of Lyutov.

The increase in usage of this type of transfer in four of the other *skaz* categories[404] is explained by its suitability for invective and jocularity: 'Roll, Wheel,'[405] puns a Cossack in 'Kombrig dva', as he addresses the ever-progressing Kolesnikov. Irony is intended in the nickname used for Vasiliy the cook, whose grossness is portrayed in his love-making with a washer-woman in 'Vecher'. Lyutov records: 'Four feet with fat heels were thrust out into the cool, and we saw Irina's amorous calves and Vasiliy's big toe with its crooked black nail. – My little cornflower, [Vasilyok,] – whispered the woman.'[406] Vasiliy, the owner of the crooked black toenail, who had earlier wooed his partner by inviting her to squash fleas with him,[407] now becomes 'a little cornflower/vasilyok'. Lyutov's irony and pejoration rely on more subtle imagery, hence the dearth of animate – inanimate transfer in his prose. Nevertheless, in 'Kvaker' the narrator of the first cycle has recourse to it when depicting Ston's woodenness and his inability to relate to his fellow men. Our grotesque view of him is created from the outset by tropes such as: 'He behaved with wooden immobility' and 'What was Ston? A bald brow at the top of a pole.' (ll.11–12 and 7 respectively, 'Kvaker') Imagery of this farcical nature is more akin to the language of Konkin or Pavlichenko; the fact that it occurs in the narrator's language of the first cycle indicates a blurring of the latter's psyche with those of subsequent Cossack narrators and points to the process of refinement that Babel's *skaz* technique and use of imagery underwent in his creation of Lyutov.

Sensuous transfer in Konarmiya —— All Babel's narrators and protagonists evince a strong preference for visual imagery but it is Lyutov who employs a greater degree of like-visual transfer in his metaphors. In 'Solntse Italii', for example, only 6 per cent of Sidorov's metaphors are of this type while Lyutov employs 46 per cent in an approximately equivalent amount of prose. In 'Perekhod cherez Zbruch', visual imagery creates a world of gentle animation: fields of poppy flower, the midday wind plays in the yellowing rye, and virginal buckwheat rises on the horizon like a monastery. However, the tranquillity recedes with the Arcadian province of Volhynia which swoons and expires in imagery of visual personification: 'Peaceful Volhynia curves away, Volhynia recedes from us into the pearly haze of birch groves, it crawls into flowery knolls and with weakened arms becomes entangled in the undergrowth of hops.'[408] Visual imagery continues the break with tranquillity, foreshadowing the turbulent events to come in symbolically violent and martial images: 'An orange sun rolls across the sky, like a severed head, a gentle light glows in the gorges of the storm-clouds, the standards of the sunset fly above our heads.'[409] The visual impact of war's destruction and menace is felt in Lyutov's description of Novograd-Volynsk, a town that he situates on the Zbruch.[410] Here in the scorched town amid, 'broken columns and dug into the earth the hooks of old womens' malicious little fingers',[411] the night is torn by the milk of the moon and the face of Sidorov, his Cossack persecutor is a 'lifeless mask'.[412]

Cossacks, like Sidorov or Balmashov, employ fewer metaphors with a totally visual transfer. In 'Sol'', for example, 25 per cent of Balmashov's metaphors comprise a like-visual transfer while 60 per cent employ an abstract to visual transfer, thus indicating a greater need on his part to visualize abstract concepts than the primary narrator displays.[413] Indeed, the considerably greater use of this type of synaesthetic transfer by protagonists other than Lyutov is in the form of cliché or colloquial language, appropriate to Cossack or peasant roots. Galin, in a dense paragraph of abstract to visual synaesthetic figures in 'Vecher', describes Lyutov's future readiness to act when the revolutionary struggle is won: 'a little time will pass, you'll see this kernel cleaned, then you'll take your finger out of your nose'.[414] In 'Sol'', Balmashov paints a picture of criminal misdoings at Fastov railway station, but then reminds himself that he should report only what he has seen: 'don't go dragging the lord's dirt about'[415] – 'the lord's dirt' is his image for the concept of wrongdoing. The railwaymen, harassed by the presence of the black marketeers, are given time, not to recover, but 'to let their chests heave' i.e. 'to get their breath back'.[416] Balmashov's men, influenced by his eloquent plea concerning the safety of the peasant woman, are portrayed as 'boiling over with my truth'.[417] His suspicion of the woman's deception is depicted thus: 'And a little thought flew about, like a bird',[418] and he concludes that traitors, like the woman, 'are dragging us into the pit and want to turn back the flow'.[419] Each time an abstract concept is translated into a visual image, suspicion is a flitting bird, treachery a pit, the Revolution a river, and so on. There is a hint of parody, too, in Babel's choice of image concerning Balmashov's suspicion: a bird was Gorkiy's symbol of the Revolution. Here, it is reserved for a self-proclaimed exponent of the Revolution – Balmashov – who justifies his subsequent act of murder as being in its cause.

The desire on the part of the Cossacks and other protagonists to visualize the abstract stems from a need to place, in concrete terms of reference, feelings and emotions which they cannot otherwise adequately express. It is also indicative of their need to stress the personal vividness of an experience to which they feel justice is not done through language of abstraction.

Unfortunately, any enhancement of their impressions is lost, if the image is hackneyed or obscure. Afon'ka Bida exemplifies this in 'Smert' Dolgushova'. His analogy, which compares grabbing at food or succour with rushing recklessly into battle, brings the regimental commander to heel: 'Don't trot over there, Taras Grigor'yevich, there's five versts to go; how will you cut them down when the horses are done for ... There's no need to grab – there's time aplenty to taste a virgin's fruits.'[420] Emotion makes a further sequence more obscure. The disjointed nature of the images, reflecting Bida's disturbed state of mind, is enhanced by the synaesthetic transfer of abstract stimulant to imported visual image: 'If my notion's right about the divisional commander ... if he's replaced, *then soap the withers and knock away the supports. Period.*'[421]

The use of this type of synaesthetic transfer is the principal means for the Cossacks of exercising a greater control over the events around them and their environment, just as the primary narrator does through his lenses of distortion. The inner perspective on the world of each protagonist is laid bare in his formation of imagery. Sidorov's visualizing of Italy shows a land that is ripe for his domination, for he writes of its readiness for revolution and of his own leading part in events: 'In Italy the earth is smouldering. There's much that is ready there. It only needs a couple of shots. I'll fire one of them.'[422] As with Balmashov, an abstract concept is realised in a visual cliché, that embodies a vainglorious, bombastic ring. Pavlichenko manifests an equal arrogance, although his sequence of synaesthetic metaphor and simile contains originality created by *ostraneniye*: 'Liberation lay down around me in the fields, the grass in all world rustles, the skies swing about above me like a many-keyed accordion ...'[423]

Such synaesthetic metaphor caters for each of Sidorov's needs: the casual – 'However tail to the side and joking apart ...'; the menacing – 'and whether we shall wipe your well-to-do noses for you'; the political – 'Volin rigs himself up in apostolic vestments and scrambles up to Leninism from anarchy'; and the sentimental – 'Italy has entered my heart'.[424] Lyutov's equivalent tropes reflect a psyche that is not in control, an inner being that is frightened and confused amid a sinister and largely alien world. 'Timorous destitution then closes in over my couch',[425] he writes in the first story of the cycle. War itself is seen as an enveloping force in 'Smert' Dolgushova': 'The curtains of war were drawing towards the town.'[426] Sidorov's persecution of him is visualized as the hairy paw of his spleen,[427] while the primary narrator's imagination, his avenue of temporary escape, becomes a 'blind happy peasant woman', that swirls ahead of him like July mist, an imagination which, like his dreams, 'leapt about me like kittens'[428] and can be shredded by Sidorov's words in his letter: 'Sidorov, anguished killer, tore into shreds the pink wadding of my imagination and dragged me into the corridors of his sane-minded madness.'[429]

Such tropes demonstrate Babel's mastery of the technique of *ostraneniye* or defamiliarization, a process by which the familiar is made to appear bizarre and new. *Ostraneniye* is most frequently achieved through synaesthetic metaphor and is a device which links the prose of Babel to similar effects in poetry and which, in its frequency and daring, associates him with the ornamental trend of prose-writing of the 1920s. Ermolayev points to ornamentalism in *Konarmiya*, commenting in particular on verb-only metaphors which comprise imagery associated with flowing (tech', bryzgat' – to flow, to spurt), usages which exemplify a change from nineteenth-century classical Russian prose.[430] Novitskiy writes of Babel's highly mannered style with its purpose of producing jarring effects. He attributes it to the influence of a Russian school of ornamentalism and compares Babel in his use of bright colours and lapidary figure to Gavriil Derzhavin, a baroque poet.[431] Iribarne also points to Babel's use of spectacle and compares the author in the 'physical grandeur and dazzling opalescence' of his imagery to Lyutov's hero, Pan Apolek.[432] Babel himself acknowledged a desire to retreat from such frequent use of figure in his later works, although the *ostraneniye* that obtains in the figures that he uses to illustrate this intention betokens an irony and an ambivalence that is reminiscent of the vacillant Lyutov:

> There's no need to think that a writer's talent consists in the ability to rhyme or create complicated and unexpected epithets and metaphors. I myself suffered from this at one time and hitherto have been squashing these very metaphors in my works, just like certain rather unclean people who squash insects on their person.[433]

While *ostraneniye* is a characteristic of this literary period, it is not peculiar to the twenties alone. Blok's tragic poem, 'Iz gazet' ('from the Papers'), is built on the device – everything is described from the viewpoint of small, innocent children who know nothing of their mother's suicide,[434] while the nineteenth-century poet Fet portrays a shower of rain thus:

> Two drops splashed on to the glass
> From fragrant limes came honey's scent
> Something came upon the grass
> And on cool leaves its drumming spent.[435]

Babel employs *ostraneniye* to convey Lyutov's sense of disorientation and isolation. Like Fet, he uses it to freshen or make strange natural phenomena: 'In the sky the squint-eyed lantern of the provincial sun goes out';[436] but in the prose of Cossacks or other protagonists there is at times a deliberate over-reaching or exaggeration in both metaphors of synaesthesia and in those in which like-transfer occurs. *Ostraneniye* then cedes to catachresis, the abuse of a trope, with absurd results. Babel surefootedly treads the narrow line which divides *ostraneniye* from catachresis in Lyutov's prose, although the image of the blind peasant woman swirling ahead like July mist may well have been omitted from later editions of 'Solntse Italii' because of its mixed metaphorical or catachrestic qualities. His use of abstract to visual synaesthetic transfer is usually sharp and fresh in the case of the primary narrator: 'Galin tirelessly ransacks the vaults of dead emperors'[437] refers to an account of Russian imperial history, and in 'Perekhod cherez Zbruch' it is one of the same emperors whose bidding has caused the deaths and suffering of many a peasant, 'along the unfading highway leading from Brest to Warsaw built upon the bones of peasants by Nicholas I.'[438] In a gruesomely symbolic image the peasants' bones have become the road's foundations; their dying has been instrumental in the building of the road and is thus equated with its very rubble.

Babel's Cossack narrators, however, regularly transgress the bounds of effective *ostraneniye* with farcical results. In a metaphor of like-visual transfer Balmashov writes: 'And the nice little night's tent was pitched. And in that tent were Chinese lantern stars';[439] and another Cossack voice is heard to bemoan the hardships that they have endured: 'in ordinary times and on days beyond the call, we've been choked with hunger, blistered with cold'.[440] Again, the abstract is visualized, the concepts of hunger and cold are transferred to visual images of pain, something with which the Cossack is familiar both as inflicter and here as victim. Indeed, beneath the brashly violent surface of a Balmashov or Konkin exists a softer being, capable of anger at the suffering of war and revolution, aware of the misery that it inflicts both on his fellow men and on his country: 'I galloped up to him and he'd already grabbed his sword, and down his cheeks tears are flowing, white tears, human milk'[441] – thus writes Konkin of a Polish general who has fallen prisoner to him. Konkin's emotional vulnerability emerges throughout the story; paradoxically, it is his making light of the wound that he suffers which belies the impression of him as a ruthless man of action, for the references that he makes to his own suffering are too casual and too frequent for us to ignore the fact that it has cost him a great deal in physical and emotional terms: 'I'd got a scratch from the morning but was making out O.K.'[442] Litotes is repeatedly used to make light of pain: 'and makes a hole in my leg … and made another draught in my face', and at the end, before he kills the Polish general, he portrays himself thus: 'And then I see – I'm losing more and more, a terrible sleepiness is coming over me, my boots are full of blood, I've had it with him …'[443] Apart from the emotion that he shows in his earlier killing of a horse, 'I felt sorry for the stallion. The stallion was a little Bolshevik, a pure little Bolshevik',[444] he also evinces concern for the wretched state of his fellow soldiers: 'The kids' rags were torn, their little shirts weren't enough to cover their manhood.'[445] The 'iron' of a Savitskiy or Baulin is rendered brittle in the figure of Konkin.

Balmashov, too, manifests concern when he bemoans the fact that the treacherous black marketeer does not suffer in the way that Russia, its land and its people are: 'And seeing that unharmed woman and an unspeakable Russia around us, and the peasants' fields without an ear of corn, and the violated girls, and the comrades who go much to the front but return little …'[446] The incessant beat of anaphora with the particle 'i' ('and') stresses the frenzy of Balmashov's anger whose culmination ends in his murder of the woman: 'I washed this shame from the face of the workers' land and the Republic.'[447]

Other forms of synaesthetic transfer —— The major cycle's range of synaesthetic metaphors is found in all *skaz* categories. Sidorov writes graphically
of his impressions of the front; his imagery assumes a Lyutovian distaste for
the slaughter of war, as an abstract stimulant, 'death' is realized in a two-
fold olfactive and visual image: 'What was ahead? Ahead was the front, the
Cavalry Army and soldiery, smelling of damp blood and human ashes.'[448]
The juxtaposition of the slighting collective noun 'soldatnya' ('soldiery') with
the similarly ending substantive 'Konarmiya' ('Cavalry Army') precedes
a symmetrical arrangement of dual imported images. In the peasant's wails
over a moribund horse in 'Nachal'nik konzapasa', there is a reversal of the
most frequent form of synaesthesia, a visual stimulant is realized in an
abstract image, a wretched horse becomes an orphan: 'How is she to get up,
the orphan … She'll snuff it, the orphan …'[449] Equally, in 'Berestechko',
ellipsis creates a similar transfer in the words of the political commissar
who addresses a crowd thus: 'You are the power.'[450] The concrete becomes
abstract, the animate inanimate, but the effect of such political clichés is
unconvincing and dull.

It is the tropes of Lyutov which exploit unusual synaesthetic transfer in
arresting fashion. In 'Smert' Dolgushova', the visual image of the setting
sun assumes an abstract significance as Afon'ka Bida arrives. The pre-
positive metaphor fuses visual and abstract imagery which glorifies the
Cossack: 'Framed in the nimbus of the sunset, Afon'ka Bida was galloping
towards us.'[451] By contrast, in the same story, imagery of the Cossacks or
other protagonists which also fuses the abstract and the visual has little
impact, such as the dubbing of the men as 'Devki' ('Girls') and Lyutov as
'gad' ('a skunk/vile creature').[452] Implicit in the respective visual images
are the concepts of inconstancy and baseness, although the first is uttered in
jocular fashion.

But the synaesthetic versatility of Lyutov's tropes is apparent in an
example from 'U svyatogo Valenta'. Here an auditory stimulant is realized
by an imported visual image of violence: 'A hoarse wail *tore* our hearing
asunder.'[453] The dramatic moment occurs at the end of the story when a
picture of a persecuted Christ is revealed in the desecrated church. Lyutov,
who deems it the most extraordinary image of God that he had seen in his
life, subsequently twice depicts Christ's mouth as 'torn',[454] thus equating
his own and others' shock at seeing the image, with the pain portrayed in the
picture. The hoarse cry which tore their hearing could indeed have come
from the torn mouth of Christ. His pain is thus transferred to the onlookers.
In 'Kombrig dva' we see a similar transfer from the auditory to the visual
plane: 'A groaning hurrah reached us, torn by the wind.'[455] The image of a
sound being lacerated conveys the desperate mood of apprehension of the
troops uttering a reluctant greeting to their new commander, as well as
the pre-battle tension of Budyonny, Lyutov and other onlookers. A similar
moment occurs in 'Zamost'ye' when synaesthetic transfer again creates
tension, as Lyutov, gazing at the town, is made aware of the murder taking
place there: 'and in the silence I heard the distant whiff of a groan'.[456] The

auditory stimulant is realized in a pre-positive image which is simultaneously visual, auditory, olfactory and tactile.

Silence is invested with the power of murder in 'Perekhod cherez Zbruch': 'Everything is deadened by silence',[457] writes Lyutov as an auditory stimulant is again realized in a pre-positive imported visual image, that is charged with a tension, enhanced by the juxtaposition of the harsh sounding figurative participle 'ubito' (deadened/killed') and the incongruously soft stimulant 'tishinoy' ('silence/hush'). This metaphor directly follows one which embodies a visual to abstract transfer, that is to say a reversal of Babel's most common synaesthetic type. Destitution assumes the role of darkness as Lyutov settles down to sleep: 'Timorous destitution closes in over my couch.'[458] Both tropes ominously foreshadow the story's climax, when Lyutov discovers that he had bedded down beside the violently murdered corpse of the father of the household.

In the tropes-saturated second paragraph of the same story, another metaphor gains in prominence because of its unique synaesthetic properties. I have already referred to the vivid quality of the tropes of 'Perekhod cherez Zbruch',[459] tropes which convey the passage of time from noon to sunset, from peace to war, and which effect a contrast in nature, and the narrator's moods. Among them is a figure which has a pivotal function, uniting the paradisaic calm of the opening visual images with the roaring confusion and cacophony of the closing ones. It finally halts the languid pace, changes the mood and moves the visually perceptible world of day into the audibly received world of night. The preceding visual figures of epic grandeur are succeeded by a metaphor whose stimulant is both visual and olfactive, and whose imported image focuses attention, not on the glory of war, but on the ugliness and unseemliness of its counterpart, death.

> An orange sun rolls across the sky like a severed head, a gentle light glows in the gorges of the storm-clouds, and the standards of the sunset fly above our heads. *The smell of yesterday's blood and slaughtered horses drips into the cool of evening.* The blackened Zbruch roars and twists the foaming knots of its rapids.[460]

As with the example quoted above from 'Zamost'ye',[461] the imported image is perceptible on more than one sensuous level, as indeed is the stimulant. We see and smell the dried blood and we see, hear and feel it being spilt. It is as if our senses are taunted by Babel and we become aware of life trickling away. The power of the image is exceptional, even among the figures of *Konarmiya*. It brings the trail of glory to a sickening halt and links the visual imagery that has dominated to the auditory imagery that follows. 'Kaplet' ('drips') simultaneously crystallizes, on visual, auditory and tactile planes, a microcosm of horror which both complements and contrasts with the fury to be unleashed in the waters of the Zbruch: 'it is full of din, whistling and singing which thunders above snaking moon trails and gleaming hollows'.[462] The crescendo of noise of the river in spasm is heightened by the lull, the false calm that 'kaplet' ('drips') induces. The metaphor encapsulates the nausea that the narrator repeatedly feels in the cycle.

Auditory transfer —— I have already commented on the originality of imported auditory images as part of Babel's range of synaesthetic metaphors. His versatility is also seen in figures of a like-auditory transfer, although their use is almost entirely restricted to the primary narrators of both cycles. Indeed, only one example is to be found in all the other *skaz* categories, 'Not far from us a little 12-centimetre cat mewed.' (ll.53–4, 'Semeystvo papashi Maresko') The pre-positive auditory figure revitalizes the hackneyed visual image with which it is juxtaposed. The Cossacks and other protagonists do not assail our ears with auditory imagery; this is left to Lyutov to exploit, albeit sparingly in comparison with his use of visual imagery.[463] Its relative infrequency, however, does not diminish the powerful and disconcerting effect it can have. In 'Solntse Italii', a story which draws symbolically on visual images of light and shade to emphasize the polarities existing between Lyutov and Sidorov, auditory imagery also finds a place. The final visual imagery of menace is preceded by an auditory image that echoes Lyutov's sense of disquiet: '*And there's the night full of distant and wearisome pealing*, a square of light in the damp gloom and in it Sidorov's deathly face, a lifeless mask, suspended above the yellow flame of the candle.'[464] Such isolated, brief use of sound is rare in Babel's cycles, however, for when it does occur, auditory imagery is usually concentrated in a rapid succession of images which build to a crescendo. In 'Vecher', Babel exploits just such a sequence to create bathos, by depicting the sudden subsidence of noise:

> The thundering machinery of the train's printing press began to creak and fell silent, the dawn drew a line at the earth's edge, the door to the kitchen gave a whistle and opened slightly. Four feet with fat heels were thrust out into the cool, and we saw Irina's amorous calves and Vasily's big toe with its crooked, black nail.[465]

The opening three auditory images are interrupted by a visual image of an incongruously grandiose kind. After the final screech of the printing press comes silence and the dawn is poetically viewed in the distance. A second rapid closing-in of Lyutov's focus then follows which brings us swiftly back to earth and the sordidness of the scene which confronts the primary narrator. An almost coy whistle of the door signals the act of copulation which follows, and contributes to the generally bathetic tone that is struck by the primary narrator throughout the story. Lyutov's lens moves swiftly between close-up and distance with a speed that creates anti-climax and enhances the satirical effect.

Such auditory series can, however, produce the opposite effect: climax instead of anti-climax. In 'Smert' Dolgushova', with Lyutov and his driver Grishchuk stranded between two walls of fire and facing a volley of shots from a Polish scout, Lyutov records: 'Grishchuk turned back, all four wheels of his cart *squealing*. – Grishchuk! – I cried through the *whistling* and the wind. – It's a laugh, – he answered gloomily. – We're done for! – I exclaimed ...'[466] The auditory images I have emphasized are unremarkable, yet their proximity, coupled with the alliterative repetition of sibilants and the terse interchange of the protagonists, enhances the drama of the occasion. Enemy bullets are also the focus of auditory imagery in a sequence of the same story; again, it is the concentration of sound imagery, this time with onomatopoeia, that creates drama: 'Bullets whine and scream. Their plaintiveness grows unbearably.' 'Puli skulyat i vzvizgivayut. Zhaloba narastayet nevynosimo.'[467] The three auditory images are then complemented by three visual ones, as Lyutov moves from one sensuous plane to another: 'Bullets wound the earth and swarm in it, quivering with impatience.'[468]

In 'Kombrig dva' the process is reversed. The narrator has followed events visually, to the point where Kolesnikov whirls in pillars of dust and leads his men off to battle. The Cossack's earlier lonely walk back to his men, bearing his burden of new office, is described in a process of reverse artistic foreshortening, a whole landscape is dominated by the figure of a man: 'And suddenly – on the expanse of the earth, on the furrowed and yellow nakedness of the fields we could see only the narrow back of Kolesnikov, with his dangling arms and sunken grey-capped head.'[469] The narrator's eyes, a pair of binoculars, and the reports of an observer in a tree above him, provide further visual details of events. But as we approach the climax and Kolesnikov's leading of his men into battle is acknowledged by a curt 'yest'' ('right')[470] from Budyonnyy, Babel switches Lyutov's perception from the visual mode to the auditory. Lyutov's ears and not his eyes become our filter. Four sound images follow each other in rapid succession and the tension is further increased in a final metaphor of paradox: 'The hurrah fell silent. The cannonade was stifled. Needless shrapnel burst over the wood. *And we heard the pregnant silence of slaughter.*'[471] Three of the four images depict the abatement of noise, and Lyutov, now more remote from events, conveys his anguish in a masterly paradoxical image which portrays the sudden onset of silence. The fourth figure creates a new level of suspense and in its inclusion of a final, chilling, visual image, 'rubki' (literally a 'chopping' or 'felling'), encapsulates the horror of mass slaughter.

Yevtushenko, in his moving denunciation of anti-Semitism and mass slaughter in 'Babiy Yar' employs a similarly paradoxical image and oxymoron:

Wild grasses rustle above Babiy Yar.
The trees look sternly
                                     judgemental.
In everything here the scream of silence
                                  and, bareheaded,
I feel,
                                  myself slowly greying.
I am myself
                                  like a *scream of*
                                  unbroken *silence*,
above the buried thousands upon thousands.[472]

The first published version of 'Kombrig dva'[473] differs substantially from any subsequent editions at this point of paradox. The fact that the second publication and further editions omit the passage quoted below indicates that the alterations to the original text were by Babel himself, alterations which illustrate the author's honing of his technique of imagery formation. The first published version is far more verbose:

– Right, – answered Budyonnyy.
And at that moment *the first Polish shell began to trace its wailing flight above us.*
– They're cantering, – said an observer.
– Right, – answered Budyonnyy, lit a cigarette and closed his eyes.[474]
A barely audible hurrah receded from us like a gentle song.
– They're at full gallop, – said the observer, shaking the branches.
Budyonnyy was smoking, not opening his eyes.
The cannonade filled the air with dust, intensified, flashed like lightning, darkened the firmament, which it hammered with crashes of thunder.
– The brigade is attacking the enemy, – sang out the observer from up above.[475]

Here Babel's auditory imagery, which I have emphasized, is not concentrated but interspersed with trite visual imagery which diminishes rather than heightens the dramatic effect. The observer's comments also are obtrusive and superfluous. The second auditory image of a scarcely audible 'hurrah' which moved away like a tender song strikes altogether the wrong note and clashes with the tense atmosphere created by the earlier successful synaesthetic metaphor: 'A groaning hurrah, torn by the wind reached us.'[476] The third sequence, with its trite hyperbolic images of thunder and lightning, appears forced and effete in comparison with the tautness and tension of the ensuing sequence which Babel did retain: 'The hurrah fell silent. The cannonade was stifled. Needless shrapnel burst over the wood. And we heard the pregnant silence of slaughter.'[477] These last tropes illustrate the clumsy over-reaching of the preceding sequence and justify Babel's omission of it. Indeed, the sureness of touch that he demonstrated in paring the verbose pedestrianism of Vidal's prose is in evidence here in the revision of his own work.

Animation (ii) —— There are, as I have already noted, close similarities between the two cycles in the amount of like and unlike transfer of animate and inanimate imagery within each respective pair of skaz categories.[478] Where the primary narrators differ from the rest of the protagonists is in their relative rejection of like-animate transfer in preference for unlike transfer, that is to say in the realization of an inanimate stimulant by an imported animate image. More than half their respective metaphors include this while the Cossacks, French soldiers and other protagonists use it in only a quarter or less of theirs. This difference in metaphor formation helps explain, at least in Lyutov's case, the greater range of synaesthetic metaphors in his prose and indicates another feature of Babel's development in figurative imagery between his first and second cycles. Animation of the inanimate is a further dimension of synaesthetic transfer which enhances the originality of Lyutov's tropes and lends them an aesthetically pleasing quality. The most common synaesthetic metaphor in any *skaz* category is that of an abstract – and hence inanimate – stimulant becoming an imported image that is visual and animate, as for example in Lyutov's reporting of Apolek's heretical story of Christ, in which: 'the bee of sorry had stung him on the heart'. [479] In the introduction to 'Pan Apolek' another example of the same synaesthetic type is found in Lyutov's first description of an Apolek painting: 'I remember: between straight, bright walls *stood* the *gossamer* stillness of a summer morning.' [480] The peaceful beauty of a summer morning is captured in the dual pre-positive pairing of verb and epithet. The completely fossilized 'stoyala' ('stood') is revitalized through its juxtaposition with 'the gossamer stillness'; it is as if the silence or peace stands suspended between the two walls, a calm that is, in the light of what follows, both incongruous and fragile.

Stories which display a high proportion of inanimate to animate transfer in Lyutov's tropes include 'Perekhod cherez Zbruch' (70 per cent) and 'Smert' Dolgushova' (76.5 per cent). By comparison, in the latter only some 5.9 per cent of the metaphors of both Cossacks or other protagonists comprise the same transfer. [481] So often in Lyutov's prose is the inanimate imbued with life; Babel's primary narrator tends to slap rather than to breathe life into his surroundings. Before we hear the screaming lamentation of bullets and witness their infestation in 'Smert' Dolgushova', 'the sun wallowed in the purple dust'. [482] In 'Vecher', the incongruous vitality with which Lyutov invests the abstract and the inanimate is a prime means of reflecting his incongruity with his milieu and his general disorientation. The endowment of human characteristics and capabilities upon the inert and the lifeless by the central narrator creates satire. The printing press roars and screeches, 'the darting lights of the printing press burn irrepressibly, like the passion of machinery', [483] and passion of another sort, 'the hollow and absurd muttering of love', [484] is evident as dawn draws a line, a door whistles, and 'in the black seaweed of the sky drag the stars ...' [485] The vigour of the Communist Party's regulations has not only 'laid headlong rails' [486] for the benefit of literati but has transformed three reprobates into newspaper correspondents, their fervour tearing holes through the motley collection assembled: 'and in the barren dust of the rear the *rebellion and fire* of their leaflets *wear down* the ranks of the dashing Cossacks on leave, the cheating reservists reckoned to be Polish interpreters, and the girls sent to the Political Section of our train as a rest-cure from Moscow.' [487]

Animation of the inanimate contributes to the alien atmosphere of 'Solntse Italii'. Lyutov's surroundings are invested with a dynamism that is wilful and malevolent, sinister and demonic: he sat 'at the live grumbling stove';

he watched the Zbruch as it 'rolled a dark, glassy wave'; he felt the inexhaustible force of the moon pouring down on 'the broken columns and dug into the ground the hooks of old womens' malicious little fingers';[488] and he witnessed how a 'hunchbacked candle ... gasped for breath'[489] while his own dreams 'leaped ... like kittens'.[490]

Lyutov's more restricted use of like-animate transfer[491] seems pallid by comparison however. At the end of the same story, he describes Sidorov's photograph of the Italian royal family, concluding with the phrase 'and with a whole *brood* of princesses'.[492] The thematic equation of human and animal status is reversed in a figure of like-animate transfer in 'Prishchepa'; an abandoned calf is endowed with emotions, as the Cossack completes his revenge: 'The earth smoked beneath him, a blue ring of flame flew out of the chimney and melted away, and in the stable an abandoned bull-calf *began to sob.*'[493]

The real power of the primary narrator to disconcert us rests in those figures where an unlike transfer is made either on a sensuous or animate level or often both. In 'Pesnya' even the pleasurable nostalgia that a Kuban song brings to the narrator is described in prosopopoeia of violence: 'Reverie broke my bones, reverie shook the rotting hay beneath me.'[494] 'Zamost'ye' contains a number of synaesthetic tropes which convey the desperation of weariness and defeat in a hostile world: 'All the stars were stifled by the ink-distended storm-clouds.'[495] The stifling power of the rain distended clouds foreshadows the narrator's preoccupation with death. Later editions replace 'zadusheny' ('stifled') with 'potusheny' ('extinguished'), an altogether less powerful and affecting image, which does not strike the consistent and menacing note of violence, death or hopelessness of other tropes in the story, and which therefore does not seem to be an alteration made by Babel.

'The smoke of unseen killing wandered around us'[496] exemplifies Lyutov's preoccupation with death and, in another figure, the inanimate is imbued with a demonic and distastefully seductive force as the narrator wraps his cloak round himself and prepares to sleep in a water-filled hole: 'The sodden earth opened to me the comforting embrace of the grave.'[497] Above or below ground, visions of death continue to haunt Lyutov; dead mice float past him, the very trees of autumn symbolize a hostile world in a pair of metaphors which comprise inanimate to animate transfer: 'Autumn's ambush encircled our hearts, and the naked corpses of trees, set upright on both feet, began to sway at the crossroads.'[498] Even when transient relief is glimpsed, it is portrayed in terms of menace as Lyutov, in desperation, lights a pile of straw in order to force his landlady into fetching him some food: 'The liberated flame flared up and darted towards me.'[499] Inanimate to animate transfer sometimes also helps to convey a sense of well-being on Lyutov's part, although such occasions are far fewer in number. Significantly, it is only in a dream that the narrator experiences relief or escape from the miseries portrayed in 'Zamost'ye': 'I was stretched out on a *noiseless* couch, and the hay's *caress* on my nape was driving me out of my mind.'[500] In his vision of a paradisaic July evening the sunset plays an active role 'The chalices of the sunset tilted backwards over the village',[501] while in 'Perekhod cherez Zbruch' it is the moon which proffers comfort to the narrator amid his gloom: 'Silence deadened everything, and only the moon, grasping with blue hands, its round, shining, carefree head, roams beneath my window.'[502]

The Cossacks and animate transfer —— '[T]he peasants and their horses are hiding themselves away from our red *eagles* in the woods.'[503] Cossack narrators, like Kurdyukov in this extract show a predilection for like-animate transfer. Here the 'author' of 'Pis'mo' employs a trite image of ennoblement to refer to fellow soldiers. In 'Sol'' and 'Konkin' some 48 per cent of each narrator's metaphors are of this variety, with a consequent diminishing of impact and effect,[504] and a characterizing of their formulators. In his introduction, Balmashov concludes the opening paragraph with the declaration that he will relate only what he himself has seen at Fastov railway station: 'Therefore I'll describe to you only what my eyes have seen *at first hand*.'[505] The figurative adverb creates a clumsy mixed metaphor which exemplifies the Cossack's farcical literary style. A little further on we encounter more examples of fossilized figures comprising totally animate transfer, as the actions of the black marketeers are described: 'Fearlessly they grabbed the handrails, those evil enemies did, they *galloped about* the iron roofs, *circled and swarmed around* and in each hand featured the not unfamiliar salt, up to five poods a bag.'[506] They gallop, encircle and stir things up. Konkin, in his figures of bravado, likewise employs totally animate transfer, as he refers to his personal annihilation of the Poles: 'We were giving them the chop down at Belaya Tserkov' and 'I'll dirty their chasubles for them'.[507]

Neither narrator is averse, however, to the use of unlike transfer in their figures, and while its frequency does not approach that of Lyutov, it does represent an increase above the average for the Cossacks or soldiers of either cycle.[508] It also explains how Balmashov and Konkin are able to include figures of vitality and originality alongside pallid figures of the variety quoted above. The inanimate is imbued with a bizarre life of its own. In 'Sol'', the train is personified in affectionate terms: 'Our little old rascal isn't whirring';[509] the night pitches its tent: 'And the nice little night's tent was pitched', and then goes off duty: 'the night had relinquished its post'; suspicion persistently nags at Balmashov: 'And a little thought flew about like a bird'; and sleep deserts him: 'I get up from my couch, which sleep was hurrying from, like a wolf from a pack of villainous dogs.'[510]

Konkin's tropes can be equally vivid. His use of unlike transfer between stimulant and imported image contributes to the general hyperbolic tone and, in its straining of the bounds of credibility, reveals a Cossack who bears a veneer of bravado and violent ways disguising sensitivity and a deep sense of pain. The exaggerated nature of both his and Balmashov's imagery evokes a sense of disorientation, bewilderment and bitterness akin to that of an equally farcical Lyutov in 'Vecher'. 'We was giving it to them hot and strong, even the trees bent low', boasts Konkin at the beginning of his story, yet in almost the next breath a softer, poetic image follows: 'The little day, I remember, was already bowing out to evening.'[511] Later, as the cornered Polish general obstinately persists in his refusal to surrender, Konkin talks vividly of his anger, which he renders both visually concrete and inanimate: 'A red sea *opened* before me. The insult felt like salt *entering* a wound, because I can see the old boy doesn't believe me.'[512] His anger was earlier translated into action in the four-fold reference to the high-ranking Pole as 'tuz' ('big-shot/ace').[513] This fossilized metaphor of unlike transfer depersonalizes the Pole, relegating him to the rich trimmings of his office: a watch-chain, gold watch and a general's braid – 'And I take aim at a big-shot. A crimson big-shot lads, with a gold watch and a little chain.'[514] As with Maresko in the minor cycle, Babel employs a reverse of the norm in his realisation of an animate stimulant by an imported inanimate image with consequent pejorative effect.[515] The callousness that Konkin displays is nevertheless countered, and by a further example of animate to inanimate transfer. Respect, even affection, for the old general is evident in Konkin's words at the end of his account when he describes the Pole's final gesture: 'There's my old boy sitting on the ground, kissing some talisman or other, he breaks his sword in two, and two lampions light up in his eyes, *two lanterns over the dark steppe.*'[516] The image is an elevatory one, the Pole's ennoblement is confirmed by Konkin's relating of the latter's final request to him: 'Forgive me … and kill me like a soldier …'[517] Compassion too is a sentiment that Konkin betrays, this time in a figure of totally inanimate transfer: 'I galloped up to him, but he'd already grabbed his sword, and down his cheeks tears are flowing, *white tears, human milk.*'[518] Thus Babel exploits a range of transfers in his figures to portray different and often polarized psychological facets of his protagonists.

Sensuous and animate transfer in Na pole chesti —— I have already commented on the extent to which both primary narrators employ figurative visual imagery.[519] *Na pole chesti*'s narrator in fact uses a proportionally greater amount of imported visual images than Lyutov (74.2 per cent compared with 67 per cent); the former's imagery can be as graphic as the latter's, as for example in the cycle's opening paragraph when his focus, for once panoramic, captures temporal panic and slaughter mirrored in the heavens: 'The sky, its dark blue intense heat shining, was slowly turning crimson, swelling and misting over.' (ll.3–4, 'Na pole chesti') Yet this very predilection for the visual is a reason for the smaller range and versatility of the metaphors of the first cycle. Lyutov's prose in *Konarmiya* embodies a greater range of metaphors of both like and unlike transfer. Only two of the narrator's metaphors of *Na pole chesti* comprise a like-auditory transfer, whereas the 10.4 per cent of Lyutov's of this variety are found usually in clusters which tighten the dramatic knot; auditory-derived tension is largely lacking in the first cycle and there are no crescendos of suspense. The closest that we come to one is, ironically, a whisper, namely Ratin's threat to the crouching Bidu in the opening story: 'No force could make him get up. Then the captain approached the very edge of the hole and hissed especially quietly.' (ll.32–3, 'Na pole chesti') The only other instance of like-auditory transfer occurs near the end of 'Kvaker'; its immediate succession by two images of different sensuous planes accentuates the banality of this first metaphor. Despite its pre-positive formation, it is pallid in comparison with the final, visual metaphor: *'The cannonade thundered ceaselessly. The earth gave off a stench, the sun rummaged in upturned corpses.'* (ll.82–4, 'Kvaker')[520]

The difference in versatility between the figures of the two narrators is more marked when one looks at metaphors of unlike transfer. While *Na pole chesti* manifests Babel's early predilection for metaphor comprising an abstract to visual transfer, it does not include the range of synaesthetic metaphor of the major cycle, neither in the figures of its narrator nor of its soldiers or other protagonists. Indeed, only one different type of synaesthetic figure obtains, in which an abstract stimulant realizes an auditory image: 'Immediately the voice of duty addressed him vehemently ...' (ll.20–1, 'Kvaker') The image is deliberately trite, its grandiloquence deriding the conventions by which the Quaker lives. Ston, 'a slave to his conscience' following 'a higher position', (l.4, 'Kvaker') reacts at seeing a neglected horse. Animals gain his compassion, men his disdain: 'People, through their sins, seemed less worthy of respect to him; but for animals he felt an indescribable compassion.' (ll.49–51, 'Kvaker')

Some 50 per cent of the minor cycle's metaphors are of the abstract to visual synaesthetic variety. Statistics for the narrator's and the soldiers' tropes equate with those of the non-Lyutov categories of *Konarmiya*; Lyutov alone employs fewer of this type of transfer, which often performs a characterizing role of banality or farce.[521] In 'Dezertir', emotions assume visual qualities: the good captain Zhem'ye loved France 'with a tenderness that devoured his heart', while his hatred for the barbarians defiling his country 'was as unquenchable'. (ll.3–4 and 5 respectively, 'Dezertir') In 'Kvaker' a whole series is devoted to Ston. The Quaker considered himself 'invested by Providence with a special mission ... Ston's zeal bore fruit', yet his conscience and the violent events around him conspired to give him no peace: 'Within a week his conscience had set about its nagging [literally nibbling/gnawing] task. ... The last bloody days had left a terrible mark on him ...' (ll.48–9, 62, 85–6 and 96–7 respectively, 'Kvaker') Only occasionally does a synaesthetic figure emerge from the narrator with a power that foreshadows Lyutov; one such is Babel's transformation of Vidal's 'les mots les plus durs' into the 'arid hail' of abuse.[522] Generally, however, synaesthetic metaphor in the first cycle lacks the power to disconcert; its pedestrianism links the narrator with imagery found in other non-Lyutov *skaz* categories, as indeed does his proportion of like-abstract transfer. Lyutov supplies the least amount of figures of this variety, while his counterpart in *Na pole chesti* approaches in degree of usage the Cossacks in *Konarmiya*: 16.1 per cent compared with the Cossacks' 19.3 per cent; Lyutov employs 9.4 per cent.

Nevertheless, totally abstract transfer in the lesser cycle can assume a significance that is perhaps not apparent on first reading. Ston's physical ungainliness is summarized thus in a simile: 'His every movement was no less *than a victory*, won by mind over matter', (ll.9–10, 'Kvaker') and the victory, later accorded him in an epithet describing his gait, is as hollow as the groom's derisive laughter which accompanies the Quaker's departure. 'And he withdrew with a measured, *solemn/triumphant* step, heedless of the guffawing resounding behind him. The square jutting chin of the youth testified convincingly to an *unconquerable* stubbornness.' (ll.34–7, 'Kvaker') The three tropes which I have emphasized link the leitmotifs of personal triumph and disaster which permeate both cycles. Ston is literally a walking disaster, yet his air at the beginning of the story is one of triumph and jauntiness. Maresko's arrival in the family vault, and the laboured, yet finally successful communication of his intent to the lieutenant, represent triumphs born of disaster, while the breaking free from military discipline and establishment expectations of Bidu and Bozhi respectively, no matter how fleeting, are moments of respite and personal triumph in a world that subsequently repays them by removing their lives. Lyutov too experiences moments of respite or personal triumph which are as hollow and fleeting as those of the protagonists of *Na pole chesti*. 'Moy pervyy gus' recounts a hard-won acceptance that the primary narrator has gained among some Cossacks, an acceptance whose bloody and pathetic achievement is witnessed by a moon, whose tawdriness betokens the cheapness of his own action, and which fills his own heart with anguish.[523] In 'Istoriya odnoy loshadi', a nostalgic Lyutov recalls in lyrical vein how he used to enjoy the companionship of Khlebnikov, a Cossack squadron commander, subsequently demobilized as unfit for service: 'we were shaken by the same passions. We both looked at the world as at a meadow in May, a meadow traversed by women and horses.'[524] Even in 'Argamak', which Babel added to *Konarmiya* some years later, Lyutov's triumph is no more than his ceasing to be a pariah among Cossack horsemen: 'The months passed. My dream was fulfilled. The Cossacks stopped following me and my horse with their eyes.'[525]

Whereas a greater range of like and unlike sensuous transfer obtains in *Konarmiya* and points to developments in Babel's use and formation of tropes, the same cannot be said for the use that he makes of animation in either cycle. Both narrators favour unlike transfer, between an inanimate stimulant and an imported animate image, to an almost identical degree: 54.8 per cent in *Na pole chesti* and 56.5 per cent in *Konarmiya*. This dimension of tropes' formation was thus not something that Babel developed in his major war cycle, it had already been exploited in the writing of his first. Its coupling with sensuous synaesthetic transfer at times invests the narrator's language there with the power and originality of a Lyutov: 'the sun rummaged in upturned corpses'. (ll.83–4, 'Kvaker') The soldier-narrator of 'Semeystvo papashi Maresko' is also not averse to inanimate–animate transfer in his evocation of the macabre: 'Decayed corpses *tumble* out of the coffins, smashed by shells … If we are destined to increase the population of this chilly corner, well we've made the rotting old men *dance* first to the march of our machine-guns.' (ll.5–6 and 8–10 respectively, 'Semeystvo papashi Maresko')[526]

The success of such imagery to arrest and focus attention upon the horrors of war is unmistakable, but the narrator of *Na pole chesti* scarcely wears the distorting lens of Lyutov. That the world of Bozhi, Bidu, Ston and Maresko is an alien place, with which each is incompatible, is indisputable, just as the harshness and uncompromising nature of Lyutov's reality is for him in his war-torn surroundings. Yet there exist but glimmerings in the first war cycle of the identity of the primary narrator of the second cycle. The narrator of the former is indistinct; only in the prologue and the concluding paragraph of the final story is the first person used (apart from the soldier-narrator's tale, 'Semeystvo papashi Maresko'), and in three aspects of tropes' formation the narrator resembles the Cossacks and other protagonists of *Konarmiya*. Two have already been mentioned: a strong preference for abstract to visual transfer in metaphor to the virtual exclusion of other synaesthetic types, and a heavier use of the usually banal like-abstract transfer.[527] Thirdly, while both primary narrators exploit inanimate to animate transfer it is *Na pole chesti*'s narrator who employs the reverse type, the realization of an animate stimulant by an imported inanimate image, a feature that is virtually absent from the tropes of Lyutov and reserved either for puns or unwitting self-satire on the part of Cossacks and other protagonists or for the pejoration of Maresko by the officer-narrator.[528] Ston is the subject of these figures and in the farcical nature of his portrayal one senses the bombast of a Konkin, Pavlichenko or Balmashov: 'What was Ston? *A bald brow at the top of a pole.*[529] The Lord had bestowed a body on him merely to elevate his thoughts above the terrible sorrows of this world.' (ll.7–9, 'Kvaker') There is thus a blurring of the narrator's voice, a confounding of it with the voices of others; his prism is at times Lyutovian in the starkness and lapidary quality of the images that it filters, but more often we perceive the farce or banality of protagonists who possess neither the sensitivity nor singular neuroses of a Jew and an intellectual like Lyutov.

Pejoration and elevation

This section of my analysis examines the effect of the metaphors of Babel's protagonists in the two cycles of war. I have dealt so far with aspects of their composition but turn now to an analysis of the effect that imported images have on their respective stimulants, examining whether the latter are enhanced in status or depreciated or whether neither effect is achieved. Section III, Table 4, reveals that there is a greater proportion of depreciatory imagery in *Konarmiya* than is the case in *Na pole chesti*. The principal reason for this is the difference in their effect of the metaphors of the cycles' respective primary narrators. While 75 per cent of Lyutov's metaphors embody a disparaging view of their respective main ideas, the first cycle's narrator maintains a more even balance between the elevatory and the depreciatory, with some 45.2 per cent of the former and 51.6 per cent of the latter. It is noticeable how few metaphors have a neutral effect in either cycle; in

Lyutov's case for example, it is 7.4 per cent and in the narrator's of the minor cycle only one such example occurs. Babel's tropes convey the emotions of his protagonists and in turn they engender emotion from his readers. The Cossacks and soldiers respectively follow the trend shown by Lyutov; while their imagery is a little less markedly pejorative than his, the statistics show that they share a jaundiced view of their respective worlds, indicating a basic unwillingness to be the agents of revolution or defenders against Teutonic barbarism. As Trilling states in an introduction to a translation of *Konarmiya*: 'There was anomaly at the very heart of the book, for the Red cavalry of the title were Cossack regiments, and why were Cossacks fighting for the Revolution, they who were the instrument and symbol of Tsarist repression?'[530] 69.5 per cent of the Cossacks' metaphors are depreciatory, while in the case of the French soldiers the figure is even higher, at 73.3 per cent. Only in the tropes of *Konarmiya*'s other protagonists is there a slight shift towards the elevatory, 42 per cent compared with 54.8 per cent that are depreciatory.

Such unanimous pejoration, at least on the part of the majority of protagonists, results in a dearth of imagery which has the reverse effect of ennoblement or elevation. Lyutov is the most grudging in this respect, with only 17.3 per cent of metaphors of this type; the Cossacks and French soldiers are a little less so with 20.3 per cent and 26.7 per cent respectively. But it is the author-narrator of *Na pole chesti* who reveals a more benign outlook with some 45.2 per cent of elevatory images. The reasons for this difference in the narrators' perspectives lie in the fact that the narrator of the French cycle is neither as closely involved in what takes place nor is he as evolved or distinct a protagonist as Lyutov is. Whether he is an officer, a reporter or an observer, he does not engender in his milieu the hostility that a Jewish intellectual does, who cannot ride a horse: '... a Jew in a Cossack regiment was more than an anomaly, it was a Joke, for between Cossack and Jew there existed not merely hatred but a polar opposition'.[531] We can see clearly which cycle reveals the personal experiences of its author. Babel had witnessed and experienced, at least to a degree, the alienation and violence that confronts Lyutov, whereas his narrator in *Na pole chesti* is created third-hand via the memoirs of another, and at a time when Babel himself had barely tasted the horrors of war or indeed any violence at all.[532]

Why, however, do the metaphors of the men ostensibly purveying the violence and persecution, the Cossacks and French officers, almost coincide in their amount of pejoration with that of *Konarmiya*'s primary narrator? The answer lies in the harshness of their respective roles: both live by – and at times for – violence and in doing so their imagery reflects their brash and brutalized perspectives. Pavlichenko in his autobiographical story reveals that even in courtship his thinking is inextricably concerned with martial imagery: 'Nastya, – I answer, – there's no answer to give you, my head's not a gun, there's no front sight on it nor no back sight ...'[533] In the story's conclusion his second rejection of a firearm is engendered by a desire to wreak the bloodiest revenge possible upon his master Nikitinskiy:

And then I trampled on my master Nikitinskiy. I trampled him down for an hour or more and during this time I got to know life thoroughly. With shooting, – I'll put it this way, – you only get rid of a man, shooting's – a pardon for him, and a despicable let off for yourself, with shooting you'll never get to the soul, to where it is in a man and how it reveals itself. But I, as a matter of fact, don't spare myself, I'll trample an enemy down in fact for an hour or more. I need to get to know life, what it's like with us ...[534]

Babel is also informing us that these inflicters of such violence are also its victims, not merely because men such as Pavlichenko have themselves been persecuted by their masters, but because their souls have been brutalized by their respective circumstances. Each of Babel's major protagonists in both cycles fulfils the role of hero and victim; the balance may waver but the degree of pejorative imagery that obtains weights the scales firmly on the side of suffering; each is more victim than hero. The officers of *Na pole chesti* foreshadow this. Their ironic taunts of inadequates like the masturbating Bidu: 'You've found a wife here, swine!'; their threats: 'Stand up, Bidu, or I'll soak you from head to foot'; and their clinical despatching of the young soldiers: 'Ratin finished him off with two shots from the revolver. The soldier's body did not even twitch' – all form their responses to the dilemmas with which war confronts them. (ll.17, 34 and 41–3 respectively, 'Na pole chesti') 'Without hurrying he took the revolver from the youth's wet hands, stepped back three paces and shot him through the skull.' (ll.55–6, 'Dezertir') – Zhem'ye's act, like Ratin's before, had been forced upon him through the behaviour and cowardice of another.

Balmashov is equally a victim. Duped by a woman black marketeer in 'Sol'', his tropes betoken his deteriorating outlook, a perspective which is further exacerbated by events in 'Izmena', where he is hospitalized and, in his opinion, humiliated. 75.5 per cent of the Cossack's metaphors in 'Sol'' produce a depreciatory effect, while only 15.5 per cent create the reverse. Like Lyutov he is in disharmony with his milieu, and like the officers of *Na pole chesti* his solution to his dilemma is violence. The brutal outcome of 'Sol'', the killing of the peasant woman, is hinted at in Balmashov's various references to women. They are firstly referred to as 'the female sex' among black marketeers: 'these evil enemies, among whom there was also a countless force of the female sex ...'[535] Later when the 'imposing woman',[536] whose cause Balmashov had earlier argued with his men, is exposed as deceiving them, she becomes a 'harmful ... vile woman ...'[537] Balmashov's final act then ensues, portrayed in a figurative sequence masterful for its depiction of clinical brutality: 'I washed this shame from the face of the workers' land and the Republic.'[538] The 'vile citizen' has been relegated still further in status. In a metonymy that links with metaphor, she is no more than Balmashov's shame, a stain to be wiped away. The abstract noun 'pozor' ('shame/infamy') is all that she finally represents in the eyes of the Cossacks and their abashed spokesman.

183

Sidorov is ostensibly the ascendant protagonist in 'Solntse Italii', bearing the upper hand over the oppressed Lyutov with whom he shares a billet: 'Returning home, I dreaded meeting Sidorov, my neighbour, who nightly lowered upon me the hairy paw of his anguish.'[539] The anguished prose of the Cossack's letter reveals that he too is as much a victim of his situation as the primary narrator. 'Solntse Italii', with its balance between Cossack *skaz* and Lyutov-based prose, allows us to examine in juxtaposition the cumulative effect within the story of the respective metaphors. Both protagonists exhibit the same tendency: 73.1 per cent of Lyutov's metaphors and 84.8 per cent of Sidorov's embody a pejorative effect. The results indicate the profound disharmony that both men feel in their partly shared, partly private worlds. In tropes which comprise significantly similar imagery, Babel writes of their respective intoxication. Lyutov, returning home from Apolek's quarters, is portrayed thus: 'My soul, filled with the wearisome *intoxication* of reverie', while Sidorov comments in his letter to his fiancée: 'The state's wisdom is driving me out of my mind, the tedium is intoxicating.'[540] Escape for both men lies in their dreams. The odious surroundings of the room assume a perverse animation for Lyutov: 'everything in it breathed the dank odour of night ... On the table the guttering candle gasped for breath ... a hunchbacked candle, sinister beacon of dreamers.'[541] It is the moon alone which provides alleviation and for which Lyutov reserves rare images of aggrandizement. The inexhaustible force of its naked light causes ruins to flower,[542] and roads to flow with life-giving succour: 'the milk of the moon ... Blue roads flowed past me, like streams of milk, spurting from many breasts', while at the end the moon's presence suggests passion and hope: 'and only the window, filled with moonlight was shining like a deliverance'.[543]

For Sidorov, escape lies in dreams engendered not by the moon but by Italian sunshine. He had become disillusioned, firstly with the campaign of the Ukranian anarchist, Makhno, in which he had participated, 'a tedious swindle and nothing more ...', then with the Soviet regimentation of Moscow, where he finds himself hospitalized because of a wound: 'in Moscow, I grew dumb with misery. Each day nurses would bring me a little gruel. Bridled with awe they would drag it on a big tray, and I grew to hate this shock-brigade gruel, these uncalled for supplies and regimented Moscow.'[544] With his fighting instincts thwarted,[545] he turns his thoughts to Italy and alters his figures of pejoration to those of expectation and exaltation. The country is ready for revolution: 'In Italy the earth is smouldering. There is much that is ready there ... Italy has entered my heart like an obsession. The thought of this country that I have never seen, is as sweet to me as a woman's name.'[546] Reality is liable to reassert itself for both men, however; Sidorov's bathetic coupling of 'Italian sunshine and bananas'[547] and Lyutov's moonlit vision of an ethereal town cede to the presence of a guttering, hunch-backed candle in a dark and gloomy room in which breathes the dank odour of a clamorous night, 'night, full of a distant and wearisome pealing',[548] while 'in the wings a morose electrician keeps a finger on the button of the moon-extinguisher'.[549]

184

A characteristic of Lyutov's imagery is exemplified in 'Kladbishche v Kozine', namely the juxtaposition of a metaphor of aggrandizement with one of depreciation. In isolation the figurative verb 'poyut' ('sing') ennobles the four generations of rabbis whose burial vaults Lyutov is contemplating: 'and the tablets, the greening tablets sing of them',[550] but the immediacy of the succeeding image damns it and in so doing renders the pejoration that much greater: 'and the tablets, the greening tablets sing of them *with the floridity of a bedouin's prayer ...*'[551] The final substantive is disparaging and exemplifies the tone of wretchedness for the primary narrator, not only amid the kitsch of this Jewish graveyard in weed-grown Volhynia, but throughout the cycle. The song that the tablets render amounts to the prayer of a wandering tribesman; the comparison is to a people without roots and conveys the isolation and ostracism which Jews have suffered throughout history, and to which Lyutov personally seeks solutions. The image does nothing to ennoble the four generations of rabbis at his feet 'in this tomb, lowly as a water-carrier's dwelling',[552] nor do the seven metaphors which follow. The tombs' inscriptions comprise incongruous, grandiose images of hyperbole which increase the damning effect: Azriil is the mouth of Jehova; his son, Iliya, a brain that enters into single combat; while Vol'f is a prince prematurely abducted from the Torah.[553] The elevatory designation 'prince' is immediately negated by the precious, mock-epic 'robbed from the Torah in his nineteenth spring'.[554] In a three-fold sequence of metaphor, death is reproached for its predatory qualities. Its personification continues the epic tone but the juxtaposition of two images in which the vulgarity of the latter punctures the loftiness of the former renders the prosopopoeia parodic: 'Oh, death, oh, *selfish one*, oh, *greedy thief*, why have you not spared us if but once?'[555]

Such a mixture obtains to a greater degree in 'Vecher'. Many of the metaphors when examined in isolation exalt their respective stimulants; however, when viewed in context, in their sequences or with their adjacent imagery, the cumulative effect is very much one of depreciation. This device is a prime means for Babel in creating irony. While appearing to praise, he derogates; the more exaggerated the imagery, the greater the bathos. *Krasnyy kavalerist*, the journal of the cavalry army for which Babel and Lyutov worked, is the newspaper in 'Vecher' which three decrepit heroes have made into a 'boisterous paper, full of boldness and crude gaiety'.[556] Its appearance towards nightfall is portrayed ostensibly in exalted fashion by Lyutov, as a 'dynamite fuse laid beneath the army'.[557] The coming of night, however, is seen in the next image by the primary narrator as the extinguishing of the provincial sun, the thematic antithesis of the previous image: 'In the sky the squint-eyed lantern of the provincial sun goes out ...'[558] The image is deliberately incongruous and, like the first, one of *ostraneniye*. It negates the previous metaphor, puncturing its dramatic, elevatory effect. Lyutov continues the theme of illumination, first exalting, 'the darting lights of the printing press burn irrepressibly', then deflating, 'like the passion of machinery'.[559] The fervour of the printing press lights resembles the passion of machinery. It is in this blaze of light, at this moment of anti-climax ('towards nightfall ... towards midnight'[560] are phrases which recur as respectively the newspaper and Galin appear) that the hero makes his appearance. He leaves the ardent presses in the railway carriage 'to shudder at the stings of unrequited love for the washerwoman Irina'.[561] The linking of passion in the person of the hapless Galin with the noise and fire of press machinery reduces both their 'products' – his love and the army newspaper – to absurdity. The squinting, provincial sun has thus made way for a small-minded newspaper concocted by absurd little men. The moon too, far from being the fount of maternal love and symbol of salvation that it represents for Lyutov in 'Solntse Italii', also plays a depreciatory role. Bathed in its light as he recounts imperial history to Irina, Galin is not illuminated by any nimbus of glory as Cossacks like Lyovka or Bida are elsewhere,[562] the moon has become a virago of displeasing appearance: 'Hunched up he is bathed in light by the moon, sticking out up there like a sore thumb ...'[563] The simile is repeated when Galin's beloved Irina with the swollen mouth has gone off to 'squash fleas'[564] with his successful rival, the cook Vasiliy. The awkwardness of the moon portrayed in the participle 'torchashchey' ('sticking out') mirrors that of Galin, its cheap ugliness that of Irina. Both luminaries are thus employed at times by Babel in depreciatory roles. The investing of the inanimate with life, a device common in Babel's synaesthetic metaphors, does not have an elevatory effect. Generally, the bestowal of animal and even human faculties upon the inert produces pejoration. The sun, a forager among corpses in 'Kvaker', 'The sun rummaged in upturned corpses' (ll.83–4, 'Kvaker') is a concomitant of the bloodshed in 'Smert' Dolgushova', as it wallows in purple dust in the aftermath of a battle, while scouts search the fields for the dead: 'The sun wallowed in purple dust. In the trenches wounded men were having something to eat ... Afon'ka's scouts were roaming the field searching out corpses and equipment.'[565]

Seeming, momentary exaltation, followed by tropes of depreciation with a consequent intensifying of the process of denigration and the creation of irony, is a device that is not peculiar to *Konarmiya*. It is found in 'Dezertir' for example, in the narrator's portrayal of the French captain. Zhem'ye is a man, we are told, who does not waver on the battlefield, yet in private life makes allowances for small misdemeanours. His patriotism is stressed; he loved his native land with tenderness and he hated the enemy who were defiling France, yet Babel combines the praise with figures that immediately reverse any positive effect. The visual imagery employed is excessive, sits uneasily with its abstract stimulants and straightway decries the captain: 'He loved France with a tenderness, *that devoured his heart*, that is why his hatred for the barbarians profaning her ancient soil, was *as unquenchable, ruthless, prolonged as life*.' (ll.3–5, 'Dezertir')[566] The reverse of this device is also found. In the cycle's first story, a depreciatory epithet is used to enhance the elevatory effect of two successive epithets. The idiot-boy Bidu is berated by his superior officer, Ratin; his dual guilt of cowardice and indecency renders him contemptible in the officer's eyes:

– Do your buttons up, Bidu, – the captain said icily. – Why are you here?

– I ... I can't tell you this ... I'm afraid, captain! ...

– You've found a wife here, swine! You dare tell me to my face that you're a coward, Bidu. You've abandoned your comrades at the very hour the regiment is attacking. Ben, mon cochon! ... (ll.14–19, 'Na pole chesti')

Yet the narrator's first reference to the boy stresses his humanity, his vulnerability: '300 metres from the trenches Ratin caught sight of a human figure. It was Bidu the soldier, Bidu the idiot. He was sitting cowering at the bottom of a damp hole.' (ll.9–11, 'Na pole chesti') It is this human fallibility that is conveyed in the ensuing description of the youth's despair. The seemingly derogatory epithet 'svinnykh' ('piggy') paradoxically enhances the elevatory effect of the subsequent epithets. The youth's animal eyes frame subtle, human emotions: 'The idiot laid his head on his knees, put his two arms around it and started to cry. Then he looked at the captain, and in the chinks of his *piggy* little eyes a *timid, tender* hope was reflected.' (ll.23–5, 'Na pole chesti')[567] Such instances are rare, however, the juxtaposition of elevatory and depreciatory imagery usually strengthens the pejorative impression that we receive.

Babel also exploits this device to create ambivalence. We can often be left wondering whether the stimulant or main idea of a figure is intended to be totally or partially denigrated or, more rarely, exalted. It is at such moments that we sense the mind of the author toying with us. As Trilling states:

> one could not at once know just how the author was responding to the brutality he recorded, whether he thought it good or bad, justified or not justified. Nor was this the only thing to be in doubt about. It was not really clear how the author felt about, say, Jews; or about religion; or about the goodness of man. He had – or perhaps, for the sake of some artistic effect, he pretended to have – a secret.[568]

Nowhere is this sense of the enigmatic felt more strongly than in the imagery formulated by the Cossack secondary narrators, such as Konkin and Pavlichenko. The portrait that Babel allows his secondary narrators to paint of themselves is both depreciatory and elevatory. Amid the braggart, self-assertive colloquialisms of these men of violence one hears echoes of noble protagonists of *Slovo o polku Igoreve* (The Lay of Igor) or the *bogatyri* ('heroes') of the *byliny* ('Russian epic tales'). Konkin's allusion to the trees' obeisance to him in his eponymous story: 'We were giving it to them hot and strong, even the trees bent low',[569] recalls lines of pathetic fallacy in *The Lay of Igor*:

> The grass droops for pity,
> and the tree has bent
> in sorrow to the ground.[570]

In the *byliny,* repetition, refrain and tautology abound. Whole episodes or single words are repeated, which draw attention to significant events in the narrative and create dramatic tension.[571] A series of negative sentences can be used to create drama and to introduce a positive statement of ennoblement:

> It is not a green oak bending low to the earth,
> nor paper leaves fluttering down to the ground, –
> a son is falling down before his father,
> and begging his blessing:[572]

Pavlichenko uses the same technique when stressing his fallibility to Nastya: 'my head's not a gun, there's no front sight on it nor no back sight, but my heart is known to you ...'[573] Balmashov employs a negative sequence in 'Sol'' with ironic and dramatic effect when he queries the suspicious bundle of the peasant woman: 'That's an odd kid, comrades, that doesn't ask for the teat, doesn't wet skirts and doesn't disturb people's sleep ...'[574] and his subsequent reiteration has the quality of a refrain: 'but you, incalculable citizen, with your odd kids that don't ask for food or need the pot ...'[575]

But it is in the themes of the imagery of the Cossack narrators that one feels most strongly the beat of the mediaeval epic. The tautologous comparison of the Polish general's eyes in 'Konkin' exemplifies this: 'and two lampions light up in his eyes, two lanterns over the dark steppe',[576] or Nastya's laughter in 'Zhizneopisaniye Pavlichenki, Matveya Rodionycha' which has the same epic backdrop of the steppe: 'she laughs rashly, full-throatedly over the whole steppe, as if she's playing a drum'.[577] Balmashov's sleep which had deserted his couch in 'Sol'' – '[which] sleep was hurrying from like a wolf from a pack of villainous dogs',[578] might well have been disturbed by Polovtsian carts screeching like liberated swans:

> at midnight carts screech,
>   like swans that have been released.[579]

Lyutov too is not averse to metaphors of epic proportions. Significantly, one is found in the opening paragraph of *Konarmiya* which describes the cavalry army's following of an ancient route between Poland and Russia: 'our staff was stretched out in a noisy rearguard along the highway that goes from Brest to Warsaw, a highway built upon the bones of peasants by Nicholas I'.[580] The last image and the repeated references to death in the plans: 'Everything is strewn with corpses, completely inconspicuous amid the rye ... A field strewn with corpses.' (Battle of Brody, p.490) are reminiscent of descriptive details of slaughter contained in *The Lay of Igor*:

> The black earth beneath the hooves
> was sown with bones,
> was watered with blood,
> and across the Russian land trouble burgeoned.[581]

The passage that I have quoted from *Konarmiya* presages the events which are about to unfold in the cycle, events of violence and sadness of which Lyutov tries to make sense and by which he is sickened.

But parallels other than similar instances of imagery can be drawn between the stories of *Konarmiya* and heroic poems such as *The Lay of Igor*, the *byliny* and other genres like the *istoricheskiye pesni* ('historical songs') and *dukhovnyye stikhi* ('spiritual poems'). Like the composers of the *istoricheskiye pesni*, Babel wrote his stories fairly soon after the events that they commemorate, and both his primary narrator, Lyutov, and his secondary narrators, are comparable to the *skaziteli,* or peasant bards, who gave unique renderings of the subject matter that they portrayed, each lending his individual colouring to the events. The following description of a *skazitel'* can apply equally well to Lyutov, Konkin or Pavlichenko:

> The role of the *skazitel'* is … of prime importance. He may develop an individual style and be skilled at producing particular effects by his manner of narration. He may give the *bylina* a particular colouring, according to his own character or background. Humour and dramatic quality especially depend on the individual *skazitel'*.[582]

Research has shown too that the belief that the Olonets region of Northern Russia was the sole repository of the *byliny* is fallacious. They have survived in other parts of the north, in Siberia and 'among the Cossacks in the extreme south and south-east of Russia';[583] their setting too is mainly around Kiev in the south. The official Soviet claim that the *byliny* are purely imaginative creations, embodying the general hopes and aspirations of the common people, conflicts with the view widely held before 1936 and promulgated by the so-called 'historical school'[584] that the *byliny* represent an accurate oral record of Russian history.[585] Such a distortion of the truth by the Soviet authorities has a familiar ring when one considers the establishment's reception of *Konarmiya*. Budyonnyy for example, was vociferous in his condemnation of Babel's portrayal of events, while the suppression of the author's works, his arrest and death by firing squad in 1939[586] testify to the authorities' fear of a writer who exposed the brutality, vacillations and vulnerability of the exponents of the revolution and its times.

A story in *Konarmiya*, 'Pan Apolek', has affinities with a third genre of mediaeval tales, the *dukhovnyye stikhi*. These spiritual poems were sung by blind or crippled beggars to musical accompaniment. Their songs of Christ or the saints would often be inspired by icons and not only glorified the Lord but told also of concessions won from him by the common people. One such is 'Vozneseniye', an account of the Ascension in which Christ is made to bequeath his name to the poor for their sustenance.[587] Babel would indeed seem to have drawn on the themes and exponents of such *dukhovnyye stikhi* in his creation of 'Pan Apolek'. The itinerant painter and his blind musical accompanist, Gottfried, resemble in parodic fashion the *kaliki prokhozhiye* (itinerant beggars), of the spiritual poems.[588] The pair develop to extremes the slight irreverence that is discernible in 'Vozneseniye'.[589] In his sacrilegious painting, Apolek realizes the hopes and aspirations of the common people by his elevation of them to sainthood; he provides a sense of achievement for them, which, in the words of one, the Church has never done: 'And isn't there more truth in the pictures of Pan Apolek, who satisfies our pride, than in your words, full of abuse and arrogant wrath ...'[590] Blind Gottfried, his name – 'the peace of God' – ambivalently ironic, 'listens to the never-ending music of his blindness'[591] while his eternal friend, Apolek, whose name evokes the irridescent, god-like abilities of Apollo,[592] paints on, creating his heretical metaphors with his brush and hatching the irreligious stories which so whetted Lyutov's appetite.

But what is Babel's purpose in drawing upon these oral heroic poems of long ago? Is it to create humour through parody? Did he see these heroic poems as forerunners of his unique and varied use of *skaz*, or is he attempting to create heroes of epic proportions in their great revolutionary struggle? The answer lies partly in all three. Humour abounds in his work for, intermingled with the epic tones of his imagery, farce frequently asserts itself, as with Konkin, who is both casual and dramatic, both grandiose and crude: 'The little day I remember, was already bowing out to evening ... Keep puffing, Spir'ka, – I say, – anyway I'll dirty their chasubles for them ...'[593] The same Spir'ka is referred to in imagery whose flavour is at once epic and farcical: 'And here's Spiridion before me, like a leaf before grass. His person's all of a lather, his eyes are hanging from his mug on threads.'[594] A similar instance occurs in 'Zhizneopisaniye Pavlichenki, Matveya Rodionycha' as Pavlichenko describes his journey to confront his master Nikitinskiy. His prose comes closest to that of a *bylina*'s *skazitel'* for it has singing, rhythmical qualities with its repetitions, tautologies, final mock-epic images and tonic beat:

> And the old man made off without further ado,
> but my legs covered twenty versts of ground that day,
> my legs covered a fair bit of ground that day,
> and in the evening I appeared at the Lidino estate,
> at my merry master, Nikitinskiy's.
> He was sitting in an upper room, the old old fellow was,
> taking three saddles to pieces: an English one, a dragoon one
> and a Cossack one, – and I grew in his doorway, like a burr,
> > a whole hour I grew, like a burr, and all to no avail.

> I starets bezuslovno, pustilsya ot menya khodom,
> a ya oboshol v tot den' moimi nogami dvadtsat' verst zemli,
> bol'shoy kusok zemli oboshol ya v tot den' moimi nogami,
> i vecherom vyros v usad'be Lidino,
> u vesyologo barina moyego Nikitinskogo.
> On sidel v gornitse, staryy starik, i razbiral tri sedla:
> angliyskoye, dragunskoye i kazatskoye, – a ya ros u yego dverey,
> > kak lopukh, tsel'nyy chas ros, i vsyo bez posledstviy.[595]

What Babel takes from the oral heroic poems and adapts in unique fashion is an extension of the device which I have examined earlier, the facility to exalt and deride simultaneously, and in so doing to create ambivalent pictures of the exponents of the Revolution, to stress their dynamism and their vulnerability.[596] He forges a link between the Cossack soldiers that Lyutov encounters and the *bogatyri* of heroic, superhuman qualities. Warriors such as Prince Igor or Il'ya Muromets, with their legendary, fantastic deeds, find twentieth-century counterparts in Konkin, Pavlichenko, Savitskiy, Baulin and Bida. Like the villagers sanctified by the brush of Apolek, Babel's pen exalts the Cossack peasant-warriors of the Galician campaign. Yet at the same time he decries the brutality and cruelty of their deeds and the times that they and he live in. Bathos abounds in the tropes concerning them; as one image exalts, another renders the protagonist ridiculous. Konkin is just such a hero and villain, oppressor and victim, who is worthy of our admiration and contempt, our sympathy and derision. His gloriously braggart qualities are exemplified in the comment that he makes to his companion as they take on eight men in battle: 'Let's die for a sour cucumber and the world revolution …'[597]

Elevatory and depreciatory imagery in the tropes of other protagonists ——
While Babel's versatility in *skaz* formulation is as evident in this category as it is elsewhere, the metaphors display a less jaundiced viewpoint than those of Lyutov or the Cossacks, with 42 per cent comprising elevatory imagery. Pejoration still predominates, however, with 54.8 per cent containing images of depreciation. They can vary between the emotive litotes of Sashka's mother: 'Our children have gone out feet first'[598] to a peasant's despair at man's animalism in 'Ivany': 'We call ourselves human beings, but foul things up worse than jackals. You feel ashamed for the earth …'[599] Sashka, 'the lady of every squadron',[600] uses tropes imbued with a crude imagery, comparable to any Cossack's. Her tough stance reveals a fighting spirit, akin to theirs, an intolerance of weakness and an accustomedness to the vicissitudes of war: 'Tomorrow you'll be gone, – Sashka said, wiping Shevelyov who lay in a cold sweat. – Tomorrow you'll be gone, it's in your guts, death …',[601] she tells her dying lover in 'Vdova'. In 'Chesniki' she chides the reluctant Step'ka for not releasing his stallion to cover her mare: 'You'll get going most likely, when you're over fourteen, – Sashka muttered and turned away. – Over fourteen most likely, and nothing'll come of it, you'll only blow bubbles …';[602] while in 'Posle boya' her criticism of the alleged cowardice of the Cossacks and then Lyutov is vehement: 'I've thought better of drinking tea with you, Vorob'yev, because I saw you heroes today and I saw your villainy, commander … Cocks only care about one thing, – said Sashka, – smacking each other in the mouth, and I just want to hide my eyes from the deeds that have been done today.'[603]

In contrast with such pejorative imagery is the confused optimism of Gedali, whose very question implies the existence of a better world – 'where is the sweet revolution?'[604] – and who, in imagery of exaltation, cherishes the sacredness of a mother's memory in 'Rabbi': 'A mother's memory feeds compassion in us, as the ocean, the boundless ocean feeds the rivers dissecting the universe ...'[605] Pejoration and disillusionment reassert themselves, however, in the dying words of the rabbi's son, Il'ya, for whom nothing is sacred any more: 'A mother in a revolution is an episode, – he whispered, his voice fading. – My letter came, the letter B, and the organisation sent me to the front ...'[606]

Galin, however, has a vision of a brighter future; he is still absurdly capable of optimism despite the sordidness of his surroundings and his unrequited love: 'we're cleaning the kernel of its shell for you; a little time will pass, you'll see this kernel cleaned',[607] and in his peroration he concludes: 'The revolutionary curve has thrown into the front line the free Cossacks steeped in many prejudices, but the CC in its manoeuvring will wear them down with a brush of iron ...'[608] His imagery encapsulates the ambivalent role of the Cossacks, brutal and heroic on the one hand, vulnerable and victims of circumstance on the other.

Originality

In my final section, on the originality of the metaphors in both cycles, I have used three designations. Those possessing no freshness or originality I have called 'fossilized', while those designated 'living' possess an impact which is immediate because of the quality of their imagery. I acknowledge the subjectivity of judgement that I have exercised in arriving at the results in Table 4, but would argue that no study of Babel's metaphors would be complete without comment on the degree and the use that he makes of both living and fossilized metaphor. To these two categories I have added a third, that of 'revitalization'. This category concerns metaphors which in isolation are unremarkable yet because of their juxtaposition breathe fresh life into one another. In Lyutov's prose, which contains most instances of this in either cycle (8.3 per cent), the most common occurrences arise from sequences of metaphor and simile. In 'Pan Apolek', for example, the primary narrator describes the stillness of a garden at night, a garden which, like him, seems to have drawn breath in expectation of Apolek's imminent, irreverent story of Christ and which dare not breathe again, lest the painter be dissuaded from his path. 'Aroused by the opening of Apolek's story I pace the kitchen floor and await the cherished hour. *And night beyond the window stands like a black column.* Beyond the window the live dark garden lies torpid.'[609] The phrase 'stoit noch'' ('night stands') represents a fossilized metaphor; the use of 'stoyat'' ('to stand') for 'byt'' ('to be') has in normal circumstances no figurative capacity, yet the simile 'like a black column' reminds us of the verb's literal meaning, 'stands' and imbues the phrase with fresh life, rendering it figurative once more in its evocation of an atmosphere of brooding sombreness.[610]

Lyutov's figures, unsurprisingly, embody the greatest degree of originality of both cycle's protagonists. Not only are his metaphors more numerous, but they are created, as we have seen, in more diverse ways. The variation of sensuous transfer and the exploitation of differently based synaesthetic metaphor, the animation of the inanimate and the sequencing of metaphor with other tropes – in particular simile, metonymy and synecdoche – all contribute to an impression of a prose saturated in figure, and teeming in living imagery. Lyutov's tonal range, his lyricism, his epic stance, his condemnation of circumstances and events befalling him and his sense of dislocation and hopelessness are conveyed in startling and memorable fashion through Babel's versatile figurative techniques. His metaphors present moments of piercing insight and emotion. In 'Eskadronnyy Trunov' Trunov's battle-hardened companion Andrey Vos'miletov confronts a young Polish prisoner of superior mien, whose clean-cut Germanic looks and woollen underwear enrage the Cossack.[611] The gulf between their worlds and the ambivalence of their respective roles as both victim and oppressor are conveyed in tiny metaphoric details whose pathos is enhanced by alliteration:

– Otkuda spodniki dostal?
– Matka vyazala, – otvetil plennyy i pokachnulsya.
– Fabrichnaya u tebya matka, – skazal Andryushka, vsyo priglyadyvayas', *i podushechkami paltsev potrogal u polyaka kholennyye nogti*, – fabrichnaya u tebya matka, nash brat takikh ne nashival …'[612]

– Where did you get the undies?
– Ma knitted them, – the prisoner answered and swayed.
– A proper little factory your ma, – Andryushka said, still peering *and with the pincushions of his fingers touched the Pole's manicured nails*, – a proper little factory your ma, our brothers don't get to wear things like this.

The Pole's manicured nails bespeak privilege, while Andrey's thickened fingers are those of a rustic turned soldier, whose hands now grasp both power and the fate of the former.

With battle about to commence in 'Chesniki', metaphor is used to create suspense and to lend an epic dimension in its presaging of the violence and defeat to come: 'The men yelling moved on after them, *and pale steel flashed in the ichor of the autumnal sun*. But I heard no unanimity in the Cossacks' cry.'[613] The ichor of the autumnal sun evokes the image of a weeping wound; the steel's paleness equates with the men's half-heartedness; everyone and everything is subdued, fearful of the worst.

Even when Lyutov's imagery appears fossilized or bears the stamp of triteness,[614] as in 'Kladbishche v Kozine', it creates a mood, an atmosphere. The dearth of living imagery in this story conveys a world of barren, Jewish decay. The trite figurative epitaphs to the dead rabbis portray their effeteness in life. The empty bluster of the inscriptions equates with the sterility of a living rabbi, portrayed earlier in the cycle:

We entered a room – stony and empty like a morgue. Rabbi Motale was sitting at a table, surrounded by liars and the possessed. He wore a sable

193

cap and a white dressing gown, tied with a cord. The rabbi was sitting with his eyes closed, digging with his thin fingers in the yellow down of his beard.[615]

His residence resembles the stone tombs of Kozin and his appearance foreshadows the figures of rabbis crudely hewn in the granite there. Like them he wears a fur cap and his gown is belted.[616] His closed lids, the anguished picking at his beard and the colour of his gown, with its resemblance to a death-shroud,[617] foreshadow the eyeless, stone rabbis of Kozin: 'Depictions of rabbis in fur caps. Rabbis' narrow hips girdled with a belt. And beneath eyeless faces the curved stone line of their curly beards.'[618]

Babel's ability to create atmosphere and convey emotion through metaphor is more often seen in *Konarmiya* than in *Na pole chesti*. Only 32.3 per cent of the narrator's metaphors of the first cycle merit the label 'living', while it is the soldier-narrator of 'Semeystvo papashi Maresko' who employs a greater amount of living imagery with some 46.7 per cent. In *Konarmiya,* by comparison, only 23.9 per cent of Cossacks' metaphors can be termed 'living', since Babel frequently employs fossilized, colloquial metaphor to characterize the many Cossack protagonists as a collective, yet distinct whole. The fashioning of the soldier-narrator of 'Semeystvo papashi Maresko' is done in a way that foreshadows both Lyutov and the individual Cossack narrators of *Konarmiya*. The lieutenant has a unique role in the cycle. Like Lyutov he is a filter and like him he records details of horror in similar fashion: 'Around us broken Crucifixes, pieces of monuments, grave-stones, played havoc with by the hammer of some unknown defiler. Decayed corpses tumble out of the coffins, smashed by shells.' (ll.3–6, 'Semeystvo papashi Maresko') Lyutov employs a similarly figurative animation in his description of the churchyard and church in Novograd: 'A corpse stripped of clothing lies down the slope. And moonlight streams over dead legs thrust out apart … The gates of the church had been opened, I enter and to meet me two silver skulls gleam on the lid of a broken coffin.'[619] Then in subsequent musing on his situation, the French lieutenant includes figures which foreshadow the Cossack humour of Konkin or Balmashov: 'If we are destined to increase the population of this chilly corner, well we've made the rotting old men dance first to the march of our machine-guns.' (ll.8–10, 'Semeystvo papashi Maresko') But it is in a sequence of metaphor and metonymy that the narrator of 'Semeystvo papashi Maresko' creates imagery of a quality to compare with Lyutov. Two epithets prepare for the subsequent final comment on the abject status of the civilian, Maresko: 'The character makes his entrance. *A worn, faded* creature. Got up in a Sunday frock-coat.' (ll.21–2, 'Semeystvo papashi Maresko')[620] Together with the neuter substantive and pronoun ('sushchestvo' and 'ono') they precipitate Maresko's capitulation as a human being in the officer's eyes: 'The Sunday frock-coat turned pale and huddled up.' (l.53, 'Semeystvo papashi Maresko')

The Cossacks of the major cycle are also capable of living imagery, but it is by no means the dominant feature that it is in the tropes of Lyutov.[621] It occurs mostly in those stories in which Lyutov is replaced as narrator and not in the speech of Cossacks who make appearances elsewhere. In both situations, however, the Cossacks' language frequently comprises hackneyed figures which employ colloquial language and which embody invective, references to peasant lifestyles, to love of horses, or to violence or lust, thereby characterizing the roots and the preoccupations of their formulators. Examples abound; some are crude like Kurdyukov's description of this father: 'my father was a dog',[622] others combine insult with violence, as Lyutov discovers from Savitskiy: 'What a little wretch ... They send you without asking, and they cut down specs here.'[623] Yet the barrage of insults in 'Moy pervyy gus' cedes to figures which betoken ingenuousness as well as a rustic upbringing. A Cossack comments thus on an article by Lenin that Lyutov had just read aloud: 'Truth tickles everyone's nostril, said Surovkov, when I'd finished, – and how do you drag it from the heap, but he hits it straightway, like a chicken with grain ...'[624] Horsemanship offers many opportunities for metaphor, some of which can be humorous or esoteric: 'Tail to the side and joking apart ...';[625] 'if he's replaced, then soap the withers and knock away the supports. Period.'[626] Physical passion is alluded to in Pavlichenko's metaphors concerning his recent marriage, and again animalism and violence obtain: 'We were hot all night, in winter we were hot, we went bare all night long and tore the hide off one another.'[627]

Seventy-one per cent of Cossacks' metaphors are of the fossilized or trite variety but others occur whose imagery is living and whose relative infrequency contributes to their impact. Sidorov's assessment of Italy's readiness for revolution, 'In Italy the earth is smouldering',[628] and his desire to be its instigator compares with the pent-up energy, centre-stage arrogance and sense of anticipation that obtains in Pavlichenko's description of the steppe. The whole world lies open to him, but in his use of 'polegla' ('lay down') he likens his freedom to crops that have been flattened. His freedom lies prone with them, yet it is ready to spring up when the right moment comes: 'until the little year eighteen came to visit me, a wastrel',[629] when he can cease to be a herdsman on the Lidino estate, and embark upon his path of becoming a Red general. 'Liberation lay down around me in the fields, the grass in all the world rustles, the skies swing about above me like a many-keyed accordion.'[630]

Even less living metaphor is encountered in the language of other protagonists; most of their figures comprise fossilized cliché or invective similar to that of the Cossacks:[631] 'The Pole is an evil dog', declares Gedali. 'He takes the Jew and tears out his beard, ah the cur! And now they're beating him, the evil dog.'[632] But it is Gedali's confused, allegorical manner of discourse that also supplies some of this category's living imagery and renders its spokesman unique in the cycle: 'A mother's memory feeds compassion in us, as the ocean, the boundless ocean feeds the rivers dissecting the universe ... In the passionate edifice of Hassidism the doors and windows have been broken open, but it's immortal, like a mother's soul ...'[633] Less lofty sentiments are uttered in typically banal fashion by the beggarwoman

in 'Sashka Khristos': 'it's pure circus with you ...', [634] she declares to Tarakanych for the rough advances that he makes to her. But amid the bluster
and cliché of the itinerant whore lies the crude humour that is so often
associated with the Cossacks: 'A little rain on an old woman, – she laughed,
– I'll give twelve hundred kilos an acre ...' [635]

Original figure is indeed more common in the prose of Lyutov but this is
hardly surprising, since ostensibly he is recording events and impressions
via the written word, while the Cossacks and other protagonists for the most
part are speaking. Indeed, the tiny proportion of the cycle that the speech of
Lyutov represents (1.1 per cent) also embodies a mixture of fossilized figure
with the occasional instance of a living trope: 'we're done for, old man!' [636]
he shouts to Grishchuk in 'Smert' Dolgushova', to whom he later bemoans
the loss of Bida's friendship: 'today I lost Afon'ka, my first friend ...' [637] But
in 'Gedali' there are instances of living imagery in the speech of the primary
narrator which compare with the versatility of his written tropes. In reply to
Gedali's naïve wish for an International of good people, the primary narrator observes that 'It's served up with gunpowder ... and seasoned with the
best blood ...', [638] and then, in nostalgic mood since it is the Sabbath, he asks
the Jewish shopkeeper: 'Where can you get ... a little of that dismissed god
in a glass of tea? ...' [639]

CONCLUSION

While the proliferation of tropes in *Konarmiya* links Babel with the ornamental trends of the twenties, [640] his tropes in general and his metaphors in
particular are never merely ornaments to some supposed non-metaphorical
language: they lie at the very heart of his use of language and are central to
depicting the respective psyches of each of his narrators and protagonists.
The aspirations and fallibilities of Lyutov, of Cossacks like Sidorov, Balmashov, Konkin or Pavlichenko, of soldiers such as Maresko's lieutenant, of
protagonists like Gedali or Apolek and of little men like Bidu, Bozhi and
Maresko, become apparent through the tropes formed by them or about
them. Babel's metaphors may seem enigmatic, for, often laced with irony,
they are intrinsic to the essential ambivalence that each of his protagonists
embodies, yet far from being obfuscatory they shed a light that is for the
most part visually brilliant and piercing in the insights that it affords.

In my study generally I have shown how Babel portrays the ugliness and
savagery of the conflicts and dilemmas which confront Lyutov and the little
men of *Na pole chesti*. This has been achieved through a close study of
particular aspects of the tropes that Babel uses. My analysis of form indicates Lyutov's predilection for verb-only metaphors which lend dynamism
and visual force and yet create contrasting moods of gentleness and violence,
stasis and movement. I also show in 'Kladbishche v Kozine' how a predom-
inance of metaphors formed from concrete substantives betokens sinister
grandeur and the oppressive presence of death amid the decaying face of a

Judaism which contrasts with the vibrancy of the bubbling Jews that Lyutov had known in the south. Form is an equally important aspect of the Cossacks' tropes; they manifest a desire to deal in basic concepts, in tangible images, more readily than the primary narrator does. Lyutov's greater level of visual to abstract transfer befits a man of intellect who is more at ease with abstraction, which he exploits to create astringent satirical images in stories like 'Vecher'. The author's choice of form is thus an integral element in his process of character delineation and in his creation of mood or atmosphere.

Babel's prose is justly noted for the passages of his primary narrator which abound in imagery, yet it is the language of protagonists other than Lyutov which embodies a greater clustering of images. It is the sequential linking of the primary narrator's tropes, however, which distinguishes them from those of others in both cycles. One trope begets another and leads into a third. Such sequences not only arrest and shock, but they also link one story to another in subtle ways, binding the cycle into a unified whole that is at first not apparent. Epithets depicting the primary narrator's changing moods recur; insight and ambivalence result from the interplay of metaphorical nuances, such as the use of 'polzti/to creep' in 'Smert' Dolgushova', where the verb portrays firstly the passage of the doomed Dolgushov's entrails over his knees, and secondly the spread of the narrator's fear as he is threatened with death. The verb's recurrence links the circumstances of the two men and exemplifies the blurring of their respective roles, a leitmotif of the two cycles: both are simultaneously oppressor and victim, persecutor and persecuted.

Sequencing and the subtle recurrence of imagery are very largely missing from the trope clusters of the language of the Cossacks or other protagonists. Their tropes occur often in series of discrete images, which sit in incongruous fashion with one another; in the minor cycle the telescoped fusing of images common to the prose of Lyutov is largely lacking although occasional glimpses give notice of what is to come in *Konarmiya*.

Babel also exploits pre-positive imagery in his figures, a device which helps freshen and lend greater impact through seemingly illogical inversion. His tropes acquire the flavour of poetry through the unification of a number of thematically incongruous elements in an unusual order. The effect is either to fashion aesthetic imagery which has an epic flavour or to create irony or satire, which the Cossacks in particular are made to utter in unwitting fashion. Such syntactic inversion also affords a means of reflecting Lyutov's distorted Weltanschauung.

In my discussion of theme I have stressed Babel's predilection for imagery recruited from the human sphere. Nature, the environment, and the artefacts of man are made to subserve the feelings of Lyutov. The inanimate and the inert are quickened in sinister fashion by the primary narrator and testify to an obsessive self-preoccupation. The Cossacks, soldiers and other protagonists of both cycles employ imagery which likewise reflects their respective personalities and perceptions; the alternating view of the Revolution, for example, as both an epic battle and a love affair, as portrayed by Pavlichenko in a mixture of masculine- and feminine-based imagery, is indicative of the forces of violence and lust which motivate the Cossacks.

Yet a relative lack of explicitly violent or militaristic imagery reflects Babel's philosophy of 'understatement', of forcing his reader to forge a network of interactions from the language employed and then to select appropriate associations and connotations. Such reactive, emotional participation is demanded in particular by Lyutov. The rustic imagery and explicit invective which are the hallmarks of the Cossacks again delineate character and contrast with the subtle framework of pejoration that flows in far more damning fashion from the pen of Lyutov.

My analysis of the transfer that is effected between stimulant and imported image in Babel's metaphors reveals, more than any other aspect, the development that his use of figurative language has undergone between the writing of his two cycles. The period between 1920 and 1925 was the time when ornamentalist tendencies were at their peak in Soviet prose and while Babel's language cannot be described as gratuitously ornamental, his considerable use of tropes in *Konarmiya* and *Odesskiye rasskazy* (a cycle that still awaits exhaustive analysis) bears testimony to the literary trend of the times. While *Konarmiya* does not embody the linguistic experiments of a Belyy, Pil'nyak or Gladkov, it does contain a synaesthetic richness in its imagery that others, such as Olesha who has also been placed on the ornamentalist register, exploit in their creation of fresh and powerfully affective images.

Babel's portrayal of war is largely visual, yet in his range of synaesthetic metaphors he embodies the fusion of unlike generic entities with startling results. While auditory imagery is used to create crescendos of suspense in the major cycle, there is only occasional recourse to the other senses of smell, taste and touch. Considerable figurative tactile contact, as with smell and taste, would place the reader too much in the centre of events; the author prefers to keep him at a distance, mostly viewing through Lyutov's prism or listening to his sound-track, observing and reacting from the outside, rather than seeing and feeling from within.

My study of Babel's use of synaesthetic transfer also supports the earlier stated view that his protagonists manifest the desire to control or subjugate the environment for their own purposes or ends. Such a desire stems from their sense of insecurity and uncertainty. The Cossacks and French soldiers more frequently employ abstract to visual transfer in their imagery, thereby manifesting a greater desire than Lyutov to visualise and 'concretize' (and thus to control) concepts like 'freedom', which for Pavlichenko lies ready to spring up like flattened crops, or 'revolution' which is symbolized in the smouldering earth of Italy by Sidorov. Lyutov, however, invests his tropes with *ostraneniye*, a device which exposes the disorientation and sense of isolation that he feels. His dwelling on the ugliness of war is graphically realized in a harnessing of imagery which, while mostly visual, occasionally appeals to other senses simultaneously. Babel's prime aim is to disconcert, to impart to his reader Lyutov's anxiety and uncertainty as he confronts the issues of life and death, friendship and enmity, bravery and cowardice amid the alien environment of his existence. *Na pole chesti*'s narrator in no way possesses the distinctive prism of a Lyutov and is often closer to the Cossacks of *Konarmiya* in the type of transfer that he effects in his figurative language. His preference for abstract to visual transfer, his heavier use of the usually banal like-abstract transfer, and his use of the rare animate to inanimate transfer which is reserved for puns or explicit invective and which Lyutov almost totally eschews, all testify to this.

My analysis finally shows that Babel's portrayal of war, whatever its context, France in 1918 or the Galician campaign of 1920, is pejorative. That the first cycle is less markedly so is due to the fact that Babel had had very little personal experience of what he wrote. It was written at second-hand and bestowed upon the narrator a perception which is less distinct, less individualistic than Lyutov's. As the author's diary testifies, by the time that he wrote *Konarmiya* he had experienced violence, brutality and death at first-hand and it is these impressions which inform the brutalized perspective of his Cossack narrators and the angst-ridden perception of his central persona. The elevatory imagery that obtains is often directly juxtaposed with the depreciatory and is used to create an intensified and cumulatively ironic and damning effect. The links with the *byliny* and medieval heroic poems allow Babel the opportunity to exalt and deride simultaneously, to create ambivalent pictures which stress the dynamism and the vulnerability of his Cossack protagonists, Cossacks whose veneer of dash and bravado at times approaches the superhuman qualities of the *bogatyri* and yet conceals the anguish and vulnerability of a Sidorov, Konkin or Balmashov.

It is the primary narrator's metaphors, in their intensity, range and richness, which undoubtedly distinguish him from each of the other protagonists and Babel's second war cycle is distinct from his first not least for the quality of figure that he employs, for the telescoped sequences of tropes, the variety of synaesthetic transfer and the range of sensuous images. Yet within the confines of the first cycle we discern the glimmerings of the masterpiece to come. In the narrator's references to natural phenomena, for example, we experience the jarring originality of a Lyutovian image: Ratin's abusive words fall on Bidu as arid hail, and on the battlefield of 'Kvaker' the sun rummages in upturned corpses.[641] In the metonymy and metaphor of the French lieutenant we hear not only the tones of Lyutov but the arrogance and sense of farce of Cossack narrators such as Konkin, Balmashov or Pavlichenko as the civilian Maresko becomes a shabby, faded frock-coat.[642] From Babel's exploitation in the lesser cycle of pre-positive figures, images of *ostraneniye*, and the portrayal of men such as Ston, have come the marvellously mock-heroic and unwittingly self-condemnatory tropes of Cossacks like Balmashov and protagonists like Galin, together with the obverse, Lyutovian figures of epic and poetic grandeur; and while at times in *Konarmiya* the orchestrating hand of Babel is glimpsed amid the various *skaz* registers,[643] it is rare that the individual voices blur, that Cossack crudity is confounded with the diction of Lyutov, for the latter's is a unique language which bespeaks a unique perception.

Epilogue

The portrayal of people's behaviour and feelings in times of war, their respective reactions to the personal dilemmas which confront them, are subjects of endless fascination for Babel. He relentlessly pursues the psyche of war heroes and, just as he blurs historical details and points to the timelessness of man's tyranny in inflicting violence upon his fellows,[644] so do his heroes and his victims merge, each forming part of the other. *Na pole chesti*'s victims are indeed the cycle's heroes, heroic figures of *Konarmiya* such as Kolesnikov and Konkin are as much victims in their vulnerability as Bozhi or Bidu.

There can be no doubt, however, that the depiction of suffering, the portrayal of the negative aspects of war, is a prime purpose of the author, for the pejoration conveyed by Lyutov in *Konarmiya* consistently exceeds any depreciatory tone contained in the diary. This is effected by a process of distortion which can result in a reversal of what is originally recorded in the diary entries, and although Babel transfers to Lyutov a sense of awe for Cossack heroes and a nostalgic affection for his Jewish roots, he also imbues him with a revulsion from the brutality of the former and a palpable loathing for the degradation in which the Jews live.

In tracing the origin of stories such as 'Eskadronnyy Trunov' we see how Babel builds into Lyutov this increased sense of horror. The changing stance of author-narrator is exemplified firstly in Babel's adaptation of Vidal's stories in *Na pole chesti*, and is seen again in the major cycle when diary, plans and finished stories are examined together. It is effected often through tiny metaphorical embellishments, which also link stories and forge a cyclical unity, as, for example, the imagery of sterility that is reserved by Lyutov for both living and dead rabbis in 'Rabbi' and 'Kladbishche v Kozine' respectively.[645]

Lyutov is an agent of distortion: he more usually stamps his mood on nature, his perspective on the surroundings, as in 'Vecher', than vice-versa. His lenses filter his inner moods to us as they focus on events and circumstances around him. His imagery encapsulates his vacillating love-hate relationship with war and its purveyors, whose own accounts like those of the primary narrator reflect their own tensions and those of other protagonists. Lyutov indeed represents the sufferings of all victim-protagonists of both cycles, and he shares too in their fleeting, shortlived triumphs. A part of each protagonist resides in him – the little men of *Na pole chesti*; the victimized woman of 'Perekhod cherez Zbruch'; old Gedali, the lonely and confused Jew; the now ascendant now disgraced Savitskiy; the vengeful

Pavlichenko. But it is the heroic stoicism of victims like Grishchuk with which he most closely identifies. The omission of his story from *Konarmiya* renders Grishchuk an enigmatic figure in the cycle. Yet the figures of Grishchuk and Lyutov merge and interact in a revealing way when the diary entries and eponymous story are read in conjunction with 'Ucheniye o tachanke' and 'Smert' Dolgushova'. 'Grishchuk', in concert with the other stories, completes Babel's portrayal of Lyutov's driver, yet for once the balance is destroyed by the story's omission.

Lyutov's triumphs may seem on a different level from the glory that is Savitskiy's or Kolesnikov's, yet they emulate it, both in their personal significance and in their fleetingness. His killing of the goose, for example, allows him an entrée into a Cossack world, which, as Savitskiy had earlier and cuttingly implied, would be inaccessible to him. That Lyutov is quickly revolted by his own act[646] is but another detail which contributes to the heavily pejorative portrayal of war that both cycles represent. Lyutov's final act of triumph which is celebrated in *Konarmiya*'s last line: 'My dream was fulfilled. The Cossacks stopped following me and my horse with their eyes',[647] in fact conceals his greatest one, that of his own survival in a world alien to him. It is not a triumph that Babel himself was to share. Perhaps he foresaw his own fate as he created Lyutov's damning, astringent tropes, tropes which constitute such a bitter indictment of man's capacity for violence and inhumanity. Yet a note of optimism was sounded at least by another of Babel's protagonists for whom life was ambivalent also: 'For victories which were defeats, for defeats which became victories, for life and death my recompense has been a paltry one ... But I feel no anger. I do not feel it because I know that I shall not die before I have snatched one more – and it will be my last ... golden sovereign.'[648] Whether Babel ever snatched a last golden moment from life before his death we cannot say; that he supplied his readers with many is beyond doubt.

Equally indubitable is the irony of Babel's Weltanschauung. In my prologue, I quote a remark made by the author to Paustovskiy: 'I have no imagination ... I cannot invent. I must know everything to the last jot, otherwise I can write nothing.'[649] The major transformation that Babel effects between the pedestrian tone of Vidal's stories and the vitality of his own; the minor transmogrification of possessions into events in references to the priest Tuzinkevich between diary entry[650] and 'U svyatogo Valenta'; the changing of the bare facts of Apanasenko's military renown, as listed in the plans,[651] into a portrayal of his psyche and his earlier life in 'Zhizneopisaniye Pavlichenki, Matveya Rodionycha' – all belie this statement and point to an imagination that was fertile and inventive in the extreme. It was an imagination too at which many have marvelled and some in their admiration may have copied. A fellow Odessan, Lev Slavin, wrote a story entitled 'Tysyacha i odna noch'', which is set in Odessa at a time of famine.[652] It relates how a pair of black marketeers accost an old man bearing a mysterious sack. They use their position of influence in the underworld to negotiate a deal with the owner for its contents, which they believe to be food. The sack in fact contains the wretched remains of another old man who has died of hunger. The irony, black comedy and mock-heroic treatment of the black marketeers bear very distinctly the stamp of Babel', just as the macabre outcome is reminiscent of 'Semeystvo papashi Maresko'. Babel's little men, his Maresko, his Lyutov, Slavin's old man and Babel himself might well have uttered in unison the bitter-sweet words quoted above of the author's literary protagonist, as, like him, they view their lives retrospectively: 'For victories which were defeats, for defeats which became victories, for life and death my recompense has been a paltry one ...'[653]

Notes

PART ONE

1. Reported in J. Stora-Sandor, *Isaac Babel' 1894–1941, L'homme et L'oeuvre* (Paris, 1968), p.15.
2. K. Paustovskiy, *Povest' o zhizni*, in Sobr. soch., ed. V. Borisova, vol. 5 (Moscow, 1967), p.117.
3. Stora-Sandor, op. cit., p.7.
4. Paustovskiy, op. cit., p.137.
5. Gaston Vidal, *Figures et anecdotes de la Grande Guerre* (Paris, 1918).
6. 'Probuzhdeniye' and 'V podvale'.
7. 14/10/31; *Vozdushnyye puti*, no. 3 (New York, 1963).
8. Paustovskiy, op. cit., p.118.
9. Only part of this diary is preserved (June–Sept 1920) and is in the possession of the author's widow, A. N. Pirozhkova, who published it in *Isaak Babel' Sochineniya v dvukh tomakh*, (Moscow, Khudozhestvennaya Literatura, 1990). Extracts have been published in *Literaturnoye nasledstvo*, LXXIV (Moscow, 1965) and in E. R. Sicher, ed., *Isaak Babel': Detstvo i drugiye rasskazy* (henceforth cited: *Isaak Babel* (1979)) (Israel, 1979); See also notes 2 and 14 of Part Two.
10. *Lava* (Odessa, 1920) was published in June 1920 and claimed to be a literary and political journal, but was shortlived.
11. *Lava*, ibid.
12. Vidal, op. cit.
13. Nathalie Babel includes translations by Max Hayward of *Na pole chesti* in *Isaak Babel, You must know everything. Stories 1915–1937* (London, 1970).
14. E. Sicher, 'The Works of I. E. Babel (1894–1941) with special reference to tradition and innovation in the style of his narrative prose of the 1920s', unpublished thesis (Oxford, 1979).
15. Danuta Mendelsohn, *Metaphor in Babel's Short Stories* (Ann Arbor, 1982), pp.91–2.
16. R. de Wilde, *De Liége à l'Yser. Mon Journal de Campagne* (Brussels, 1918).
17. M. Lekeux, *Mes cloîtres dans la tempête* (Brussels, 1922).
18. In *30 dney*, no. 6 (Moscow, 1932). In a discussion of the story in *Smena* nos. 17–18 (1932), Babel attributes its writing to 1920–2.

19. See, for example, *Isaak Babel* (1979), p.359.
20. *Sobraniye sochineniy G. de Mopassand*, ed. I. Babel, (Moscow–Leningrad, 1926–7), 3 vols.
21. *Isaak Babel* (1979), p.86.
22. From a letter from Babel to Gorkiy written on 26 June 1925 and published in *Literaturnoye nasledstvo*, LXX, pp.39–40 and in *Izbrannoye: I. Babel'* (Moscow, 1966), pp.431–2, and 481.
23. See p.50 for my comments on this.
24. *Isaak Babel* (1979), p.89.
25. The texts of Babel's and Vidal's stories are printed in appendices A and B below. They are taken from the sources named (see footnotes 5 and 10) and quotations are taken from these versions; translations are my own.
26. 'Dezertir' and 'Semeystvo papashi Maresko'.
27. It is with these words that Paustovskiy entitles a chapter of his *Povest' o zhizni*, op. cit., p.135. He reports Babel as using these words on p.142.
28. 'Na pole chesti'.
29. Vidal uses 1,520 words; Babel uses 530.
30. Babel's alteration of the names used by Vidal is commented on below. See p.30.
31. This and other quotations from *Konarmiya* are taken from *Isaak Babel* (1979). This quotation comes from p.225. Preparation of the text, commentaries and bibliography are by E. Sicher, who states on p.5: 'The majority of the works of Isaac Babel presented in this book are printed according to the texts of early publications, often appearing in unavailable journals and papers of the twenties. In this way the present collection differs from preceding collections of selected works of the author.'
32. I. A. Smirin, 'Iz planov i nabroskov k *Konarmii*', in *Literaturnoye nasledstvo*, LXXIV (Moscow, 1965).
33. See, for example, Anne M. Iverson, 'The Ancient Greek "Death" Aspect of Spring in Mandelstam's Poetry', in *Slavic and East European Journal*, XX, no.1 (1976).
34. Vidal's version merely states: 'Je regarde les herbes.'
35. *Isaak Babel* (1979), p.148.
36. Ibid., p.149.
37. Smirin, 'Iz planov i nabroskov k *Konarmii*, op. cit., p.490.
38. Ibid., p.491.
39. *Isaak Babel* (1979), p.101.
40. T. W. Clyman, 'Babel as Colorist', in *Slavic and East European Journal*, XXI, Part 3 (1977), p.334.
41. *Isaak Babel* (1979), p.224.
42. Ibid., p.125.
43. Ibid., p.126; 'menya' is Lyutov.
44. Ibid., p.228. In his commentary, Sicher says, on p.390, that the second sentence of the three that I have quoted has been omitted in all editions of Babel's works since his rehabilitation and the omission is therefore due to censorship.

45. Their bravery and willingness to face danger are commented on, for example, in Ragna Grøngaarde, *I. Babel's 'Red Cavalry' – an Investigation of Composition and Theme* (Aarhus, 1979), translated by Daniel R. Frickleton.

46. 'Deux actes devant une conscience'; see Appendix B, below.

47. The first spelling of the name is the transliterated Russian, the second is the French spelling. I shall use the transliterated Russian spelling unless I refer to the French version. For discussion of Babel's use of names see pp.30–1.

48. I. A. Smirin. 'U istokov voyennoy temy v tvorchestve I. Babelya', in *Russkaya literatura*, Part 1 (1967), pp.203–4.

49. See, for example, the stories 'Perekhod cherez Zbruch', 'Kombrig dva', 'Afon'ka Bida', 'Eskadronnyy Trunov'.

50. *Isaak Babel* (1979), p.136.

51. Ibid., p.104.

52. For discussion on the definition and characteristics of *skaz* see Martin P. Rice, 'On *Skaz*', in *Russian Literature Triquarterly*, XII (Michagan, Spring 1975). Rice states that *skaz* is a loosely used term and has no firm definition as yet. I shall use the term, as I do here, in the conventionally accepted sense of language written in the oral manner of a character or protagonist to further authenticity, atmosphere and colour in a piece of literature.

53. J. N. Cru, *Témoins: Essai d'analyse et de critique des souvenirs de combattants édités en français de 1915–1928* (Paris, 1929), pp.408–10.

54. Thomas Rothschild, 'Issak Babel – Eine Monographie', unpublished thesis (Vienna University, 1967), p.98.

55. *Isaak Babel* (1979), p.181.

56. For comment on the names of the protagonists of the *Na pole chesti* cycle that have no links with Vidal's work, namely Ston and Bekker of 'Kvaker', see pp.14–15 and p.51.

57. *Isaak Babel* (1979), p.174.

58. Babel uses a popular form of the French 'bien'.

59. T. Rothschild, 'Zur Form von Isaak Babel's Erzählungen', *Wiener Slavistisches Jahrbuch,* Part 16 (Vienna, 1970), pp.127–8.

60. Published originally in 1923, in *Ogni*, VI (Kiev, 9 February 1913), but forgotten until its republication in April 1967 in *Gorizont* (Odessa), pp.68–71.

61. Rothschild, 'Zur Form von Isaak Babel's Erzählungen', op. cit., p.127.

62. Mendelsohn, op. cit., p.92. She may have thought that this line was a forerunner of a metaphor in 'Gedali': 'tak nachinayet Gedali i obvivayet menya sholkovymi remnyami svoikh dymchatykh glaz' ('thus begins Gedali and entwines me with the silky straps of his smoky eyes'). *Isaak Babel* (1979), p.126.

63. See for example pp.28, 32, 38.

64. Cf I. A. Smirin, 'Na puti k *Konarmii*', in *Literaturnoye nasledstvo*, LXXIV (Moscow, 1965), pp.478–9.

65. *Isaak Babel* (1979), p.191.
66. Ibid., p.187.
67. Ibid.
68. Published in *Krasnaya nov'*, no. 7 (December 1923) as a variant of 'Skazka pro babu', published in *Siluety*, No. 8–9 (Odessa, 1923) the previous year.
69. *Isaak Babel* (1979), p.101.
70. Ibid., p.102.
71. Ibid., p.160.
72. V. Propp, *Morfologiya skazki*, (Leningrad, 1928); L. Seyfullina, *O Literature* (Moscow, 1958).
73. See for example, the beginning and end of 'Pis'mo', or the ending of 'Sashka Khristos' or 'Istoriya odnoy loshadi' respectively.
74. See p.44. Babel may have been influenced here in his choice of imagery by a simile that Gogol used; 'khozyain tak zhe trudno opredelit', kak tsvet iznoshennogo syurtuka.' (N. Gogol, sobr. soch., vol. 3, eds S. I. Mashinskiy, N. L. Stepanov and M. B. Khrapchenko (Moscow, 1966–7), p.248). For further comment on Gogolian influence see p.159 and note 365 of Part Three.
75. My emphasis.
76. i.e. the second of the four sections that I noted on p.24.
77. Alice Lee comments specifically on this in 'Epiphany in Babel's *Red Cavalry*', in *Russian Literature Triquarterly*, III (Michigan, 1972), pp.249–60.
78. Compare, for example, a passage in 'Smert' Dolgushova' where Lyutov, harangued by Afon'ka Bida for not dispatching the mortally wounded Dolgushov, is threatened with death: 'I vzvyol kurok. Ya poyekhal shagom, ne oborachivayas', chuvstvuya spinoy kholod i smert'.' *Isaak Babel* (1979), p.144).
79. Ibid., p.141. Analysis and discussion of this sequence is given in Part Three; for comment on revitalized metaphor, see my section entitled 'Originality' in Part Three.
80. *Isaak Babel* (1979), p.103.
81. See pp.14–15.
82. For example, Afon'ka Bida in the eponymous story: 'Kon' – on drug, – otvetil Orlov. – Kon' – on otets, – vzdokhnul Bitsenko, – beschislenno raz zhiznyu spasayet. Propast' Bide bez konya …' *Isaak Babel* (1979), p.181. Other stories include 'Istoriya odnoy loshadi' and 'Prodolzheniye istorii odnoy loshadi'.
83. Something that he achieves in the final story 'Argamak', which Babel published in 1932, several years after the remainder of the cycle. In 1990, however, Babel's widow, A. N. Pirozhkova, published a two-volume edition of Babel's collected works in which she added another story 'Potseluy' (published in 1937) to the end of the *Konarmiya* cycle, claiming that he had always intended to do so himself.
84. See, for example, 'Kostyol v Novograde', 'Rabbi', 'Gedali'.

85. From 'Moy pervyy gus', *Isaak Babel* (1979), p.130.

86. See p.47.

87. An episode from the story concerning some prisoners is also to be found in two other fragmentary versions, 'Ikh bylo devyat'' published in *Novyy zhurnal*, no. 95 (New York, June 1969), pp.16–20, and 'Ikh bylo desyat'', the handwritten manuscript of which is in the possession of Babel's widow, Pirozhkova. For further discussion of the origins and thematic strands of 'Eskadronnyy Trunov', see my section, 'The Trunov Complex', in Part Two.

88. *Isaak Babel* (1979), p.189.

89. Ibid.

90. *Krasnaya nov'*, no. 2 (Feb, 1925); and *Shkval*, no. 13 (Odessa, 1925).

91. *Isaak Babel* (1979), p.190 (the first five words are included in all editions).

92. Ibid., p.188.

93. Babel's respective, pejorative comparison of Ston and the Galician to Don Quixote contradicts the positive associations which had been created in the literary imagination by Turgenev's essay, 'Hamlet and Don Quixote', in I. S. Turgenev, *Polnoye sobraniye sochineniy i pisem*, VIII (Moscow–Leningrad, 1964), pp.171–92, first published in *Sovremennaya*, no. 1 (1860), pp.239–58.

94. *Isaak Babel* (1979), p.189.

95. Ibid., p.190.

96. Ibid.

97. Ibid., pp.189–90.

98. From 'uvidel pered soboy galichanina', to 'goryachiy blesk nebes', ibid.

99. See pp.19–20. The relevant quotations which I have included on p.20 are: 'Zemlya izdavala zlovoniye, solntse kopalos' v razvorochennykh trupakh' (ll.83–4, 'Kvaker') and 'Ubityye, zarublennyye, solntse, pshenitsa … Bleshchushchiy den'. Vsyo useyano trupami, sovershenno nezametnymi sredi rzhi.' (Plans and Sketches, p.490).

100. *Isaak Babel* (1979), p.132.

101. Ibid. 'uzhe' is excluded in later editions; its inclusion implies that the moon had witnessed Lyutov's bloody act, just as the stars illuminate his bloodstained conscience, his feelings of guilt, at the end of the story.

102. Ibid.

103. 'Tak umer Selestin Bidu, normandskiy krest'yanin, rodom iz Ori, 21 goda – na obagryonnykh krov'yu polyakh Frantsii.' (ll.44–5 'Na pole chesti').

104. At times in *Konarmiya*, Lyutov plays a minor role, appearing only briefly, e.g. in the stories 'Sashka Khristos' and 'Istoriya odnoy loshadi'.

105. 'nosim' was a misprint in the original text for 'nosil', literally, 'he was wearing' (l.97 'Kvaker').

106. *Isaak Babel* (1979), p.189.

107. See for example the use of 'yozhilsya' on which I have commented on p.44.

108. Paustovskiy, op. cit., p.141, attributes this phrase to Babel.
109. This is the sub-title of a book on Babel by James E. Falen (Tennessee, 1974).
110. Cru, op.cit., p.410.

PART TWO

1. This is the title of Smirin's article, op.cit.
2. See note 9 of Part One. The missing portion is usually considered to be only pages 69–89, 6 June–11 July 1920, but Babel's widow, A. N. Pirozhkova, disputes this. The handwritten manuscript of the diary in an exercise book which she showed me in 1987 begins at page 55. When she had asked Babel about the whereabouts of the first 54 pages, he replied: 'Ne znayu'. Her conclusion is that there is a substantial first part to the diary of which there is no trace. Babel's statement at a conference in 1938 seems to confirm this; see p.71 and note 69 of Part Two. Pirozhkova published the extant part of the diary in 1990 in a two-volume edition of Babel's works, *Isaak Babel' Sochineniya* (Moscow, 1990).
3. Smirin, 'Iz planov i nabroskov k *Konarmii*', op. cit.
4. Ibid., p.497.
5. Issue no. 175, under the heading 'Iz dnevnika'.
6. This is corroborated by L. Livshits in his article 'Materialy k tvorcheskoy biografii I. Babelya', in *Voprosy literatury*, no. 4 (1964).
7. Smirin, 'Iz planov i nabroskov k *Konarmii*', op. cit., pp.492–3.
8. *Isaak Babel* (1979), p.164 and 203 respectively.
9. Smirin, 'Iz planov i nabroskov k *Konarmii*', op. cit., p.493.
10. L. Livshits, op. cit., p.113.
11. Ibid.
12. Ibid.; Gareth Williams in 'The Rhetoric of Revolution in Babel's *Konarmija*', in *Russian Literature* XV (Holland, 1984), pp.290–1, points to a similarity between the openings of Babel's stories and the section of soldiers' writings in *Krasnyy kavalerist*.
13. Livshits, op.cit., p.114. He blames the damning nature of Babel's treatment of war on the fact that he was portraying events in an imperialist war, and bemoans a lack of positive portrayal of the Revolution on Babel's part. Yet there is evidence of Babel's protagonists embracing the Revolution wholeheartedly, for, as Gareth Williams shows, even the speech patterns of protagonists reflect the monumental nature of the event: 'Rhetoric of Revolution', op. cit., pp.279–98).
14. Each quotation from Babel's diary is followed by its entry date for the year that it was written, 1920. I have culled these extracts from a variety of sources. Those in Russian have been taken from Smirin's notes on 'Novyye Materialy', published by A. N. Pirozhkova, *Litera-*

turnoye nasledstvo, LXXIV (Moscow, 1965), p.467–99: this quotation comes from p.498. Also see Livshits, op. cit. and *Isaak Babel* (1979). Short passages are also quoted in I. Erenburg, *Lyudi, gody, zhizn,* vol. 3, ch. 15 (Moscow, 1966), and in *Novyy mir,* 9 (1961), pp.146–52. Any quotations from Babel's diary will be followed by the name of the editor from whose publication they have been taken. Other quotations from the diary that appear in English are my translations from German, French or Hungarian, as extracts from Babel's diary have appeared in those languages, and occasionally add to what is available in Russian. The sources of these foreign language versions are: F. Mierau, ed., *Die Reiterarmee mit Dokumenten und Aufsätzen im Anhang* (Leipzig, 1969), pp.183–202; H. Pross-Weerth, *Ein Abend bei der Kaiserin* (Neuwied, 1970), pp.121–43; J. Catteau, tr. and ed., *Isaac Babel' Cavalerie Rouge suivi des récits du cycle de 'Cavalerie Rouge' des fragments du journal de 1920, des plans et esquisses* (Paris, 1971), pp.162–71; A. Gereben, 'Babel naplója', in *Valóság,* 12 (Budapest, 1981), pp.81–102.

15. The first 7 words would appear to be what has been excluded by Smirin, op.cit., p.498.

16. M. Gorkiy, 'Otvet S. Budyonnomu', *Pravda,* 27 November 1928.

17. Babel worked on the *Odessa Tales* between the summer of 1921 and the spring of 1923. 'Korol' first appeared in *Moryak,* no. 100 (Odessa, 23 June 1921'; 'Kak eto delalos' v Odesse' in *Izvestiya Odesskogo gubispolkoma, gubkoma KP(b)U i gubprofsoveta,* no. 1025 (5 May 1923); 'Otets' and 'Lyubka Kazak' in *Krasnaya nov',* no. 5 (Aug–Sept, 1924).

18. 'Tabak (Pis'mo iz Abkhazii)', in *Zarya Vostoka,* 29 October 1922. Seven examples of Babel's journalistic writing with *Zarya Vostoka* have been republished in N. Stroud, ed., *Zabytyy Babel'* (Ann Arbor, 1979), pp.130–53. They are entitled and dated as follows: 'V dome otdykha', 24/6/1922; '"Kamo" i "Shaumyan" (Pis'mo iz Batuma)', 31/8/1922; 'Medresse i Shkola', no. 73, 14/9/1922; 'Bez rodiny', no. 73, 14/9/1922; 'V Chakve', 3/12/1922; 'Remont i chistka', 14/12/1922; 'Gagry', 1922. All are signed K. Lyutov except the second which is unsigned and the first, fifth, sixth and seventh also bear Babel's name.

19. *Isaak Babel* (1979), p.228. For discussion of the themes that Babel employs in his metaphors in *Konarmiya,* see pp.155–63.

20. '"Kamo" i "Shaumyan" (Pis'mo iz Batuma)', in *Zarya Vostoka,* 31 August 1922.

21. See Clyman, op. cit., for a discussion of the emotional significance of Babel's use of colour, as well as my references to this in Part One, pp.20–1.

22. *Isaak Babel* (1979), p.129.

23. Babel's attitude to visual description, to the use of both line and colour in writing is given in the form of a debate in *Liniya i tsvet* which was published just a year after his stay in the Caucasus and immediately

211

before the first publication in 1924 of 'Moy pervyy gus', i.e. in *Kras-naya nov'*, no. 7 (Dec, 1923).

24. *Isaak Babel* (1979), p.129.
25. '"Kamo" i "Shaumyan" (Pis'mo iz Batuma)'.
26. Ibid.
27. *Isaak Babel* (1979), p.165.
28. Ibid.
29. '"Kamo" i "Shaumyan" (Pis'mo iz Batuma)'.
30. *Isaak Babel* (1979), p.166.
31. 'V dome otdykha', in *Zarya Vostoka*, 24 June 1922.
32. *Isaak Babel* (1979), p.132.
33. Ibid., p.118.
34. Ibid., p.126.
35. Ibid., p.174.
36. Livshits, op. cit., p.127.
37. Ibid., p.126.
38. Ibid., p.127.
39. This phrase occurs in an article written by Babel in *Literaturnaya gazeta*, 5 September 1932.
40. Ibid., my emphasis.
41. Smirin, 'Iz planov i nabroskov k *Konarmii*', op. cit., pp.490–9. All quotations from the plans are from this source, which I shall henceforth refer to only as the 'plans', with a title and page reference following in parentheses.
42. See Part 2, note 2.
43. Nathalie Babel, op. cit., pp.viii–ix.
44. Smirin, 'Iz planov i nabroskov k Konarmii', op. cit., p.496.
45. 'Grishchuk' was first published in *Izvestiya Odesskogo Gubispolkoma*, 23 February 1923, and was not republished until March 1967 in *Zvezda Vostoka* (Tashkent). For my examination of the story and its links with *Konarmiya* see pp 91–7. 'Ikh bylo devyat'' was not published until June 1969 in *Novyy Zhurnal*, no. 95 (New York) pp.16–20. For earlier comment on this, see note 87 of Part One. The story has never been published in the Soviet Union. An earlier English translation by Max Hayward, 'And Then There Were None', appeared in *Dissent* (Nov–Dec 1966). The author's widow, A. N. Pirozhkova, holds a handwritten manuscript of another fragment, 'Ikh bylo desyat'', which has never been published. She intended to include 'Ikh bylo devyat'', together with 'Potseluy' and 'Grishchuk' in the *Konarmiya* cycle (thus increasing it to 38 stories) in her two-volume publication of Babel's works, which was due in 1988 or 1989. She told me that she feels these stories rightfully belong to *Konarmiya*. While I believe 'Grishchuk' has some claim to inclusion, for reasons that I outline later, I do not feel that either of the other two stories belongs to the cycle. 'Eskadronnyy Trunov' has subsumed the episode in 'Ikh bylo devyat'' and 'Potseluy' was not published until 1937, some 5 years

after 'Argamak', which itself was added 8 years after the rest of the cycle. ('Argamak' was published in *Novyy mir*, no. 3 (March 1932) with the footnote 'Nenapechatannaya glava iz Konarmii' and dated 1924–30; 'Potseluy', which has no such footnote nor date of composition, however vague, was published in *Krasnaya nov'*, No. 7 (July 1937)). Pirozhkova's edition, op. cit., appeared in 1990 and in fact includes only 'Potseluy' from among the extra stories mentioned above.

46. D. Furmanov in *Sobraniye Sochineniy v chetyryokh tomakh*, vol. 4 (Moscow, 1961), p.340, writes of Babel's intention to complete fifty chapters.
47. Smirin, 'Na puti k *Konarmiya*', op. cit., p.467.
48. Ibid., p.474.
49. Ibid., p.476.
50. Ibid.
51. Smirin quotes these entries from Babel's diary but does not date them, ibid., p.476.
52. *Isaak Babel* (1979), p.169.
53. See pp.69–70 for further comment.
54. Brackets in the Russian text of the plans and in references to them denote completions by Smirin of words that Babel had left in abbreviated form.
55. Smirin has stressed these two words, possibly to draw attention to some indiction of emphasis by the author himself.
56. Smirin, 'Na puti k *Konarmii*', op. cit., p.473.
57. A. Gereben, '*Isaak Babel's diary and his Red Cavalry*', in *Hungaro-Slavica* (Budapest, 1983), p.56.
58. Brackets in the Russian text of the diary or, in this case a letter, indicate the respective editor's completion of words, which Babel had left in abbreviated form.
59. This first diary entry of 3 June 1920 contains material that is used in 'Gedali' and 'Rabbi'. Podolski is the forerunner of the shopkeeper, Gedali.
60. Gereben, 'Isaak Babel's diary', op. cit., p.55.
61. Ibid., p.58.
62. From a conversation with the captured American pilot, Mosher, Babel records: 'I bury myself in the past' (14/7/20, Mierau, p.187).
63. This abbreviation is the editor's, Livshits' and stands for 'nerazborchivo' or 'indecipherable' and indicates the illegibility of Babel's handwriting at this point in the diary entry.
64. Babel added the words '2 days' in brackets at the end of this diary entry, possibly indicating that the contents occurred not over one day but two, although the entire diary entry is dated 3 June 1920.
65. The South Russian Telegraph Agency, a predecessor of T.A.S.S.
66. *Isaak Babel* (1979), pp.169–70.
67. See p.101.

68. *Literaturnaya gazeta*, 5 September 1932.

69. From a report on a conference of young Soviet writers held on 30 December 1938, and kept in the manuscript department of IMLI; see also note 2 of this part of my book.

70. See pp.69–70; the diary entry referred to is for 7 August 1920.

71. W. Cuckiermann, writing of Babel's *Odesskiye rasskazy*, states: 'Throughout there are strong suggestions of dynamically rising and falling intonation, typical of Jewish speech … it can be felt in the frequent questions, and answers to them, which repeat the same words or phrases'. ('The Odessan Myth and Idiom in Some Early Works of Odessa Writers', in *Canadian–American Slavic Studies*, 14, no. 1 (Spring, 1980), pp.42–3). Sicher's unpublished thesis on Babel's works explores the author's roots in Jewish culture. He makes the general claim that Babel 'has more, than is generally thought, in common with contemporary Hebrew and Yiddish literature' and points specifically to his habit of carrying words over from one sentence to the next, which he designates 'paratactic parallelism', op. cit., pp.iii and 214 respectively).

72. *Isaak Babel* (1979), p.109.

73. Ibid., p.157.

74. She appears in four: 'U svyatogo Valenta', 'Vdova', 'Chesniki' and 'Posle boya'.

75. Babel's widow, A. N. Pirozhkova, knows of four journalistic pieces that Babel wrote for *Krasnyy kavalerist* (the newspaper of the political department of the First Cavalry army); 'Yeyo den'' is the best known and was published in issue no. 235, 19 September 1920; it has been republished in *Literaturnoye nasledstvo*, LXXIV (Moscow, 1965), p.488. Of the three others, 'Nedobytyy ubiytsa', 'Pobol'she takikh Trunovykh' and 'Rytsary tsivilizatsii', I have managed to trace the second and the third, the last of which, published on 14 August 1920, describes the torturing of a Jewish chemist with a burning iron by some Poles. 'Pobol'she takikh Trunovykh' has been republished in *Zabytyy Babel'* prepared by N. Stroud, op. cit., p.115 and was first published in *Krasnyy kavalerist*, no. 208 on 13 August 1920. In grandiloquent, vainglorious language it extols the bravery and virtuous example set by the 34th Cavalry regiment commander, Konstantin Trunov, who was killed in action on 3 August. It concludes with the article's title and the following words: 'Pobol'she takikh Trunovykh – kogda kryshka panam vsego mira'. Babel would seem to have heeded his own words in his creation of Pavel Trunov in *Konarmiya*'s 'Eskadronnyy Trunov'.

76. *Krasnyy kavalerist*, no. 235, 19 September 1920. This and the other extant journalistic writings for *Krasnyy kavalerist* were signed K. Lyutov, as were his earlier pieces in another newspaper, *Zarya Vostoka* in the Caucasus.

77. *Isaak Babel* (1979), p.223. The earlier quotation from 'Perekhod cherez Zbruch' is from pp.102–3.

78. Ibid., p.223.

79. Ibid., p.219.

80. Livshits, op. cit., p.131, gives this quotation from Babel but states neither source nor date. He precedes it with a lament over Babel's choosing to open his 'volume' on women in *Red Cavalry* 'with such a dirty page'. 'Why did he note down' the details on Sashka, he asks, implying that the quotation is part of a rough draft of one of the stories in which she is to appear.

81. *Isaak Babel* (1979), p.207.

82. Ibid., p.219; 'mne' refers to Lyutov. This extract was omitted in later editions of *Konarmiya*. As it last appeared in the 1928 edition, its omission from versions published in the thirties points to censorship and not the author as the cause.

83. 'Put' v Brody', 'Smert' Dolgushova', 'Afon'ka Bida', 'U svyatogo Valenta'.

84. For earlier comment on this see pp.30–1 of Part One.

85. See pp.71–2.

86. Smirin, 'Na puti k *Konarmii*', op. cit., p.478.

87. Ibid.

88. From the biography of I. R. Apanasenko, published in *Krasnyy kavalerist*, No. 95, 9 April 1920.

89. *Isaak Babel* (1979), p.145. For discussion of this figure and others containing animate-inanimate transfer see pp.164–5 of Part Three.

90. See pp.29–31 of Part One.

91. *Isaak Babel* (1979), p.146.

92. Ibid. 'I' refers to Lyutov and the emphasis is mine. From 1931 'gustoy/thick' replaced 'goluboy/blue'; see note 127 of Part Two for comment on this adjective of colour.

93. Ibid., pp.145–6.

94. Ibid., p.146; my emphasis.

95. Paustovskiy, op. cit., p.142. For further discussion of this passage of 'Kombrig dva' which differs greatly from the first published version, see p.175 of Part Three.

96. Before the battle Lyutov had referred to Kolesnikov's 'boltayushchimisya rukami' (*Isaak Babel* (1979), p.146).

97. Ibid.

98. 'a light, not dreary, but defeated and subdued town' (3 July, Mierau, p.183).

99. *Isaak Babel* (1979), p.125.

100. Ibid.

101. Ibid., p.127.

102. Ibid., p.125; Babel describes Gedali as a 'pyostraya ptichka' in 'Rabbi', ibid., p.134, thus linking the metaphor with this image of the feather duster and stressing Lyutov's view of Gedali as a source of animation amid inanimate surroundings of death and desolation.

103. Ibid., p.126; 'me' refers to Lyutov.

104. Others have commented on Babel's habit of changing names, dates and settings, for example Norman Davies who states that Babel 'was totally disinterested in history'. N. Davies, 'Izaak Babel's *Konarmiya* Stories and The Polish–Soviet War', in *The Modern Language Review*, vol. 67, no. 4 (October 1972), p.846.

105. *Isaak Babel* (1979), p.133.

106. Ibid.

107. Ibid., p.135; Babel's development of the figure of the Rabbi's son in this story renders him unrecognizable in comparison with the figure in the passing reference of the diary. In focusing on him, Babel was laying the foundations for the story with which he originally intended to end the *Konarmiya* cycle – 'Syn Rabbi'. Il'ya is a significant figure for Lyutov, for he is a Jew who has attempted to break free from religious and family ties to embrace the revolutionary cause. Both men thus share a common bond; apart from their anxiety to escape Rabbi Motale's funereal and predatory presence they had or were to embark on respective quests of acceptance in an alien world.

108. Ibid.

109. Ibid., p.168.

110. Ibid., p.169.

111. Mierau, p.196.

112. *Isaak Babel* (1979), p.169.

113. Ibid.

114. Ibid., p.168.

115. By placing the stories apart, Babel stresses their independence, yet he also creates cyclical unity in doing so, as is the case with the stories 'Gedali', 'Rabbi' and 'Syn Rabbi', none of which is consecutively placed with the other.

116. *Isaak Babel* (1979), p.183; my emphasis.

117. Ibid.

118. The translation is Walter Morison's in *The Collected Stories, Isaac Babel* (London, 1961), p.105.

119. *Isaak Babel* (1979), p.184.

120. Ibid.

121. Ibid.

122. Post-1928 versions omit this phrase and replace it by the single word 'Vnachale'.

123. *Isaak Babel* (1979), p.186.

124. Ibid.

125. Ibid.; 'it' refers to 'raka' – 'a shrine'.

126. Ibid.

127. Babel often associates the colour 'blue' with death. In 'Perekhod cherez Zbruch' Lyutov's sleeping companion turns out to be the violently murdered corpse of the father of the household: 'Glotka yego vyrvana, litso razrubleno popolam, sinyaya krov' lezhit v yego borode, kak kusok svintsa'. While in 'Kombrig dva', Kolesnikov's gesture of bravado

before he leads his men into a crucial battle takes place 'v stolbakh goluboy pyli', as if his intention is to cheat the very portal of death (ibid., pp.102 and 146 respectively).

128. *Isaak Babel* (1979), p.186.

129. Ibid., p.105.

130. Ibid., p.104.

131. Smirin, 'Iz planov i nabroskov k *Konarmii*', op. cit., pp.492–4.

132. For earlier discussion of 'Eskadronnyy Trunov' and of its links with 'Kvaker' please see p.36 and pp.50–1 of Part One, including notes 64 and 87, the latter of which contains details of the publication or whereabouts of these fragments. The name Trunov probably originates from an article that Babel wrote for *Krasnyy kavalerist* in honour of a Cavalry regiment commander, Konstantin Trunov, killed in action on 3 August 1920, 'Pobol'she takikh Trunovykh', 13 August 1920; see note 75 of Part Two.

133. Sicher states on p.385, *Isaak Babel* (1979), that a Sedrik E. Faunt-Le-Ro did command a Polish air squadron in which American volunteers served but that he cannot have been present at the taking of Sokal on 26 August 1920 since he had transferred to the Sixth Polish Army in the middle of July. Thus he could not have been Trunov's assailant and Babel has again blurred historical details.

134. *Isaak Babel* (1979), p.195; 'we' refers to Lyutov's fourth squadron. In the diary the American's name appears as Font-le-Ro, in the story as Faunt-le-Ro.

135. Nathalie Babel dates it 20 August 1920; both Sicher and Smirin, 30 August.

136. Post-1928 editions have replaced 'gordoy/proud' with 'beloy/white'.

137. *Isaak Babel* (1979), p.193.

138. Ibid., p.192.

139. Plate 16 of Francisco Goya Y Lucientes' *The Disasters of War* (New York, 1967), first published as *Los Desastres de la Guerra* (Madrid, 1863).

140. See my discussion of this concerning 'Solntse Italii' on p.128, Part Three.

141. One faction were Hasidic Orthodox Jews, supporters of the Rabbi of Bel's, the other comprised moderate Jews, supporters of the Rabbi of Gusyatin, an opponent of Hasidism.

142. Il'ya-Gaon, a Jewish religious figure, persecutor of the Hasidic sect, who lived in Vil'no.

143. *Isaak Babel* (1979), p.188.

144. 'shchoki yego byli useyany ranami, yazyk vyrvan. … i rot yego, nabityy razlomannymi zubami,' ibid.

145. Ibid., p.189; 'them' refers to the arguing Jewish factions.

146. Quoted above from plans, Sokal' 2, p.493.

147. Smirin, 'Na puti k *Konarmii*', op. cit., p.478.

148. *Isaak Babel* (1979), p.202.

149. Ibid., p.203.

150. Ibid., pp.163–4; 'uzhasno/terribly' is omitted in post-1928 editions.

151. 'sochinyonnaya po vsem pravilam gazetnoy ritoriki', Smirin, 'Na puti k *Konarmii*', op. cit., p.478.

152. Savitskiy, nachdiv shest', vstal, zavidev menya, i ya udivilsya krasote gigantskogo yego tela. On vstal i purpurom svoikh reytuz, malinovoy shapchonkoy, sbitoy nabok, ordenami, vkolochennymi v grud', razrezal izbu popolam, kak shtandard razrezayet nebo. Ot nego pakhlo nedo-syagayemymi dukhami i pritornoy prokladoy myla. Dlinnyye nogi yego byli pokhozhi na devushek, zakovannykh do plech v blestyash-chiye botforty ...
    Ty gramotnyy?
    – Gramotnyy, – otvetil ya, Zaviduya zhelezu i tsvetam etoy yunosti ... (*Isaak Babel* (1979), p.129).
    The choice of 'iron' as one of Savitskiy's attributes is not without significance, for the same substantive is used in the trite metaphor that occurs in the 'funeral oration' concerning the Communist Party and which Savitskiy himself uses in his shallow reply to Khlebnikov. For further discussion of Babel's figurative use of this substantive see pp.135–6 of Part Three.

153. 'Moy pervyy gus', 'Istoriya odnoy loshadi' and 'Prodolzheniye istorii odnoy loshadi'.

154. *Isaak Babel* (1979), p.195.

155. Ibid., p.188.

156. Ibid.

157. 'gordoy etoy falange', ibid.

158. For earlier discussion of this episode and its links with 'Kvaker' please see pp.50–1 of Part One.

159. Paustovskiy, 'Povest' o zhizni', p.142; see also note 27 of Part One.

160. Smirin, 'Na puti k *Konarmii*', op. cit., p.477.

161. Until 1966 it had been published only in English (see note 45 of Part Two). The story was published in Russian in *Novyy zhurnal* (New York, June 1969) and has now been published in Russia in Pirozh-kova's two-volume edition of 1990 (op.cit.).

162. 'vsemirnogo geroya', The plans, Sokal' 2, p.493 and elsewhere.

163. 'V *Konarmii* ... dayotsya khudozhestvennoye osmysleniye vsego etogo pyostrogo potoka vpechatleniy'. Smirin, 'Na puti k *Konarmii*', op. cit., p.477.

164. For analysis and discussion of the 'Demidovka episode' see my con-cluding subsection of Part Two, pp.97–103.

165. It was first published under the heading 'Iz knigi Konarmiya' in *Izvestiya odesskogo gubispolkoma*, part no. 967 (23 February 1923), with five other stories that later appeard in *Konarmiya*. It was not republished until May 1967 in *Zvezda Vostoka* (Tashkent), pp.110–11.

166. 14, 19, 21, 22, 23, 26, 29 July 1920.

167. 26/7/20; Livshits, op. cit., p.115.

168. 'Grishchuk', *Zvezda Vostoka*, p.110.

169. Unlike Ston, however, we are told in the diary entry of 24/7/20 that Grishchuk disliked and did not understand horses and thereby incurred the disrespect of the desperate Prishchepa, another of Lyutov's drivers and a protagonist in *Konarmiya*. For discussion on Prishchepa see pp.97–103 of Part Two.

170. Smirin, 'Na puti k *Konarmii*', op. cit., p.474.

171. 'Ucheniye o tachanke' and 'Smert' Dolgushova'.

172. 'Grishchuk', *Zvezda Vostoka*, p.110; 'my' refers to Lyutov.

173. Ibid.

174. Ibid.; 'I' refers to Lyutov, 'we' to Grishchuk and Lyutov.

175. *Isaak Babel* (1979), p.132; 'we' refers to Lyutov and a group of Cossacks.

176. My emphasis.

177. 'Grishchuk', *Zvezda Vostoka*, p.111.

178. See p.51 of Part One.

179. In February and May 1923 respectively, in *Izvestiya Odesskogo gubis-polkoma*', nos. 967 and 1022 respectively.

180. *Isaak Babel* (1979), p.138.

181. Ibid., p.140.

182. Ibid., p.143; 'I' refers to Lyutov.

183. Tachanka! Eto slovo sdelalos' osnovoy treugol'nika, na kotorom zizh-detsya nash obychay: rubit'-tachanka-kon' … Pulemyot, zakopannyy pod skirdoy, tachanka, otvedyonnaya v krest'yanskuyu klunyu, – oni perestayut byt' boyevymi edinitsami. Eti skhoronivshiyesya tochki, predpolagayemyye, no ne oshchutimyye slagayemyye, dayut v summe stroyeniye nedavnego ukrainskogo sela-svirepogo, myatezhnogo i korystolyubivogo. (Ibid., 138–139).

184. '–Ty vsyo molchish', Grishchuk, – skazal ya yemu, zadykhayas', – kak ya poymu tebya, tomitel'nyy Grishchuk?..', ('Grishchuk', *Zvezda Vostoka*, p.110) and the diary entries of 19, 22 and 26 July 1920 respectively.

185. *Isaak Babel* (1979), p.141.

186. Ibid., p.143.

187. Livshits, op. cit., p.115.

188. *Isaak Babel* (1979), p.143.

189. 'Grishchuk', *Zvezda Vostoka*, p.110.

190. *Isaak Babel* (1979), p.144; 'he' refers to Afon'ka Bida, the first person references in the final sentence to Lyutov.

191. Ibid.

192. The two acts are symmetrically complementary: in 'Grishchuk' Lyutov had given food to save the other's life; this had led to the forming of a bond of friendship between the driver and Lyutov. In 'Smert' Dolgu-shova' Grishchuk had saved the narrator's life and then offered him friendship in the form of a wrinkled apple.

193. *Isaak Babel* (1979), p.144. This concluding sentence is omitted from post-1928 editions of *Konarmiya*.

194. Grishchuk features little in the plans; a passing reference occurs

in Belev-Boratin, p.395, where he is only named, and previously in Leshnyuv (29 July, p.494), where the narrator is mainly concerned with the unceasing rain and unsettled night: 'setku dozhdya ... Trevozhnaya noch' – Govinskiy i Grishchuk ... Sostoyaniye ozhidaniya i ustalosti'.

195. See·note 45 of Part Two concerning the publication of 'Grishchuk' *inter alia* in *Konarmiya*.
196. 'sobiratel'nyy den'', p.496.
197. 'Bunt dushi', p.495.
198. For my earlier comments see pp.72–4.
199. Firstly, with the heading 'Iz knigi *Konarmiya*' in *Izvestiya Odesskogo gubispolkoma*, no.1060 (17 June 1923), then in *Lef*, no.4 (Aug–Dec, 1923).
200. The only other grouping given greater coverage is 'Boy pod Brodami', pp.490–2, from which, as I have mentioned earlier, eight *Konarmiya* stories emerge. (See the section entitled 'The diary and the plans' of Part Two).
201. Smirin notes that there is evidence of Babel's intention to write at least three stories concerning Prishchepa, one entitled 'V Dubno', which only remained in the diary, the second 'Demidovka' upon which he was working and the third which realised the *Konarmiya* story, 'Prishchepa'. (Smirin, 'Na puti k *Konarmii*, op. cit., p.481).
202. *Isaak Babel* (1979), p.159.
203. Ibid.
204. Ibid.; the diary reference is 'belyy bashlyk', (23 July, Smirin, p.499).
205. 'prost, kak trava,'.
206. Since 'Demidovka' had never been published, or as far as I know, written as a finished story by Babel, I use the term 'narrator' instead of Lyutov's name for Prishchepa's companion, when he is referred to in the plans. When my source is a diary entry the first person of course refers to Babel himself. I would add that there are many instances when the thoughts or actions of the narrator in the plans or the author in the diary are consistent with those of *Konarmiya*'s primary narrator.
207. *Isaak Babel* (1979), p.140.
208. See pp.72–4 of Part Two.
209. *Isaak Babel* (1979), p.104.
210. Ibid.
211. 'We' refers to Babel and Prishchepa. In the plans (Smirin, pp.495, 496 and 499) Babel refers to the Jewish religious festival as '9 Aba', whereas the Jewish critic, Sicher, uses '9 Ava' in his reference to it, *Isaak Babel* (1979), p.377.
212. *Isaak Babel* (1979), p.131.
213. Ibid., p.132; the final pair of verbs recall Lyutov's description of his killing of the goose and directly links his anguish with his earlier action: 'gusinaya golova tresnula pod moim sapogom, tresnula i potekla'., (ibid., 131). See also p.52 of Part One.

214. The 9 Ava festival was held to commemorate this event.
215. *Isaak Babel* (1979), pp.168 and 169.
216. 25 July, Smirin, p.499; Smirin's quotation from Babel's diary omits the last 8 words which Mierau has included in his German translation.
217. 'Ya rasskazom uvlekayu vsekh– dol'she vsekh soprotivlyayetsya Dora Aronovna. –', (p.496).
218. *Isaak Babel* (1979), p.159; 'my' refers to Lyutov.
219. Smirin, in his introduction to the footnotes on 'Iz planov i nabroskov k *Konarmii*', op. cit., p.497.
220. T. V. Ivanova, *Moi sovremenniki, kakimi ya ikh znala* (Moscow, 1987), p.273. She also reiterated this to me at Peredelkino on 29/10/87.
221. *Literaturnaya gazeta*, 5 September 1932.
222. Nash *sovremennik*, no. 4 (1964), based on Babel's speech to the Writers' Union made on 28 September 1937.

PART THREE

1. Isaak Babel, *Literaturnaya Gazeta*, 31 March 1936.
2. A. Kvyatkovskiy, *Poeticheskiy Slovar'* (Moscow, 1966), p.269 and Rice, op. cit. For my interpretation of *skaz* please see note 52 of Part One.
3. Mendelsohn, *op. cit.*, p.116.
4. e.g. Yu Benni, 'I. Babel', in *Pechat' i revolyutsiya*, no. 3 (1924), pp.135–9 and A. Lezhnev, 'Sredi zhurnalov', in *Krasnaya nov'*, no. 4 (1924), pp.304–13.
5. Mendelsohn, *op. cit.*, p.116.
6. P. Carden, *The Art of Isaac Babel* (Ithaca, 1972), p.35.
7. This was Babel's answer to a question about his method of working in an article entitled: 'O tvorcheskom puti pisatelya', based on a speech made at a conference of the Union of Soviet Writers held on 28 September 1937 and reported in *Nash Sovremennik*, no. 4 (1964), p.100.
8. The opening story of *Odesskiye rasskazy* is entitled 'Korol'', which refers to Benya Krik.
9. I. Babel, *Izbrannoye* (Moscow, 1966), p.164.
10. Carden, op. cit; she discusses this in ch. 6.
11. See Table 1.
12. Carden's term; see note 10.
13. *Isaak Babel* (1979), pp.106 and 109–10. The proportion of the cycle in the *skaz* category, 'Cossacks', is 19 per cent. At one point in Kurdyukov's letter, however, Lyutov records a conversation which has unmistakable Yiddish rhythms; see pp.71–2 of Part Two for comment on this.
14. Carden's term; see note 10.
15. See the opening, Appendix B.
16. Carden, op. cit., p.90. Vassiliy is Kurdyukov's first name.
17. *Isaak Babel* (1979), p.101.

18. Ibid., p.102; 'for me' is omitted in later editions.
19. Mendelsohn, op. cit., p.124.
20. Furmanov, op. cit., p.343.
21. See, for example, J. S. Bruner, 'The Course of Cognitive Growth', in *American Psychologist*, no. 19 (1964), pp.1–15, and 'The Ontogenesis of Symbols', in *Essays to Honour Roman Jakobson*, vol. 1 (The Hague, 1967), pp.427–46; or A. Roland, 'Imagery and Symbolic Expression in Dreams and Art', in *International Journal of Psychoanalysis*, no. 53 (1972), pp.531–9.
22. Mendelsohn, op. cit., p.24.
23. B. Tomashevskiy, *Teoriya Literatury (Poetika)* (Moscow, 1928); B. Leondar, 'The Structure and Function of Metaphor', Ph.D. thesis (Harvard University, 1968).
24. Mendelsohn, op. cit., pp.25–6.
25. Ibid., p.27. P. Ricoeur, 'Metaphor and the Main Problem of Hermeneutics', in *New Literary History*, no. 6 (1974), pp.95–111.
26. Mendelsohn, op. cit., p.46–8.
27. *Times Literary Supplement*, London, 14 October 1926.
28. A. Sabatier, *L'Apôtre Paul'*, 74, quoted by Stephen J. Brown, *The World of Imagery* (London, 1927), p.12.
29. S. Brown, op. cit., p.19.
30. Ibid.
31. Ibid., p.23.
32. Tomashevskiy, op. cit., p.28.
33. S. Brown, op. cit., p.29.
34. Frederico Garlanda, *Philosophy of Words* (London, 1888), pp.36–7.
35. S. Brown, op. cit., p.32.
36. Further reference to these terms will be made without the use of inverted commas, as will be the case with each methodological term after its introduction.
37. F. Brinkmann, *Die Metaphern, Studien über den Geist der modernen Sprachen* (Bonn, 1878).
38. M. Müller, 'Lectures on the Science of Language', Second Series, pp.328–9, quoted by Gertrude Buck, *Figures of Rhetoric: A Psychological Study* (Ann Arbor, 1896), p.7.
39. S. Brown, op. cit., p.37.
40. Aristotle, *Poetics*, ch. 21 (Oxford, 1909), p.63, translated by I. Bywater.
41. Quintilian, *Institutes of Oratory*, Book 9, ch. 1 (London, 1920–2), translated by H. E. Butler.
42. Cicero, *De Oratore* (London, 1942), p.43.
43. S. I. Ozhegov, *Slovar' russkogo yazyka* (Moscow, 1973), p.320.
44. *Oxford English Dictionary* (Oxford, 1930).
45. Funk and Wagnall, ed., *The Standard Dictionary* (New York, 1903).
46. Michel Béal, *La Sémantique*, quoted by S. Brown, op. cit., p.46.
47. J. Hastings, *Dictionary of the Apostolic Church*, vol. II (Edinburgh, 1915–18), p.30.

48. B. Keach, *Tropologia or a key to open Scripture Metaphors* (1779, republished Waterford, 1858).

49. Hastings, op. cit., p.31.

50. Seeley and Abbott, *English lessons for English People* (London, 1890), p.42.

51. J. Earle, *English Prose: Its Elements, History and Usage* (London, 1890), p.75.

52. Seeley and Abbott, op. cit., p.42.

53. Earle, op. cit., p.75.

54. *Isaak Babel* (1979), p.132.

55. Brown uses this term in *The World of Imagery*, op. cit., p.48.

56. Ibid.

57. Ibid.

58. *Isaak Babel* (1979), p.133.

59. Whateley, *Rhetoric*, part 3, ch. 2, quoted by G. Buck, op. cit., p.16.

60. Buck, op. cit., pp.15–16.

61. S. Brown, op. cit., p.51.

62. Quintilian, op. cit.

63. Buck, op. cit., pp.16 and 24.

64. S. Brown, op. cit., p.51.

65. Ibid.

66. Ibid., p.52; 'main notion' is another term for 'main idea'.

67. Ibid., p.54.

68. Ibid.; Brown states that this is demonstrated by Th. Ribot in 'Essai sur l'imagination créatrice', ch. 2: 'Le facteur émotionel' (Paris, 1921).

69. Ibid., pp.54–6.

70. J. Andrew, 'Structure and Style in the Short Story: Babel's "My First Goose"', in *Modern Languages Review*, 70, no. 2 (April 1975), p.367.

71. 'Moy pervyy gus'' has a trope density of 1:12.3 words (the average for *Konarmiya* is 1:13.3) and a metaphor density of 1:19.6 words (the average for this cycle is 1:24). 62.7 per cent of the story's tropes are metaphors, while the average for the cycle is 55.3 per cent. See Tables 2 and 3 respectively.

72. *Isaak Babel* (1979), p.121; these lines are omitted from later editions.

73. For further discussion of this sequence please see p.168.

74. R. P. Prat, *Etudes*, vol. 135 (Paris, 1913), p.109.

75. Gogol was a prolific creator of similes; Proffer tells us that he has a ratio of 1 simile to 306 words in the first part of 'Myortvyye dushi'. (See Carl R. Proffer, *The Simile and Gogol's 'Dead Souls'* (The Hague, 1967)). Babel embodies an average of 6 similes per *Konarmiya* story which gives a ratio of 1 simile to 152.1 words. His average density of metaphor is 1:24 words.

76. J. G. Jennings, *Metaphor in Poetry* (1915), p.33, quoted in S. Brown, op. cit., p.57.

77. S. Brown, op. cit., p.73.

78. J. S. Hart, *Rhetoric,* quoted by Brown, op. cit., p.76.

79. S. Brown, op. cit., p.82.
80. An exception to this occurs in 'Istoriya odnoy loshadi' where we meet a sensually striking vehicle in a simile which depicts Savitskiy's Cossack mistress: 'I ona poshla k nachdivu, nesya grud' na vysokikh bashmakakh, grud', shevelivshuyusya, kak zhivotnoye v meshke.' (*Isaak Babel* (1979), p.161). For discussion of the themes of Babel's metaphors in the two cycles please see pp.155–63.
81. Middleton Murray, *The Problems of Style* (London, 1925), quoted by Brown, op. cit., p.89.
82. Babel's ex-wife, Tamara Ivanova, disputes the commonly held belief that he frequently revised his work in writing and also asserts that he did not write different versions of the same story (see T. Ivanova, *Moi sovremenniki, kakimi ya ikh znala*, op. cit., p.272: 'Babel' vovse ne pisal variantov.'). She tells of his pacing up and down mentally rehearsing his stories before he committed them finally to paper. A. N. Pirozhkova, Babel's widow, however, corroborates Paustovskiy's statement and states that Babel did amend his stories in writing frequently. There would seem to be truth in both impressions, however. Mental and written rehearsal were surely concomitant processes of the 'katorzhnaya rabota' (Paustovskiy, op. cit., p.142) which his work represented for him. These statements were made to me when I visited T. V. Ivanova and A. N. Pirozhkova on consecutive days in October 1987 in Peredelkino and Moscow respectively.
83. S. Brown, op. cit., p.92.
84. Ibid., p.96.
85. I. A. Richards, *Principles of Literary Criticism* (London, 1925), p.241.
86. S. Brown, op. cit., p.100.
87. Ibid.
88. Cicero, op. cit., Book 3.
89. Proffer, op. cit., p.23. I have adopted the terms 'tenor' and 'vehicle' in my references to Babel's similes.
90. *Isaak Babel* (1979), p.193.
91. Ibid., p.189.
92. Ibid., p.190.
93. Proffer, op. cit., p.23.
94. *Isaak Babel* (1979), p.197.
95. S. Brown, op. cit., p.120. This quotation is attributed to Goldsmith.
96. Ibid.
97. *Isaak Babel* (1979), p.137.
98. S. Brown, op. cit., p.120.
99. For discussion of Babel's tropes' sequences please see pp.141–51.
100. Including the pointing word(s).
101. *Isaak Babel* (1979), p.192. The imagery embodies the epic flavour of the byliny, a device which Babel used to elevate his Cossack protagonists to heroic proportions. For discussion of this please see pp.187–91.
102. Ibid., p.101.

103. Earle, op. cit., quoted by Brown, op. cit., p.121. See p.119 for the quotation from Goldsmith.

104. *Isaak Babel* (1979), p.132.

105. See pp.159 and 161.

106. There are 381 instances of metonymy in *Konarmiya*, (15.8% of the tropes used) and 200 instances of synecdoche (8.3%), while *Na pole chesti* employs them in less proportion, 8 or 9% (metonymy) and 4 or 4.5% (synecdoche). Babel's greater use of them in his major cycle points to an increased subtlety in the imagery of *Konarmiya*; this claim is further supported by the respective proportions of hyperbole. The bluster and grandiloquence of this trope type is proportionally more dominant in the minor cycle, with 13.5% compared with 8.4% in *Konarmiya*. See Table 3.

107. *Isaak Babel* (1979), p.103.

108. Ibid., pp.228–9.

109. S. Brown, op. cit., p.160.

110. W. G. Weststeijn, *Velimir Khlebnikov and the Development of Poetical Language in Russian Symbolism and Futurism*, Studies in Slavic Literature and Poetics, vol. 4 (Amsterdam, 1983), p.90.

111. B. S. Meylakh, 'O metafore kak element khudozhestvennogo myshleniya', in *Trudy otdela novoy russkoy literatury* (Moscow–Leningrad, 1948), pp.207–32, quoted by Weststeijn, op. cit., p.262.

112. See pp.107–11.

113. *Isaak Babel* (1979), p.149.

114. Ibid., p.161.

115. Ibid., p.219.

116. See for example 'Moy pervyy gus' and 'Pesnya'.

117. Mendelsohn, op. cit., pp.92–8. Mendelsohn considers that the story 'Spravedlivost' v Skobkakh, Na pomoshch'' (Odessa, 1921, republished only once in *Prostor*, No. 1, Alma-Ata, 1974) marks the beginning of the metaphor-orientated stage of Babel's stylistic development. She has also conducted a count of figurative expressions in all Babel's stories, but does not distinguish between types of tropes, merely labelling all as metaphoric. I disagree strongly both with her word counts – at times she makes some *Konarmiya* stories nearly twice as long – and with her metaphor totals. For example Mendelsohn's version of 'Kvaker' has 1,102 words with two instances of metaphor (mine 875 words and 20 metaphors), while in *Konarmiya* her version of 'Vdova' comprises 1,936 words and 18 metaphors which compares with my totals of 1,090 words and 46 metaphors. (See Appendix B in Mendelsohn, op. cit., pp.136–7).

118. The third *skaz* category (5.9% of the cycle) realizes 5.6% of the tropes.

119. See Table 2.

120. *Isaak Babel* (1979), p.191. The Pole's words in correct Russian would be: Eta voyna zakonchena … vse ofitsery uderzhali, eta voyna zakonchena … / Etimi pyat'yu pal'tsami ya vykhodil svoyu sem'yu.

121. Prosopopoeia is a figure by which abstract things are represented as persons, or absent persons as speaking. I have used the term 'epithet' as a figurative adjective, that is to say as 'expressing some quality or attribute ... characteristic of a person or thing' used in a way that deviates from the normal'. (*Shorter Oxford English Dictionary* (Oxford, 1965), pp.624 and 697 respectively.) Ozhegov speaks of its poetic function as an attribute lending greater expressiveness to the designation of an object (op. cit., pp.835–836).

122. See pp.120–1.

123. *Isaak Babel* (1979), p.121.

124. Ibid., p.127.

125. Ibid., p.126.

126. Ibid., p.157.

127. Ibid., p.155; my emphasis.

128. Ibid., p.204.

129. 'I stali my zhit' s Nastey kak umeli, a umet' my umeli. Vsyu noch' nam zharko bylo, zimoy nam zharko bylo, vsyu dolguyu noch' my golyye khodili i shkuru drug s druzhki obryvali.' *Isaak Babel* (1979), pp.153–4.

130. Ibid., p.204; my emphasis.

131. Ibid., p.206; 'he' refers to the enemy.

132. Ibid., p.149; my emphases.

133. Ibid., p.205.

134. Ibid.

135. See pp.110–26.

136. See for example, Louis H. Leiter, 'A Reading of Isaac Babel's Crossing into Poland', in *Studies in Short Fiction*, III, no. 2 (1965–6), pp.199–206; J. van der Eng, 'La description poétique chez Babel', in *Dutch Contributions to the Fifth International Congress of Slavicists* (The Hague, 1963), pp.79–92; A. B. Murphy, 'The Style of Isaac Babel', in *The Slavonic and East European Review*, XLIV, no. 103 (London, 1966), pp.361–80; as well as the monographs of Carden, op. cit., and Falen, *Isaac Babel,* op. cit.

137. *Isaak Babel* (1979), p.119; my emphasis.

138. 'i mertvit smolistuyu dukhotu yeli, razbrosannoy po kukhne.', ibid.

139. Ibid., p.121; my emphases.

140. I have counted 349 epithets in *Konarmiya*, these represent 10.9% of the total adjectives used.

141. See for example pp.135–6 and 148.

142. *Isaak Babel* (1979), p.121; my emphasis.

143. Obgorelyy gorod – perelomlennyye kolonny i vrytyye v zemlyu kryuchki zlykh starushech'ikh mizintsev – on kazalsya mne podnyatym na vozdukh, udobnym i nebyvalym, kak snoviden'ye. Golyy blesk luny lilsya na nego s neissyakayemoy siloy. Syraya plesen' razvalin tsvela, kak mramor opernoy skam'i. (ibid., p.121) ... Nasha komnata byla temna, mrachna, vsyo dyshalo v ney nochnoy syroy von'yu, i tol'ko okno,

zapolnennoye lunnym ognem, siyalo, kak izbavleniye. (ibid., p.124).

144. Ibid., p.121.
145. Ibid., p.124.
146. Ibid., p.121.
147. Ibid., p.122.
148. For comment on this please see p.48 of Part One and pp.144–5 of Part Three.
149. *Isaak Babel* (1979), p.122. This sentence is omitted in later editions.
150. A narrower margin exists in the cycle as a whole; although Lyutov still employs more verb-only metaphors than the Cossacks, namely 31.3% compared with 29.85%, the latter use more concrete substantive-verb metaphors than Lyutov, 14.2% compared with 6.8%.
151. *Isaak Babel* (1979), p.121.
152. Ibid., p.122. The vehicle of the simile was included only in the first published edition in *Krasnaya nov'*, no. 3 (April–May 1924).
153. Ibid., p.122; my emphases.
154. Ibid., p.123.
155. Ibid., p.122; 'it' refers to 'gruel'; my emphasis.
156. Ibid.
157. Makhno was a Ukrainian anarchist associated with banditry, slaughter and Jewish pogroms, who fought both against the White Guard army and the Red Army. Several times, however, he became the temporary ally of the latter.
158. See my discussion of the tropes of Balmashov, Konkin and Pavlichenko on pp.133–6, 154, 155–6, 157, 158, and 159–60.
159. *Isaak Babel* (1979), p.121; my emphases.
160. Ibid., p.101; my emphasis.
161. Shklovsky first introduced this term into Russian poetics. Kvyatkovskiy defines it as signifying a description in an artistic production of a man, an object or phenomenon which is as if glimpsed for the first time and which then acquires new signs. Thus an accustomed and recognized object can be shown as unusual or strange. (A. Kvyatkovskiy, op. cit., pp.188–9).
162. *Isaak Babel* (1979), p.101.
163. Ibid.
164. Ibid.
165. Ibid., p.140.
166. Ibid., p.169.
167. Ibid., p.140.
168. 21 July, Pelga-Voratin, p.374. The penultimate word is written in French.
169. Ibid., p.140.
170. Ibid., p.125; my emphasis.
171. Ibid., p.158.
172. Ibid.; my emphases.
173. Ibid.; for discussion of the tension that is created here between elevatory and pejorative images please see p.185.

174. Ibid.
175. Ibid.
176. 31.3%, see Section IA, Table 4.
177. 27.2% concrete nouns, 14.3% abstract.
178. *Isaak Babel* (1979), p.143. This trope is interposed between two more physiological details: 'Zhivot u nego byl vyrvan, ... i udary serdtsa byli vidny.' They recall the three-fold description of the mutilated body of an old man in 'Perekhod cherez Zbruch': 'Glotka yego vyrvana, litso razrubleno popolam, sinyaya krov' lezhit v yego borode, kak kusok svintsa.' (ibid., 102). Apart from the same participle 'vyrvan(a)' the colour blue, which is often associated with death in Babel's war stories, reappears concerning the dying Dolgushov: 'Dolgushov razlozhil po zemle siniye ladoni', (ibid., 143). See also the return of Sashka Khristos and his stepfather amid 'golubykh prostorakh gorizonta' to a home recently afflicted by death (ibid., 148 and see pp.20–1 of Part One and note 246 of Part Three for further comment on Babel's use of colours).
179. Ibid., p.141; for further discussion of other aspects of this sequence please see pp.143 and 173 respectively.
180. Ibid., p.142.
181. Ibid.
182. Ibid., p.143; my emphasis.
183. Ibid., p.141; my emphasis.
184. Both *Konarmiya* and *Na pole chesti* portray the respective dilemmas of misfits and their attempts to resolve the situation. 'Moy pervyy gus', 'Posle boya' and 'Argamak' illustrate this in the case of Lyutov, as does each of the minor cycle's stories for Bozhi, Bidu, Maresko and Ston respectively.
185. *Isaak Babel* (1979), p.143; 'us' refers to Lyutov and Grishchuk.
186. Ibid., p.143.
187. 44.1% compared with Lyutov's 27.2%, see Section I, Table 4.
188. *Isaak Babel* (1979), p.142.
189. Ibid., p.144.
190. This is the designation Balmashov gives himself at the end of 'Sol''; ibid., p.174.
191. 30.3% and 38.1% respectively.
192. *Isaak Babel* (1979), p.165; my emphasis.
193. Ibid.
194. Ibid.
195. Ibid., p.142.
196. 27.2% in the whole cycle.
197. *Isaak Babel* (1979), p.165. 'tuz' in its figurative and colloquial sense is a 'big-shot', literally it is the 'ace' in a suit of playing cards.
198. Ibid., the metaphors refer to Konkin's comrade Spir'ka Zabutyy.
199. 14.3% of Lyutov's metaphors consist of a figurative abstract substantive, while 9% of the Cossacks embody the same in *Konarmiya*.

200. *Isaak Babel* (1979), p.164; my emphasis.
201. Ibid., p.165.
202. Ibid., p.166.
203. Ibid.
204. 54.5% compared with 46.3%.
205. Hardly any of Babel's tropes in any *skaz* category of either cycle embody a concrete to abstract transfer between stimulant and imported image.
206. 89%.
207. 1 metaphor to 32.3 words, compared to an average in *Konarmiya* of 1:24 words.
208. 4 of the figures are epithets.
209. In 'Istoriya odnoy loshadi' Khlebnikov had been aggrieved at having his white stallion taken from him by his divisional commander Savitskiy. After unsuccessful attempts to retrieve it he withdrew from the Communist Party and was demobilized as medically unfit for service. This story, the sequel, portrays the former's forgiveness of the latter.
210. Smirin, 'Iz planov', p.494 and see p.88 of Part Two.
211. *Isaak Babel* (1979), p.203; my emphasis.
212. Ibid.
213. Ibid., 176. For further discussion of the tropes of 'Vecher' please see pp.136–8.
214. Ibid., p.177. CC = Central Committee (of the Communist Party).
215. See p.128.
216. *Isaak Babel* (1979), p.129; my emphases.
217. Ibid., 203; my emphasis.
218. *Krasnaya nov'*, no. 3 (April, 1925) under the general heading 'Iz dnevnika'.
219. *Isaak Babel* (1979), p.174; my emphasis. RCP = Russian Communist Party.
220. It should not be forgotten also that the newspaper *Krasnyy kavalerist*, its printing press, etc., was housed on a train.
221. *Isaak Babel* (1979), p.174.
222. These instances occur respectively in 'Pan Apolek' and 'Kostyol v Novograde'. Sashka Khristos, the syphilitic aspirant pastor and the role of pimp that Christ plays in *Iisusov grekh* further exemplify both within and without *Konarmiya* Babel's particular exploitation of the Jewish disregard for Christ.
223. *Isaak Babel* (1979), p.174.
224. Ibid.
225. Bathos enhances the derision, for it is not just Cossacks on leave who feel the inspiration of their writing but 'rezervnykh zhulikov, chislyashchikhsya pol'skimi perevodchikami, i devits, prislannykh k nam v poyezd politotdela na popravku iz Moskvy.', ibid.
226. Ibid; for comment on other protagonists of this category and type please see pp.108, 144 and 145.
227. See Part Two, pp.97–103.

228. *Isaak Babel* (1979), p.178.
229. Ibid., p.177.
230. Ibid., pp.176–7; my emphasis. 'me' refers to Lyutov.
231. Ibid., p.176; my emphasis. 'Noch' uteshala nas v nashikh pechalyakh'.
232. Ibid.
233. Ibid., p.175; my emphasis.
234. Ibid., p.176; the first 13 words referring to the Party were omitted in later editions.
235. Lyutov's metaphors comprise 20.4% concrete and 8.2% abstract substantives. See Table 4, Section IA.
236. *Isaak Babel* (1979); my emphasis.
237. *Na pole chesti* comprises ten figurative concrete substantives and eleven abstract ones.
238. The first edition was published in *Lef*, no. 4 (Aug–Dec, 1923). Another story which bore the name of its Cossack hero, D'yakov, and was first published with 'Kombrig dva' is *Nachal' nik konzapasa*.
239. S. M. Budyonnyy was a Cossack who, from 1919, commanded the first Cavalry Army, having formed a Cossack detachment of cavalry after the Revolution. He subsequently took a strongly negative view of Babel's portrayal of the Cavalry Army and vented his anger in 'Babizm Babelya iz *Krasnoy novi*', in *Oktyabr*, no. 3 (1924), pp.196–7.
240. *Isaak Babel* (1979), p.145.
241. Ibid., pp.145–6.
242. Ibid., p.145.
243. Ibid.
244. 'Ne toropyas' on vynul revol'ver iz mokrykh ruk yunoshi', (l.55, 'Dezertir'); 'he' refers to Captain Zhem'ye.
245. The Captain found Bozhi sobbing and prostrate on his second return. 'Paltsy yego, lezhavshiye na revol'vere, slabo shevelilis'.' (l.51, 'Dezertir').
246. In *Konarmiya* ,'red' is often referred to concerning the grandeur of the Cossacks' uniforms: 'Kazaki v krasnykh sharovarakh' ('Syn Rabbi', *Isaak Babel* (1979), p.29), Budyonnyy v krasnykh sharovarakh ('Kombrig dva', ibid., p.145), the athletic D'yakov whose face and trousers are red, 'krasnorozhiy ... krasnykh sharovar.' ('Nachal' nik konzapasa', ibid., p.111) and in one instance the colour's dazzling quality makes the Cossacks appear larger than life: 'Shtab armii, roslyye genshtabista v shtanakh krasneye, chem chelovecheskaya krov'' ('Chesniki', ibid., p.217, omitted in later editions). Benya Krik, Babel's flamboyant hero of *Odesskiye Rasskazy,* together with his men, is also associated with shades of red in his dress: 'On byl odet v oranzhevyy kostyum' ('Korol'); 'Aristokraty Moldavanki, oni byli zatyanuty v malinovyye zhilet,' ('Korol'); 'Tut Benya sdelal pauzu. Na nyom byl ... malinovyye shtiblety' ('Kak eto sdelalos' v Odesse') I. Babel, *Izbrannoye* (Moscow, 1966), pp.161, 163 and 170 respectively.

247. *Isaak Babel* (1979), p.146.

248. Ibid.

249. See pp.139–40.

250. 'Vizhu, kak stroyatsya v kolonnu, tsepi idut v ataku ... net lyudey, yest' kolonny,' (3 August, Smirin, p.498). For comment on Babel's changing of the image from pejoration to elevation please see p.77 of Part Two.

251. *Isaak Babel* (1979), p.146.

252. Ibid.

253. Ibid., p.145.

254. Smirin, 'Iz planov i nabroskov k Konarmii', op. cit., p.490, and in 'Kvaker', 'Gremela, ne perestavaya, kanonada. Zemlya izdavala zlovoniye, solntse kopalos' v razvorochennykh trupakh.' (ll.82–4). See p.20 of Part One for further discussion of this.

255. The river Zbruch and the Volhynian countryside.

256. *Isaak Babel* (1979), p.101.

257. See Section IB, Tables 3 and 4 respectively. I have discounted the results of the 'others' category in *Na pole chesti* since only two tropes occur there.

258. See pp.171–2.

259. *Isaak Babel* (1979), p.148.

260. See pp.19–20 of Part One for my discussion of Babel's associating spring with death.

261. *Isaak Babel* (1979), p.168.

262. Ibid., p.184.

263. Ibid., p.167.

264. Ibid., p.186.

265. Ibid., p.121.

266. Ibid.; my emphasis.

267. Ibid., p.141.

268. Ibid.

269. Ibid., p.168.

270. Ibid., p.169. 'Zdes' skoplyayutsya za mnogo dney chelovech'; otbrosy i navoz skotiny. Unyniye i uzhas zapolnyayut katakomby yedkoy von'yu i protukhshey kislotoy isprazhneniy.'

271. Ibid., p.184.

272. Just as the narrator's use of the adjective 'mokrykh' denotes pathos and dejection in 'Dezertir': 'Ne toropyas', on vynul revol'ver iz mokrykh ruk yunoshi, otoshol na tri shaga i prostrelil yemu cherep' (ll.55–6; 'on' refers to Captain Zhem'ye, 'yemu' to the deserter, Bozhi). This follows a reference to the prostrate, sobbing soldier in which again liquid 'l' sounds predominate: 'Kogda kapitan vernulsya, soldat vskhlipyval lezha na zemle. Pal'tsy yego, lezhavshiye na revol'vere, slabo shevelilis.' (ll.50–1, 'Dezertir').

273. *Isaak Babel* (1979), p.184; my emphasis.

274. Ibid.; 'ikh' refers to 'zvuki organa'.

275. Ibid., p.143; my emphasis.
276. Ibid., p.144.
277. Ibid.; 'I' refers to Lyutov.
278. I have counted only four instances in both cycles.
279. *Isaak Babel* (1979), p.131; my emphasis. 'tovarishch' refers to Lyutov.
280. Ibid., p.132.
281. Ibid.
282. Ibid., p.131.
283. 56% and 52.6% respectively compared with Lyutov's 38.8%.
284. *Isaak Babel* (1979), pp.111–12.
285. Ibid., p.112.
286. Ibid., p.122.
287. Ibid., 'zdravomyslyashchego svoyego bezumiya'.
288. Ibid., p.122; the 'Tseka' is the 'Tsentral'nyy Komitet' while the word 'tsek' means a factory department.
289. Ibid., p.123.
290. Ibid., p.130.
291. Ibid.
292. Ibid., p.132.
293. Ibid., p.122.
294. One further trope employed by Sidorov seems Lyutovian in quality; his description of the nurses as they brought him his food daily: 'Vznuzdannyye blagogoveniyem,', ibid.
295. *Krasnaya Nov'*, no. 3 (April–May, 1924). The story was dated Novograd, June 1920 by the author.
296. For a discussion of this see Alice Lee, op. cit., pp.249–60.
297. *Isaak Babel* (1979), p.148.
298. Ibid., p.149.
299. Ibid., p.144; my emphasis.
300. Ibid., p.142.
301. Ibid., p.126.
302. Ibid.
303. Ibid.
304. Ibid., p.127; the 'International' was the organization responsible for promoting unity between the Communist Parties of the world between 1919 and 1943.
305. Ibid.
306. Ibid., p.133.
307. Cuckierman, op. cit., p.42.
308. Ibid., pp.42–43.
309. *Isaak Babel* (1979), p.133. The last sentence contains imagery from Babel's plans: 'Khasidizm s vytekshimi glaznitsami.' (Brody, p.492).
310. 3 June, Zhitomir.
311. *Isaak Babel* (1979), p.126.
312. See p.144.
313. 48.4% compared with 38.8%.

314. The two tropes attributed to Ston, the only source of figurative language in the third *skaz* category, are independent, non-adjacent metaphors.
315. My emphasis.
316. My emphasis.
317. *Isaak Babel* (1979), p.133.
318. 'bran" also possesses the poetic meaning of 'field of battle'; the resulting figure of a blasphemous battlefield descending upon Bidu's head would indeed seem catachrestic. However, a *double entendre*, which contains the possible interpretation of Bidu's incurring the universal condemnation of the military world, is not without credence.
319. My emphasis.
320. 29.2% of the cycle's metaphors are epithets.
321. My emphasis.
322. *Isaak Babel* (1979), p.103; my emphasis.
323. Ibid., pp.103, 104, 105 respectively; 'he' is Pan Romuald, the priest's assistant.
324. 'dykhaniye nevidannogo uklada mertsalo pod razvalinami doma ksyondza, i vkradchivyye yego soblazny obessilili menya.', ibid., p.104.
325. Ibid.; my emphasis.
326. Ibid., pp.145–146; my emphasis.
327. Ibid., p.146; my emphasis.
328. Ibid., p.101; my emphases.
329. Ibid., p.172; my emphasis.
330. Ibid., p.154.
331. Ibid., p.176.
332. Ibid., p.175.
333. Ibid.; my emphasis.
334. Ibid.; 'torchashchey tam, vverkhu, kak derzkaya zanoza'.
335. Percentages of imported images with a violent theme are Lyutov 13, Cossacks 11.2, others 10.5; *Na pole chesti*'s narrator 9.7, soldiers 13.3; and those with a military theme: Lyutov 0.9, Cossacks 2.8, others 0, *Na pole chesti*'s narrator 3.2, soldiers 0. The 'others' category of the lesser cycle only comprises 2 metaphors and is discounted for statistical purposes.
336. Although a simile does too, while another metaphor embodies a military image.
337. *Isaak Babel* (1979), p.101.
338. Ibid., p.164.
339. Ibid., p.165.
340. Ibid., pp.122 and 121 respectively.
341. Ibid., p.121.
342. Ibid., p.172.
343. Ibid., p.101.
344. Ibid., pp.142 and 144 respectively. See p.148 for my discussion of this.

345. Ibid., p.144.

346. Ibid., p.213.

347. Ibid., p.173.

348. Ibid., p.224.

349. Ibid.

350. Lyutov and the narrator of *Na pole chesti* are in fact the most conservative users of animal imagery with 6.5% and 6.4% respectively.
The Cossacks use twice as many, 11.2%, other *Konarmiya* protagonists 15.8% and the soldiers of the second cycle 33.3%.

351. *Isaak Babel* (1979), pp.122 and 123 respectively; my emphases.

352. Ibid., p.121.

353. Ibid., p.200.

354. Ibid., p.174.

355. See also pp.133–4 concerning Konkin.

356. *Isaak Babel* (1979), pp.171 and 172 respectively; my emphasis. 'Mol-
odnyaka' is a collective noun in Russian for the 'young of animals'.

357. Seven (13.2%) of Balmashov's metaphors in 'Sol'' employ animal
imagery, 2% more than the average for the Cossacks.

358. See Section ID, Table 4.

359. Only the soldiers of the minor cycle import more images from another
sphere, namely 'animals' and then in only one more instance.

360. *Isaak Babel* (1979), p.224.

361. Ibid., p.121. Babel locates Novograd-Volynsk on the Zbruch, when in
fact it is situated on the river Sluch. There are many instances of the
author's blurring of dates and locations. See Part Two pp.79–80 for
my discussion of this, as well as N. Davies, 'Izaak Babel's Konarmiya
stories and the Polish–Soviet War', *The Modern Language Review*,
vol. 67, no. 4 (Oct 1972), pp.845–57.

362. In 'Moy pervyy gus'', 'Solntse Italii' and 'Posle boya' respectively.

363. *Isaak Babel* (1979), p.137.

364. Ibid.

365. As for example 'litsa tochno durno vypechennyy khleb ...', N. Gogol,
op. cit., p.228; see also P. Spycher's interpretation of 'Nos' in
N. V. Gogol, 'The Nose: A Satirical Comic Fantasy Born of an
Impotence Complex', in *Slavic and East European Journal*, vol. 7,
no. 4 (Winter 1963), pp.361–75. See also note 74 of Part One of
this book.

366. *Isaak Babel* (1979), p.158; my emphasis.

367. 28.7% and 33.3% respectively.

368. See pp.260–261.

369. *Isaak Babel* (1979), p.155.

370. Ibid.

371. Ibid.

372. Ibid.

373. Ibid.

374. My emphasis.

375. 'Yesli nam suzhdeno uvelichit' naseleniye etogo prokhladnogo ugolka, chto-zh – my snachala zastavili gniyushchikh starikov poplyasat' pod marsh nashikh pulemyotov.' (ll.8–10, 'Semeystvo papashi Maresko').
376. See for example pp.20, 140–1 and 159.
377. 'Luna visela uzhe nad dvorom, kak deshyovaya ser'ga.', *Isaak Babel* (1979), p.132. Gareth Williams discusses the respective roles of the sun and moon in 'Two Leitmotifs in Babel's *Konarmiya*', in *Die Welt der Slaven*, Book 1 (Cologne, 1972), pp.308–17.
378. Ibid., p.121; 'it' is the town Novograd-Volynsk.
379. For further discussion of this, see pp.187–8 of Part Three.
380. *Isaak Babel* (1979), p.164; my emphasis.
381. Ibid., p.165.
382. Ibid., p.132; 'it' refers to truth, 'he' to Lenin.
383. Ibid., p.176.
384. 'Deux actes devant une conscience', Appendix B.
385. My emphases.
386. My emphasis.
387. *Isaak Babel* (1979), p.103.
388. Ibid., p.141.
389. Ibid., p.137.
390. Ibid., p.118.
391. Ibid., p.132.
392. See Section IIIA, Table 4 and my discussion of this on pp.181–2, 184 and 185–6.
393. *Isaak Babel* (1979), p.234.
394. 40%.
395. *Isaak Babel* (1979), p.167.
396. Ibid., p.166; 'me' refers to Konkin.
397. Ibid., p.213; 'us' refers to Balmashov and his two wounded comrades in 'Izmena', Golovitsyn and Kustov.
398. Ibid., p.216.
399. 'O smert', ..., o, zhadnyy vor,' ibid., p.158.
400. This term, and others designated 'like-...' mean that the same sense is used to perceive both stimulant and imported image.
401. *Odesskiye rasskazy*, written in roughly the same period as *Konarmiya*, also exemplify this. Danuta Mendelsohn's work, op. cit., which is concerned with the Odessa cycle in particular, scarcely touches upon the tropes of *Konarmiya* and makes scant reference to *Na pole chesti*.
402. 6.2% of the tropes of Cossacks and other protagonists together employ synaesthetic transfer of the visual to abstract variety, while 7.8% is of other synaesthetic types. Lyutov's respective figures are 5.7% and 7.5%.
403. 16.1% compared with 19.3% (Cossacks), 13.3% (soldiers), 12.5% (other protagonists of *Konarmiya*).
404. 2.6% (Cossacks), 5.4% (other protagonists of *Konarmiya*), 6.5% (narrator of *Na pole chesti*), 13.3% (French soldiers).

405. *Isaak Babel* (1979), p.145.

406. Ibid., p.176.

407. '– Nochnoye vremya, Arisha ... I zavtra u lyudey den'. Ayda blokh davit' ...', ibid., p.176.

408. Ibid., p.101.

409. Ibid.

410. See note 361.

411. *Isaak Babel* (1979), p.121.

412. Ibid., p.124.

413. 30.2% of Lyutov's metaphors are of the abstract to visual variety of transfer, while the Cossacks employ 54.6% and the other protagonists 62.5%.

414. *Isaak Babel* (1979), p.176.

415. Ibid., p.170.

416. Ibid., p.171.

417. Ibid., p.172.

418. Ibid.

419. Ibid., p.174.

420. Ibid., p.142.

421. Ibid.; my emphasis.

422. Ibid., p.123.

423. Ibid., pp.152–3.

424. Ibid.; the first three quotations are from p.122 and the fourth from p.123.

425. Ibid., p.102.

426. Ibid., p.141.

427. 'Ya strashilsya vstrechi s Sidorovym, moim sosedom, opuskavshim na menya po nocham volosatuyu lapu svoyey toski.', ibid., p.121.

428. Ibid.; both quotations are from p.121.

429. Ibid., p.122.

430. H. Ermolayev, *Mikhail Sholokhov and his Art*, Princeton, 1982, p.196.

431. P. I. Novitskiy, 'Babel', in *I. E. Babel': Stat'i i materialy*, ed. Yu. Tynyanov (Leningrad, 1928), p.52.

432. L. Iribarne, 'Babel's *Red Cavalry* as a Baroque Novel', in *Contemporary Literature*, no. 14 (1973), p.67.

433. G. Munblit, 'Iz vospominaniy', *I. Babel', Vospominaniya sovremennikov* (Moscow–Leningrad, 1960), pp.308–9.

434. A. Blok, *Sobr. soch.*, eds. V. N. Orlov, A. A. Surkov and K. I. Chukovskiy, vol. 1: *Stikhotvoreniya 1897–1904* (Moscow–Lenigrad, 1960), pp.308–9.

435. A. Fet, *Stikhotvoreniya* (Moscow, 1970), p.262. This is the last verse of a poem entitled 'Vesenniy dozhd''.

436. *Isaak Babel* (1979), p.175.

437. Ibid.

438. Ibid., p.101.

439. Ibid., p.172.

440. Ibid.
441. Ibid., p.165.
442. Ibid., p.164.
443. Ibid., pp.165 and 167 respectively.
444. Ibid., p.165.
445. Ibid., p.164.
446. Ibid., pp.173–4.
447. Ibid., p.174.
448. Ibid., p.123.
449. Ibid., p.112.
450. Ibid., p.170.
451. Ibid., p.144.
452. Ibid., pp.142 and 144 respectively.
453. Ibid., pp.186–7; my emphasis.
454. 's razodrannym ... rtom ... Rot yego byl razodran, kak guba loshadi,', ibid., pp.186–7. 'yego' refers to Christ.
455. Ibid., p.146.
456. Ibid., p.210.
457. Ibid., p.102.
458. Ibid.
459. See p.130.
460. *Isaak Babel* (1979), p.101; my emphasis.
461. 'I v tishine ya uslyshal otdalyonnoye dunoveniye stona.', ibid., p.210.
462. Ibid., p.101.
463. 36.8% of Lyutov's metaphors employ a like-visual transfer compared with 10.4% that comprise a like-auditory transfer.
464. *Isaak Babel* (1979), p.124; my emphasis.
465. Ibid., p.176.
466. Ibid., p.143; my emphases.
467. Ibid., p.141; see p.143 for earlier reference.
468. Ibid.
469. Ibid., p.146.
470. Ibid.
471. Ibid.; my emphasis.
472. *Yevgenii Yevtushenko: Selected Poetry*, ed. R. Milner-Gulland (Oxford, 1963), p.138; my emphases.
473. *Lef*, no. 4 (1923), p.70–2, under the title, 'Kolesnikov'.
474. This sentence is the only one retained in all other publications of the story.
475. *Lef*, no. 4 (1923), p.71; my emphases.
476. *Isaak Babel* (1979), p.146.
477. *Lef*, no. 4 (1923), p.71.
478. See pp.164–5 and Section IIB, Table 4.
479. *Isaak Babel* (1979), p.120; 'him' refers to Christ.
480. Ibid., p.113; my emphasis.
481. 64.7% embody a totally animate transfer.

482. *Isaak Babel* (1979), p.141.
483. Ibid., p.175.
484. Ibid.
485. Ibid.
486. Ibid., p.174.
487. Ibid.; my emphasis.
488. Ibid., the last three quotations are from p.121.
489. Ibid., pp.121 and 124.
490. Ibid., p.121.
491. 18.5% in the cycle as a whole.
492. *Isaak Babel* (1979), p.124; my emphasis.
493. Ibid., p.160; my emphasis. 'him' refers to Prishchepa.
494. Ibid., p.227.
495. Ibid., p.208.
496. Ibid., p.210.
497. Ibid., p.209.
498. Ibid., p.211.
499. Ibid.
500. Ibid., p.209; my emphasis.
501. Ibid.
502. Ibid., p.102.
503. Ibid., p.107; my emphasis.
504. To be precise, 48.8% in 'Sol'' and 48.3% in 'Konkin'.
505. *Isaak Babel* (1979), p.170; my emphasis.
506. Ibid., p.171; my emphasis.
507. Ibid., pp.164 and 164–5 respectively.
508. Lyutov's use of inanimate to animate transfer occurs in 56.5% of his metaphors; for *Konarmiya*'s Cossacks it is 24.8% and *Na pole chesti*'s soldiers 28.6%, while Balmashov employs it in 33% of his metaphors and Konkin in 31%.
509. *Isaak Babel* (1979), p.171.
510. Ibid., the last four quotations are from p.172.
511. Ibid., both quotations are from p.164.
512. Ibid., p.166; my emphases.
513. Ibid., all on p.165; see also note 197.
514. Ibid.
515. I refer to the soldier's reference to the civilian as a huddled, frightened frock-coat: 'Voskresnyy syurtuk blednel i yozhilsya.' (l.53, 'Semeystvo papashi Maresko').
516. *Isaak Babel* (1979), p.166; my emphasis.
517. Ibid., p.167.
518. Ibid., 165; my emphasis.
519. See pp.163–4 and 165–9.
520. My emphases.
521. 54.8% (the narrator) and 46.7% (the soldiers) of metaphors in *Na pole chesti* embody abstract to visual transfer, while the Cossacks and

others of *Konarmiya* employ 54.6% and 62.5% respectively. Lyutov uses this type of transfer in 30.2% of his metaphors.

522. 'V nego poletel sukhoy grad tekh otvratitel'nykh, yarosnykh i bessmyslennykh slov,' (ll.27–8, 'Na pole chesti'). The quotation from Vidal is from 'Deux actes devant une conscience', Appendix B.

523. 'Luna visela uzhe nad dvorom, kak deshyovaya ser'ga. .... i tol'ko serdtse moyo, obagrennoye ubiystvom, skripelo i teklo.' *Isaak Babel* (1979), p.132.

524. Ibid., p.164.

525. Ibid., p.235. 'Argamak' was first published in *Novyy mir*, no. 3 (1932), with the footnote, 'Nenapechetannaya glava iz *Konarmii*', dated 1924–1930, and included in the 7th–8th edition (1933).

526. My emphasis.

527. See p.164.

528. See pp.139–40 and 164–5 for examples from *Konarmiya*. The tropes in question from *Na pole chesti* are: 'Personazh delayet svoy vykhod. *Ponoshennoye, vytsvetsheye sushchestvo.*' (l.21, 'Semeystvo papashi Maresko'; my emphasis).

529. My emphasis.

530. W. Morison, ed., *Isaac Babel Collected Stories,* op. cit., p.10.

531. Ibid.

532. Although his semi-autobiographical story of childhood, 'Istoriya moyey golubyatni' depicts the suffering of his family in a pogrom, his elder daughter, Nathalie, states that this was not the case. (See her introduction to *The Lonely Years: 1925–1939*, ed. Nathalie Babel, op. cit., p.xv). Babel himself also confirms that the stories of his childhood cycle are not based solely on fact. In a letter to his mother, written on 14 October 1931, he states that in them 'privrano, konechno, mnogoye i peremeneno – kogda knizhka budet okonchena – togda stanet yasno, dlya chego mne vsyo eto bylo nuzhno.' (*Vozdushnyye puti*, no. 3 (New York, 1963), pp.101–15). Babel did in fact serve briefly on the Romanian front in October 1917. He volunteered for army service although he had been exempted in 1914, but soon fell ill with malaria and was sent back to Odessa in 1918.

533. *Isaak Babel* (1979), p.153.

534. Ibid., p.157.

535. Ibid., p.171.

536. Ibid.

537. Ibid., p.173.

538. Ibid., p.174.

539. Ibid., p.121; the first person references are to Lyutov.

540. Ibid., pp.121 and 123 respectively; my emphasis. The first quotation is omitted from later editions.

541. Ibid., the first two quotations are from p.124, the last from p.121.

542. 'Syraya plesen' razvalin tsvela, kak mramor oper'noy skam'i,', ibid., p.121.

543. Ibid., pp.121 and 124 respectively; 'me' refers to Lyutov.

544. Ibid., pp.122 and 122–3 respectively.

545. 'Teper' budem govorit' delo. V armii mne skuchno. Yezdit' verkhom iz-za rany ya ne mogu, znachit ne mogu i drat'sya.', ibid., p.123.

546. Ibid., p.123.

547. Ibid.

548. Ibid., p.124.

549. Ibid., p.121.

550. Ibid., p.158.

551. Ibid.; my emphasis.

552. Ibid.

553. 'Azriil, syn Ananii, usta Yegovy. Iliya, syn Azriila, mozg, vstupivshiy v yedinoborstvo s zabveniyem. Vol'f, syn Ilii, prints, pokhishchennyy u Tory na devyatnadtsatoy vesne.' ibid.

554. Ibid.

555. Ibid.; my emphasis.

556. Ibid., p.174.

557. Ibid., p.175.

558. Ibid.

559. Ibid., both quotations are from p.175.

560. Ibid.

561. 'chtoby sodrognut'sya ot ukusov nerazdelyonnoy lyubvi k poyezdnoy nashey prachke Irine.', ibid., p.175.

562. In 'Vdova', Lyovka, a Cossack driver is boasting of former violent and amorous exploits: 'Do poslednego lech', – povtoryaet Lyovka s vostorgom, i protyagivayet ruki k nebu, okruzhaya sebya noch'yu kak nimbom.', ibid., p.205. Bida carries out a killing Lyutov cannot in 'Smert' Dolgushova': 'Obvedyonnyy nimbom zakata, k nam skakal Afon'ka Bida.', ibid., p.144.

563. Ibid., p.175.

564. 'blokh davit' …', ibid., p.176.

565. Ibid., p.141.

566. My emphasis.

567. My emphasis.

568. Morison, ed., *Collected Stories*, op. cit., p.10.

569. *Isaak Babel* (1979), p.164.

570. *Slovo o polku Igoreve*, ed. and tr. I. P. Eremin (Moscow, 1957), p.58.

571. For a discussion of the use of repetition in the *byliny* see D. P. Costello and I. P. Foote, ed., *Russian Folk Literature* (Oxford, 1967), pp.68–70.

572. 'Pervaya Poyezdka Il'i Muromtsa. Il'ya i Solovey – Razboynik', Dmitriy Obolenskiy, ed., *The Penguin Book of Russian Verse* (London 1965).

573. *Isaak Babel* (1979), p.153.

574. Ibid., p.172.

575. Ibid., p.173.

576. Ibid., p.166.

577. Ibid., p.153.

578. Ibid., p.172.

579. *Slovo o polku Igoreve*, op. cit., p.55.

580. *Isaak Babel* (1979), p.101.

581. *Slovo o polku Igoreve*, op. cit., p.58.

582. *Russian Folk Literature*, op. cit., p.67.

583. Ibid., p.63.

584. V. F. Miller, M. N. Speranskiy *inter alia*.

585. In 1936, the Soviet authorities officially condemned the historical school as mistaken and 'bourgeois', but there were, however, Soviet scholars such as D. S. Likhachov and B. A. Rybakov, who claimed that 'the byliny originated as a direct record of historical fact.'; see *Russian Folk Literature*, op. cit., pp.64–5.

586. In an interview that I had with Babel's widow, A. N. Pirozhkova in Moscow in October 1987, she told me of her conviction that Babel had died in 1940, not 1941, as had been earlier thought. She based her assumption on a purchase that she made in a Soviet store in 1956 or '57 of a calendar, among whose pages for 13 July (Babel's birthday) she found a picture of her husband, in which his dates of birth and death were given respectively as 1894 and 1940. She poignantly related how she had hoped until then that Babel might return from the concentration camp. Her hopes had been falsely raised by an alleged fellow inmate, a man called Zavatskiy from Brest, who had told her in 1948 that he had been with Babel in the concentration camp and that he was alive and well. It has, however, become clear, with the demise of the Soviet regime and the consequent accessibility of KGB files, that Babel was shot shortly after his arrest in 1939. Pirozhkova's two-volume edition of Babel's works, published in 1990 (op.cit.), includes a fuller version of her memoirs than was available prior to this (A. N. Pirozhkova, 'Babel v 1932–39 godakh [iz vospominaniy]', in *I. Babel' Vospominaniya sovremennikov* (Moscow, 1972), pp.292–373)), as well as all the extant portion of his 1920 diary, which had not been published previously in Russian.

587. Published in *Russian Folk Literature*, op. cit., p.172.

588. These were usually blind or crippled itinerant beggars who survived by singing outside churches in return for alms; 'kalika' was used in Russian for 'pilgrim', but later denoted only these beggars; it is also related to 'kaleka' (a 'cripple').

589. **ВОЗНЕСЕНИЕ**

Как вознесся Христос на небеса,

Расплакалась нищая братья,

Расплакались бедные-убогие, слепые и хромые:

— Уж ты истинный Христос, царь небесный!

Чем мы будем бедные питаться?

Чем мы будем бедные одеваться, обуваться?

Тут возговорил Христос царь небесный:

— Не плачьте вы, бедные-убогие!
Дам я вам гору да золотую,
Дам я вам реку да медвяную:
Будете вы сыты да и пьяны,
Будете обуты и одеты.
     Тут возговорит Иван да Богословец:
— Ведь ты истинный Христос да царь небесный!
Не давай ты им горы да золотыя,
Не давай ты им реки медвяныя:
Сильные-богатые отнимут;
Много тут будет убийства,
Тут много будет кровополитья,
Ты дай им свое святое имя:
Тебя будут поминати,
Тебя будут величати, –
Будут они сыты да и пьяны,
Будут и обуты и одеты.
     Тут богговорит Христос да царь небесный:
— Ты Иван да Богословец,
Ты Иван да Златоустый!
Ты умел слово сказати,
Умел слово рассудити!
Пусть твои уста да золотые,
Пусть те в году праздники частые.

THE ASCENSION

     As Christ ascended to heaven,
Broke forth in tears the lowly brethren,
Broke forth in tears the poor and wretched, the blind and
crippled:
— Indeed you are the veritable Christ, the Heavenly Father!
With what shall we poor people be fed?
With what shall we poor people be clothed and shod?
     Then proclaimed Christ the Heavenly Father:
— Do not weep, you poor and wretched!
I will give you a mountain of gold,
I will give you a river of honey:
You will be sated and ebrious,
You will be clothed and shod.
     Then proclaims John the Divine:
— Indeed you are the veritable Christ and the Heavenly Father!
Do not give them mountains of gold,
Do not give them rivers of honey:

The rich and strong will deprive them;
Much will be the slaughter here,
Much will be the bloodshed here.
Give them your holy name:
They will speak of you,
They will honour you –
They will be sated and ebrious,
They will be clothed and shod.
　　Then proclaims Christ the Heavenly Father:
— You are John the Divine,
You are John the Golden-Tongued!
You knew the words to speak,
You knew the words to weigh!
May your lips be gilded,
May those days of celebration be oft repeated in the year.

590. *Isaak Babel* (1979), p.118; 'your' refers to a representative of the Church's commission sent to investigate what had happened.
591. 'on slushayet neskonchayemuyu muzyku svoyey slepoty', ibid., p.119.
592. Apollo, who was the god of light and often identified with the sun also presided over the fine arts, music, poetry and eloquence.
593. *Isaak Babel* (1979), pp.164 and 164–5 respectively.
594. Ibid., p.165.
595. Ibid., p.154; the arrangement of the lines is mine.
596. See pp.185–8.
597. *Isaak Babel* (1979), p.165.
598. Ibid., p.149.
599. Ibid., p.201.
600. Ibid., p.219.
601. Ibid., p.206.
602. Ibid., p.220.
603. Ibid., pp.223 and 224 respectively.
604. Ibid., p.126.
605. Ibid., p.133.
606. Ibid., p.230.
607. Ibid., p.176; 'you' refers to Lyutov and others who complain of their fate.
608. Ibid., pp.176–7. CC = Central Committee.
609. Ibid., pp.118–9; my emphasis.
610. For discussion of other examples of revitalized figures please see pp.44 and 175.
611. 'yunosha, pokhozhiy na nemetskogo gimnasta iz khoroshego tsirka, yunosha s gordoy nemetskoy grud'yu', *Isaak Babel* (1979), p.193; in later editions 'beloy' replaces 'gordoy'. The Poles had discarded their clothes so that the officers were indistinguishable from the men.
612. Ibid., my emphasis.

613. Ibid., pp.218–9, my emphasis; 'them' refers to Voroshilov and Budyonnyy; the former became a Marshal and chairman of the Presidium of the Supreme Soviet of the U.S.S.R. 'I' refers to Lyutov.

614. 30.6 per cent.

615. *Isaak Babel* (1979), p.133.

616. This was a sign among Hasidic Jews that they were praying.

617. While a dressing-gown forms a part of Hasidic dress, a white gown is not common and is only worn by rabbis in a few Hasidic groups.

618. *Isaak Babel* (1979), p.158.

619. Ibid., p.104.

620. My emphasis.

621. 61.1% of Lyutov's tropes are living compared with 23.9% of the Cossacks'.

622. *Isaak Babel* (1979), p.110.

623. Ibid., p.130.

624. Ibid., p.132.

625. Ibid., p.122.

626. Ibid., p.142; this is Bida's way of conveying his fear of the removal of his divisional commander.

627. Ibid., p.153.

628. Ibid., p.123.

629. Ibid., p.155.

630. Ibid., p.153.

631. Only 17.9% is 'living', 82.1% fossilized metaphor.

632. *Isaak Babel* (1979), p.126.

633. Ibid., p.133.

634. Ibid., p.147.

635. Ibid., p.148.

636. Ibid., p.143.

637. Ibid., p.144.

638. Ibid., p.127; 'it' refers to 'an International'.

639. Ibid.

640. See pp.167–8 for comment on this.

641. 'v nego poletel sukhoy grad tekh otvratitel'nikh, yarostnykh i bessmyslennykh slov,' (ll.27–8, 'Na pole chesti'; 'nego' refers to Bidu); 'solntse kopalos' v razvorochennykh trupakh.' (ll.83–4, 'Kvaker').

642. 'Ponoshennoye, vytsvetsheye sushchestvo. Ono oblacheno v voskresnyy syurtuk … Voskresnyy syurtuk blednel i yozhilsya.' (ll.21–2 and 53 respectively, *Semestvo papashi Maresko*).

643. See examples from 'Solntse Italii' on p.147.

644. As in the Demidovka episode which I have examined in Part Two, pp.97–103.

645. See pp.193–4 of Part Three.

646. '– Ty iz kinderbal'zamov, – zakrichal on, smeyas', – i ochki na nosu, kakoy parshiven'koy … Shlyut vas ne sprosyas', a tut rezhut za ochki. Pozhivyosh' s nami, shto l'? ('Ty' refers to Lyutov, 'on' to Savitskiy)

'Ya videl sny i zhenshchin vo sne, i tol'ko serdtse moyo, obagry-onnoye ubiystvom, skripelo i teklo.' (the first person references are to Lyutov), *Isaak Babel* (1979), pp.130 and 132 respectively.

647. Ibid., p.235.
648. 'Moy pervyy gonorar', in *Vozdushnyye puti*, no. 3 (1963) republished in N. Stroud, ed., *Zabytyy Babel'*, op. cit., p.291. The author's dating of the story is 1922–8.
649. K. Paustovskiy, op. cit, vol. 5, p.117.
650. 7 August 1920.
651. 'unter – ofitser. 4 Georgiya. Syn svinopasa. – Sobral derevnyu. Deystvoval na svoy strakh i risk. Soyedinilsya s Budyonnym. – Astrakhanskiy pokhod. –', *Zhizneopisaniye Apanasenki*, p.495.
652. L. Slavin, 'Tysyacha i odna noch', in *Siluety*, no. 2 (Odessa, Dec–Jan 1922–3), p.7.
653. 'Moy pervyy Gonorar', in *Zabytyy Babel'*, op. cit., p.291.

Tables of Analysis

TABLE 1 Proportions of *skaz* in the two cycles of war stories

KONARMIYA	LYUTOV				COSSACKS		OTHERS		Total number of words
	Narrated words	Uttered words	Total words	%	Words	%	Words	%	
Perekhod cherez Zbruch	413	6	419	84.3	–	–	78	15.7	497
Kostyol v Novograde	681	8	689	100.0	–	–	–	–	689
Pis'mo	135	9	144	11.5	1,104	88.5	–	–	1,248
Nachal'nik konzapasa	399	–	399	80.6	66	13.3	30	6.1	495
Pan Apolek	1,599	3	1,602	83.5	–	–	317	16.5	1,919
Solntse Italii	491	–	491	53.1	433	46.9	–	–	924
Gedali	427	52	479	61.4	–	–	301	38.6	780
Moy pervyy gus'	707	39	746	81.0	164	17.8	11	1.2	921
Rabbi	391	12	403	63.1	–	–	236	36.9	639
Put' v Brody	363	–	363	76.7	110	23.3	–	–	473
Ucheniye o tachanke	675	–	675	100.0	–	–	–	–	675
Smert' Dolgushova	560	21	581	75.1	118	15.3	74	9.6	773
Kombrig dva	339	–	339	92.6	27	7.4	–	–	366
Sashka Khristos	987	–	987	80.0	232	18.3	47	3.7	1,266
Zhizneopisaniye Pavlichenki, Matveya Rodionycha	–	–	–	–	1,523	100.0	–	–	1,523
Kladbishche v Kozine	134	–	134	100.0	–	–	–	–	134
Prishchepa	278	–	278	100.0	–	–	–	–	278
Istoriya odnoy loshadi	683	–	683	69.2	304	30.8	–	–	987
Konkin	34	–	34	4.6	702	95.4	–	–	736
Berestechko	694	–	694	97.3	7	1.0	12	1.7	713
Sol'	–	–	–	–	1,024	100.0	–	–	1,024
Vecher	475	11	486	74.1	–	–	170	25.9	656
Afon'ka Bida	1,394	2	1,396	93.3	100	6.7	–	–	1,496

	AUTHOR	NARRATOR	AUTHOR/NARRATOR		SOLDIERS		OTHERS		Total number of words
	Words	Words	Words	%	Words	%	Words	%	
U svyatogo Valenta	1,109	–	1,109	99.6	4	0.4	–	–	1,113
Eskadronnyy Trunov	1,688	25	1,713	88.8	194	10.1	21	1.1	1,928
Ivany	1,222	25	1,247	74.0	347	20.6	91	5.4	1,685
Prodolzheniye istorii odnoy loshadi	32	–	32	11.0	259	89.0	–	–	291
Vdova	720	–	720	66.7	338	31.3	22	2.0	1,080
Zamost'ye	758	25	783	87.9	35	3.9	73	8.2	891
Izmena	–	–	–	–	1,208	100.0	–	–	1,208
Chesniki	679	9	688	71.0	207	21.4	74	7.6	969
Posle boya	725	19	744	80.2	119	12.8	65	7.0	928
Pesnya	635	–	635	86.2	35	4.7	67	9.1	737
Syn rabbi	493	33	526	92.1	–	–	45	7.9	571
Argamak	1,119	45	1,164	86.7	179	13.3	–	–	1,343
TOTAL	21,039	344	21,383	66.9	8,839	27.7	1,734	5.4	31,956
AVERAGE PER STORY	601.1/65.8%	9.8/1.1%	610.9	66.9	252.5	27.7	49.5	5.4	913

NA POLE CHESTI	AUTHOR/NARRATOR		SOLDIERS		OTHERS		Total number of words
	Words	%	Words	%	Words	%	
Na pole chesti	333	81.0	78	19.0	–	–	411
Dezertir	356	70.6	148	29.4	–	–	504
Semeystvo papashi Maresko	–	–	513	100.0	–	–	513
Kvaker	740	84.6	–	–	135	15.4	875
TOTAL	1,429	62.0	739	32.1	135	5.9	2,303
AVERAGE PER STORY	357.3	62.0	184.8	32.1	33.8	5.9	575.8

TABLE 2 Proportions of tropes in relation to *skaz* in the two cycles of war stories

KONARMIYA	Number of tropes	Number of words	Density of tropes (T to W*)	LYUTOV-BASED		COSSACKS		OTHERS	
				Skaz %	Tropes: no./%	Skaz %	Tropes: no./%	Skaz %	Tropes: no./%
Perekhod cherez Zbruch	43	497	1:11.6	84.3	43/100	–	–	15.7	0/0
Kostyol v Novograde	56	689	1:12.3	100.0	56/100	–	–	–	–
Pis'mo	39	1,248	1:32.0	11.5	6/15.4	88.5	33/84.6	–	–
Nachal'nik konzapasa	46	495	1:10.7	80.6	35/76.1	13.3	8/17.4	6.1	3/6.5
Pan Apolek	246	1,919	1:7.8	83.5	222/90.2	–	–	16.5	24/9.8
Solntse Italii	105	924	1:8.8	52.9	62/59.0	47.1	43/41.0	–	–
Gedali	75	780	1:10.4	61.4	40/53.3	–	–	38.6	35/35.4
Moy pervyy gus'	75	921	1:12.3	81.0	53/70.7	17.8	22/29.3	1.2	0/0
Rabbi	58	639	1:11.0	63.1	35/60.3	–	–	36.9	23/39.7
Put' v Brody	65	473	1:7.3	76.7	55/84.6	23.3	10/15.4	–	–
Ucheniye o tachanke	75	675	1:9.0	100.0	75/100	–	–	–	–
Smert' Dolgushova	53	773	1:14.6	75.1	25/47.2	15.3	20/37.7	9.6	8/15.1
Kombrig dva	19	366	1:19.3	92.6	14/73.7	7.4	5/26.3	–	–
Sashka Khristos	50	1,266	1:25.3	80.0	33/66.0	18.3	12/24.0	3.7	5/10.0
Zhizneopisaniye Pavlichenki, Matveya Rodionycha	139	1,523	1:11.0	–	–	100.0	139/100	–	–
Kladbishche v Kozine	20	134	1:6.7	100.0	20/100	–	–	–	–
Prishchepa	18	278	1:15.4	100.0	18/100	–	–	–	–
Istoriya odnoy loshadi	59	987	1:16.7	69.2	43/72.9	30.8	16/27.1	–	–
Konkin	74	736	1:9.9	4.6	0/0	95.4	74/100	–	–
Berestechko	62	713	1:11.5	97.3	59/92.2	1.0	0/0	1.7	3/4.8
Sol'	95	1,024	1:10.8	–	–	100.0	95/100	–	–
Vecher	69	656	1:9.5	74.1	52/75.4	–	–	25.9	17/24.6
Afon'ka Bida	100	1,496	1:15.0	93.3	92/92.0	6.7	8/8.0	–	–

	Number of tropes	Number of words	Density of tropes (T to W*)	AUTHOR/NARRATOR		SOLDIERS		OTHERS	
				Skaz %	Tropes: no./%	Skaz %	Tropes: no./%	Skaz %	Tropes: no./%
U svyatogo Valenta	165	1,113	1:6.7	99.6	165/100	0.4	0/0	–	–
Eskadronnyy Trunov	69	1,928	1:27.9	88.8	48/69.6	10.1	16/23.2	1.1	5/7.2
Ivany	75	1,685	1:22.5	74.0	33/44.0	20.6	37/49.3	5.4	5/6.7
Prodolzheniye istorii odnoy loshadi	26	291	1:11.2	11.0	0/0	89.0	26/100	–	–
Vdova	82	1,080	1:13.2	66.7	56/68.3	31.3	21/25.6	2.0	5/6.1
Zamost'ye	48	891	1:18.6	87.9	41/85.4	3.9	3/6.3	8.2	4/8.3
Izmena	72	1,208	1:16.8	–	–	100.0	72/100	–	–
Chesniki	37	969	1:26.2	71.0	17/46.0	21.4	13/35.1	7.6	7/18.9
Posle boya	46	928	1:20.2	80.2	33/71.7	12.8	9/19.6	7.0	4/8.7
Pesnya	38	737	1:19.4	86.2	31/81.6	4.7	5/13.1	9.1	2/5.3
Syn rabbi	51	571	1:11.2	92.1	50/98.0	–	–	7.9	1/2.0
Argamak	56	1,343	1:24.0	86.7	43/76.8	13.3	13/23.2	–	–
TOTAL	2,406	31,956	1:13.3	66.9	1555/64.6	27.7	700/29.1	5.4	151/6.3
AVERAGE PER STORY	68.7	913	1:13.3	66.9	44.4/64.6	27.7	20.0/29.1	5.4	4.3/6.3

NA POLE CHESTI	Number of tropes	Number of words	Density of tropes (T to W*)	AUTHOR/NARRATOR		SOLDIERS		OTHERS	
				Skaz %	Tropes: no./%	Skaz %	Tropes: no./%	Skaz %	Tropes: no./%
Na pole chesti	15	411	1:27.4	81.0	12/80.0	19.0	3/20.0	–	–
Dezertir	15	504	1:33.6	70.6	7/46.7	29.4	8/53.3	–	–
Semeystvo papashi Maresko	25	513	1:20.5	–	–	100.0	25/100	–	–
Kvaker	34	875	1:25.7	84.6	29/85.3	–	–	15.4	5/14.7
TOTAL	89	2,303	1:25.9	62.0	48/53.9	32.1	36/40.5	5.9	5/5.6
AVERAGE PER STORY	22.25	575.8	1:25.9	62.0	12/53.9	32.1	9/40.5	5.9	1.25/5.6

* Tropes to Words

TABLE 3 Types of tropes

KONARMIYA	METAPHOR			METONYMY			SYNECDOCHE			SIMILE		
	a	b	c	a	b	c	a	b	c	a	b	c
Perekhod cherez Zbruch	31	72.1	1:16	4	9.3	1:124.3	3	7.0	1:165.7	5	11.6	1:99.4
Kostyol v Novograde	38	67.9	1:18.1	9	16.1	1:76.6	2	3.6	1:344.5	4	7.1	1:172.3
Pis'mo	24	61.5	1:52	4	10.3	1:312	1	2.6	1:1248	3	5.1	1:624
Nachal'nik konzapasa	35	76.1	1:14.1	3	6.5	1:165	2	4.3	1:247.5	3	6.5	1:165
Pan Apolek	109	44.3	1:17.6	110	44.7	1:17.4	10	4.1	1:191.9	12	4.9	1:159.9
Solntse Italii	76	72.4	1:12.5	12	11.4	1:77	2	1.9	1:462	10	9.5	1:92.4
Gedali	40	53.3	1:19.5	6	8.0	1:130	12	16.0	1:65	5	6.7	1:156
Moy pervyy gus'	47	62.7	1:19.6	7	9.3	1:131.6	5	6.7	1:184.2	10	13.3	1:92.1
Rabbi	40	69.0	1:16	–	–	–	5	8.6	1:127.8	8	13.8	1:79.9
Put' v Brody	41	63.1	1:11.5	6	9.2	1:78.8	12	18.5	1:39.4	5	7.7	1:94.6
Ucheniye o tachanke	44	58.7	1:15.3	2	2.7	1:337.5	21	28.0	1:32.1	4	5.3	1:168.8
Smert' Dolgushova	38	71.7	1:20.3	1	1.9	1:773	2	3.8	1:386.5	3	5.7	1:257.7
Kombrig dva	16	84.2	1:22.9	–	–	–	–	–	–	2	10.5	1:183
Sashka Khristos	27	54.0	1:46.9	8	16.0	1:158.3	–	–	–	2	4.0	1:633
Zhizneopisaniye Pavlichenki, Matveya Rodionycha	64	46.0	1:23.8	19	13.7	1:80.2	20	14.4	1:76.2	9	6.5	1:169.2
Kladbishche v Kozine	9	45.0	1:14.9	6	30.0	1:22.3	2	10.0	1:67	1	5.0	1:134
Prishchepa	10	55.6	1:27.8	4	22.2	1:69.5	1	5.5	1:278	1	5.5	1:278
Istoriya odnoy loshadi	35	59.3	1:28.2	4	6.8	1:246.8	7	11.9	1:141	7	11.9	1:141
Konkin	30	40.5	1:24.5	15	20.3	1:49.1	6	8.1	1:122.7	10	13.5	1:73.6
Berestechko	26	41.9	1:27.4	7	11.3	1:101.9	15	24.2	1:47.5	5	8.1	1:142.6
Sol'	53	55.8	1:19.3	9	9.5	1:113.8	7	7.3	1:146.3	7	7.3	1:146.3
Vecher	42	60.9	1:15.6	–	–	–	3	4.3	1:218.7	7	10.1	1:93.7
Afon'ka Bida	67	67.0	1:22.3	3	3.0	1:498.6	5	5.0	1:299.2	10	10.0	1:149.6
U svyatogo Valenta	48	29.1	1:23.2	91	55.1	1:12.2	2	1.2	1:556.5	13	7.9	1:85.6

	METAPHOR			METONYMY			SYNECDOCHE			SIMILE		
	a	b	c	a	b	c	a	b	c	a	b	c
Eskadronnyy Trunov	38	55.1	1:50.7	8	11.6	1:241	4	5.8	1:482	11	15.9	1:175.3
Ivany	46	61.3	1:36.6	9	12.0	1:187.2	4	5.3	1:421.3	7	9.3	1:240.7
Prodolzheniye istorii odnoy loshadi	9	34.6	1:32.3	3	11.5	1:97	2	7.7	1:145.5	1	3.9	1:291
Vdova	46	56.1	1:23.5	7	8.5	1:154.3	7	8.5	1:154.3	6	7.3	1:180
Zamost'ye	35	72.9	1:25.5	2	4.2	1:445.5	3	6.3	1:297	6	12.5	1:148.5
Izmena	41	56.9	1:29.5	7	9.7	1:172.6	7	9.7	1:172.6	5	6.9	1:241.6
Chesniki	18	48.7	1:53.8	3	8.1	1:323	3	8.1	1:323	7	18.9	1:138.4
Posle boya	25	54.3	1:37.1	2	4.4	1:464	7	15.2	1:132.6	5	10.9	1:185.6
Pesnya	21	55.3	1:35.1	2	5.3	1:368.5	5	13.1	1:147.4	4	10.5	1:184.3
Syn rabbi	27	52.9	1:21.1	5	9.8	1:114.2	10	19.6	1:57.1	3	5.9	1:190.3
Argamak	35	62.5	1:38.4	3	5.3	1:447.7	3	5.3	1:447.7	10	17.8	1:134.3
TOTAL	1,331	55.3	1:24.0	381	15.8	1:83.8	200	8.3	1:159.7	210	8.7	1:152.1
AVERAGE PER STORY	38.0			10.9			5.7			6		

	METAPHOR			METONYMY			SYNECDOCHE			SIMILE		
NA POLE CHESTI	a	b	c	a	b	c	a	b	c	a	b	c
Na pole chesti	10	66.7	1:41.1	–	–	–	–	–	–	–	–	–
Dezertir	6	40.0	1:84	2	13.3	1:252	–	–	–	2	13.3	1:252
Semeystvo papashi Maresko	12	48.0	1:42.8	4	16.0	1:128.3	2	8.0	1:256.5	–	–	–
Kvaker	20	58.8	1:43.8	2	5.9	1:437.5	2	5.9	1:437.5	5	14.7	1:175
TOTAL	48	53.9	1:48.0	8	9.0	1:287.9	4	4.5	1:575.8	7	7.9	1:329
AVERAGE PER STORY	12.0			2.0			1.0			1.75		

a=number; b=percentage; c=density

Table 3 continued

KONARMIYA	HYPERBOLE			LITOTES			OTHER TROPES	TOTAL	
	a	b	c	a	b	c	Name & number	Number	Density
Perekhod cherez Zbruch	–	–	–	–	–	–	–	43	1:11.6
Kostyol v Novograde	2	3.6	1:344.5	–	–	–	Apostrophe (1)	56	1:12.3
Pis'mo	7	17.9	1:178.3	1	2.6	1:1248	–	39	1:32
Nachal'nik konzapasa	2	4.3	1:247.5	–	–	–	Oxymoron (1)	46	1:10.7
Pan Apolek	1	0.4	1:1919	4	1.6	1:479.8	–	246	1:7.8
Solntse Italii	3	2.9	1:308	1	0.9	1:924	Oxymoron (1)	105	1:8.8
Gedali	7	9.3	1:111.4	2	2.7	1:390	Apostrophes (3)	75	1:10.4
Moy pervyy gus'	1	1.3	1:921	4	5.3	1:230.3	Zeugma (1)	75	1:12.3
Rabbi	5	8.6	1:127.8	–	–	–	–	58	1:11.0
Put' v Brody	1	1.5	1:473	–	–	–	–	65	1:7.3
Ucheniye o tachanke	2	2.7	1:337.5	–	–	–	Zeugmas (2)	75	1:9.0
Smert' Dolgushova	–	–	–	7	13.2	1:110.4	Zeugma (1) Irony (1)	53	1:14.6
Kombrig dva	1	5.3	1:366	–	–	–	–	19	1:19.3
Sashka Khristos	11	22.0	1:115.1	2	4.0	1:633	–	50	1:25.3
Zhizneopisaniye Pavlichenki, Matveya Rodionycha	16	11.5	1:95.2	8	5.8	1:190.4	Apostrophes (3)	139	1:11.0
Kladbishche v Kozine	1	5.0	1:134	–	–	–	Apostrophe (1)	26	1:6.7
Prishchepa	2	11.1	1:139	–	–	–	–	18	1:15.4
Istoriya odnoy loshadi	5	8.4	1:197.4	1	1.7	1:987	–	59	1:16.7
Konkin	6	8.1	1:122.7	7	9.5	1:105.1	–	74	1:9.9
Berestechko	9	14.5	1:79.2	–	–	–	–	62	1:11.5
Sol'	14	14.7	1:73.1	5	5.3	1:204.8	–	95	1:10.8
Vecher	14	20.3	1:46.9	2	2.9	1:328	Apostrophe (1)	69	1:9.5
Afon'ka Bida	14	14.0	1:106.9	1	1.0	1:1496	–	100	1:15.0
U svyatogo Valenta	11	6.7	1:1012	–	–	–	–	165	1:6.7

	HYPERBOLE			LITOTES			OTHER TROPES	TOTAL	
	a	b	c	a	b	c	Name & number	Number	Density
Eskadronnyy Trunov	6	8.7	1:321	1	1.45	1:1928	Irony (1)	69	1:27.9
Ivany	9	12.0	1:187.2	–	–	–	–	75	1:22.5
Prodolzheniye istorii odnoy loshadi	9	34.6	1:32.3	2	7.7	1:145.5	–	26	1:11.2
Vdova	10	12.2	1:108	6	7.3	1:180	–	82	1:13.2
Zamost'ye	1	2.1	1:891	–	–	–	Oxymoron (1)	48	1:18.6
Izmena	11	15.3	1:109.8	1	1.4	1:1208	–	72	1:16.8
Chesniki	4	10.8	1:242.3	2	5.4	1:484.5	–	37	1:26.2
Posle boya	3	6.5	1:309.3	4	8.7	1:232	–	46	1:20.2
Pesnya	5	13.5	1:147.4	1	2.6	1:737	–	38	1:19.4
Syn rabbi	6	11.8	1:95.2	–	–	–	–	51	1:11.2
Argamak	3	5.35	1:447.7	2	3.6	1:671.5	–	56	1:24.0
TOTAL	202	8.4	1:158.1	64	2.7	1:499.2	18/0.8%/1:1774.7	2,406	1:13.3
AVERAGE PER STORY	5.8			1.8			0.5	68.7	1:13.3

	HYPERBOLE			LITOTES			OTHER TROPES	TOTAL	
NA POLE CHESTI	a	b	c	a	b	c	Name & number	Number	Density
Na pole chesti	1	6.7	1:411	3	20.0	1:137	Oxymoron (1)	15	1:27.4
Dezertir	3	20.0	1:168	–	–	–	Irony (2)	15	1:33.6
Semeystvo papashi Maresko	5	20.0	1:102.6	1	4.0	1:513	Irony (1)	25	1:20.5
Kvaker	3	8.8	1:291.7	2	5.9	1:437.5	–	34	1:25.7
TOTAL	12	13.5	1:191.9	6	6.7	1:383.8	4/4.5%/1:575.8	89	1:25.9
AVERAGE PER STORY	3.0			1.5			1.0	22.25	1:25.9

a=number; b=percentage; c=density

TABLE 4   Analysis of metaphors in the two cycles of war stories

	KONARMIYA			NA POLE CHESTI		
	Lyutov %	Cossacks %	Others %	Narrator %	Soldiers %	Others *
Section IA – Form						
Verb only	31.3	29.85	17.9	32.25	20.0	–
Verb + concrete substantive	6.8	14.2	12.5	6.5	6.7	–
Verb + abstract substantive	6.1	4.5	7.1	9.7	13.3	[1]
Concrete substantive only	20.4	29.85	41.1	9.7	26.7	–
Abstract substantive only	8.2	4.5	8.9	9.7	6.7	[1]
Epithet	27.2	16.4	10.7	32.3	26.7	–
Others	–	0.7	1.8	–	–	–
Section IB – Trope series						
Adjacent metaphors	38.8	56.0	52.6	48.4	53.3	–
Non-adjacent metaphors	61.2	44.0	47.4	51.6	46.7	[2]
Proportion of metaphors connecting with:						
Simile	17.5	6.7	10.0	13.3	–	–
Metaphor	66.7	78.7	83.3	73.3	62.5	–
Metonymy or synecdoche	8.8	6.6	–	6.7	12.1	–
Hyperbole or litotes	7.0	8.0	6.7	6.7	25.0	–
Section IC – Position of imported image to stimulant or main idea						
Pre-positive	38.1	40.3	45.6	64.5	53.3	–
Post-positive	61.9	59.7	54.5	35.5	46.7	[2]
Section ID – Theme of imported image						
Human or body	50.0	28.7	33.3	41.9	26.7	[1]
Animal	6.5	11.2	15.8	6.4	33.3	–
Violence	13.0	11.2	10.5	9.7	13.3	–
[Insult]	[–]	[9.1]	[1.75]	[–]	[6.7]	[1]
Military	0.9	2.8	–	3.2	–	–
Natural phenomena	11.1	7.0	5.3	19.4	–	–
Fabric	1.85	2.1	1.75	9.7	13.3	–
Miscellaneous	16.7	40.0	31.6	9.7	6.7	–

Table 4 continued

	KONARMIYA			NA POLE CHESTI		
	Lyutov %	Cossacks %	Others %	Narrator %	Soldiers %	Others*

Section II – Transfer between stimulant or main idea and imported image

A – Sensuous transfer

Visual–Visual	36.8	21.0	16.0	19.4	33.3	–
Auditory–Auditory	10.4	–	–	6.4	6.7	–
Synaesthetic:						
Abstract–Visual	30.2	54.6	62.5	54.8	46.7	[1]
Visual–Abstract	5.7	0.8	5.4	–	–	–
Other	7.5	4.2	3.6	3.2	–	–
Abstract–Abstract	9.4	19.3	12.5	16.1	13.3	[1]

B – Animate and inanimate transfer

Animate–Animate	18.5	53.0	48.2	16.1	46.7	–
Synaesthetic:						
Inanimate–Animate	56.5	24.8	21.4	54.8	26.7	[1]
Animate–Inanimate	0.9	2.6	5.4	6.5	13.3	–
Inanimate–Inanimate	24.1	19.6	25.0	22.6	13.3	[1]

Section III – Evaluation

A – Effect on stimulant

Elevatory	17.6	20.3	42.0	45.2	26.7	–
Depreciatory	75.0	69.5	54.8	51.6	73.3	[2]
Neutral	7.4	10.2	12.0	3.2	–	–

B – Degree of originality

Fossilized	30.6	71.0	82.1	64.5	46.7	[1]
Revitalizing	8.3	5.1	–	3.2	6.6	[1]
Living	61.1	23.9	17.9	32.3	46.7	–

*As only two metaphors belong in this category, the results are not given as percentages but as numbers in parentheses.

257

Appendix A(i)
На поле чести

Печатаемые здесь рассказы - начало моих заметок о войне. Содержание их заимствовано из книг, написанных французскими солдатами и офицерами, участниками боев.[1] В некоторых отрывках изменена фабула и форма изложения, в других я старался ближе держаться к оригиналу.

На поле чести

Германские батареи бомбардировали деревни из тяжелых орудий. Крестьяне бежали к Парижу. Они тащили за собой калек, уродцев, рожениц, овец, собак, утварь. Небо, блиставшее синевой и зноем, - медлительно багровело, распухало и обволакивалось дымом.

5 Сектор у N занимал 37 пехотный полк. Потери были огромны. Полк готовился к контр-атаке. Капитан Ратен[2] обходил траншеи. Солнце было в зените. Из соседнего участка сообщили, что в 4 роте пали все офицеры. 4 рота продолжает сопротивление.

В 300 метрах от траншеи Ратен увидел человеческую фигуру. Это
10 был солдат Биду, дурачок[3] Биду. Он сидел скорчившись на дне сырой ямы. Здесь когда-то разорвался снаряд. Солдат занимался тем, чем утешаются дрянные осарикашки в деревнях и порочные мальчишки в общественных уборных. Не будем говорить[4] об этом.

- Застегнись, Биду, - с омерзением сказал капитан. - Почему ты
15 здесь?

- Я ... я не могу этого сказать вам ... Я боюсь, капитан! ...

- Ты нашел здесь жену, свинья! Ты осмелился сказать мне в лицо, что ты трус, Биду. Ты оставил товарищей в тот час, когда полк атакует. Ben, mon cochon! ...
20 - Клянусь вам, капитан! ... Я все испробовал ... Биду, сказал я себе, будь рассудителен ... Я выпил бутыль чистого спирту для храбрости. Je peux pas, capitaine ... Я боюсь, капитан! ...

Дурачок положил голову на колени, обнял ее двумя руками и заплакал. Потом он взглянул на капитана, и в щелках его свинных
25 глазок отразилась робкая и нежная надежда. Ратен был вспыльчив. Он потерял двух братьев на бойне, и у него не зажила рана на шее. На солдата обрушилась кощунственная брань, в него полетел сухой град

тех отвратительных, яростных и бессмысленных слов, от которых кровь стучит в висках, после которых один человек убивает другого.

30   Вместо ответа Биду тихонько покачивал своей круглой рыжей похматой головой, твердой головой деревенского идиота.

    Никакими силами нельзя[5] было заставить его подняться. Тогда капитан подошел к самому краю ямы и прошипел совершенно тихо:

    – Встань, Биду, или я оболью тебя с головы до ног.

35   Он сделал как сказал. С капитаном Ратен шутки были плохи. Зловонная струя с силой[6] брызнула в лицо солдата. Биду был друак, деревенский дурак, но он не перенес обиды. Он закричал нечеловеческим и протяжным криком; этот тоскливый, одинокий, затерявшийся вопль прошел по взбороненным полям; солдат
40 рванулся, заломил руки и бросился бежать полем к немецким траншеям. Неприятельская пуля пробила ему грудь. Ратен двумя выстрелами прикончил его из револьвера. Тело солдата даже не дернулось. Оно осталось на полдороге, между вражескими линиями.

    Так умер Селестин Биду, нормандский крестьянин, родом из Ори,
45 21 года – на обагренных кровью полях Франции.

    То, что я рассказал здесь – правда. Об этом написано в книге капитана Гастона Видаля – Figures et anecdotes de la grande[7] Guerre. Он был этому свидетелем. Он тоже защищал Францию, капитан Видаль.

Дезертир

Капитан Жемье был превосходнейший человек, к тому же философ. На поле битвы он не знал колебаний, в частной жизни умел прощать маленькие обиды. Он любил Францию с нежностью, пожиравшей его сердце, поэтому ненависть его к варварам, осквернившим древнюю ее
5 землю, была неугасима, беспощадна, длительна, как жизнь.

    Что еще сказать о Жемье? Он любил свою жену, сделал добрыми гражданами своих детей, был фрацузом, патриотом, книжником, парижанином и любителем красивых вещей.

    И вот – в одно весеннее сияющее розовое утро капитану Жемье
10 доложили что между французскими и неприятельскими линиями задержан везоружный[8] солдат. Намерение дезертировать было очевидно, вина несомненна, солдата доставили под стражей.

    – Это ты, Божи?

    – Это я, капитан, – отдавая честь, ответил солдат.

15   – Ты воспользовался зарей, чтоб подышать чистым воздухом? Молчание.

    – C'est bien. Оставьте нас.

    Конвой удалился. Жемье запер дверь на ключ. Солдату было двадцать лет.

20 - Ты знаешь, что тебя ожидает? - Voyons, объяснись.

Божи ничего не скрыл. Он сказал, что устал от войны. - Я очень устал от войны, mon capitaine! Снаряды мешают спать шестую ночь …

Война ему отвратительна. Он не шел предавать, он шел сдаться.

Вообще говоря, он был неожиданно красноречив, этот маленький
25 Божи.

Он сказал, что ему всего двацать лет, mon Dieu, c'est naturel, в двацать лет можно совершить ошибку. У него есть мать, невеста, де[7] bons amis. Перед ним вся жизнь, перед этим двадцатилетним Божи, и он загладит свою вину перед Францией.

30 -- Капитан, что скажет моя мать, когда узнает, что меня расстреляли, как последнего негодяя?

Солдат упал на колени.

- Ты не расжалобишь меня, Божи! - ответил капитан. Тебя видели солдаты. Пять таких солдат, как ты, и рота отравлена. C'est la défaite.
35 Cela jamais. Ты умрешь, Божи, но я спасаю тебя в твою последнюю минуту. В мэрии не будет известно о твоем позоре. Матери сообщат, что ты пал на поле чести. Идем.

Солдат последовал за начальником. Когда они достигли леса, капитан остановился, вынул револьвер и протянул его Божи.
40 - Вот способ избегнуть суда. Застрелись, Божи! Я вернусь через пять минут. Все должно быть кончено.

Жемье удалился. Ни единый звук не нарушил тишину леса. Офицер вернулся. Божи ждал его сгорбившись.

- Я не могу, капитан, - прошептал солдат. - У меня не хватает
45 силы …

И началась та же капитель - мать, невеста, друзья, впереди жизнь …

- Я даю тебе еще пять минут, Божи! Не заставляй меня гулять без дела.
50 Когда капитан вернулся, солдат всхлипывал лежа на земле. Пальцы его, лежавшие на револьвере, слабо шевелились.

Тогда Жемье поднял солдата и сказал, глядя ему в глаза, тихим и душевным голосом:

- Друг мой, Божи, может быть ты не знаешь, как это делается?
55 Не торопясь, он вынул револьвер из мокрых рук юноши, отошел на три шага и прострелил ему череп.

И об этом происшествии рассказано в книге Гастона Видаля. И, действительно, солдата звали Божи. Правильно ли данное мною капитану имя Жемье - этого я точно не знаю. Рассказ Видаля
60 посвящен некоему Фирмену Жемье в знак глубокого благоговения. Я думаю, посвящения достаточно. Конечно, капитана звали Жемье. И потом, Видаль свидетельствует, что капитан, действительно, был патриот, солдат, добрый отец и человек, умевший прощать маленькие обиды. А это не мало для человека - прощать маленькие обиды.

Семейство папаши Мареско

Мы занимаем деревню, отбитую у неприятеля. Это маленькое пикардийское селеньице – прелестное и скромное. Нашей роте досталось кладбище. Вокруг нас сломанные Распятия, куски надгробных памятников, плитья, развороченные молотом неведомого
5 осквернителя. Истлевшие трупы вываливаются из гробов, разбитых снарядами. Картина достойна тебя, Микель Анджело!

Солдату не до мистики. Поле черепов превращено в траншеи. На то война. Мы живы еще. Если нам суждено увеличить население этого прохладного уголка, что-ж – мы сначала заставили гниющих
10 стариков поплясать под марш наших пулеметов.

Снаряд приподнял одну из надгробных плит. Это сделано для того, чтобы предложить мне убежище, никакого сомнения. Я водворился в этой дыре, que voulez-vous,[9] on loge où on peut. И вот – весеннее, светлое ясное утро. Я лежу на покойниках, смотрю на жирную траву,
15 думаю о Гамлете. Он был неплохой философ, этот бедный принц. Черепа отвечали ему человеческими словами. В наше время это искусство пригодилось бы[10] лейтенанту французской армии.

Меня окликает капрал.

– Лейтенант, вас хочет видеть какой-то штатский.
20 Какого дьявола ищет штатский в этой преисподней?

Персонаж делает свой выход. Поношенное, выцветшее существо. Оно облачено в воскресный сюртук. Сюртук забрызган грязью. За робкими плечами болтается мешок, на половину пустой. В нем, должно быть, мороженный картофель; каждый раз, когда старик
25 делает движение, что-то трешит[11] в мешке.

– Eh ben, в чем дело?

– Моя фамилия, видите-ли, монсье Мареско, – шепчет штатский и кланяется. – Потому я и пришел …

– Дальше?
30 – Я хотел бы похоронить мадам Мареско и все семейство, господин лейтенант! …

– Как вы сказали?

– Моя фамилия, видите-ли – папаша Мареско. Старик приподнимает шляпу над серым лбом! Может быть, слышали, господин
35 лейтенант! …

Папаша Мареску? Я слышал эти слова. Конечно, я их слышал. Вот она – вся история. Дня три тому назад, в начале нашей оккупации, всем мирным гражданам был отдан приказ эвакуироваться. Одни ушли, другие остались; оставшиеся засели в погребах. Бомбардировка
40 победила мужество, защита камня оказалась ненадежной. Появились убитые. Целое семейство задохлось под развалинами подземелья. И это было семейство Мареско. Их фамилия осталась у меня в памяти – настоящая французская фамилия. Их было четверо – отец, мать и две дочери. Только отец спасся …

45 – Мой бедный друг, так это вы, Мареско? Все это очень грустно. Зачем вам понадобился этот несчастный погреб, к чему?

Меня перебил капрал.

– Они, кажется, начинают, лейтенант …

Этого следовало ожидать. Немцы заметили движение в наших
50 траншеях. Залп по правому флангу, потом левее. Я схватил папашу Мареско за ворот и стащил его вниз. Мои молодцы, втянув головы в плечи, тихонько сидели под прикрытием, никто носу не высунул.

Воскресный сюртук бледнел и ежился. Недалеко от нас промяукала кошечка в 12 сантиметров.
55 – Что вам нужно, папаша, говорите живее. Вы видите, здесь кусаются.

– Mon lieutenant, я все сказал вам, я хотел бы[12] похоронить мое семейство.

– Отлично, я прикажу сходить за телами.
60 – Тела при мне, господин лейтенант!

– Что такое?

Он указал на мешок. В нем оказались скудные остатки семьи папаши Мареско.

Я вздрогнул от ужаса.
65 – Хорошо, старина, я прикажу их похоронить.

Он посмотрел на меня, на человека, выпалившего совершенную глупость.

– Когда стихнет этот проклятый шум, начал я снова, мы выроем им превосходную могилу. Все будет сделано, père[13] Marescot, будьте
70 спокойны …

– Но , но у меня фамильный склеп …

– Отлично, укажите его нам.

– Но, но …

– Что такое - но?
75 – Но, mon lieutenant, мы в нем сидим все время.

Квакер

Заповедано – не убий. Вот почему. Стон – квакер записался в колонну автомобилистов. Он помогал своему отечеству, не совершая страшного греха человекоубийства. Воспитание и богатство дозволяли ему занять более высокую должность, но раб своей совести, он принимал
5 со смирением невидную работу и общество людей, казавшихся ему грубыми.

Что был Стон? Лысый лоб у вершины палки. Господь даровал ему тело лишь для того, чтобы возвысить мысли над жалкими скорбями мира сего. Каждое его движение было не более, как победа, одержанная духом над материей. У руля своего автомобиля, каковы бы ни были грозные обстоятельства он держался с деревянной неподвижностью проповедника на кафедре. Никто не видел, как Стон смеется.

Однажды утром, будучи свободен от службы, он возымел мысль выйти на прогулку для того, чтобы преклониться перед Создателем в его творениях. С огромной Библией под мышками Стон пересекал длинными своими ногами лужайки, возрожденные весной. Вид ясного неба, щебетание воробьев в траве – все заливало его радостью.

Стон сел, открыл свою Библию, но в ту минуту увидел у изгиба аллеи непривязанную лошадь с торчащими от худобы боками. Тотчас же голос долга с силой заговорил в нем, – у себя на родине Стон был членом общества покровительства животным. Он приблизился к скотине, погладил ее мягкие губы и, забыв о прогулке, направился к конюшне. По дороге, не выпуская из рук своей Библии с застежками – он напоил лошадь у колодца.

Конюшенным мальчиком состоял некий юноша, по фамилии Бэккер. Нрав этого молодого человека издавна составлял причину справедливого гнева Стона: Бэккер оставлял на каждом привале безутешных невест.

– Я бы мог, – сказал ему квакер, – объявить[14] о вас майору, но надеюсь, что на этот раз и моих слов будет достаточно. Бедная, больная лошадь, которую я привел и за которой вы будете ухаживать, достойна лучшей участи, чем вы.

И он удалился размеренным, торжественным шагом, не обращая внимания на гоготание, раздававшееся позади него. Четырехугольный, выдвинутый вперед подбородок юноши с убедительностью свидетельствовал о непобедимом упорстве.

Прошло несколько дней. Лошадь все время бродила без призору. На этот раз Стон сказал Бэккеру с твердостью:

Исчадие сатаны, – так приблизительно начиналась эта речь, – Всевышним позволено вам, может быть, погубить свою душу, но грехи ваши не должны всею тяжестью пасть на невинную лошадь. Поглядите на нее, негодяй. Она расхаживает здесь в величайшем беспокойстве. Я уверен, что вы грубо обращаетесь с ней, как и пристало преступнику. Еще раз повторяю вам, сын греха: идите к гибели с той поспешностью какая вам покажется наилучшей, но заботьтесь об этой лошади, иначе вы будете иметь дело со мной.

С этого дня Стон счел себя облеченным Провидением особой миссией – заботой о судьбе обиженного четвероногого. Люди, по грехам их, казались ему мало достойными уважения; к животным же он испытывал неописуемую жалость. Утомительные занятия не препятствовали ему держать нерушимым его обещание Богу. Часто по ночам квакер выбирался из своего автомобиля, – он спал в нем, скорчившись на сиденьи - для того , чтобы убедиться, что лошадь находится в приличном отдалении от бэккеровского сапога, окованного гвоздями. В хорошую погоду он сам садился на своего любимца и кляча, важно попрыгивая, рысцой[15] носила по зеленеющим полям его тощее, длинное тело. С своим бесцветным желтым лицом, сжатыми бледными губами, Стон вызывал в памяти бессмертную и потешную фигуру рыцаря печального образа, трусящего на Росинанте среди цветов и возделанных полей.

Усердие Стона приносило плоды. Чувствуя себя под неусыпным наблюдением, грум всячески изловчался, чтобы не быть пойманным на месте преступления. Но наедине с лошадью он вымещал на ней ярость своей низкой души. Испытывая необъяснимый[16] страх перед молчаливым квакером – он ненавидел Стона за этот страх и презирал себя. У него не было другого средства поднять себя в собственных глазах, как издеваться над лошадью, которой покровительствовал Стон. Такова презренная гордость человека. Запираясь с лошадью в конюшне, грум колол ее отвислые волосатые губы раскаленными иголками, сек ее проволочным кнутом по спине и сыпал ей соль в глаза. Когда измученное, ослепленное едким порошком животное, оставленное наконец в покое, боязливо пробиралось к стойлу, качаясь как пьяный, мальчишка ложился на живот и хохотал во все горло, наслаждаясь местью.

На фронте произошла перемена. Дивизия к составу которой принадлежал Стон, была переведена на более опасное место. Религиозные его верования не разрешали ему убивать, но позволяли быть убитым. Германцы наступали на Изер. Стон перевозил раненых. Вокруг него с поспешностью умирали люди разных стран. Старые генералы, чисто вымытые, с припухлостями на лице, стояли на холмикак и оглядывали окрестность в полевые бинокли. Гремела, не переставая, канонада. Земля издавала зловоние, солнце копалось в развороченных трупах.

Стон забыл свою лошадь. Через неделю совесть принялась за грызущую свою работу. Улучив время, квакер отправился на старое место. Он нашел лошадь в темном сарае, сбитом из дырявых[17] досок. Животное еле держалось на ногах от слабости, глаза его были затянуты мутной пленкой. Лошадь слабо заржала, увидев своего верного друга, и положила ему на руки падавшую морду.

– Я ни чем не виноват – дерзко сказал Стону грум, – нам не выдают овса.

– Хорошо – ответил Стон, – я добуду овес.

Он посмотрел на небо, сиявшее через дыру в потолке, и вышел.

Я встретил его через несколько часов и спросил – опасна ли дорога? Он казался более сосредоточенным, чем обыкновенно, Последние кровавые дни наложили на него тяжкую печать, он как будто носил[18] траур по сам себе.

– Выехать было нетрудно, – глухо проговорил он, – в конце пути могут произойти неприятности. И прибавил неожиданно. – Я выехал в фуражировку. Мне нужен овес.

На следующее утро солдаты, отправленные на поиски, нашли его убитым у руля автомобиля. Пуля пробила череп. Машина осталась во рву.

105   Так умер Стон – квакер из-за[19] любви к лошади.

И Бабель.

Original variants were as follows:

1. 'боевъ'
2. 'Ratin', here and in all subsequent occurrences.
3. 'дурачек'
4. 'говорит'
5. 'недьзя'
6. 'сидой'
7. 'grand'
8. 'безоружевый'
9. 'voulez vous'
10. 'пригодилось-бы'
11. 'трещить'
12. 'хотел-бы'
13. 'pére'
14. 'об'явить'
15. 'рысцою'
16. 'необ'яснимый'
17. 'дырявыхъ'
18. 'носим'
19. 'из за'

Appendix A(ii)
On the Field of Honour

The stories printed here are the beginning of my observations on war. Their contents have been borrowed from books written by French soldiers and officers, participants of the fighting.[1] In some passages the plot and form of recounting have been changed, in others I have tried to keep closer to the original.

ON THE FIELD OF HONOUR

German batteries were bombarding the villages with heavy guns. The peasants were fleeing to Paris. Behind them they dragged the crippled, the maimed, women in childbirth, sheep, dogs, chattels. The sky, its dark blue, intense heat shining, was slowly turning crimson, swelling and misting over.

The sector at N was occupied by the 37th infantry regiment. The losses had been huge. The regiment was preparing for a counter-attack. Captain Ratin[2] was making his round of the trenches. The sun was at its zenith. From the next section it was reported that all the officers in the 4th regiment had fallen. The 4th regiment was continuing its resistance.

300 metres from the trenches Ratin caught sight of a human figure. It was the soldier Bidu, the idiot[3] Bidu. He was sitting cowering at the bottom of a damp hole. A shell had exploded here at some time. The soldier was engaged in what wretched old men seek comfort from in the villages and shameful boys in public lavatories. We'll not speak[4] of this.

– Button yourself up, Bidu, the captain said with loathing. – Why are you here?

– I … I can't tell you this … I'm afraid captain! …

You've found a wife here, swine! You've dared to tell me to my face that you're a coward, Bidu. You've abandoned your comrades at the very hour that the regiment is attacking. Ben, mon cochon! …

– I swear to you, captain! … I've tried everything … Bidu, I said to myself, be reasonable … I drank a whole bottle of pure spirit for courage. Je peux pas, capitaine … I'm afraid, captain.

The idiot laid his head on his knees, put his two arms around it and started to cry. Then he looked at the captain, and in the chinks of his piggy little eyes a timid, tender hope was reflected. Ratin was quick tempered. He had lost two brothers in the war, and the wound on his neck had not healed.

Blasphemous abuse came down upon the soldier, an arid hail fell on him of those repulsive, violent and senseless words, at which the blood hammers in the temples, after which one man murders another.

Instead of an answer Bidu quietly rocked his shaggy, round ginger head, the hard head of a village idiot.

It was impossible[5] to make him get up by force. Then the captain approached the very edge of the hole and hissed especially quietly:

– Get up, Bidu, or I'll soak you from head to foot.

He did as he said. Captain Ratin was not one to be trifled with. A fetid stream spattered forcefully[6] in the soldier's face. Bidu was an idiot, a village idiot, but he did not endure the affront. He cried out with an inhuman, prolonged yell; this yell, melancholy, lonely, diminishing passed across the harrowed fields; the soldier darted up, wrung his hands and took to his heels across the fields to the German trenches. An enemy bullet pierced his breast. Ratin finished him off with two shots from a revolver. The soldier's body did not even twitch. It remained halfway, between the opposing lines.

Thus Selestin Bidu died, a Norman peasant, native of Ory, 21 years of age – on the bloodstained fields of France.

What I have related here is the truth. It has been written about in captain Vidal's book – Figures et anecdotes de la grande[7] Guerre. He was witness to this. He also defended France, captain Vidal.

THE DESERTER

Captain Zhem'ye was a most excellent man, a philosopher besides. On the field of battle he knew no hesitation, in private life he could forgive small wrongs. He loved France with a tenderness that devoured his heart, that is why his hatred for the barbarians profaning her ancient soil, was as unquenchable, ruthless, prolonged as life.

What else is there to say about Zhem'ye? He loved his wife, made good citizens of his children, was a Frenchman, a patriot, a bibliophile, a Parisian and a lover of beautiful things.

And then – on one shining pink spring morning it was reported to captain Zhem'ye that an unarmed[8] soldier had been detained between French and enemy lines. His intention to desert was obvious, his guilt manifest, the soldier was placed under arrest.

– Is that you, Bozhi?

– It's me captain – the soldier replied, saluting.

– You've availed yourself of the dawn to get some fresh air?

Silence.

– C'est bien. Leave us.

The escort moved off. Zhem'ye locked the door. The soldier was twenty.

– Do you know what's in store for you? – Voyons, explain yourself.

Bozhi concealed nothing. He said that he was tired of the war. – I'm tired of the war, mon capitaine! The shells have stopped me sleeping for six nights …

The war was repugnant to him. He hadn't gone to betray the cause, he had gone to surrender.

Generally speaking, he was unexpectedly eloquent, this little Bozhi. He said that he was only twenty years old, mon Dieu, c'est naturel, at twenty you can make a mistake. He had a mother, a fiancée, good friends. Ahead of him was his whole life, ahead of this twenty year old Bozhi, and he would redress his wrong before France.

– Captain, what will my mother say, when she finds out that I have been shot like the worst kind of villain?

The soldier fell to his knees.

– You won't move me to pity, Bozhi! – the captain answered. The soldiers saw you. Five soldiers like you and the regiment's finished. C'est la défaite. Cela jamais. You'll die, Bozhi, but I'll spare you in your last moments. They'll not know of your shame in the mairie. Your mother will be told that you fell on the field of honour. Let's go.

The soldier followed the officer. When they had reached a wood, the captain stopped, took out a revolver and proffered it to Bozhi.

– That's the way you escape from here. Shoot yourself, Bozhi! I'll return in five minutes. Everything must be finished.

Zhem'ye withdrew. Not a single sound broke the silence of the wood. The officer returned. Bozhi was waiting for him hunched up.

– I can't, captain, the soldier whispered. I don't have the strength … And the same rigmarole began – mother, fiancée, friends, life ahead of him …

– I'll give you five more minutes, Bozhi! Don't make me walk about for the sake of it.

When the captain returned, the soldier lay on the ground sobbing.

His fingers, lying on the revolver, stirred feebly.

Then Zhem'ye picked the soldier up and, looking him in the eyes, said in a voice of quiet emotion:

– Bozhi, my friend, perhaps you don't know how it's done?

Unhurriedly he withdrew the revolver from the damp hands of the youth, fell back three paces and shot him through the skull.

And this event is recounted in Gaston Vidal's book. And the soldier's name really was Bozhi. Whether Zhem'ye, the name given to my captain, is right, I really don't know. Vidal's story was dedicated to a certain Firmen Zhem'ye as a mark of deep veneration. I think the dedication is sufficient. Of course the captain's name was Zhem'ye. And then, Vidal testifies that the captain really was a patriot, a soldier, a good father and a man who knew how to forgive small wrongs. And it's no small thing for a man – to forgive small wrongs.

THE FAMILY OF OLD MAN MARESKO

We are occupying a village recaptured from the enemy. It's a small Picardy village, charming and modest. The cemetery fell to our regiment's lot. Around us are broken crucifixes, pieces of monuments, gravestones played havoc with by the hammer of an unknown defiler. Decayed corpses tumble out of coffins, smashed by shells. A picture worthy of you, Michael Angelo!

A soldier can't be a mystic. The field of skulls is turned into trenches. But that's war. We are still alive. If we are destined to increase the population of this chilly corner, well we've made the rotting old men dance first to the march of our machine-guns.

A shell had slightly raised one of the gravestones. This has been done to offer me shelter, no doubt. I have installed myself in this hole, que voulez-vous,[9] on loge où on peut. And it's a bright, clear, spring morning. I lie on the dead men, look at the rich grass, think of Hamlet. He wasn't a bad philosopher, that poor prince. The skulls answered him with human words. This skill would have been useful[10] nowadays to a lieutenant of the French army.

A corporal calls to me.

– Lieutenant, some civilian or other wants to see you.

What the devil is a civilian looking for in this nether world?

The character makes his entrance. A worn, faded creature. Got up in a Sunday frock coat, the frock coat is bespattered with mud. A sack dangles over timid shoulders, half empty. There must be frozen potatoes in it; each time that the old man makes a movement something cracks[11] in the bag.

– Eh ben, what is it?

– My surname, you see, is Monsieur Maresko – the civilian whispers and bows. – The reason why I've come …

– Well?

– I should like to bury Madame Maresko and all the family, monsieur lieutenant! …

– What did you say?

– My surname, you see is old man Maresko. The old man raises his hat a little above his grey brow! Perhaps you've heard, monsieur lieutenant! …

Old man Maresko? I had heard these words. Of course I had heard them. Here's the whole story. Three days ago, at the beginning of our occupation, the order to evacuate was given to all peaceful citizens. Some left, others stayed; those who stayed did not leave their cellars. The bombardment vanquished courage, stone defences proved hopeless. Dead appeared. A whole family suffocated beneath the ruins of their underground prison. And this was the family Maresko. Their name had stayed in my memory – a real French name. There were four of them – father, mother and two daughters. Only the father escaped …

– My poor friend, so you're Maresko? It's all very sad. Why did you need this wretched vault, what for?

The corporal interrupted me.

– It seems they're starting, lieutenant …

270

This was to be expected. The Germans had noticed the movement in our trenches. A volley on the right flank, then to the left. I grabbed old man Maresko by the collar and dragged him down. My lads were sitting quietly beneath the covering, their heads hunched on their shoulders, no one dared stick their noses out.

The Sunday frock coat turned pale and huddled up. Not far from us a 12 centimetre 'cat' mewed.

– What do you need, old man, come to the point. You can see they're giving us stick.

– Mon lieutenant, I have told you everything, I would like to bury my family.

– Fine, I'll order the bodies to be fetched.

– The bodies are with me, monsieur lieutenant!

– What's that?

He pointed at the bag. The meagre remains of the family of old man Maresko were to be found in it.

I trembled with horror.

– Good, old man, I'll order them to be buried.

He looked at me, as at someone mouthing a sudden and utter absurdity.

– When this accursed din has quietened down, I began again, we'll dig out an excellent grave for them. It will all be done, père[13] Marescot, rest assured …

– But, but I have a family vault …

– Excellent, show it to us.

– But, but …

– What do you mean – but?

– But, mon lieutenant, we've been sitting in it all the time.

THE QUAKER

It is commanded – thou shalt not kill. Here's why. Ston a Quaker had enlisted as a driver. He was helping his fatherland without committing the terrible sin of murder. Upbringing and wealth permitted him to occupy a higher position, but a slave to his conscience he meekly accepted the unenviable work and the society of people who to him appeared coarse.

What was Ston? A bald brow at the top of a pole. The Lord had bestowed a body on him merely to elevate his thoughts above the terrible sorrows of this world. His every movement was no less than a victory won by mind over matter. At the wheel of his vehicle, no matter how threatening circumstances were, he behaved with the wooden immobility of a priest at the pulpit. No one saw Ston laugh.

One morning when he was off duty, he conceived the notion of going out for a walk in order to bow down before the Creator in his creation. A huge Bible under his arm, Ston with his long legs crossed the lawns regenerated by spring. The sight of the clear sky, the twittering of sparrows in the grass – all flooded him with joy.

271

Ston sat down, opened his Bible, but at that moment at a bend in the path he caught sight of an untethered horse, its meagre flanks projecting. Immediately the voice of duty addressed him vehemently, – at home Ston was a member of a society for the protection of animals. He approached the animal, stroked its soft lips and forgetting about his walk, made his way to the stable. Still clutching his Bible with the fastenings, he let the horse drink from a well along the road.

The stable lad was a certain youth named Bekker. This young man's disposition had long since furnished a reason for Ston's justifiable anger: Bekker would leave inconsolable brides at every halting place.

– I could have reported [14] you to the major, the Quaker told him, but I hope that this time my words will be enough. The poor, sick horse which I have brought and which you will look after, is worthy of a better fate than you.

And he moved away with a measured, solemn step, unheedful of the guffawing resounding behind him. The square jutting chin of the youth testified convincingly to an unconquerable stubbornness.

A few days passed. The whole time the horse wandered about neglected. This time Ston spoke harshly to Bekker:

Spawn of Satan – thus more or less did this speech begin – The Almighty has perhaps permitted you to destroy your own soul, but your sins must not fall with all their weight upon an innocent horse. Have a look at her, wretch. She is walking up and down in the greatest distress. I am sure you're treating her as roughly as you would a criminal. Once more I repeat to you, son of sin: go to hell with that thoughtlessness which is your trademark, but trouble yourself with this horse, otherwise you'll have me to deal with.

From that day Ston considered himself invested by Providence with a special mission – concern for the fate of the badly treated quadruped. People through their sins seemed less worthy of respect to him; but for animals he felt an indescribable compassion. Arduous chores did not prevent him from keeping inviolable his promise to God. Often at night the Quaker would crawl out of his vehicle – he used to sleep in it, bent up on the seat – to satisfy himself that the horse was at a proper distance from the hobnailed Bekker boot. In good weather he himself would mount his pet and the prancing jade would bear his long, emaciated body at a trot [15] across the verdant fields. With his insipid yellow face, pale compressed lips, Ston recalled the immortal and amusing figure of the knight of mournful appearance, trotting on Rosinante amid the flowers and cultivated fields.

Ston's zeal bore fruit. Sensing he was under constant observation, the groom took great pains not to be caught at the scene of the crime. But alone with the horse he vented the fury of his base soul upon her. Feeling an inexplicable fear before the taciturn Quaker – he hated Ston for this fear and despised himself. He had no other means of raising his own self esteem than taunting the horse whose protector Ston was. Such is man's contemptible pride. Locking himself in the stable with the horse, the groom pierced her limp, hair-covered lips with burning needles, lacerated her back with a wire whip and poured salt into her eyes. When the exhausted animal, blinded by the caustic powder, was finally left in peace and timidly picked its way to the stall, swaying like a drunk, the boy lay on his belly and roared with laughter, revelling in his revenge.

At the front a change had occurred. The division, to whose ranks Ston belonged, was moved to a more dangerous place. His religious beliefs did not permit him to kill, but allowed him to be killed. The Germans were attacking the Yser. Ston was transporting the wounded. Around him people of different countries were promptly dying. Old generals, freshly washed, with swellings on their faces, stood on hillocks and examined the locality through field-glasses. The cannonade thundered ceaselessly. The earth gave off a stench, the sun rummaged in upturned corpses.

Ston forgot his horse. Within a week his conscience had begun to gnaw away at him. Finding some time, the Quaker set off for his old haunt. He found the horse in a dark shed, knocked together from planks full of holes.[17] The animal could barely stay on its feet from weakness, its eyes were covered in a dull film. Seeing her trusty friend the horse began to neigh weakly and laid her drooping muzzle in his hands.

– I'm not to blame for anything – the groom told Ston boldly – they're not issuing any oats.

– Fine – Ston answered – I'll get some oats.

He looked at the sky shining through a hole in the ceiling and left.

I met him some hours later and asked whether the road was dangerous. He seemed more tense than usual. The last bloody days had left a terrible mark on him, it was as if he were in[18] mourning for himself.

– Driving out wasn't difficult, he uttered in a muffled voice – you could meet trouble at the end of the line. And he added unexpectedly – I came out foraging. I needed oats.

The following morning soldiers on a search party found him dead at the wheel of his car. A bullet had pierced his skull. The car had stopped in a ditch.

So died Ston the Quaker on account of[19] love for a horse.

I. Babel

Appendix B
Figures et anecdotes de la Grande Guerre
Gaston Vidal

DEUX ACTES DEVANT UNE CONSCIENCE
A Firmin Gemier, en témoignage de vive admiration.

Le capitaine V... était, ce soir-là, en veine de confidences.

Un hasard nous avait réunis à la même table, pendant une permission passée à Paris où nous avions l'un et l'autre des parents et des amis à voir. Je connais V... depuis des mois. C'est à la guerre un lion qui rugit, au repos un aigle qui médite. A la guerre, tout à l'aventure terrible et sanglante, il se donne corps et âme à son pays, rien qu'à son pays, seul objet de ses pensées. Il a l'âme qu'il faut aux chefs. Il ne connaît ni la peur pour lui, ni la pitié pour l'ennemi, ni l'indulgence pour ses propres hommes quand ceux-ci commettent des erreurs ou des fautes. Il se fait un cerveau de maître, se verrouille le coeur, commande avec une fermeté qui n'admet ni le recul ni la faiblesse. Au repos, il redevient le doux homme des temps de paix, bon père et bon époux comme on dit, affable et serviable, oublieux des petits tots qu'on put avoir envers lui, sachant pardonner, sachant se faire aimer, sachant aussi philosopher. Péremptoire sous l'épaulette, il vous écoute obligeamment dans le civil, discute sans entêtement vos raisons, s'y soumet si vraiment elles emportent sa persuasion. Or, voici ce qu'il me dit, ce jour de printemps, au moment du café, cigare aux lèvres, l'oeil doux et le geste rond.

– Mon cher, je me rends très bien compte des deux hommes qui se trouvent en moi pendant cette unique, cette extraordinaire période de ma vie, que je ne croyais jamais connaître, je vous le jure. J'étais un paisible, un bourgeois, un lettré goutant la conversation et les livres, et, sinon un sceptique, du moins un être enclin à accepter volontiers les doctrines les plus diverses et même à concilier les thèses les plus contradictoires, estimant qu'en chacune il est des possibilités, des étincelles de vérité. L'agression allemande a bouleversé ce citoyen tranquille, l'éclairant d'une lumière brutale sur la certitude où l'on est parfois de supprimer la raison au nom d'un instinct plus profond qu'elle, d'agir en certains cas avec un parti pris absolu. La guerre est un de ces cas. Je n'ai plus à discuter mais à me défendre, à défendre la patrie en danger. Alors j'accomplis des actes qui, en d'autres heures, m'eussent semblé discutables, monstrueux peut-être. Et je n'en éprouve nul regret. Voulez-vous me permettre de vous en raconter deux et de vous faire juge?

– Pourquoi juge, puisque vous les avez résolus dans la plénitude d'une conscience sans reproche? J'écoute tout de même. Cela passe le temps!

– Voici, fit-il après un court recueillement où passait je ne sais quel effort semblable à celui d'une personne qui fait une confession. Un matin, le capitaine de térritoriale Jean L... à son nom importe peu, vous ne le connaissez pas – me dit qu'on a trouvé entre nos lignes et celles de l'ennemi un soldat désarmé dont la volonté de déserter ne faisait aucun doute, et qu'on va me l'amener. En effet, peu de minutes après, j'aperçois un garçon que je connaissais bien, et qui, l'air accablé, marchait entre deux territoriaux.

– Tiens, fis-je quand it fut à dix pas, la main à la tempe, c'est toi, Bridoux?

– C'est moi, mon capitaine, répondit-il, pâle comme une serviette.

– Il paraît qu'on te réintègre dans nos rangs, car tu nous brûlais la politesse?

– Mon capitaine …

Il n'en dit pas plus, tremblant, vrai chien battu.

– Ton silence est un aveu. C'est bien, laissez-nous, vous autres.

Je reste en tête-à-tête avec le jeune poilu qui, d'ailleurs, ne mérite plus ce beau nom. Il a vingt ans. J'ais dû déjà user de mansuétude avec lui pour des peccadilles, sans doute, preuves toutefois de son insubordination.

– Tu comprends ce que tu as fait et ce que tu mérites cette fois, n'est-ce pas? Voyons, en deux mots, dis-moi franchement ce que tu fichais entre les lignes.

Il ne chercha pas à dissimuler. Il dit sa lassitude, son dégoût de la guerre, me jurant qu'il ne voulait pas trahir, mais simplement se rendre, et reconnut toutefois que sa fatigue était criminelle, n'en appelant qu'à ma générosité pour une erreur qu'il regrettait.

– Je t'ai déjà pardonné deux ou trois fois des négligences de service. Mais tu viens de commettre une faute contre l'honneur, et cela ne se pardonne pas.

Il se jeta à mes pieds:

– Mon capitaine, le désespoir, la dépression physique m'ont seuls conduit à un crime que je sais grave. Ayez pitié de moi!

– J'aurais peut-être eu pitié, une fois encore. Mais on t'a vu. Le capitaine L... a fait son rapport. Des soldats t'ont ramené, sachant ce que tu allais oser, toi, un Français. Cette lâcheté, te dis-je, est impardonnable. Voudrais-je te pardonner que je ne le peux même pas. On m'accuserait de mauvaise indulgence et surtout de déplorable injustice. Te pardonner serait pardonner d'advance à ceux qui, sur la même pente que toi, demain lèveraient, eux aussi, les bras en criant 'kamarades' comme les bandits d'en face. C'en serait dès lors fini de la discipline, de la résistance. C'est la démoralisation gagnant la compagnie, et par elle, le bataillon, le régiment, le corps d'armée. C'est la défaite. Cela, jamais. Il faut un exemple. Tant pis pour toi!

Il me cria sa peur et tâcha de m'attendrir par les arguments ordinaires. Que dira sa mère en apprenant qu'on a fusillé son fils pour un acte pareil! Et peut-on sévir jusqu'à donner la mort à un garçon de vingt ans, qui a une fiancée, des amis, l'existence devant lui s'ouvrant toute large? Fichtre! Le gaillard, pour assez rustre qu'il paraissait, se montra soudain d'une singulière éloquence. Mais il ne fallait pas que je me laisse séduire, je ne le pouvais, ni pour moi, ni pour ses compagnons.

– Rien à faire, déclarai-je. Le conseil de guerre et le poteau d'exécution...

Puis je me ravisai:

–Ecoute, si, peut-être, il y a un moyen d'éviter, non la mort, car tu es condamné, mais ton déshonneur, et le déshonneur des tiens. Car tu sais ce qui t'attend: l'affichage, à ta mairie, de ton infamie, et de la punition qu'elle nécessita. C'est la honte pour ta mère, tes parents, tes connaissances, ton village même qui n'oubliera jamais qu'un de ses enfants a trahi le plus sacré des devoirs. Or, cela je veux te l'éviter. Suis-moi.

Et il me suivit, docilement. Je l'emmenai dans un bois proche. Quand nous fûmes bien seuls, je tirai mon revolver et le lui tendis.

– Le moyen, le seul moyen d'échapper à la honte, le voici. Brûle-toi la cervelle.

– Oh! mon capitaine...

– Tu as compris, hein? Supprime-toi. Je ne serai pas forcé de dire que tu t'es fait justice. Il y a des balles perdues, n'est-ce pas? tu seras porté comme mort, mort au champ d'honneur.

J'appuyai sur les mots, et, pour en finir:

– Je te laisse et je reviens dans cinq minutes.

Je m'éloignai. Nulle détonation ne parvint jusqu'à mes oreilles. Je retournai près de mon homme. Il était là, hébété, immobile.

– Les cinq minutes sont passées.

– Je n'ai pas le courage, bêle-t-il … non, je n'ai pas le courage.

Et il sanglote, recommence l'histoire … sa mère … sa jeunesse … le pardon … l'assurance de se battre avec courage à l'avenir.

– Rien à faire, t'ai-je dit. Je te donne encore cinq minutes … Ne me fais pas marcher comme ça...

Je m'éloigne à nouveau. Et puis je reviens. Il est toujours à la même place, tournant l'arme dans ses doigts.

Je compris l'impossibilité d'obtenir le geste de bravoure et de repentir. Je compris aussi qu'il était douloureux pour la mère, là-bas, de savoir la vérité. Je sauvai de la catastrophe ce qui pouvait en être sauvé: le nom du malheureux. Je m'approchai et lui dis simplement:

– Peut-être ne sais-tu pas t'en servir?

Je lui arrachai le revolver des mains, d'un petit coup sec et froidement, *sûr de faire un acte juste et bon*, je lui brûlai la cervelle … Que pensez-vous de cela?

– Vous avez, entre deux formes du malheur pour lui, choisi la moins épouvantable … Et l'autre histoire?

– L'autre histoire diable! elle est plus corsée. Excusez les détails. C'est tout à fait 'poilu'.

– Allez-y … Je ne suis pas une fillette à qui on coupe ses tartines.

– Voici ma tartine … j'abrège … J'étais, l'an dernier, en tournée avec un de mes lieutenants, dans la campagne avoisinant les tranchées, quelques heures avant un assaut. Nous avisons tout à coup, au fond d'un entonnoir creusé par quelque gros obus, un de nos types accroupi, frissonnant, les yeux égarés. Ce dialogue assez … naturaliste s'engage:

– Qu'est-ce que tu f … là-dedans, toi?

– Ah mon capitaine … je peux pas vous dire … j'ai … j'ai peur, quoi!

– Tu as peur? … Ben, mon cochon! … Et tu oses le dire! Et tu oses quitter les camarades, te cacher, te … ah! par exemple...

– Je vous jure, mon capitaine, je ne peux pas … j'ai essayé tout … de me raisonner, de m'engueuler, de boire de la gniole … Rien n'y fait … J'ai le trac … J'en ai fait dans mon pantalon...

Excusez que je dise ça … C'est pour que vous compreniez … Y a pas moyen, quoi...

– Bougre de lâche, va! feignant! saligaud!...

Les mots les plus durs pleuvent sur le misérable … Mon lieutenant, un qui n'a pas froid aux yeux, lui en débite encore plus que moi … Rien n'y fait, il l'a dit … Pas moyen d'obtenir qu'il sorte de son trou. Alors une folle colère prend le lieutenant. Il cherche comment il pourrait exprimer son dégoût suprême, et finalement s'écrie:

– Lève-toi, bon Dieu! ou je te pisse dessus!

Et il fait comme il dit! Et son geste me gagne. Et nous voilà l'un et l'autre inondant le malheureux de toute l'abjection possible … Alors, sous l'outrage énorme, il bondit, hurlant, et se met à courir vers l'ennemi. Deux minutes après, une balle en pleine poitrine permettait de dire qu'il était mort en héros.

Celle-là, qu'en dites-vous? … Sur le moment je fus ravi du résultat … Et maintenant, voilà, je ne sais pas … Et pourtant...

Nous nous tûmes, pensifs.

HISTOIRE SHAKESPEARIENNE

(Extrait d'un Carnet de route)

A Emile Marchand.

… Depuis huit jours, nous sommes dans ce petit village que l'ennemi laissa entre nos mains après un dur combat. C'est un hameau picard, humble et charmant. J'en occupe, avec ma section, le cimetière. Et cela ne laisse pas de me porter à la rêverie. Habiter un cimetière vous a je ne sais quelle saveur romantique à laquelle ne vous habitue guère la paix bourgeoise. Et habiter ce lieu de mort en un temps où la mort se multiplie, rehausse encore cette saveur d'un goût terrible, d'un fantastique intense.

Autour de nous, des croix brisées, des fragments de couronnes, des dalles cassées comme à coups de marteau par on ne sait quel vampire profanateur, un grand christ qui gît à terre, fracassé, Dieu mort ainsi par deux fois, des cercueils entr'ouverts laissant échapper des ossements, et qui font songer à la Résurrection en une étrange vallée de Josaphat. D'ailleurs, n'a-t-on pas ici entendu la trompette, évocatrice d'une sorte de Jugement Dernier? Tableau digne du pinceau de Michel-Ange! Et pourtant, la Guerre a mis sa marque et ramène aux réalités. Car tout ce champ des trépassés est bouleversé, retourné par nos tranchées. Vaste et nécessaire sacrilège! Hélas! Nous nous sentons des vivants, âpres à la lutte, décidés à la défense. Et s'il nous faut mourir, ajouter nos cadavres à ces cadavres, nous voulons que ce ne soit pas sans avoir chèrement vendu notre peau!

Un obus a soulevé une dalle. Abri tout trouvé! Je m'y suis installé. J'en ai fait une sorte de funèbre cagnat. On loge où l'on peut!

Ce matin, il fait clair. J'allais dire il fait gai. La nuit et la brume se sont dissipées. Un large soleil nous inonde, indifférent à ces horreurs, à l'aspect de ces tombeaux, à l'acharnement de cette sombre tuerie. Lui, là-haut, n'a cure des batailles, des haines. Il luit paisiblement, impassiblement, fait éclore les fleurs, enivre les papillons. Plus de gelée nocturne. Beau temps pour les artilleurs!

Je regarde les herbes, et le mot d'*Hamlet* me revient en mémoire. Que de philosophie dans ces humbles graminées! Et ces milliers de livres savants sur les lois morales, les voilà combien déchirés sous les coups de dents de l'implacable Histoire!

Soudain, quelqu'un m'interpelle. Un caporal me dit (je n'avais alors que deux galons d'argent):

— Mon lieutenant, un civil envoyé par le commandant...

Un civil! Qu'est-ce qu'un civil vient faire dans cette galère? Qu'est-ce qu'il vient faire au milieu de ma songerie? Encore quelque réclamation! Une tuile peut-être. Je ne peux donc pas rêver tranquillement cinq minutes d'affilée?

L'homme approche. Il a l'air d'un pauvre bougre bien inoffensif, et je regrette le ton hargneux que j'étais sur le point de prendre. Vêtu de noir, endimanché me semble-t-il, d'ailleurs maculé de boue, il tient les deux manches d'une brouette sur laquelle un grand sac est posé. Un sac de pommes de terre, je suppose, à moitié plein, qui fait un bruit singulier quand le porteur lâche son véhicule pour chercher gauchement son laissez-passer.

— Qu'est-ce que c'est?

— Voilà, bafouille-t-il ... je viens, par rapport que je suis M. Marescot ... et que je voudrais enterrer ma famille...

— Comment ça ... enterrer votre famille! Vous êtes, dites-vous?...

— M. Marescot, le père, vous avez peut-être entendu parler...

C'est vrai, je me souviens du nom. Il y a deux jours, au début de l'occupation, on a donné l'ordre, ou tout au moins le conseil d'évacuer. Plusieurs sont partis. D'autres ont voulu rester, se sont cachés dans les caves. Mais le bombardement a vaincu la bravoure, et la protection des pierres. Des gens du village ont écopé. Il y eut des blessés, des morts. Presque toute une famille a même été enterrée, quasi totalement carbonisée dans le souterrain où elle s'était réfugiée. Et c'était la famille Marescot ... Le nom m'est resté dans la mémoire, un nom bien français. Il y avait le père, la mère, deux filles. Le père seul est sorti sain et sauf de la catastrophe.

– C'est vous Marescot, le père? … Mon pauvre ami, je sais le malheur qui vous est arrivé. Je vous plains … Mais aussi pourquoi diable...

J'allais le sermonner de son imprudence quand le caporal m'interrompit:

– Mon lieutenant! Attention, voilà qu'ils recommencent!

– Il fallait s'y attendre! On a vu notre remue-ménage. Une salve à droite. Une en arrière. Mille dieux! Tout le monde dans les trous!

Chacun de disparaître. D'un geste brusque, je tire le bonhomme et le colle à côté de moi, cependant que mon regard embrasse d'un coup le cimetière pour savoir si tous mes gars sont à l'abri. Pas un nez de chasseur dehors. C'est bien. Je reprends la conversation.

– Alors, c'est vous Marescot le père...

Il a pâli en entendant le miaulement des 77. Il reste immobile, abruti, replié sur lui-même comme une bête traquée. Je reprends:

– Mais, mon brave, vous ne pouvez rester là. Vous voyez, ça barde. A chaque instant, une alerte. Voyons, qu'est-ce que vous voulez?

– Je vous l'ai dit, mon lieutenant … enterrer ma famille.

– Soit, J'irai faire prendre les corps...

– Ils sont là, mon lieutenant.

– Où ça?

Il me montre le sac. Ce que j'avais pris pour des tubercules, c'étaient les restes, les pauvres restes des trois victimes. Le bruit singulier que j'avais entendu, c'était le heurt de leurs os. J'eus un bref sursaut de stupéfaction, de pitié, mais je me reconquis vite:

– Eh bien! ne vous tourmentez pas, je vais les faire enterrer.

Il me regarde. On aurait cru que je disais une énormité.

– Mais oui, repris-je, mes chasseurs vont creuser une tombe, au premier moment de répit … Vous pouvez avoir confiance.

– C'est que … j'ai un caveau de famille.

– Bien! … Indiquez-le nous...

– C'est que...

– C'est que quoi?

– C'est que, mon lieutenant, nous sommes déjà dedans!

Bibliography

WORKS BY BABEL

'And then there were None', tr. M. Hayward, *Dissent* (Nov–Dec, 1966).

'Argamak', *Novyy mir*, no. 3 (1932).

'Grishchuk', under heading 'Iz knigi *Konarmiya*', *Izvestiya Odesskogo gub-ispolkoma, gubkoma KP(b)U i gubprofsoveta*, subsequently republished in *Zvezda Vostoka* (March 1967), pp.110–11.

'Gyui de Mopassan', in *30 dney*, no. 6 (Moscow, June 1932). This story was subsequently discussed by Babel in *Smena*, no. 17–18 (1932).

'Iisusov grekh', in *Krasnaya nov'*, no. 7 (Dec 1923) and in *Krug*, no. 3 (Moscow, 1924). A variant of the story entitled 'Skazka pro babu' had appeared in *Siluety*, no. 8–9 (Odessa, 1923), pp.5–6.

'Ikh bylo desyat'', manuscript in possession of Babel's widow A. N. Pirozhkova.

'Ikh bylo devyat'', in *Novyy zhurnal*, no. 95 (New York, June 1969), pp.16–20.

Isaak Babel' Cavalerie Rouge suivi des récits du cycle de 'Cavalerie Rouge', des fragments du journal de 1920, des plans et esquisses, tr. and ed. J. Catteau, Paris, 1971.

Isaak Babel' : Detstvo i drugiye rasskazy, ed. E. R. Sicher (Israel, 1979). This edition includes the earliest published version of the *Konarmiya* stories, *Odesskiye rasskazy*, other stories and extracts of Babel's 1920 diary, with notes on each.

Isaak Babel', Racconti proibite e lettere intime (Milan, 1961).

Isaac Babel' : You Must Know Everything, Stories 1915–1937, ed. Nathalie Babel, tr. M. Hayward (New York, 1969 and London, 1970).

Isaak Babel' : Sochineniya v dvukh tomakh (ed.), A. N. Pirozhkova, Khudo-zhestvennaya Literature (Moscow, 1990).

Izbrannoye (Moscow, 1957).

Izbrannoye (Moscow, 1966).

"Kombrig dva', *Lef*, no. 4 (Augt–Dec 1923), under the heading 'Kolesnikov'.

Konarmiya (Moscow, 1928), 3rd ed., reprint (London, undated).

'Moy pervyy gonorar', in *Vozdushnyye puti*, no. 3 (New York, 1963), pp.101–15.

Na pole chesti, in *Lava* (Odessa, 1920), pp.10–13. Three of the stories 'Dezertir', 'Semeystvo papashi Maresko' and 'Kvaker' have subsequently been republished in *Filologicheskiy sbornik*, Alma Ata, no. 8/9 (1968), pp.199–202. The remaining story 'Na pole chesti' has been republished in *Vozdushnyye puti*, 3 (New York, 1963), pp.52–3.

'O rabotnikakh novoy kul'tury', subtitle 'Iz rechi tov. I Babelya', *Literaturnaya gazeta*, no.19 (31 March, 1936).

'O tvorcheskom put: pisatelya', *Nash sovremennik*, no.4 (1964) pp.96–100.

'Nachal'nik konzapasa', in *Lef*, no. 4 (Aug–Dec 1923).

'Probuzhdeniye', in *Molodaya gvardiya*, no. 17–18 (Sept 1931).

'Solntse Italii', in *Krasnaya nov'*, no. 3 (April–May 1924).

'Spravedlivost' v Skobkakh', in *Na pomoshch* (Odessa, 1921), republished in *Prostor*, no. 1, Alma-Ata (1974).

'Staryy Shloime', in *Ogni*, no. 6 (Kiev, 9 February 1913). Not republished until it appeared in *Gorizont* (Odessa, April 1967), pp.68–71.

The Lonely Years: 1925–1939, ed. Nathalie Babel, tr. MacAndrew and Hayward (New York, 1964).

'V podvale', in *Novyy mir*, no. 10 (Oct 1931).

'Vecher', in *Krashnaya nov'*, no. 3 (April 1925).

'Vyderzhki iz pisem I. E. Babelya k materi i sestre', in *Vozdushnyye puti*, no. 3 (1963), pp.101–15.

Zabytyy Babel', ed. N. Stroud, (Ann Arbor, 1979), including various journalistic pieces for *Krasnyy kavalerist* and *Zarya Vostoka* usually with the pseudonym K. Lyutov.

OTHER WORKS

Abrams, M. H., *A Glossary of Literary Terms* (New York, 1961).

Alexandrova, V., *A History of Soviet Literature, 1917–64: From Gorky to Pasternak* (New York, 1963).

Andrew, J. M., 'Structure and Style in the Short Story: Babel's *My First Goose*', in *Modern Language Review*, 70, no. 2 (April 1975), pp.366–79.

Annenkov, Yu., 'Isaak Babel', in *Dnevnik moikh vstrech* (New York, 1966), pp.299–308.

Aristotle, *Poetics*, ch. 21 (Oxford, 1909), tr. I. Bywater.

Baun, S. and Bowlt, J. E., eds., *Russian Formalism* (Edinburgh, 1973).

Benni, Yu., 'I. Babel', in *Pechat' i revolyutsiya*, no. 3 (1924), pp.135–9.

Blake, P. and Hayward, M., eds. *Dissonant Voices in Soviet Literature* (New York, 1962).

Blok, A., *Sobr. soch.*, eds. V. N. Orlov, A. A. Surkov and K. I. Chukovskiy, vol. 1: *Stikhotvoreniya 1897–1904* (Moscow–Leningrad, 1960).

Bondarin, S., 'Razgovor so sverstnikom', in *Nash sovremennik*, no. 5 (1962), pp.175–92.

Brinkmann, F., *Die Metaphern*, Studien über den Geist der modernen Sprachen (Bonn, 1878).

Brodal, J., 'Fathers and Sons: Isaack Babel and the Generation Conflict', in *Scando–Slavica*, no. 17 (1971), pp.27–43.

Brown, E. J., *Russian Literature since the Revolution*, London, 1969.

Brown, S. J., *The World of Imagery* (London, 1927).

Browning, G. L., 'Russian Ornamental Prose', in *Slavic and East European Journal*, vol. 23, no. 3 (1979), pp.346–52.

Bruner, J. S., 'The Course of Cognitive Growth', in *American Psychologist*, no. 19 (1964), pp.1–15.

——'The Ontogenesis of Symbols', in *Essays to Honour Roman Jakobson*, vol. 1 (The Hague, 1967), pp.427–46.

Buck, G., *Figures of Rhetoric: A Psychological Study*, no. 1 (Ann Arbor, 1896).

Budyonnyy, S., 'Babizm Babelya iz *Krasnoy novi*', in *Oktyabr'*, no. 3 (1924), pp.196–7.

——'Otkrytoye pis'mo M. Gor'komu', in *Pravda* (26 October 1928).

Buznik, V. V., *Russkaya sovetskaya proza dvadtsatykh godov* (Leningrad, 1975).

Carden, P., *The Art of Isaac Babel* (Ithaca, 1972).

Catteau, J., 'L'épopé babélienne', in *Revue des Etudes Slaves*, 49 (Paris, 1973), pp.103–18.

Choseed, B., 'Jews in Soviet Literature', in *Through the Glass of Soviet Literature*, ed., E. J. Simmons (New York, 1953), pp.110–58.

Cicero, *De Oratore* (London, 1942).

Clyman, T. W., 'Babel' as Colorist', in *Slavic and East European Journal*, XXI, no. 3 (1977), pp.332–343.

Costello, D. P. and Foote, I. P., ed., *Russian Folk Literature* (Oxford, 1967).

Cru, J. N., *Témoins: Essai d'analyse et de critique des souvenirs de combattants édités en français de 1915–1928* (Paris, 1929).

Cuckierman, W., 'The Odessan Myth and Idiom in Some Early Works of Odessa Writers', in *Canadian–American Slavic Studies*, 14, no. 1 (Spring 1980), pp.36–51.

Davies, N., 'Izaak Babel's *Konarmiya* Stories and the Polish–Soviet War', in *Modern Language Review*, 67, no. 4 (Oct. 1972), pp.845–57.

Deutsch, B., *Poetry Handbook, A Dictionary of Terms* (New York, 1957).

Domnitz, M., *Judaism* (London, 1970).

Earle, J., English Pose: *Its Elements, History and Usage* (London, 1890), p.75.

Eng, J. van der, 'La description poétique chez Babel', in *Dutch Contributions to the Fifth International Congress of Slavicists* (The Hague, 1963), pp.79–92.

——'Red Cavalry: A Novel of Stories', in *Russian Literature*, 33–2/3 (1 April 1993), pp.249–64.

Eremin, I. P., ed. and tr. *Slovo o polku Igoreve* (Moscow, 1957).

Erenburg, I., 'I. E. Babel', in *I. Babel', Izbrannoye* (Moscow, 1957), p.5–10.

——'*Lyudi, gody, zhizn'*. Kniga tret'ya,' in *Novyy mir*, 9 (1961), pp.146–52, and vol. 3, ch.15 (Moscow, 1966).

Ermolayev, H., *Mikhail Sholokhov and his Art* (Princeton, 1982).

Eykhenbaum, B., *Leskov and Modern Prose* (Munich, 1925).

Falen, J. E., 'A note on the fate of I. Babel'', in *Slavic and East European Journal*, II (1967), pp.398–404.

Falen, J. E., *Isaak Babel – Russian Master of the Short Story* (Tennessee, 1974).

Fet, A., *Stikhotvoreniya* (Moscow, 1970).

Friedman, N., 'Imagery: From Sensation to Symbol', *Journal of Aesthetics*, vol. 12 (1953), pp.25–37.

Furmanov, D. M., *Sobr. soch. v chetyryokh tomakh*, vol. 4 (Moscow, 1961), p.343.

Garlanda, F., *Philosophy of Words* (London, 1888), pp.36–7.

Gereben, A., 'Uber die Kohärenz einer epischen Gattung', in *Studia Hungaro–Slavica*, XXVII (Budapest, 1981).

——'Babel' naplója', in *Valóság,* 12 (Budapest, 1981), pp.81–102.

——'Isaac Babel's Diary and His *Red Cavalry*', in *Hungaro–Slavica* (Budapest, 1983), pp.55–9.

——'The Writer's "Ego" in the Composition of Cycles of Short Stories', in *Essays in Poetics*, vol. 9, no. 1 (Keele, 1984).

——'*Konarmiya* I Babelya v literaturnoy kritike 20-kh godov', in *Slavica* XX (Budapest, Dec 1984), pp.119–37.

——'The syntactics of cycles of short stories', in *Essays in Poetics*, vol. 11, no. 1 (Keele, 1986), pp.44–75

Gogol, N., *Polnoye sobr. soch.*, vol. 6, ed., N. L. Meshcheryakov (Leningrad, 1937–52).

——*Sobr. soch.*, eds. S. I. Mashinskiy, N. L. Stepanov and M. B. Khrapchenko (Moscow, 1966–7).

Goldmann, L., *The Hidden God*, tr. P. Thody (London, 1964).

Gorkiy, M., 'Otvet S. Budyonnomu', in *Pravda* (27 November 1928).

Goya, F., *The Disasters of War*, intro. P. Hofer (New York, 1967); original edition entitled *Los desastres de la guerra* (Madrid, 1863).

Grøngaarde, R. I., *I. Babel's 'Red Cavalry' – an Investigation of Composition and Theme*, tr. D. R. Frickleton (Aarhus, 1979).

Gukovskiy, G., 'Zakat', in *I. E. Babel': Stat'i materialy*, ed. Yu. Tynyanov (Leningrad, 1928), pp.73–99.

Gustafson, R. F., 'Tjutcev's Imagery and What It Tells Us', in *Slavic and East European Journal*, vol. 4, no. 18 (1960).

Hallet, R. W., *Isaac Babel* (Letchworth, 1972).

Hastings, J., *Dictionary of the Apostolic Church*, vol. II (Edinburgh, 1915–18).

Herod, F.G., *What men believe* (London, 1968), pp.75–82.

Hornstein, L.H., 'Analysis of Imagery: A Critique of Literary Method', P.M.L.A., vol. 57, no. 1 (1942), pp.638–53.

Hyman, S. E., 'Identities of Isaac Babel'', in *Hudson Review*, 4 (1956), pp.620–7.

——'New Voices of Isaac Babel', in *New Leader* (20 July 1964), pp.16–17.

Iribarne, L., 'Babel's *Red Cavalry* as a Baroque Novel', in *Contemporary Literature*, no. 14 (1973), pp.58–77.

Isachenko, A. V., *Grammaticheskiy stroy russkogo yazyka v sopostavlenii s slovatskim*, 2 vols. (Bratislava, 1954).

Ivanova, T. V., Babel's second widow, interviewed at Peredelkino, 29 October 1987.

——*Moi sovremenniki, kakimi ya ikh znala* (Moscow, 1987).

Iverson, A. M., 'The Ancient Greek "Death" Aspect of Spring in Mandelstam's Poetry', in *Slavic and East European Journal*, XX, no. 1 (1976).

Jordan, M., *Andrey Platonov* (Letchworth, 1973).

Keach, B., *Tropologia or a key to open Scripture Metaphors*, (1779, republished Waterford, 1858).

Klotz, M. B., 'Poetry of the Present: Isaak Babel's *Red Cavalry*', in *Slavic and East European Journal*, 17, no. 2 (Summer 1974), pp.160–9.

Kruchenykh, A. E., *Zaumnyy yazyk u: Seifullinoy, Vs. Ivanova, Leonova, Babelya, I. Sel'vinskogo, A. Veselogo i drugikh* (Moscow, 1925, reprint Ann Arbour, 1960).

Kvyatkovskiy, A., *Poeticheskiy slovar'* (Moscow, 1966).

Lee, A., 'Epiphany in Babel's *Red Cavalry*', in *Russian Literature Triquarterly*, III (Michigan, 1972), pp.249–60.

Leiter, Louis H., 'A Reading of Isaac Babel's "Crossing into Poland"', in *Studies in Short Fiction*, III, no. 2 (Winter 1966), pp.199–206.

Lekeux M., *Mes cloîtres dans la tempête* (Brussels, 1922).

Leondar, B., 'The Structure and Function of Metaphor', Ph.D. thesis (Harvard University, 1968).

Levin, F. I., *Babel': ocherk tvorchestva* (Moscow, 1972).

Lezhnev, A., 'Sredi zhurnalov', Krasnaya nov', no. 4 (1924), pp.304–13.

Livshits, L., 'Materialy k tvorcheskoy biografii I. Babelya', in *Voprosy literatury*, no. 4 (April 1964), pp.110–35.

Lucas, F. L., *Literature and Psychology* (Edinburgh, 1951).

Luplow, C., *Isaac Babel's 'Red Cavalry'* (Ann Arbor, 1982).

——'Paradox and the Search for Value in Babel's *Red Cavalry*', in *Slavic and East European Journal*, vol. 23, no. 2 (1979), pp.216–32.

Macguire, R. A., *Red Virgin Soil: Soviet Literature in the 1920s* (Princeton, 1968).

Markish, S., 'La littérature russo-juive et Isaac Babel", *Cahier du Monde Russe et Soviétique*, vol. 18, no. 1–2 (1977), pp.73–92.

Mathewson, R. W. Jr., *The Positive Hero in Russian Literature* (Stanford, 1958).

de Maupassant, G., *Contes et Nouvelles published between 1875 and 1884* (Paris, 1974).

Mendelsohn, D., *Metaphor in Babel's Short Stories* (Ann Arbor, 1982).

Meylakh, B.S., 'O metafore kak element khudoshestvennogo myshleniya', in *Trudy otdela novoy russkoy literatury* (Moscow–Leningrad, 1948), pp.207–32.

Middleton, Murray J., *The Problem of Style* (Oxford, 1922).

——*Countries of the Mind* (London, 1931).

Mierau, F., ed., *Die Reiterarmee mit Dokumenten und Aufsätzen im Anhang* (Leipzig, 1969).

Mooij, J. J. A., 'Tenor, Vehicle and Reference' in *Poetics*, no. 4 (1975), pp.257–72.

Munblit, G., 'Iz vospominaniy', I. Babel', *Vospominaniya sovremennikov* (Moscow-Leningrad, 1960), pp.308–9.

Murphy, A. B., 'The Style of Isaac Babel", in *The Slavonic and East European Review*, 44 (1966), pp.361–80.

Novitskiy, P., 'Babel", in *I. E. Babel': Stat'i i materialy*, ed. Yu. Tynyanov (1928), pp.45–69.

Obolenskiy, D., ed., 'Pervaya Poyezdka Il'; Muromtsa. Il'ya i Solovey–Razboynik', *The Penguin Book of Russian Verse* (London, 1965).

O'Connor, F., *The Lonely Voice: A Study of the Short Story* (Cleveland and New York, 1965).

O'Toole, L. M., 'Structure and Style in the Short Story: Chekhov's "The Student"', University of Essex Language Centre Occasional Papers 4 (June 1969), pp.1–29.

——*Structure, Style and Interpretation in the Russian Short Story* (New York, 1982).

Oulanoff, H., *The Serapion Brothers: Theory and Practice* (The Hague, 1966).

Oxford English Dictionary (Oxford, 1930).

Ozhegov, S. I., *Slovar' russkogo yazyka* (Moscow, 1973).

Parijanine, M., 'Introduction' to I. Babel, *Cavalerie Rouge* (Paris, 1930).

Paustovskiy, K., *Povest' o zhizni*, Sobr. soch., ed. V. Borisova, vol. 5 (Moscow, 1967).

Pertsov, V., 'Kakaya byla pogoda v epokhu grazhdanskoy voyny?' in *Novyy let*, no. 7 (1927), pp.36–45.

Petrovskiy, M. A., 'Morfologiya Novelly' (Moscow, 1928).

Pirozhkova, A. N., ed., 'Babel v 1932–39 godakh (iz vospominaniy)' in *I. Babel', Vospominaniya sovremennikov* (Moscow, 1972).

——Babel's widow and Lid'ya, their daughter, interviewed in Moscow, 30 October 1987. [She is Babel's third child; he had a son by T. V. Ivanova and a daughter by his first wife, Yevgeniya Borisovna Gronfein. Babel scarcely knew any of his children.]

Platonov, A., *Velichiye prostykh serdets* (Moscow, 1976).

Poggioli, R., 'I. E. Babel', in *The Phoenix and the Spider* (Cambridge, 1957), pp.229–38.

Polyak, L., 'I. Babel', in *I. Babel, Izbrannoye* (Moscow, 1966), pp.3–22.

Prat, R. P., *Etudes*, vol. 135 (Paris, 1913), p.109.

Povartsov, S. N., 'Ob ideyno – khudozhestvennom svoyeobrazii "Konarmii" I. Babelya', in *Uchonyye Zapiski*, vol. 187 (Moscow, 1967), pp.55–66.

Proffer, C. R., 'Notes on the Imagery in Zamjatin's "We"', in *Slavic and East European Journal*, vol. 7, no. 3 (1963).

——*The Simile and Gogol's 'Dead Souls'* (The Hague, 1967).

Propp, V., *Morfologiya skazki* (Leningrad, 1928).

Pross-Weerth, H., 'Nachwort' to *Ein Abend bei der Kaiserin*, which includes extracts from Babel's 1920 diary (Neuwied, 1970), pp.121–43.

Quintilian, *Institutes of Oratory*, Book 9, ch. 1 (London, 1920–2), tr. H. E. Butler.

Reformatskiy, A. A., *Opyt analiza novellisticheskoy kompoziyey* (Moscow, 1922).

Rice, M. P., 'On *Skaz*, in *Russian Literature Triquarterly*, no. 12 (Michigan, Spring, 1975).

Richards, I. A., *Principles of Literary Criticism* (London, 1925)

Ricoeur, P., 'Metaphor and the Main Problem of Hermeneutics', in *New Literary History*, no. 6 (1974), pp.95–111.

Roland, A., 'Imagery and Symbolic Expression in Dreams and Art', in *International Journey of Psychoanalysis*, no. 53 (1972), pp.531–9.

Rothschild, T., 'Isaak Babel – Eine Monographie', unpublished doctoral thesis (Vienna University, 1967).

——'Zur Form von Isaak Babel's Erzählungen', in *Weiner Slavistisches Jahrbuch*, part 16 (Vienna, 1970), pp.112–34.

Rzhevskiy, L., 'Babel' – stylist', in *Vozdushnyye puti*, 3 (1963), pp.217–41.

Seeley and Abbot, *English lessons for English People* (London, 1890).

Seyfullina, L., *O Literature* (Moscow, 1958)

Shklovskiy, V. I., 'Babel' (Kriticheskii romans)', *LEF*, no. 2.vi (1924), pp.152–5.

——'O Babele', in *Zhili-byli* (Moscow, 1964), pp.390–3.

——'O teorii prozy', in *Krug* (Moscow–Leningrad, 1925).

Shorter Oxford English Dictionary (Oxford, 1965).

Sicher, E. R., 'The works of I. E. Babel (1894–1941) with special reference to tradition and innovation in the style of his narrative prose of the 1920s', unpublished D.Phil. thesis (Oxford University, 1979).

——'The Road to a Red Cavalry: Myth and Mythology in the Work of Isaak Babel in the 1920s', in *Slavonic and East European Review*, vol. 60, no. 4 (October 1982), pp.528–46.

Sinkó, E., *Roman eines Romans* (Cologne, 1962).

Sinyavskiy, A., 'Babel" in *Major Soviet Writers*, ed., E. J. Brown (Oxford, 1973).

Slavin, L., 'Tysyacha i odna noch", in *Siluety*, no. 2 (Odessa, Dec–Jan, 1922–3).

Slonim, M., *Soviet Russian Literature, 1917–77* (Oxford, 1977).

Smirin, I.A., 'Iz planov i nabroskov k *Konarmii*', in *Literaturnoye nasledstvo*, LXXIV (Moscow, 1965), pp.490–9.

——'K probleme traditsii N. V. Gogolya i I. S. Turgeneva v *Konarmii* I. Babelya', in *Rol' traditsii v razvitii literatury i fol'klora*, ed. B. Shalaganov (Perm, 1974).

——'Na puti k *Konarmii*', in *Literaturnoye nasledstvo*, LXXIV (Moscow, 1965), pp.467–82.

——'U istokov voyennoy temy v tvorchestve I. Babelya', in *Russkaya literatura*, part 1 (1967), pp.203–4.

Spurgeon, C., *Shakespeare's Imagery and What It Tells Us* (Cambridge, 1935).

Spycher, P., 'N. V. Gogol's "The Nose": A Satirical Comic Fantasy Born of an Impotence Complex', in *Slavic and East European Journal*, vol. 7, no. 4 (Winter 1963), pp.361–75.

Stepanov, N., 'Novella Babelya' in *I. E. Babel': stat'i i materialy*, ed. Yu. Tynyanov (Leningrad, 1928), pp.13–41.

Stora-Sandor, J., *Isaak Babel'*, *1894–1941, L'homme et L'oeuvre* (Paris, 1968).

Stroud, N., 'The Art of Mystification: The "Prehistoric" Isaac Babel', in *Russian Literature Triquarterly*, no. 13 (Ann Arbor, 1975).

Sullivan, E. D., *Maupassant The Short Stories* (London, 1962).

Terras, V., 'Line and Colour: The Structure of I. Babel's Short Stories in *Red Cavalry*', in *Studies in Short Fiction*, III, no. 2 (Winter 1966), pp.141–56.

The Standard English Dictionary, ed. Funk and Wagnall (New York, 1903).

Thompson, E. M., *Russian Formalism and Anglo–American New Criticism: A Comparative Study* (The Hague, 1971).

Times Literary Supplement (London, 14 October 1926).

Tomashevskiy, B., *Teoriya Literatury (Poetika)* (Moscow, 1928).

Trilling, L., 'Introduction', in *Isaak Babel: Collected Stories,* ed. and tr., W. Morrison (London and New York, 1961), pp.9–37.

Turgenev, I. S., 'Gamlet i Don-Kikhot', in *Polnoye sobraniye sochineniy i pisem,* VIII (Moscow–Leningrad, 1964), pp.171–92, first published in *Sovremennaya*, no. 1 (1860), pp.239–58.

Tynyanov, Yu., *Arkhaysty i Novatory* (Leningrad, 1929 and Munich, 1967).

Vinogradov, I., *Bor' ba za Stil'* (Moscow, 1937).

Vinogradov, V. V., *O Poezii Anny Akhmatovoy* (Leningrad, 1925, reprinted The Hague, 1969).

——'Problema avtora v khudozhestvennoy literature', in *O teorii khudozhestvennoy rechi* (Moscow, 1971).

Wellek, R. and Warren, A., *Theory of Literature*, 3rd edition (New York, 1956).

Weststeijn, W. G., 'Velimir Khlebnikov and the Development of Poetical Language in Russian Symbolism and Futurism', in *Studies in Slavic Literature and Poetics*, vol. 4 (Amsterdam, 1983).

Wheelwright, P., *Metaphor and Reality* (Indiana, 1962).

de Wilde, R., *De Liége à l'Yser. Mon journal de Campagne* (Brussels, 1918).

Williams, G., 'The Rhetoric of Revolution in Babel's *Konarmija*', in *Russian Literature*, XV (North Holland, 1984), pp.279–98.

——'Two Leitmotifs in Babel's *Konarmija*', in *Die Welt der Slaven*, Book 1 (Cologne, 1972), pp.308–17.

——'Uneasy Rider: Babel and his Reader in *Konarmiya*', unpublished paper (Oxford, 1984).

Yarmolinskiy, A., 'Isaac Babel' (1894–1941) An Odessa Maupassant?' in *The Russian Literary Imagination* (New York, 1969), pp.131–85.

Yevtushenko, Ye., *Selected Poetry*, ed. R. Milner-Gulland (Oxford, 1963).

Zavalishin, V., *Early Soviet Writers* (New York, 1958).